Death in the Tiergarten

Death in the Tiergarten

Murder and Criminal Justice in the Kaiser's Berlin

Benjamin Carter Hett

HARVARD UNIVERSITY PRESS

Cambridge, Massachusetts

London, England • 2004

To my first history teachers,
Robert and Eileen Hett,
with love and gratitude

Copyright © 2004 by the President and Fellows of Harvard College
All rights reserved

Library of Congress Cataloging-in-Publication Data
Hett, Benjamin Carter.
Death in the Tiergarten : murder and criminal justice in the
Kaiser's Berlin / Benjamin Carter Hett.
p. cm.
Includes bibliographical references and index.
ISBN 0-674-01317-4 (alk. paper)
1. Criminal justice, Administration of—Germany—Berlin—History—20th century.
2. Criminal justice, Administration of—Germany—Berlin—History—19th century.
3. Criminal courts—Germany—Berlin—History—20th century. 4. Criminal courts—Germany—Berlin—History—19th century. 5. Trials (Murder)—Germany—Berlin—History—20th century. 6. Trials (Murder)—Germany—Berlin—History—19th century. I. Title.
HV9680.B4H48 2004
345.43'15501—dc22   2003067617

Contents

	Acknowledgments	vii
	Introduction	1
1	In Moabit	11
2	The Berlin of Surrogates	55
3	Honorable Men	104
4	Justice Is Blind	145
5	"Were People More Pitiless Fifteen Years Ago?"	179
	Epilogue	220
	Appendix: Regimes and Rulers	237
	Abbreviations	239
	Notes	241
	Archival and Primary Sources	277
	Index	287

Acknowledgments

This book was probably born in the class on "the practice of criminal law" taught by Edward Greenspan, Q.C., at the University of Toronto Law School in 1989. Sitting directly under the "no smoking" sign and defiantly chain-smoking, Mr. Greenspan would glare around the table at the eager students and growl, "If you want to see democracy in action, forget elections. Go and sit for a day in the criminal courts, and watch how hard the state has to work to put someone in jail. *That's* democracy." Many years and much research later, I still agree.

It is a great pleasure to thank some of the people who have helped me through graduate school and through this project. I am grateful to the lawyers of Russell & DuMoulin in Vancouver, and Blake, Cassels & Graydon in Toronto, who tried to teach me something of the art and science of trial advocacy. I would especially like to mention two superb advocates, Murray Tevlin and Dinyar Marzban, both formerly of Russell & DuMoulin. I think they would get on like a house afire with Alsberg, Sello, and the other great trial lawyers in these pages.

I am very grateful for financial assistance for this research from the Social Sciences and Humanities Research Council of Canada (SSHRC), the Deutsche Akademische Austauschdienst (DAAD), and the Minda de Gunzburg Center for European Studies through its Program for the Study of Germany and Europe.

My debts to the scholars who have gone before in these subjects will be clear from the notes, but I do want to add that where I have sometimes differed from their findings, this in no way diminishes my respect and gratitude for their work. For advice on sources, reading of drafts, and general encouragement I am especially grateful to William Alford, Alison Frank,

Peter Fritzsche, Karsten Hecht, Christina von Hodenberg, Eric Johnson, Maximo Langer, Kenneth Ledford, Corinna Treitel, Detlev Vagts, Richard Wetzell, and the participants at the conference on German criminal law that Richard convened at the German Historical Institute in 2001. The editors of *Central European History* have kindly given permission to use material in this book that originally appeared in my article "The Captain of Köpenick and the Transformation of German Criminal Justice, 1891–1914."

For several years the faculty, staff, and students of Harvard College's History and Literature Concentration, the Harvard Law School Graduate Program, and the Minda de Gunzburg Center for European Studies have provided a constantly stimulating home from which I have learned immensely. Special thanks to Steven Biel, Charitini Douvaldzi, William Alford, Gail Hupper, and Anne-Marie Slaughter. Michael Olson at Harvard's Widener Library, and Stephen Helfer and Philip Satterfield at the International Legal Studies Library, have gone to amazing lengths to find obscure reading matter. Since September 2003, my new colleagues in the History Department of Hunter College, CUNY, have been wonderfully welcoming.

In Berlin, Constantin Goschler and Julianna Mehls were admirable hosts and landlords, and made my time there incomparably more rewarding than it would otherwise have been. Siegfried Weichlein introduced me to a range of cultural experiences from operas to soccer games; and the gang at the Bundesarchiv provided very welcome diversions on many lunch breaks and evenings (special thanks to Caroline Fricke). The archivists at the Geheime Staatsarchiv Preussisicher Kulturbesitz, the Bundersarchiv Berlin-Lichterfelde, the Landesarchiv Berlin, and the Brandenburgische Landeshauptarchiv were unfailingly friendly and helpful (special thanks to Herr Torsten Zarwel at the Bundesarchiv for retrieving all of the *Ehrengerichtshof* files), as were the staff at the Staatsbibliothek Berlin.

I am very grateful to Kathleen McDermott at Harvard University Press for taking an early interest in this project, and for her patience and encouragement with the delivery of the final manuscript. The fine editorial assistance of Kaesmene Harrison and Charlotte Maurer has saved me from myriad crimes against the English language.

I have been extraordinarily lucky with my history teachers, both at the University of Toronto and at Harvard. Timothy Alborn, Thomas Bisson, Michael McCormick, Susan Pedersen, James Retallack, Anne Robson, and Wesley Wark have not only been great teachers, they have regularly gone above and beyond the call of duty with endless reference letters, help with jobs and funding, and general moral support. Special thanks to my dissertation committee, David Blackbourn, Charles Maier, and Charles Donahue. About David Blackbourn, my advisor at Harvard, I can only echo what one of his students told me on my first day: "He's the platonic ideal of the graduate supervisor." Outstanding scholar, conscientious teacher, gentleman; it is a pleasure as well as an honor to be his student.

My beautiful wife, Corinna Andiel, has cheerfully borne all of the drawbacks of an academic husband. She also reminds me that there is more to life than historical research and in all respects keeps me going. I can't imagine life without her.

My parents, Eileen and Robert Hett, have been a constant source of love and support throughout my life, and even took stoically the alarming prospect of their son leaving the legal profession for the uncertainties of academe. I hope the dedication of this book is some small acknowledgment of the enormous debt I owe them.

I finished the first draft of this book on September 10, 2001. No one who lived through the next day will ever forget it. Painted on the wall of the main jury courtroom of Wilhelmine Berlin one could find the words, "Where there is a court, there is peace." In its humble way, this book is dedicated to the hope that the slow and civilized values of the law may yet triumph over the flames of barbarism.

Early in their legal education many law students pick up a virus from some unknown source that drives them to ask of each case, what does it stand for? They seem to assume that the cases are building blocks, that each has an understandable shape and will fit neatly into a little wall of law, snugly and certainly. The correct answer to the question is that the case "stands for" what it is, a little segment of human history, history of an event or of an idea, or of both. The important question is: What is to be done with this case?

J. B. MILNER
MILNER'S CASES AND MATERIALS ON CONTRACTS

Introduction

This book takes up a subject that has no history: the criminal trial in Germany in the last years before the First World War.

The reader may find this statement surprising. "No history?" There are venerable histories of criminal law in Germany,[1] and a good deal of recent work on such subjects as crime[2] and the history of the legal professions.[3] We can certainly say that German criminal justice has not enjoyed a good press since the days in which the judges of Berlin's *Kammergericht* resisted the arbitrary incursions of Frederick the Great.[4] By the late nineteenth century the proud claim of Frederick's time (1740–1786), "There are still judges in Berlin!" had been replaced by the buzzwords of a new political critique: *Klassenjustiz* and *Weltfremdheit* ("class justice" and "being out of touch"). These were the themes of countless newspaper editorials, parliamentary speeches, and pamphlets. According to this critique, German courts in the age of Kaiser Wilhelm II (1888–1918) were staffed by judges carefully selected to be from the "right" classes, fiercely loyal to the monarchical system, and bereft of any comprehension of the life lived by the majority of the population. Even juries and defense counsel were either powerless to bring popular opinion to the courtroom or, as representatives of the complacent bourgeoisie, themselves part of the problem.[5] The tumultuous years of the Weimar Republic added another catch-phrase: "easy on the right, hard on the left," the conclusion drawn by the Heidelberg statistician Emil Julius Gumbel in texts successively titled *Two Years of Political Murder* and then *Four Years of Political Murder*.[6] Judges, it was said, had simply carried their arch-conservative, authoritarian values from the Empire to the democratic Weimar Republic, constituting a fifth column against the new state.[7]

What began as a political critique, as arguments deployed by politicians and activist intellectuals, found its way into the historiography of German criminal justice after the Second World War—though not immediately. For two decades this literature was dominated by writers at least partly implicated in the horrors of justice in the Third Reich, and consequently it struck an apologetic tone. German judges, it was said, had done their best to curb the worst tendencies of Nazi rulers; to the extent that they had failed, they had been the victims of their positivist intellectual training (succinctly characterized by legal philosopher Gustav Radbruch as the belief that "orders are orders and law is law"),[8] which had left them defenseless in the face of a barbaric state. The eras preceding the Third Reich made only cameo appearances in this literature, and then only to play the role of the lost Eden, the time before the fall.[9]

But starting in the 1960s historians began to seek the roots of Nazi justice in the years before 1933. They rediscovered the oppositional political writings of people like Gumbel, Alfred Apfel, and the left-leaning intellectuals associated with journals like *Die Weltbühne* and *Die Justiz*, such as Carl von Ossietzky, Hugo Sinzheimer, and Gustav Radbruch. The contemporary accounts stressing the political and class biases of Weimar justice were rechanneled by a younger generation of historians seeking to overcome the apologetics of the early postwar literature.

The first important account in this vein came in 1966 from trial lawyer Heinrich Hannover and historian Elisabeth Hannover-Drück. For Hannover and Hannover-Drück, the political orientation of Weimar judges—"Imperial Judges in the Democratic Republic" as they put it, hostile to the Republic, to political parties left of the right-liberal DVP (German People's Party), and to the working classes in general—served as a complete explanation for the systemically slanted justice of the 1920s. They emphasized the social selectivity of judicial recruiting in prewar Germany, and the refusal of republican administrations to violate judicial independence by dismissing large numbers of those "imperial" judges. Thus, it was "a bitter discovery for the working class and its leaders" that in "their state" an "antidemocratic jurisprudence could paralyze the will of the democratic legislature." Since Hannover and Hannover-Drück, the dominant tone in the historiography of modern German criminal law, and of ancillary subjects such as crime and the professions, has been that of the baleful continuities, the degree to which the courts of the Second Reich foreshadowed those of the Third.[10]

But the sources from which this historiography tends to be written represent only one strand in a complex political debate. Attitudes to criminal justice in early twentieth century Germany were closely related to overall political outlook. The Wilhelmine Social Democratic critique (which was taken over by the Weimar Communist Party or KPD as the SPD became part of the establishment)—the critique of *Klassenjustiz* and *Weltfremdheit*—has survived to inspire our historiography. Other critiques have not survived; but there *were* others. The Wilhelmine years gave birth to a far-right critique of justice, which came to a Weimar climax in the early 1930s with the *Gefesselte Justiz* ("Justice in Chains") books and the editorials of Nazi papers like Goebbels' *Angriff*.[11] The Wilhelmine far-right critique focused on the "harsh" treatment of anti-Semitic activists by the courts, and on the increasingly lenient treatment of other kinds of offenders. That such a critique could be born in so conservative a state points to a reality of Wilhelmine German society and politics that has concerned historians for twenty years or so: there was a good deal of political territory to the right of the Imperial and Prussian governments.[12]

Another now-forgotten contemporary critique could be called the "critique of liberal despair." Around the turn of the twentieth century, many liberals began to feel that the justice system they had striven for through much of the nineteenth century, and achieved by 1879 (with national codes of procedure, a free legal profession, judges insulated from political interference, trials conducted openly and publicly, and juries for the most serious criminal matters) was under siege from unexpected enemies: from "below," from popular superstition, stupidity, and ignorance, and from the drawbacks of the very guarantees of procedural fairness that the system had adopted.[13] I certainly do not present these narratives to claim that one was true and the others false. But the fact that they all existed suggests that the picture was more complicated and more contested than historians have assumed.

We have seen the extent to which this historiography has been driven by an effort to find the roots of the corruption and horrors of justice in the Third Reich. Of these horrors there can be no doubt.[14] During the twelve years of Hitler's Reich, German courts pronounced approximately 32,000 death sentences, evenly divided between civilian and military courts, 30,000 of them after 1941.[15] From the very beginnings of the Nazi regime, jurists of Jewish background or left-leaning political affiliation could expect only the worst; many of the most brilliant and influential among them were forced into exile or suicide or were murdered in the concentration and the death camps.[16] But the question remains, how did the justice system come to such a pass?

Arguments that seek the answer in judicial ideological continuities face considerable empirical difficulties. There is little disputing that the political orientation of German judges, during the Empire as well as the Weimar Republic, tended to the conservative. But it is not at all clear that judicial outcomes can so easily be read off from political ideology. This is so even in the most overtly political trials, at least before 1918, when the judiciary demonstrated more independence than political critics of all stripes wished to acknowledge.

The argument that seeks to explain judges' performance in the Third Reich by their adherence to legal positivism encounters similar difficulties. Positivism has been made to carry a lot of explanatory weight here, beginning with the apologetic literature of the 1950s and 1960s and continuing more recently with histories of crime.[17] But the very breadth of the concept "legal positivism" should provide a clue to its explanatory shortcomings. In a famous 1958 essay, H. L. A. Hart identified five possible meanings of legal positivism, adding "there may be more." These various meanings—above all, that law is distinct from morality; that a legal system is a "closed logical system in which correct legal decisions can be deduced by logical means from predetermined legal rules without reference to social aims, policies, [or] moral standards"; and that law is nothing more than the commands of a society's recognized law-making authority[18]—were all available to early twentieth-century German judges, based on the work of such thinkers as Georg Friedrich Puchta, Bernhard Windscheid, Karl Binding, Paul Laband, and Hans Kelsen. But to argue that these diverse doctrines could of themselves produce a mechanical jurisprudence based on a slavish deference to statutes or rulers is to overlook the very large space for judicial interpretation that Germany's modern and sophisticated legal codes still left open.[19] In any case, German legal theorists were beginning to argue in the early twentieth century that it was both common and acceptable for judges to "make law," even contrary to the terms of legislation.[20] That judicial practice shows they did just this has been argued in some instances before,[21] and will be here.

But in any event the judicial mind, of whatever sort it may be, does not and cannot constitute a complete explanation for judicial outcomes. The Imperial German judicial mind could not be isolated from myriad professional, social, and political factions all clamoring for a role in shaping the justice system. Lay opinion was often vital to trial outcomes; the determination of guilt or innocence in the most serious cases was made by juries, while in the least serious cases two lay judges, recruited like jurors from the community, sat alongside one professional judge and could, at least in theory, outvote him. As we shall see, well-organized lobby groups or individual citizens exercising their rights of complaint or appeal could often intimidate or cajole officials, even justice ministers, into handling cases differently than the officials would have preferred. Defense lawyers could often decisively affect the outcomes of trials (as even prosecutors acknowledged), and prosecutors themselves did not always see cases the same way judges did. Practitioners of a range of scientific and medical disciplines—physicians, psychologists, chemists, anthropologists, sociologists, ballistics experts—were simultaneously defining new fields of inquiry and asserting their own claim to authority in the courtroom.

Above (and around) all was the press. Berlin papers were aggressive and mostly of liberal or Social Democratic political sentiment. Even the more pro-government Conservative and National Liberal papers were often just as critical of the workings of criminal justice as their left-leaning counterparts, if for different reasons. Papers of the far right, like the anti-Semitic *Staatsbürger Zeitung,* were at least as likely as papers of the left to see conspiracy behind every judge's bench, and (not coincidentally) to be prosecuted for libel. The result of all the press scrutiny was that Berlin's jurists worked in a constant glare of publicity; the slightest mistake or hint of controversy could garner headlines and serious professional consequences. Prussian justice ministers, as well as the (national) Reich secretaries of state for justice, were highly sensitive to press criticism and usually responded to attacks with the full bureaucratic arsenal of demands for reports, orders for reformed procedures, and reprimands or other disciplinary measures for the personnel involved.

This book, then, is a study of how lawyers and judges, prosecutors and jurors, criminals and police officers, reporters and expert witnesses, met and interacted. In short, it studies the culture of the criminal courtroom. In doing so it seeks to understand not only how these people did what they did, but how they thought about what they did and how they reacted to the other elements of the culture. Most of all, the book seeks to understand how this culture changed over time. Here we are back to the subject with no history. There is a history of Germany's laws, and of its institutions—

the prosecutor's office, the judiciary, the legal profession. There are histories of crimes, and of executions, and of the press. But the events that brought together these laws and institutions, these diverse people and their ideas—the trials—have been neglected.

The book focuses on a small number of Berlin trials spanning the years 1891–1913. I chose Berlin as a case study for several reasons. Looking only at cases from one municipality allows one to control for regional variations in the nature of justice. At the same time, Berlin—as contemporaries unanimously asserted—was the legal as well as the political capital of Germany, with a volume and sophistication of legal business far outstripping other centers. If any one city can stand for national patterns, it is Berlin.

Most of the trials in these pages are murder trials. This is not an accident; the seriousness of murder trials tended to ensure that all of the substantive and procedural issues of the conduct of trials received a full airing, both in the courtroom and in the public sphere. But we will also see trials for offenses ranging from sex with minors to the unauthorized wearing of a military uniform. We will see lawyers facing disbarment for transgressions from quaffing champagne in court, to challenging a prosecutor to a duel, to libeling the Russian Czar. My theoretical premise is that the career of a law really begins when it is first used in the courtroom. Every time there is a trial, every time an official makes a decision based on a statutory power, the law is created anew. I will illustrate the gulf that can separate the law as it exists in the statute book from the law as it is applied in the trial courts—even in a country said to be a land of slavish legal positivists. I will also show that great shifts took place over time in Wilhelmine Berlin in the way trials were carried out and in how they were received in the public sphere. These shifts are all the more interesting for the fact that prevailing German legal doctrines left no space for them, and historians have not noticed them.

Legal scholars will recognize in this methodological orientation the shades of American legal realism, and rightly so. Ironically, in seeking to apply the insights of the realists to German legal history, I am doing no more than sending those insights back to their homeland. Realist-in-chief Karl Llewellyn wrote strikingly in 1930 that "men talk about contracts, and trusts, and corporations, as if these things existed in themselves, instead of being the shadows cast across the front stage by the movements of the courts unheeded in the rear . . . The main thing is what officials are going to *do*."[22] This was, to put it another way, Roscoe Pound's famous distinction between "law in books and law in action." But, as American lawyers with an eye on Germany have recently begun to notice, Germans got there first. The realists' insights about the defects of formal logic in legal thought, and the inherent and inescapable politics of law, were anticipated by several decades by such German-speaking "free law" thinkers as Eugen Ehrlich, Hermann Kantorowicz, and Ernst Fuchs. Less eminent and now forgotten writers of Wilhelmine Germany, such as the Bremen lawyer and notary Richard Finger, were turning their attention to the legal-theoretical lessons to be learned from legal practice. Finger lamented in 1912 the absence of a "science of the application of law," as a sub-genre of legal science, and he called for "a *literature* of the application of law."[23]

These German thinkers directly influenced the Americans, partly through the agency of Dean Pound, the publicizer of Ehrlich's legal sociology in America, and partly through the Germanophile Llewellyn. But because of the realists' rather Freudian conflict with their elder Pound, they seldom wished to acknowledge their German influences.[24] The "realist moment" in Germany passed, leaving no noticeable trace on the methods of subsequent historiography. German legal history today remains intellectual history—doctrinal and theoretical history, narrowly conceived—and German university legal education remains as narrowly formalist as in the late nineteenth century.[25]

To what extent can the historian make generalizations based on a close study of a handful of trials—a study of law in action—about a whole system of justice? This book certainly owes a theoretical and methodological debt to the "micro-history" of Carlo Ginzburg and others, and mostly avoids the kind of sweeping statistical treatment that, in the words of Richard J. Evans, "[does] not produce very many readable books."[26] For every gain in breadth there is a loss in depth. The criminologist Franz Exner, who in 1931 authored a groundbreaking statistical study of the sentencing practice of German courts, felt obliged to answer what he felt would be an objection to the statistical study of trial outcomes: "statistics are mass-observation and oriented to the typical; judicial determination of sentence on the other hand proceeds on an individual basis."[27] What we miss in a broadly focused treatment is, for want of a better word, the *culture*. Like the miller in Ginzburg's classic book, the actors in this book's stories could move only within the "flexible and invisible cage" of their culture; they could only articulate the possibilities that were latent within it.[28]

We will find clues to the essence of the criminal justice system in Berlin in very small and localized acts: a lawyer drinking champagne in the courtroom in the course of a murder trial, or a judge offering God's blessings to a man he has just condemned to four years' imprisonment. The reactions of contemporaries to champagne-swilling lawyers or demonstratively kind judges show us where these actions can be located in that culture's spectrum of possibilities. This information can tell us things the statistics cannot. What micro-history and the related practice of "history of everyday life" have in common is an attention to the human being in history. They represent a turn away from the grand teleological theorizing of the recent past and a return to narrative on a human scale. Perhaps the professional historian is uniquely susceptible to forgetting the humanity of the past. For him or for her, the past is largely a matter of paper: crumbling, yellowing archive files, the books of colleagues and predecessors. From time to time the historian needs to be jerked out of his or her working routine and reminded: this *happened* to people.

The argument that unfolds in these pages reveals a courtroom culture that changed dramatically in the years under study. To be sure, the courts at the end of the Bismarck era, that is to say in 1890, were far from simple engines of political repression; they often displayed considerable resistance to political manipulation "from above." But at the same time the early Wilhelmine courts were unfriendly environments for the conduct of an aggressive criminal defense, and many disciplines which would soon come to be inseparable from judicial activity—psychology, sociology, to say nothing of biology and chemistry—were as yet all but unknown in the courtroom. This state of affairs forms the essential subject of Chapters 2 and 3.

Over the following two decades the courts were transformed. The prestige of criminal defense counsel rose, and with it the freedom to make arguments for which earlier defense counsel would have been reprimanded, fined, or even disbarred. The courts gave out ever-lighter punishments; ordinary prison sentences increasingly replaced hard labor, while fines increasingly replaced prison. Judges grew more willing to hear psychological evidence or evidence of the defendant's social circumstances, which could exclude or mitigate guilt. At the same time, the willingness of prosecutorial and judicial authorities to allow demagogic agitators and popular superstition to influence the conduct of cases was causing increasing concern, especially among liberals; sometimes it seemed as though the judicial system was near to breaking down altogether under the burdens it was assigned. In the press and in parliament, the long-familiar complaints from the left of "Klassenjustiz und Weltfremdheit" were challenged by the right's laments of cultural decline and judicial permissiveness. These trends will be our themes in the later part of Chapter 3 as well as in Chapters 4 and 5.

Borrowing from recent American experience, I have used the term "culture wars" to refer to the increasingly strident late-Wilhelmine debates about a complex of issues relating to the criminal law: the treatment of prisoners, the use of psychology in the courtroom, the publicity of trials, and the "moral" tone of the media in general. Some readers may find this anachronistic, yet I would contend that the nature of the arguments and their political salience are startlingly similar to what we have heard recently at Republican nominating conventions, or in such episodes as the Clinton-Lewinsky scandal. This very familiarity is part of the often shocking contemporaneity of Wilhelmine Germany.

Thus although the focus of this book is on the micro-level, I also hope to make a contribution to some of the macro-questions of German and European history. The German justice system before Hitler has been seen as static in two senses. The then-prevailing positivist school of German academic legal thought took it as axiomatic that legal codification froze the evolution of legal doctrine, providing a clear and definitive scheme of precisely measured offenses and punishments, ensuring the transparency of justice, the predictability of outcomes, and the liberty of the law-abiding citizen. In this vision of a legal system the code gave the judge clear instructions for resolving any given case; influences on trials from politicians, and from public or scientific opinion were as unthinkable as creeping, unlegislated changes in legal rules. Historiography has taken this system at its word and drawn a similarly static picture. And yet it moved; and in its movements we may draw lessons about law and society that reach well beyond Imperial Germany.

The workings of the criminal law display with absolute clarity the quality of civil liberties in a society, and thus go a long way toward illuminating that society's political culture. The practices of the occupational groups involved in criminal justice are one of the major transmission belts from the world of bourgeois culture to the realm of high politics. The echoes of trials in the public sphere help us understand the contours of public opinion on some of the most essential subjects of political, cultural, and social history. And indeed this public opinion is perhaps the hero of the story. Perhaps nothing defines the twentieth century and distinguishes it from its predecessors like the sudden arrival of the great majority of the population within the magic circle of political and cultural relevance. A cluster of events at the turn of the century—the development of a true mass politics in Germany, paralleling the development of a mass press—and new developments in other media, such as the first motion pictures and the first million-selling popular novel, showed that "the masses have come into their own."[29] So while we will focus on a number of small and discrete events, we will attempt to keep in mind some of the larger questions with which historians of Germany and Europe have wrestled.

CHAPTER

1

In Moabit

This book is about the culture of the courtroom, and that means that it is also about the culture of the city. The courts of Berlin-Moabit, the jurists, witnesses, and defendants who were caught up in them, the newspapers that made the rituals of justice truly public—these were intensely *berlinisch* phenomena, and throughout the book we will see how the place shaped the events, in large and small ways. It shaped the people, too. Berlin's lawyers, although the more famous among them developed the practice of traveling to the "provinces" to argue cases, seldom wished to leave the city permanently. "Anyone who has once lived, worked, breathed, in this city," wrote the celebrated defense counsel Erich Frey in old age, "cannot forget it. One must love Berlin and admire it, again and again." That Frey wrote from the Chilean exile to which the Nazis drove him brings home the biting poignancy of his words.[1]

All great cities have their own romance: a stock of images, ideas about places, attitudes. The romance of a city may consist largely of clichés, but the fact that many people believe it gives the romance its power; it is part of the glue that holds together the imagined metropolitan community. Certain images dominate the literature of early twentieth century Berlin: the bars of Friedrichstrasse, the factories of Siemens and AEG, Sundays in the Grunewald, the new elevated railway and the five-sided *Verkehrsturm*—Europe's first traffic light—at Potsdamer Platz. These are images of growth and innovation, of new forms of leisure and sociability. Sometimes clichés are true. The romance of Berlin received its defining image in a book published in 1910 by the art critic Karl Scheffler, *Berlin: Ein Stadtschicksal* ("Berlin: Fate of a City"). Berlin's fate, said Scheffler, was that it was damned "always to be becoming and never to be."

Anyone at the beginning of the twenty-first century who surveys the landscape of pits and cranes around Potsdamer Platz or west of the Reichstag might conclude that Scheffler was blessed with prescience of a high order, but many contemporaries agreed with him too. "Where is Berlin?" Alfred Kerr asked rhetorically in one of his weekly "Letters from Berlin" for the *Breslauer Zeitung,* a question which editor Günther Rühle recently considered representative enough to serve as the title for a published collection of Kerr's pieces. The electrical engineer Georg Siemens wrote that "Berlin at the turn of the century was the most restless city in the world . . . Everywhere streets were torn up, piles driven in *(Spundwände eingetrieben),* kilometer-long building fences set up, temporary sidewalks laid down . . . the most common vehicle in the traffic was the mortar-wagon." The Hamburg art historian Alfred Lichtwark, returning to Berlin in February 1894 after an absence of a few months, wrote "so much has changed since the summer, it is as if I were in a strange city." And everyone talked about the pace of Berlin. The future mayor of West Berlin, Ernst Reuter, arrived in 1913. He did not care for the city: "Dust and appallingly many people, who all run as if every minute cost them 10 Marks." The man who updated Scheffler's Berlin romance for the mid-twentieth century, Walther Kiaulehn, wrote that nothing was more characteristic of the Berliner than the drive for speed, expressed in the emphatic words "tempo, tempo." Parallels to the newness and energy of America were always at hand—*Spreechicago,* some said, playing on the older tag of *Spreeathen*—except when an actual American came and found, as Mark Twain did, that Berlin's neighborhoods were newer and less gracious than Chicago's.[2]

The essential novelty, impermanence, and pace of the Berlin romance were also the essential qualities of the city's criminal justice system. The workloads of Berlin's courts were always heavy, and they increased steadily throughout our period. Private lawyers, prosecutors, and judges alike were always pressed for time, often ill-prepared for their work, often exhausted and sick. The Prussian government was never willing to allocate enough money to its courts to alleviate the worst of this situation. The resulting pressures only magnified the systemic and political conflicts endemic to the justice system. The place, in short, defined the culture of the courtroom. In this chapter, then, we begin with the place.

A Sense of Place

Criminal law in Wilhelmine Berlin had two poles: Alexanderplatz in the east and Moabit in the northwest. Alexanderplatz had the quality of an outpost. Its landmarks were symbols of bustling, prosperous Berlin: the train station; the statue of Berolina, the goddess of Berlin; Hermann Tietz's department store; Aschinger's, one of the world's first chain restaurants (10 *pfennig* for an open-faced sandwich, 30 *pfennig* for beer sausage and potato salad). But beyond the square, north, east and south, were some of the most miserable of Berlin's slums. Fitting the frontier quality, Alexanderplatz was home to the giant Police Presidium, completed in 1889. With a total floor space of 11,000 square meters, it was the third largest building in Wilhelmine Berlin, surpassed only by the nearby Royal Palace and the Reichstag. Nearly 6,000 people worked at the "Alex," from humble nightwatchmen to the criminal-commissars and inspectors, many of whom were local celebrities. The Police President had his official residence here, on the first floor at the top of an imposing marble staircase. But he had to share the building with up to 700 persons in police custody, and with the police horses, whose stables were spread across parts of two floors of the building.[3]

If one walked west from Alexanderplatz, through the old medieval core of Berlin-Cölln, across the Mühlendamm, and toward Leipziger Strasse, one would arrive at the political, commercial, social, and journalistic center of Wilhelmine Berlin. When it became the capital of a united Germany in 1871, Berlin experienced a profound transformation; increasingly trade and commerce, and not government and the army, set the tone of capital city life. By the 1890s the center of the city fully reflected the changes. Three streets formed the axes of "Berlin C." To the world they were Leipziger Strasse, Unter den Linden, and Friedrichstrasse. Berliners called them "Kaufstrasse," "Laufstrasse," and "Saufstrasse"—roughly, "shopping street," "promenade street," and "boozing street." Kaufstrasse: Leipziger Strasse could boast no fewer than three huge department stores. A measure of symbolism was inescapable. The young journalist Alfred Kerr wrote in 1900 of the great shopping palaces of Tietz, Jandorf, and Wertheim that had made Leipziger Strasse "a shopping street of the first order." It had not always been so; this was the street in which the Reichstag had once met and where Bismarck "gave great speeches" when "the Reich was in its classical period." Kerr found the transformation of Leipziger Strasse symbolic: "The fundamental character of the German people today is mercantile, not political."[4] Laufstrasse: Unter den Linden had its grand central promenade, where Berlin's most eminent citizens went walking or riding, and along the way (at least at certain times of night) might encounter great flocks of the more upscale prostitutes. Saufstrasse: Mark Twain reported that Friedrichstrasse's 254 addresses played host to 257 bars or cafes. A few other districts rounded out Berlin C. Along Behrenstrasse, just south of Unter den Linden, a banking district developed. South of Leipziger Strasse was the newspaper district, the home of the great press empires of Scherl, Mosse, and Ullstein. Along Wilhelmstrasse were the Prussian and Reich ministries and state offices.[5]

Here, in the company of bankers, rulers, merchants, and drunks, were the offices of most of Berlin's better-known trial lawyers. The acknowledged king of Berlin's defense counsel, *Justizrat* Erich Sello, had his office at Leipziger Strasse 6. The near-kings, the partners Max Wronker and Ludwig Chodziesner, were not far away at Königstrasse 1; Karl Schwindt, defender of the famous "Captain of Köpenick" among many others, was on the corner of Charlottenstrasse and Französischestrasse, at the tony Gendarmenmarkt. On Zimmerstrasse in the last years before the Great War one could find a young man with the imposing title *Rechtsanwalt* Dr. Dr. Erich Frey (the characteristically German double-doctorate reflecting his pride in his philosophical as well as legal studies).[6] A Berliner seeking legal advice would need to walk a little farther to visit two other stars of criminal defense: north on Friedrichstrasse to Oranienburger Strasse, "close by the Oranienburg Gate" *(dicht beim Oranienburger Tor)* as the office letterhead read, for the young Johannes Werthauer and the even younger Max Alsberg.[7] Perhaps these men found an advantage in being closer to the clientele, for it was Berlin North, north of the Weidendamm Bridge, that generated most of their business—the world of the "control girls" and their "Louis," the underworld *Kaschemme* (dives), the mean tenements of the poor and desperate. But the young lawyers would not stay there long. Even before the Great War Berlin was shifting west; the fashionable people and the expensive shops and cafés that catered to them were leaving Friedrichstrasse for Ku'damm and Tauentzienstrasse. The lawyers would follow. In the Weimar years virtually all the famous barristers would settle like Max Wronker on Ku'damm or Alsberg at Nollendorf Platz. Erich Frey's letterhead gave a clue to his free-spirited character, identifying his office location as Potsdamer Platz, "above Café Josty."[8]

A world away from the posh cafés and shops, back in unfashionable Berlin North, the major artery of Invalidenstrasse pointed like an arrow from the districts where crimes were nurtured and carried out to the places where they were officially processed and punished. Starting at Brunnenstrasse and running past the great *Vormärz* architect Schinkel's St. Elizabeth's Church, Invalidenstrasse crossed Ackerstrasse and continued to the southwest, to Lehrterstrasse. Here one would find the *Moabiter Zellengefängnis,* the most feared prison in Berlin. Built in the 1840s, it was the first prison in Prussia constructed according to the "Pennsylvania system": the four wings of cells were arranged in a radial pattern so an overseer could watch all floors at once. Solitary confinement was the rule. Prisoners wore masks even when they attended church services or the prison school, to prevent them from recognizing or communicating with one another. Executions were carried out here too, at least until 1889, when growing official squeamishness drove the executioner further to the northwest, to the prison at Plötzensee.[9]

Moabit, this section of northwest Berlin, was settled originally by the Huguenots, who came to Berlin in the seventeenth century fleeing religious persecution in France. They gave the area its unflattering name: "La terre de Moab." In the time of Wilhelm II, Moabit was in fact "one of the most populated and cheerful districts of the new Berlin, which grows from year to year and already in many respects threatens to rival the west."[10] But despite the broad streets and elegant apartment blocks, the popular Exhibition Park and the Glass Palace, in the popular mind Moabit remained the "cursed land" it was to its first settlers. The pedestrian could see why upon reaching the end of Invalidenstrasse. Sprawling along Rathenower Strasse on one side and Alt-Moabit on the other was a building with a deceptively unpretentious address: Alt-Moabit 11, the criminal court.

Criminal law was a new arrival in Moabit. It was only at the end of the nineteenth century that the center of gravity of criminal justice in Berlin moved out from the medieval heart of the city. In the middle of the century the *Kreisgericht* (the court for the suburban districts of the capital city) and an eponymous prison were at Hausvogteiplatz; nearby on Molkenmarkt was the old Police Presidium, along with the *Stadtgericht* (the court for central Berlin) and another prison, the *Stadtvogtei*. Dispersal began with new prisons: the Lehrterstrasse in the 1840s, the women's prison at Barnimstrasse east of Alexanderplatz, and even further out, the prisons at Plötzensee and Tegel, which dated respectively from the 1860s and the 1890s. But it was the construction of the new criminal court building after 1877 that gave criminal law in Berlin its symbolic as well as physical home, and that made Moabit a buzzword across Germany.[11]

The new court was built to house all criminal trials from all levels of the Berlin courts, along with providing office space for the prosecutors and

Alt-Moabit 11: the old criminal court when it was new. (Courtesy of Dr. Simone Ladwig-Winters)

judges. The location was chosen, according to a contemporary manual of Berlin's public buildings, "in consideration of the connections that the nearby *Stadtbahn*, as well as horse-drawn streetcar *(Pferdebahn)* and omnibus lines provided." Because of the sharp angle formed by the corner of Alt-Moabit and Rathenowerstrasse, the design, from architects *Ober-Baudirektor* Hermann and *Geheimer Ober-Regierungsrat* Busse, called for an A-shaped building. The focal point of the new courthouse, at the apex of the "A", was the Great Jury Court Hall, a grand room indeed, 20.4 meters long, 11.25 meters wide and 12 meters tall. In 1902 a writer described its furnishings and interior decorations, which "correspond to the significance of the room," with wood carvings on the doors and walls, "characteristic epigrams" painted on the walls, and portraits of the late Kaisers Wilhelm I and Friedrich III behind the judges' bench. Five stained-glass windows looked out to Alt-Moabit. The hall had room for 250 spectators, and there were two special "loges" which could be reserved for prominent official spectators.[12]

Behind the Great Jury Hall, between the two arms of the "A", was the smaller jury hall. This room, too, had its interesting features. It was entirely skylit, and decorated by six oil paintings of "female ideal forms with law books in their hands." The arms of the "A" themselves provided the hearing rooms for the lay-judge courts *(Schöffengerichte)* of the Local Courts *(Amtsgerichte)* on the ground floor, the criminal chambers *(Strafkammern)* of the higher Superior Courts *(Landgerichte)* on the first floor, and office space for the state prosecutors *(Staatsanwaltschaften)*, as well as the investigating magistrates *(Untersuchungsrichter)* on the second floor. In the crossbar of the "A" were the holding cells for women awaiting trial. Behind the courthouse was the starfish-shape of the men's holding cells. The building's most striking features were the two towers flanking the main entrance, in the style of mid-Victorian church architecture.[13]

But for all its grandeur, within two decades the scale of criminal litigation and the personnel of the courts outgrew the old building. In 1906, as part of a jurisdictional reshuffling and expansion, a new courthouse opened at the corner of Turmstrasse and Rathenower Strasse, on the far side of the *Untersuchungsgefängnis* from Alt-Moabit 11. The old and new courts were joined to each other and to the holding cells by a passageway to facilitate the movement of prisoners. The design of the new criminal court never drew much enthusiasm. Carl Vohl likened it to an eighteenth-century barracks (and he was one of the architects); many others, then and since, have called it pompous. Inside, its dominant feature was the great stone staircase of the entry hall.[14]

Perhaps it was inevitable that no one ever had a kind word for these buildings; they were stern houses serving a stern function. Little effort was made to make them comfortable, although one of the major design drawbacks of the old courthouse was inadvertent. The first drafts of the Code of Criminal Procedure *(Strafprozessordnung)* envisaged that judges would hear cases in panels of three. But in some last minute parliamentary horse-trading, liberals in the Reichstag accepted some curtailment of the rights of appeal from trial judgments in return for the addition of two more judges to the panels. By this time construction was under way at Alt-Moabit 11, with the criminal chamber hearing rooms designed for three judges. As a result there was never enough space. The criminal chamber rooms were cramped places for five judges to work, and they could seat only ten spectators.[15] The architecture thus treated grandly the jury courts in which ordinary people were most involved, and shunted into closets those courts that were staffed exclusively by professional judges.

Indeed, architecture decisively stamped Moabit's trials. Looking back years later, Walter Kiaulehn, who in the 1920s covered Moabit for the *BZ am Mittag,* recalled that in the criminal chambers "People sat on top of one another, and in the dark too, and this created the unforgettable atmosphere of familiarity and lamplight in which it was totally natural for the presiding judge to call the defendant by his first name, as in the notorious Sklarek trial: 'Okay, Willi, you can remember everything else . . .'" And beyond the architecture, these rooms had other qualities which could make the work that went on in them uncomfortable and unhealthy. The *National Zeitung* complained, "it appears almost incomprehensible how people can hold out longer than five hours there without damaging their health." Alfred Kerr, attending a trial in 1897, recorded that "the air is dreadful . . . when the Chief Prosecutor . . . courteously handed his bottle of smelling salts to [the defendant], it was . . . not merely a nice and humane gesture."[16]

Perhaps the discomfort explained the popularity of Becker's Wine Bar, across Alt-Moabit from the courthouse, "much visited by judges, prosecutors and defense lawyers, naturally also an eating and refreshment spot for jurors and lay judges." Becker's was the kind of place where the reputable denizens of Moabit rubbed shoulders with the not-so-reputable, often in an effort to find out what was really going on. It was no accident that the great journalist Maximilian Harden, in one of his screeds about a celebrated trial, set a (probably at least semi-fictionalized) argument about the case "bei Peter Beckers," as he and his interlocutor awaited the verdict. Walther Kiaulehn remembered "you had to be a regular if you wanted to get the news, and learn something about the presumed outcome of trials in progress; here one knew exactly what the presiding judge thought and how many years of hard labor the witnesses had probably sworn themselves into." Some of Becker's regulars were people who did not always take the laws of perjury very seriously. "I'd like to see the oath that I wouldn't swear!" was their motto; one did not always want to ask what they did for a living, or how exactly they were interested in the outcome of the trial.[17]

The Laws

As with the buildings, and Berlin as a whole, there was something raw and unfinished about Germany's criminal laws. They were formed of a complex clay of competing historical and philosophical sources, political and social agendas; and they would prove over time to be almost infinitely malleable.

The laws that govern any system of criminal justice come in two forms. Some are *substantive,* that is, they define what kinds of actions a society holds to be crimes, and stipulate the punishments that will follow those actions. The others are *procedural,* that is, they define how the state will prosecute and judge the individual who is charged with committing a criminal act, and what rights this individual has within the process.[18] The substantive criminal law of Imperial Germany was largely contained within one statute, the Reich Criminal Code *(Reichstrafgesetzbuch)* of 1871. The procedural criminal law was defined by two statutes, the Code of Criminal Procedure *(Strafprozessordnung),* and the Judicial Code *(Gerichtsverfassungsgesetz),* both of which came into effect on 1 October 1879. All of these laws were entirely characteristic products of the "liberal era" of Prussian-German politics; none of them received any significant degree of reform in the last three-and-a-half decades of the German Empire. The problem of the administration of criminal justice in the Wilhelmine era, then, was that of how to adapt these laws to a society which, within a few decades, had been utterly transformed economically, socially, and politically from its mid-nineteenth century condition. This task fell to the courts, and from the late 1880s to the First World War the way the courts applied the laws was likewise transformed.

The Reich Criminal Code, drawn in large measure from the Prussian Criminal Code of 1851, represented the world view of mid-century liberals applied to crime. In certain respects the new Code marked a degree of liberalization unknown in countries such as Britain: flogging was formally abolished, and the death penalty nearly so, although it was retained (only for premeditated murder) after Bismarck's strenuous intervention in the parliamentary battle. The provisions of the Code assumed that law-breakers were rational creatures, fully responsible for their actions; the best punishment was one measured to the seriousness of their act (a *Tatvergeltungsstrafe),* which could also serve as a general deterrent to other rational actors in society. There was no hint that crime might have social causes; the only concession to a loss of individual responsibility was section 51, which set up a rather restrictively worded insanity defense.

But the years after 1871, and especially after 1900, witnessed a great intellectual ferment in German criminal law, as in other branches of German legal thought. The liberalism, rationalism, and positivism of the Code, and of thinkers like the Leipzig professor and judge Karl Binding (who wrote that he "found his pride" in the complete dependence of his work on the study of statutory enactments, and dismissed as "dilettantism" the inroads that criminologists, sociologists, and practitioners of forensic psychology were making in the criminal law), began to give way to a more flexible conception of law's sources and a greater concern with its social ends. The Berlin law professor Franz von Liszt, founder of the "sociological school" of criminal law, advocated the incorporation of social and medical science in the criminal law, anathema to Bindingite positivism. At the center of Liszt's teachings was the idea that the law should not focus on the *crime*, that is on the breach of a statutory provision, but rather on the *subjective factors* that drove the criminal to act. The goal was, in a utilitarian spirit, to bring about the greatest possible social protection from repeat offenders. The more radical "free law" movement, which grew in part out of Liszt's celebrated seminar, held that codified law was inevitably too feeble and filled with gaps to be definitive, and therefore judges should operate independently in the heroic mold that these writers associated with the jurists of ancient Rome and judges of modern Britain. Strongly marked by the irrationalism of Nietzsche and Schopenhauer, the ideas of "free lawyers" like Hermann Kantorowicz and Ernst Fuchs constituted an even more drastic break than did Liszt's with the Kantian presumptions of Germany's Criminal Code. As Michael Stolleis has written, the revolt against legal positivism "stood in unmistakable connection with the general *Aufbruchbewegung* of that time, with the various 'secessions' of the arts, with the youth movement and the reform movement, in short with the unfolding of the modern." With all of this ferment, very soon after its passage, the Reich Criminal Code began to seem "the conclusion of an era" rather than the opening of one.[19]

Offenses in the Code came in three forms, defined by the punishment they carried: *Verbrechen, Vergehen,* and *Übertretungen*—major, medium, and minor offenses. A *Verbrechen* was defined as an offense punishable by death, hard labor *(Zuchthaus),* or custody in a fortress *(Festungshaft)* for more than five years; a *Vergehen* was an offense punishable by custody in a fortress for less than five years, prison *(Gefängnis),* or a fine; an *Übertretung* was an offense punishable by custody in the police cells *(Haft)* or with a fine of up to 150 marks. The death sentence applied only to premeditated murder and certain special offenses outside the Code, such as killing by means of explosives and several offenses under military law. The next most serious punishment was custody in a *Zuchthaus,* which usually involved solitary confinement, enforced silence, and hard labor. Justus Olshausen, a judge on the Imperial Supreme Court and author of the most respected "commentary" on the Code, wrote that "the essence of the *Zuchthausstrafe* consists, next to the deprivation of liberty, in forced labor." A *Zuchthaus* sentence could be lifelong in the event that it was substituted for a death sentence; otherwise it was to be for a defined period between one and fifteen years. The *Gefängnis* was the second most serious form of prison. A *Gefängnis* sentence could involve some of the harsher characteristics of the *Zuchthaus,* such as hard labor, but did not have to; the language of the Reich Criminal Code was permissive in this case rather than mandatory. The minimum *Gefängnis* sentence was one day, the maximum five years, with two exceptions: if a person were convicted of several independent offenses at once *(Realkonkurrenz),* the *Gefängnis* sentence could extend to ten years. Young offenders (persons under 18) could not be sentenced to death or to a *Zuchthaus;* instead, they could be given up to fifteen years' *Gefängnis. Festungshaft* was conceived as a *custodia honesta*—a jail sentence without dishonor. Here there was no forced labor, and in general such a sentence could not be combined, as other prison sentences could, with a deprivation of civil rights *(Ehrenrechte)* for a defined period after the serving of the sentence. *Festungshaft* was generally applied to those persons convicted of political offenses, or of dueling. It could range in length from one day to fifteen years; it could also be a lifelong sentence, although in practice this was all but unheard of. The Code quantified the relative severity of these sentences: eight months of *Zuchthaus* was equal to a year of *Gefängnis;* eight months of *Gefängnis* equaled one year of *Festungshaft.* The Code also provided for the imposition of fines in certain cases. In cases of major and minor offenses, fines were set at a minimum of three marks. There was no general maximum. Certain individual offenses provided a particular maximum; for instance, for usury *(Wucher)* the maximum fine was 15,000 marks.[20]

Berliners who were sentenced to time in a *Zuchthaus* generally went either to the Lehrterstrasse, or to the prisons in the nearby towns of Brandenburg on the Havel or Sonnenberg. For *Gefängnis* sentences the usual choices were Plötzensee or Tegel. Women were usually sent to the prison on Barnimstrasse. For those convicted of *Übertretungen,* the most serious outcome was simple custody, or *Haft.* In Berlin, a *Haft* sentence was served in the cells of the Police Presidium; it could range from one day to six weeks, or in the event of *Realkonkurrenz* to three months.[21]

As there were very few amendments to the Reich Criminal Code before the First World War, the way the courts applied those penalties gives an idea of how much courtroom culture was changing in those years. The Code did not expressly provide for fines as a penalty for any of the most serious offenses (*Verbrechen* or serious *Vergehen*); in the case of less serious offenses, fines were permitted as an alternative to custodial sentences, generally only where the court made an express finding of "mitigating circumstances." In a study published in 1931, criminologist Franz Exner traced the increase in the use of fines as a punishment between, on the one hand, the years 1890–1903 and on the other, 1911–1913. He found that for trespassing, in the earlier period 51 percent of cases had been punished with fines, in the later period 65.4 percent. For fraud the percentages were 22.1 percent and 41.4 percent; for grievous bodily harm 41 percent and 66 percent. Where the law allowed no possibility of imposing a fine, the severity of prison sentences declined. For the offense of sexual assault on children, Exner found that in the period 1890–1903 22.1 percent of cases had resulted in a hard labor sentence; 22.9 percent at least one year in prison; 45.1 percent between three months and one year in prison; and 9.9 percent under three months in prison. By the period 1911–1913, these figures had shifted to 13.3 percent, 24 percent, 49.7 percent, and 12.9 percent; thus the courts were much more likely to send an offender to the lesser form of prison and for a shorter period of time.[22]

If the problem for the courts in applying the substantive criminal law was one of how to carry out a piecemeal adaptation of sentencing practices to new ideas about the causes of crime, the problem in applying the procedural laws was one of steering between the Scylla of a too-ruthless efficiency and the Charybdis of procedural gridlock. This dilemma had everything to do with the hybrid nature of the laws of Imperial German criminal procedure, marked as they were by traces of inquisitorial and adversarial procedures.

What do these terms mean? The criminal trial procedures of Anglo-American common law are of an adversarial nature. They evolved with two critical assumptions: (1) that the trier of fact—the person or persons who determine whether or not an accused person committed a certain act—should be a passive spectator at the trial; and (2) that the trier of fact was more likely to be a jury than a professional judge, and thus had to be protected from evidence which could inflame, confuse, or mislead the uninstructed. The main implication of the first assumption is that it is up to the parties, the prosecution on one side and the defense on the other, to present the evidence for their case. The theory of the adversarial trial is that the truth of the issue in question will have the best chance to emerge if two interested parties do their utmost to bring out all of the evidence which supports their case.[23] The judge is supposed to stay out of the contest: "The over-speaking judge is no well-tuned cymbal," as no less a lawyer than Lord Chancellor Francis Bacon put it.[24] The implication of the second assumption is that countries whose legal system is descended from that of Great Britain have very large and complicated bodies of evidentiary law. The classic work on the common law of evidence fills eleven volumes;[25] an exegesis of the common law of hearsay evidence alone is a subject on which books can be written.[26]

When we enter a German courtroom, however—no matter if it is in the twenty-first century or the late nineteenth—we pass into an altogether different world. The Imperial German system was, in the view of its legal scholars, a hybrid of an "accusatory" (essentially what we mean by "adversarial") and an "inquisitorial" system. Inquisitorial trial systems were typical of all continental European countries in the pre-modern and early modern eras. In their most extreme forms they were characterized by secret proceedings, in which the judge acted as investigator, prosecutor, and trier of fact and law all rolled into one, with no defense counsel present.[27] An inquisitorial system, wrote Otto Schwarz, "obliges the judge to investigate all offenses. Here there are no parties." Of the practice in Imperial Germany, he went on, "Our criminal trial has an accusatory form, but an inquisitorial content." This meant that although the raising of an indictment was, with a few exceptions, a monopoly in the hands of the state prosecutor (the vital element of an adversarial system, as it separated the accusatory from the judicial function), the court ultimately had very wide discretion to examine a case at trial, to lead and shape the proceedings, and to make whatever final determination it saw fit.[28]

The classic expression of the discretion of a court to interpret the evidence in front of it, and thus a crucial element of inquisitorial procedure, was the principle of *freie Beweiswürdigung*—"free evaluation of the evidence." Paragraph 260 of the Code of Criminal Procedure brought this principle into the modern German criminal law when it specified that "the court decides over the results of the taking of the evidence according to its free conviction, formed from the content of the proceedings." Thus the only requirement that the law imposed on the decision maker was that he base his decision on evidence presented in the trial, and not on any "private source" of knowledge about the case or any documents which had not been presented at the trial. But in dramatic contrast both to the huge body of evidentiary law in Anglo-Saxon legal systems and to the canon law's formal rules of proof, "the essence of free evaluation of the evidence consists in the fact that the judge is not bound by rules of evidence, that is, by legal norms concerning the effect of evidence, or stipulations concerning under what circumstances a fact is to be seen as proven."[29] Another implication of *freie Beweiswürdigung* foreign to the common law tradition is that, as Schwarz wrote, the defendant "is not merely a party, but rather at the same time an item of evidence." Thus even the defendant's confession did not bind the court, or indeed do away with the necessity of a trial.[30] There were no plea bargains in German law.[31]

The significance of the role of the presiding judge in German law was entirely in keeping with the principles of an inquisitorial proceeding. Apart from the principle of *freie Beweiswürdigung,* the laws of trial procedure gave the presiding judge another important legal tool to ensure his control of the courtroom. Paragraph 177 of the Judicial Code stated baldly that "it is incumbent on the presiding judge to maintain order in the sitting." Judges were often willing, as we shall see, to interpret this provision broadly in the event of disputes with defense counsel and defendants. Indeed, in an Imperial German trial, the presiding judge *(Vorsitzende)* was the star of the show. He was not only responsible for directing the trial; he alone had the right to examine the defendant, and he was chiefly responsible for questioning all other witnesses. The other judges, the prosecutor, and the defense counsel could only question witnesses when the presiding judge was finished and after requesting his permission (which, however, he was obliged to grant). And presiding judges dominated their courts. A contemporary critic noted that individual chambers were known by the names of the their presidents and that an observer who knew the presiding judge could predict the verdicts of his chamber.[32]

But other general principles governing the conduct of a German trial pointed toward an adversarial character. The most important of these was the so-called "legality principle" *(Legalitätsprinzip),* which worked together with the "indictment monopoly" *(Anklagemonopol)* of the state prosecutor's office. The legality principle required the state prosecutor's office to investigate any allegation of a criminal offense that was brought to its attention. The Code of Criminal Procedure also created a legal means by which a dissatisfied injured party could ask the court to compel the prosecutor to proceed with a case which he had abandoned. The harsh-sounding legality principle had a benign intention: it was meant to prevent the prosecutor from making arbitrary, perhaps politically influenced decisions about who was to be prosecuted and who was not. The indictment monopoly, on the other hand, meant that *only* the state prosecutor's office could raise an indictment, and thus this side of an inquisitorial system was closed to the judiciary.[33]

The other important general principles of German trials—the principles of publicity, orality, immediacy, and unity—developed in the nineteenth century as reform-minded responses to some of the procedural implications of an inquisitorial trial. The principles of publicity and orality worked together: they required all criminal trials to unfold in the presence of the public with all evidence presented in oral form. There was an important exception to the publicity requirement. Because of sensational sexual revelations in the trial of an artist named Gustav Graef in 1885, an 1888 amendment to the Judicial Code allowed the court to exclude the public from a trial, or a part of a trial, if the evidence to be heard could endanger "public order," "state security," or "morality." But it is difficult to maintain that the Wilhelmine courts abused this discretion. Trials in Berlin were often scheduled by the court administrators to be held in the largest hearing room available if they were expected to attract a great degree of public interest. Even when the public was excluded, often representatives of the press were allowed to remain, as in the Sternberg trial in 1900. And the justice ministry could be assured of a round measure of public condemnation if press and public alike were excluded, as in the murder trial of Hugo Guthmann in 1899 or the second round of the Heinze trial in 1892.[34]

The principles of immediacy and unity, like those of publicity and orality, also functioned together. The immediacy principle required that the entire proceeding, with all of the evidence, had to take place in front of the court which had proper jurisdiction. The unity principle meant that a trial counted as one indivisible unit. If a trial were adjourned, it had to be continued at the latest on the fourth day after the adjournment, or all of the evidence heard up to that point became a nullity and the entire trial had to be heard again. Since the Code of Criminal Procedure (§245) also provided that the court could not reject a motion to hear additional evidence solely on the grounds that the motion was brought too late, but that the other party could be granted an adjournment to prepare to meet the new evidence, defense lawyers in particular often stood under suspicion of raising spurious motions if a trial was not going well. They knew, so it would be objected, that the new evidence could not be secured within four days, and thus their client would get a new trial at some future date. We will see cases in which courts read this intention into a defense motion, fairly or unfairly; the rule in section 245 was one of those liberal-minded measures of German procedural law which contributed to a significant degree of delay and gridlock in the Wilhelmine courts.[35]

The pre-trial proceedings in Imperial (and present-day) German law were extensive in comparison to those of English-speaking countries. Lawyers sometimes spoke of a three-stage process: an initial investigatory phase, the *Vorverfahren;* an intermediate phase in which a motions court called the *Beschlusskammer* made a decision regarding whether the case should proceed; and finally the main event, the *Hauptverfahren.* The defendant bore a different designation in each phase as well, the sense of which cannot readily be captured in English: in the *Vorverfahren* he or she was the *Beschuldigte,* in the *Zwischenverfahren* the *Angeschuldigte,* in the *Hauptverfahren* the *Angeklagte.*[36] A rough sense of the meanings might be conveyed by *suspect, accused,* and *indicted.*

The important matter of the form of court in which the *Hauptverfahren* took place was regulated by the Judicial Code; and just as with classification of criminal offenses in the Reich Criminal Code, the choice of court was keyed to the severity of potential sentence. The Judicial Code set up for all of Germany a court system of four levels, of which the first two levels, the Local Courts *(Amtsgerichte)* and the Superior Courts *(Landgerichte)* were trial courts, hearing cases at first instance, while the third and fourth levels, the Courts of Appeal *(Oberlandesgerichte)* and the Imperial Supreme Court *(Reichsgericht)* heard appeals. Less serious cases entered the system at the Local Court, more serious ones at the Superior Court, one—high treason—at the Imperial Supreme Court.[37]

The criminal division of the Local Court was called the lay-judge court *(Schöffengericht).* Decisions in the lay-judge court were made by a bench consisting of one professional judge and two lay judges, appointed like jurors from a list prepared by every local *Gemeinde,* or community. The right to be a lay judge or juror was limited to male German citizens of at least 30 years of age who had lived in their community for at least two years and who had not received public welfare payments any time in the previous three years. The last limitation in particular injected an element of class selectivity into the pool of jurors and lay judges. Into the jurisdiction of the lay judge courts fell the most minor of criminal offenses: minor and medium offenses with a maximum sentence of three months' *Gefängnis* or a fine of 600 marks, and such offenses as assault or libel, which were launched as private prosecutions rather than being handled by the state prosecutor. The lay-judge courts were the sweat shops of criminal justice. In 1887, while there were 48,096 Superior Court trials in Prussia, there were 377,321 trials in the lay-judge courts. Ten years later Prussian Superior Courts heard 64,837 cases, the lay-judge courts 454,032.[38]

Two kinds of Superior Court panels heard criminal cases: the criminal chambers *(Strafkammern)* and the jury courts *(Schwurgerichte)*. The criminal chambers dealt with a broad middle band of offenses: all medium offenses which did not go to the lay-judge courts, and those major offenses which carried a maximum sentence of up to five years' *Zuchthaus*. In a few instances the criminal chambers heard more serious cases: these included the sexual abuse of children, all cases of offenders under 18, and serious cases of theft, fraud, and receiving stolen goods. The criminal chambers were the only trial court in which there was no lay element. They were staffed by five professional judges, one with the rank of Superior Court director who usually presided over the sittings, the others being lower-ranked judges or assessors—newly minted judges without a permanent post. The jury court, on the other hand, was similar in structure and function to the English and French models. A jury of twelve men decided the questions of fact—that is, whether the accused had committed the acts charged. Three professional judges, usually a Superior Court director and two counselors, decided questions of procedure during the trial and, if necessary, the sentence afterwards. The jury court heard the most serious cases, including all cases of premeditated and unpremeditated murder, arson, and (interestingly) perjury.[39]

When the new judicial regime came into effect in 1879, Berlin was given two Superior Courts. Superior Court I was for the city of Berlin proper, Superior Court II for the suburbs. Superior Court I had only one local court in its territory, Local Court I, whereas a string of suburban local courts fed their cases to Superior Court II. After 1906, the jurisdictional boundaries became more complicated still with the creation of Superior Court III, which also took as its territory a wide swath of the fast-growing suburbs. Although the administrative buildings and hearing rooms for the civil side of these courts were widely separated, their criminal divisions were all quartered in the sprawling justice complex of Moabit.

Whether a trial took place in the lay-judge court, the criminal chamber, or the jury court, the procedure was essentially the same. The Code of Criminal Procedure set out a program for a trial in three phases. First, the presiding judge examined the defendant; the Code (§242) specified that this questioning was to take place in the absence of all witnesses. In contrast to Anglo-American practice, the defendant was not treated as a witness, and he or she did not take an oath to assure the truth of his or her testimony. When this examination was over, the trial moved into the phase of the *Beweisaufnahme,* or the "taking of evidence," in which the presiding judge (and others upon request) questioned the witnesses and expert witnesses. If evidence existed in documentary form—for instance, published articles in a libel trial, or a transcript of a judicial examination of a witness who had since died—then the presiding judge would read the document out loud to the court. Every time the court heard from a witness, or heard the reading of a document, the presiding judge was supposed to ask the defendant if he or she had anything to say in response.

When the court had heard all the evidence, the trial moved into its last phase, that of the closing addresses *(Plaidoyer).* The prosecutor spoke first, followed by the defendant or the defendant's lawyer. The prosecutor had a right of reply, but the last word always went to the defendant. In a criminal chamber trial, the court would then withdraw to consider its verdict. In order to find the defendant guilty, at least two-thirds of the judges had to agree on the verdict. In a jury trial, after the closing addresses of prosecution and defense, the presiding judge gave the jurors their "legal instructions"; in a jury trial as in a criminal chamber trial, any decision that was made "to the disadvantage of the defendant" had to be approved by two-thirds of the jurors. If the jury found the defendant guilty, the prosecutor and the defense counsel would make submissions to the three judges on the appropriate sentence. If the judges believed (unanimously) that the jury had erred in its verdict to the *disadvantage* of the accused, they could order another trial with a new jury.[40]

In theory, the four-tier court system made generous provisions for appeals, with criminal cases able to go through two or even three instances (by contrast, Britain created a Court of Criminal Appeals only in 1907).[41] But in practice the German system functioned restrictively. To be sure, the criminal chambers were not gentle with appeals from the decisions of the lay-judge courts. These appeals, known as *Berufungen,* were in the form of a complete retrial with all of the evidence heard again. At Berlin's Superior

Court I in 1904, the 10 criminal chambers heard 4,486 *Berufungen,* and overturned the first judgment in 1,874 of them—an astonishing 41.8 percent.[42] But the situation was very different with trial decisions of the criminal chambers or the jury courts. These were appealed directly to the Imperial Supreme Court in Leipzig, and could only take the form of *Revision.* A Revision was an appeal only on questions of law, generally on procedural matters, in which the facts as found at trial had to be assumed to be correct. If a case made it to the Imperial Supreme Court, the chances of a successful appeal were slight but not impossible: the success rate hovered around 15 percent to 18 percent. But only a tiny proportion of trial decisions was appealed. In 1904, for instance, only 88 of every 1,000 Berlin *Strafkammer* judgments were appealed to the Imperial Supreme Court; the next year the rate was 90 per 1,000. For jury court decisions in the years 1901–1915 the number appealed was 66 per 1,000.[43]

Compared to the Imperial Supreme Court, the intermediate Court of Appeal played only a minor role in criminal law. The Court of Appeal for Berlin and the Province of Brandenburg was unique: the eighteenth-century *Kammergericht* was incorporated into the new system after 1879 and kept its historic name, as it does to this day. But though the court itself did not hear many criminal cases, the chief officers of the *Kammergericht* played an important managerial role in Berlin justice. The president and chief prosecutor were the administrative superiors of all judges and prosecutors, respectively, in the Province of Brandenburg, and reported directly to the Prussian justice minister. Thus they had a great influence on personnel appointments in Berlin. The *Kammergericht* was housed in its old building on Lindenstrasse (now part of the Jewish Museum) until 1913, when it moved into larger premises at Kleistpark in Schöneberg. Since the end of the cold war, the Allied Control Commission has moved out of Kleistpark and the *Kammergericht* has returned.[44]

Besides an appeal, a convicted person had two other potential remedies: if the prisoner still maintained his or her innocence, he or she could apply for a re-trial—a *Wiederaufnahmeverfahren;* or he or she could accept guilt and apply for a royal pardon. But a *Wiederaufnahme* was rarely granted, and distinguished lawyers like Erich Sello and Max Alsberg thought that process was largely a matter of chance. Reports on pardon cases were prepared by the state prosecutor's office, which had a natural inclination against undoing by royal grace what the prosecutor's labor had achieved. Even the more conventional appeal routes had critics. Erich Sello wrote with disdain that the *Revision* constituted "a pure, and often enough completely unworthy, game of chance" in which glaring miscarriages of justice could be rubber-stamped, but inconsequential technicalities—"the court clerk in a weak moment forgot to note that a witness was sworn"—could result in a case being sent back for a retrial.[45]

The framework of Imperial German criminal justice was, in sum, filled with contradictions and ambiguities. Important aspects of the system embodied the hopes and demands of liberal reformers since at least the time of the French Revolution. Holding trials in public, and requiring that all evidence be heard orally were nineteenth-century liberal demands to replace the secret trials by documents "characteristic of absolutism." The creation of the office of the state prosecutor, and the associated legality principle and indictment monopoly, were meant to guard against the abuse of prosecutorial and inquisitorial discretion. These elements of the system were the more modern historically; public and oral trials, the jury, and the prosecutor's office had all been introduced into Prussian law by the energetic Minister of Law Reform, Friedrich Karl von Savigny, in the 1840s. At the same time that criminal law was opened to the view and participation of the general public, it was supposed to be largely closed to the rulers; that the judiciary was free from political interference was dramatically and unambiguously proclaimed in the first paragraph of the Judicial Code.[46]

Judges, however, especially presiding judges, had a near-untrammeled power in the courtroom, a power of which defense lawyers and others often complained. Here was a significant holdover from the older inquisitorial practices, one which could be easily adapted to the support of authoritarian rule. There were numerous procedural provisions which could ensure that the accused person received a vigorous defense and a fair trial, including generous provisions for public defenders (obligatory in jury trials); the wide scope allowed to the defense for the calling of witnesses and the raising of other evidence at trial; and such provisions as the requirement of a two-thirds majority vote of the triers of fact for a conviction. On the other hand, the defense counsel was almost completely excluded from the lengthy pre-trial process; he was subject both to the disciplinary control of the presiding judge within the courtroom (as the prosecutor was not), and to the often severe disciplinary machinery of his own profession outside of it (as we shall explore further in Chapters 2 and 3). Similarly, the system allowed wide scope for appeals in theory while largely denying them in practice. There were, in short, tensions inherent in the fundamental structure of the system: the real conditions of practice could pull it toward inquisitorial efficiency with an attendant risk of running roughshod over defendants, or toward adversarial latitude, with the risk of degenerating into a chaos of drawn-out trials and endless appeals. How would, how did, this system work in practice?

Moabit at Work

Visitors to Moabit's courtrooms often had difficulty identifying the prosecutor. It was easy enough to spot the others: the person with a policeman on either side had to be the defendant; the man in the black robe *(Talar)* at a desk in front of the defendant must then be the defense counsel. On the high bench at the front of the courtroom, the men in black robes and round black caps *(Barrett)* were obviously the judges. In the Great Jury Hall there was no difficulty spotting the twelve citizens on the benches by the windows. But where was the prosecutor? Many found it both surprising and menacingly symbolic that the prosecutor sat alongside the judges. The pseudonymous contemporary critic "Aulus Agerius" wrote that after the prosecutor's closing speech, it was not unusual to hear the defendant exclaim "'I appeal!'" for "he has taken the declaration, which came from the podium of the court, for the judgment."[47] The appearances, as Agerius added, were important, and said much about the ambiguities of the prosecutor's position in German law (though it is interesting to note that in the early twenty-first century the prosecutor in Moabit's courtrooms still takes his or her seat next to the judges).

The most serious and fundamental criticism that could be, and was, made of the administration of justice in Wilhelmine Germany was that the prosecution overbalanced the other elements of the system. But if we probe this common contemporary criticism, we will find that it requires much qualification; and in these qualifications lie some of the essential qualities of the practice of law in Berlin's criminal courts.

Like the courtrooms he worked in and the laws he administered, the state prosecutor was a recent development. The office was a product of revolutionary France, carried into Germany by revolutionary and Napoleonic armies. Since the German Rhineland kept its French legal institutions after Napoleon's defeat, the revolution's legal innovations, including not only the office of the public prosecutor but also juries and the public conduct of trials, found a foothold in German-speaking Europe, from which they could gradually spread east. It was Savigny who brought the prosecutor to Prussia in the 1840s. His conception of the office was summed up in a memo of 1846: the prosecutor was to be the "watchman of the law," who was "just as obligated to protect the accused person as to proceed against him." Thus the institution has to be seen against the backdrop of what came before. To separate the function of raising and investigating criminal charges from the judging of them, and to put the accusatory function in the hand of a quasi-judicial figure who had to carry out his principal task in the public arena, were important steps away from the secret inquisitorial trials of the early modern era.[48]

Yet by the end of the nineteenth century the real nature of the prosecutor's role in the criminal courtroom was by no means clear to all observers. Was the prosecutor an interested party in a case or another kind of judge? Otto Schwarz, a judge in Memel, gave an answer typical of the orthodox "Savignian" position. The indictment monopoly, he argued, did not make the prosecution a party in an adversarial system. Rather, the prosecution was supposed to search out exculpatory as well as inculpatory evidence. "These principles," Schwartz concluded, "prove clearly that the prosecutor's office is no party and has a strictly objective, not subjective, activity to carry out. It should investigate the truth; that is, the inquisition principle is definitive for it."[49]

But the questions of whether the form of a criminal trial was inquisitorial or accusatorial, and (consequently) whether the prosecution was a party, were strongly contested legal issues in Imperial Germany. Schwarz himself cited Ernst Rosenfeld, a law professor in Münster, as a champion of the opposing view. Rosenfeld wrote that the accusatory form of trial avoided the great danger that the judge would lose his impartiality: "The idea that the state's criminal law is a public law . . . devoid of definite administrative arbitrariness is only realized in an accusatory trial." Elsewhere he wrote "The parties . . . are first of all the state and the defendant." But like Schwarz, Rosenfeld admitted that "every sentence here is controversial to the utmost," especially "that there are 'parties' at all in the Criminal Code."[50]

One of the most thorough criticisms of the institution and the practice of the Wilhelmine state prosecutor's office appeared in the pages of the *Preussische Jahrbücher* in 1895. Entitled "The Influence of the Prosecutor's Office on Prussian Justice," its author was that "Aulus Agerius" with whose description of the courtroom we began this section. Agerius believed that this "institution which has been taken from France" had "never become popular in Germany." The reason lay in the drastic disproportion of the influence of the prosecution—merely a proxy for the government of the day—throughout the justice system. The prosecution, said Agerius, dominated the pre-trial procedures, even when there was a judicial investigation, because the investigating magistrate was dependent on the prosecution for essential information about the case. The motions chamber was supposed to serve as a check on the raising of unfounded indictments; but in Berlin at least, wrote Agerius, if the motions court rejected an indictment, the prosecutor could count on the criminal senate of the *Kammergericht* to allow its appeal, because four of the six members of that Senate were former prosecutors. The numbers of former prosecutors appointed to the judiciary was in fact a major theme of Agerius's critique. Four of the thirteen presidents of Courts of Appeal and nineteen of ninety-two Superior Court presidents in Prussia in 1895 were former prosecutors.

If these figures did not seem to constitute a large proportion of the senior posts, Agerius argued that the number of prosecutors who received such appointments was large in comparison to the relative numbers of prosecutors and judges in Prussia: there were only 312 of the former as against 4,125 of the latter, so that prosecutors accounted for only 7.14 percent of "higher justice officials." In the courtroom, not only did the prosecutor sit next to the judges, he was not subject to the presiding judge's disciplinary control of the courtroom, embodied in section 177 of the Judicial Code. The prosecution controlled all access to the courts: if a defense counsel wished to visit a client in jail, for instance, he had to submit his request through the prosecutor's office. The carrying out of sentences, even the preparation of reports on pardon applications, were tasks put in the hands of the prosecutor. As a result, the prosecutorial view was increasingly taking hold of Prussian jurisprudence, producing outcomes which, both in procedure and in substance, were flagrant violations of the popular conception of what was right and just.[51]

Was Agerius right? A few months after its publication, his critique received a rebuttal from a judge who dubbed himself "Numerius Negidius."[52] Negidius, who disarmingly hoped that his past experience as a prosecutor—"my depraved youth"—would not taint his argument, conceded many of Agerius's criticisms of Prussian justice. But where Agerius saw "everywhere system and tendency," Negidius saw "in truth only carelessness and lack of principle [*Lässigkeit und Prinziplosigkeit*]." The essence of his critique was that the intellectual and educational caliber of judges had declined sharply since the 1870s; in the face of these human weaknesses, the justice ministers and other high officials "paid too much rather than too little tribute to the comfortable principle of laissez faire." If there were too many former prosecutors in judicial positions, that was only because of the lack of talent in the judicial ranks; given the "disorganization, which especially since 1879 has been observable in Prussian justice," the higher officials were "happy if they even have a halfway qualified person for a vacant position, and they take them where they can find them."[53]

Abundant evidence suggests that Negidius's emphasis on expediency and administrative chaos was much closer to the mark than Agerius's paranoia. These mundane bureaucratic factors placed a powerful check on the influence that the prosecution could exert in the courtroom. Indeed, just as this debate got under way, the Berlin prosecutors' offices entered a period in which their influence (as measured in convictions secured in court) waned significantly. This decline in prosecutorial influence was in part a product of the structural conditions of law in Berlin: the heavy and growing caseloads, changes in the makeup of the cases reaching the criminal chambers, strained prosecutorial resources, and the efforts of defense attorneys and journalists who had it in their power to make any trial both a battle and a public spectacle. And partly it was a product of judicial independence and resistance to certain kinds of prosecutions.

To begin, the most serious offenses in Imperial Germany were tried in the form of court most likely to acquit the defendant—the jury court. In the 1890s, the juries of Berlin's Superior Court I acquitted a full 30.1 percent of the defendants who appeared before them.[54] Prosecutors knew that it was particularly difficult to get jury convictions for certain kinds of offenses. The acquittal rate for perjury, for instance, hovered around 50 percent.[55]

The acquittal rates of Superior Court I's criminal chambers in the 1890s are no less interesting. The all-professional, five-judge criminal chambers were always less likely to acquit their defendants than were the juries. Yet in the 1890s the judges appeared to become significantly more lenient. From 1883 through 1892, the criminal chambers averaged an annual acquittal rate of 14.7 percent. Then in 1893 the rate climbed to 18.7 percent, and from 1893 through 1899 it averaged 20.8 percent. Criminal chamber acquittals actually peaked in the very year Agerius wrote his article, in 1895, at 22.7 percent. In 1900 the rate dropped to 17.1 percent, and the following year it fell again, to 15.9 percent; the average rate for the period 1900 to 1906, after which these figures were no longer reported in this form, was 17.0 percent.[56]

How might we explain the behavior of the chambers, especially the sharp increase in the rate of acquittals in the 1890s, and the slight decline after the turn of the century? Naturally, any answer to this question must retain an element of speculation, as the deliberations of criminal chamber judges were private and confidential. Nonetheless, if we keep in mind the interrelation of two factors, namely, the jurisdiction of the criminal chambers, and the kinds of crimes (or at least prosecutions of crimes) which were on the increase in the 1890s, we can offer a reasonable hypothesis.

The business of the Berlin criminal chambers increased significantly in the 1890s. From 1883 to 1890, the annual average number of persons appearing before them had been 4,620; from 1891 to 1900 it was 7,205. The caseload grew especially quickly from 1891 to 1893. One might hypothesize, then, that the higher acquittal rates of the 1890s were related to the increased burdens on the chambers, a response to overwork, or poorly prepared cases. Further support for this hypothesis comes from the fact that in 1906, the last year for which we have these figures, the so-called *lex Hagemann* significantly reduced the workload of the criminal chambers by sending more cases to the lay-judge courts. The acquittal rate of the criminal chambers then fell from 18.5 percent in 1905 to 14.9 percent in 1906, with a drop in caseload from 7,280 to 5,077 persons.[57] But since the acquittal rate fell slightly from 1900 to 1906 while the caseload remained both high and constant, the burdens of work cannot alone explain the fluctuations in acquittal rate. For the rest of the explanation we must turn to the composition of the caseload of the criminal chambers.

In Wilhelmine Berlin, as in any other time and place, some crimes were more "politicized" than others; that is to say, their prosecution was more sensitive to official mood swings, and indeed to swings in public opinion. By no means were all politicized crimes overtly political. As we shall see in the next chapter, the Heinze murder trial of 1891 set off a moral panic shared by the Kaiser and broad segments of German society. One result was that instructions went out from the "all-highest place" to prosecute the sex trade more vigorously. Prosecutorial and judicial requests for the investigation of cases of procuring *(Kuppelei)* jumped from 817 in 1890 to 1,337 in 1891, to 1,713 in 1892—a two-year increase of 110 percent. In 1890, the Berlin police arrested 148 people for procuring; in 1891, 247; in 1892,

370—a two-year increase of 150 percent, occurring in the absence of any (successful) formal legislative change.

This vigorous investigatory and prosecutorial effort did not, however, pay proportional dividends in convictions. Procuring was an offense that fell within the jurisdiction of the criminal chamber. In 1890, the judges of Superior Court I convicted 422 persons of procuring (slightly fewer than in any of the years 1884–1888); in 1891 there were 494 such convictions; in 1892 the number rose to 686.[58] The increase from 1890 to 1892 was thus 62.6 percent—dramatic, but far from proportional to the prosecutorial effort expended.

The classic political crime of Wilhelmine Berlin was *Majestätsbeleidigung*—lèse majesté or libel of the Kaiser. Here the pattern of prosecutions and convictions was similar to that for procuring. Official requests to investigate *Majestätsbeleidigung* skyrocketed with the beginning of Wilhelm II's reign. In Berlin in 1887 there were 18 such requests; in 1888, 60; the average for the years 1889–1899 was 82.5, whereas from 1882 to 1887 it had been 10.2. But again the number of convictions tells a story. From 1883 to 1887, the average number of annual convictions for *Majestätsbeleidigung* in Berlin was 22; from 1889 to 1899 it was 28.5.[59] Reich-wide statistics show a similar pattern. In 1882, 524 persons were tried for *Majestätsbeleidigung* in Germany; 94, or 17.9 percent, were acquitted. These numbers are typical of the last years of Wilhelm I's reign. In 1888, 700 persons were tried and 146, or 20.9 percent, were acquitted; in 1890, the acquittal rate was 26 percent, and it hovered around 25 percent for the remainder of the decade.[60] This pattern repeats itself again and again for all those prosecutions that were most sensitive to the official mood. We see the same trend at work in publicly prosecuted libel and slander cases, other kinds of sexual offenses, and commercial crimes. So it seems that as an official desire to prosecute certain kinds of crimes more vigorously (which, as we shall see, was *the* story of criminal justice in Berlin and elsewhere in Germany in the 1890s) made itself apparent, the courts responded by throwing out a greater proportion of prosecutions.

Prosecutions of overtly political offenses declined dramatically after the turn of the century. To follow the example of *Majestätsbeleidigung* once more, convictions in Berlin fell from twenty-four in 1898, to fourteen in 1899, to four in 1900; after 1904, the annual number hovered between zero and two. On the other hand, prosecutions of other crimes which were less sensitive to popular and official passions showed a steady rise throughout the whole of the Wilhelmine period. Property crimes, such as theft, increased at a rate well in excess of population growth; and most theft cases were heard by the criminal chambers. Prosecutions for procuring showed another kind of evolution. After 1900, many procuring prosecutions had a more solid statutory basis, as the final passage of the *lex Heinze* in the Reichstag added the so-called "pimp paragraph," section 181a, to the Reich Criminal Code. Procuring convictions showed a slight upturn after 1900: the annual average of convictions between 1896 and 1900 was 620, while between 1901 and 1905 it was 710.[61]

Taking all of the evidence together, it is highly likely that fluctuations in the criminal chambers' acquittal rate were closely related to shifts in the composition of their caseload, which was in turn shaped by the political climate and the changing nature of criminality in Berlin. It is also likely that the judges viewed some of the politically charged cases that came before them with a skeptical eye. But there were other systemic factors—the pressure of business on the institutions, the defense bar, and the vigorous Berlin press—that operated as an important check on arbitrary and ill-founded prosecutions.

Prussian Justice Ministry documents suggest that, far from deferring excessively to prosecutors, judges frequently asserted their independence, even through complaints to the justice minister. In 1896, for instance, the president of Superior Court I wrote that "as I permitted myself to explain last year," the prosecution had a tendency to combine cases and defendants in one large proceeding when separate trials would have been more efficient and logical. For their part, prosecutors often expressed vexation at judicial reluctance to accept the prosecution's case. In 1900, Berlin's most important prosecutor complained to the justice minister that "according to experience" the criminal chambers at Superior Court I "required particularly strict proof" in press libel cases, thus he doubted he could win a particular case.

Sometimes the prosecutors could not even get the police to cooperate. Erich Frey wrote of a case in which the celebrated police detective Ernst Gennat enlisted Frey's aid in slowing down a prosecution. A man named Carl Grossmann, suspected of several murders, was in custody. The prosecutors wanted to take the case to court, knowing they already had enough evidence to secure a conviction and death sentence. Gennat believed Grossmann should be kept alive while the police investigated several other unsolved murders Grossmann could have committed. "It came to a major struggle between the Alexanderplatz and Moabit," said Frey.[62]

The evidence of day-to-day practice in Moabit's courts suggests that neither defense counsel nor prosecutors really conducted their business as if they believed that the judiciary was monolithically prosecution-friendly. Attempts on both sides to "judge-shop" show more clearly than anything else what they really thought. The assignment of cases to chambers was supposed to be regulated in order to prevent any such manipulation. Every year, each of Berlin's Superior Courts made up a business plan which assigned cases to chambers by the first letter of the defendant's last name. Problems arose, however, when multiple defendants were tried in one proceeding; then the prosecution had the discretion to name the case after whichever defendant it saw fit, and thus bring the case before a preferred judge.

One of the most conspicuous examples of such manipulation was the 1905 libel trial that the prosecution chose to call Kaliski et al. In this case it was clear that the principal defendant was in fact a man named Schneidt, while Kaliski's importance was secondary. But cases beginning with K went to the Fourth Chamber, presided over by the notoriously fierce Director Oppermann, from whom the prosecution had reasonable expectations of securing a conviction. First Prosecutor Isenbiel thus named the case for Kaliski rather than Schneidt. Asked by his superior to explain this decision, Isenbiel replied, with characteristic bluntness, that it was necessary "to entrust the proceeding to a presiding judge who was in all respects equal to it." Isenbiel's claim in the next sentence, that the expectation of "particular hardness" from the president of the Fourth Chamber was not decisive, smacks of protesting too much. Kaliski was represented by no less a defense team than the brothers Karl and Theodor Liebknecht. The Liebknechts fought the assignment of the case to the Fourth Chamber—unsuccessfully—with every legal weapon at their disposal. Against the backdrop of the underhanded prosecution tactics, it is perhaps easy to miss the significance of this story. If the prosecutors could rely solely on their influence with judges, as Agerius claimed, there would be no need for Isenbiel to engage in such tactics, nor any reason for the brothers Liebknecht to resist. As a final irony, even with the assistance of Director Oppermann's Fourth Chamber, the prosecution did not win this case.[63]

Sometimes defense counsel were more forthright in acknowledging the limits of prosecutorial power. In 1901 a Berlin lawyer named Ludwig Flatau went so far as to write that the influence of defense lawyers could dangerously overbalance that of the prosecution and the judge. It was already a tremendous advantage, said Flatau, that the defense had the last word in the closing arguments and that the lawyer could help shape the proceedings with evidentiary motions. But a new and graver danger arose from the practice of the "secessionist lawyers"—those who departed from the older traditions of the bar by striving for an acquittal at all costs through the unethical exploitation of the procedural rules. Against these secessionists, Flatau believed, the courts and the laws of procedure stood defenseless. Reviewing statistics on how many cases the prosecutors stayed before opening a trial, Flatau doubted that private lawyers were ever likely to be so objective.

Flatau would probably have considered Fritz Friedmann, among the most prominent of Berlin lawyers between 1880 and 1896, a "secessionist." Friedmann, like most defense lawyers, was inclined by mental habit and professional outlook to share most of Agerius's criticisms of the prosecutor's office. He mocked the idea that "their principal and favorite occupation consists of putting together exculpatory evidence on behalf of the defendant." But, like Flatau, Friedmann knew that there were important advantages in the hands of the defense. Above all, there was the "question of gifts": private lawyers were "almost always more astute, skillful, sharp-witted, and well-spoken than the judges, and, for the most part, more than the prosecutors." Friedmann claimed that in a sixteen-year career he had managed to win two-thirds of his trials. It is impossible to judge the accuracy of this claim, but he must have done well to justify his famously high fees. The great journalist Maximilian Harden held Friedmann in contempt, and yet could not help conceding that Friedmann was good at his job: "He was an excellent defense counsel because he understood how, in every case, to hit the big 'C' in 'Common' [*bei jeder Sache das grosse A der Allgemeinheit zu treffen*]."[64] More importantly, Friedmann's claim about the imbalance in abilities between defense counsel and prosecutors, and the contention that there were other important systemic checks on the power of the prosecution, drew support from an unlikely source—from the man whom Friedmann and all the other Berlin defense lawyers might have considered to be their principal adversary.

This man was the First Prosecutor at Superior Court I, the *Oberstaatsanwalt* Hugo Isenbiel. Isenbiel's position as the head prosecutor at the biggest trial court in Germany's biggest city gave him extensive influence over all areas of the criminal justice system in Berlin. He had considerable discretion over how cases were handled (and sometimes over *which* cases were handled, as in the famous trials of Maximilian Harden and Prince

Eulenburg between 1907 and 1909). Isenbiel was a tough prosecutor and was seldom a stranger to controversy. During the statutory rape trial of millionaire banker August Sternberg, in which Isenbiel himself was confronted by a suggestion of scandal, his defiant claim that "the state prosecutor's office is the most objective authority" ensured his enduring fame as a phrase-maker. But Isenbiel also had widely acknowledged talents as an advocate and an orator; even a left-liberal paper like the *Berliner Morgenpost* could write of one of his courtroom presentations, "legal gourmets will have had their rapturous delight . . . with this truly brilliant dialectic," and concluded that Isenbiel "has unarguably shown himself as a master." Isenbiel's superiors were scarcely less enthusiastic. His immediate superior, Chief Prosecutor Wachler at the *Kammergericht*, wrote to the justice minister in 1902 that Isenbiel "is well known to your Excellency by his accomplishments," and added that "this superbly qualified jurist" should be promoted to the Imperial Supreme Court.[65]

Perhaps it was this esteem of his superiors that occasionally gave Isenbiel the self-confidence for utterances that, ordinarily, no Prussian civil servant could permit himself. Isenbiel was clearly suffering from a fit of pique on 18 October 1907 when he drafted a long memo to Chief Prosecutor Wachler to explain why the prosecutor's office at Superior Court I could sustain no further cuts in personnel.[66] If the occasion was mundane, the outcome was not. Isenbiel's memo is a remarkable record of the world of Berlin criminal law as seen by one of its principal actors. It contains many surprises.

The first surprise is Isenbiel's tone of blunt annoyance. Ordinarily, officers of the Prussian justice service were expected to observe strict forms of courtesy and deference when communicating with their superiors. One wrote of one's reports that one was "honored" to submit them; and they were submitted "most obediently" (unless one was writing to the Kaiser and King, in which case the submission was offered *untertänigst*, roughly "most subserviently"). Isenbiel began his memo by grumbling that he "must not expect that . . . weight will be put on my personal experience, formed from long years of practice." Someone at the *Kammergericht* or the ministry marked in the margin, "This remark of the First Prosecutor might require a protest," and someone—it looks like another pencil—marked the margin with a line and a large exclamation mark.[67]

Isenbiel's first substantive theme was the uniqueness of his office's workload. "The Prosecutor's Office-I Berlin [the numerical designation of the office followed that of the Superior Court to which it was attached] is a unique authority," he wrote, "which simply cannot be compared with other authorities of the same type." First of all, it was still the largest in the country, even after the administrative changes in 1906 had created a third criminal trial court for the Berlin area. But even a purely numerical assessment, Isenbiel argued, would miss the point. One could not simply compare the number of cases handled by his office with those of other offices, because to do so would be to miss the essential *qualitative* difference:

> Berlin—and particularly the business area of the inner city—is today the burning point of all political, social, and economic life of the Reich. In it are concentrated, as in a great melting pot, from a criminalistic perspective, all the combustible political material, all the criticism of the administration of the state, all the rubbish and filth of literature, all the commercial and industrial hair-splitting, all the criminal cunning, and all sense of the toughest competition in the struggle for existence. Everything that emerges from this gigantic emporium falls to the examination of the Prosecutor's Office-I for criminalistic observation, assessment, and prosecution.[68]

The workload of the central Berlin prosecutors involved, for instance, an unusually heavy amount of reading. All of the political newspapers, especially the Social Democratic and the anarchist ones, had to be checked every day for criminal content; on top of this came all the brochures and pamphlets, posters, and other forms of entertainment literature that were published in Berlin. Other duties, such as communicating with foreign authorities, and—this comment, too, drew a ministerial reader's marginal exclamation point—the "instruction of provincial authorities" also consumed a great deal of time.[69]

But even in more normal criminal matters, said Isenbiel, it would be easy to draw a misleading impression of the pressures on his prosecutors. Because so many theft cases remained unsolved in Berlin, the cases were administratively consolidated into one at the end of each month, so the statistics understated the amount of prosecutorial effort expended. Even murder cases gave the Berlin officials more and heavier work than elsewhere. And if this were not enough, one had to consider the quality and quantity of defense lawyers in Berlin. Here Isenbiel was moved to a remarkable admission, which supported Fritz Friedmann's claims:

> With the numerous and shrewd defense counsel of Berlin, who can devote without too much strain a thorough preparation and careful consideration to every case they represent, the prosecutor is in an unusually difficult position. If this prosecutor is overburdened from other work, he comes to the sitting exhausted and sometimes even starts out insufficiently prepared and distracted. He is, therefore, as daily experience unfortunately teaches, not seldom intellectually inferior to the defense lawyer from the outset.[70]

Isenbiel was not alone in complaining about Berlin's defense counsel; judges frequently did, too, and if they were not supposed to express regret that the defense impeded convictions, at least they could complain that lawyers lengthened the judicial day. In 1913, in a report to the president of the *Kammergericht*, a Berlin Superior Court director wrote that a case had been "held up by the lawyer Werthauer . . . for more than two-and-a-half hours, through endless questions to the witnesses, and especially to the expert witnesses." And in 1908, the president of the *Kammergericht* complained to the justice minister of "the heedlessness with which defenses here are often carried out."[71]

The scale of trials in the capital also helped make the life of a Berlin prosecutor harder than elsewhere. Isenbiel complained of the "many sensational trials" which "occur year in and year out, and often lead to weeks-long court proceedings." These more protracted hearings made "relatively more claim on the work and performance capacity" of the individual prosecutor "than if he is on sitting-duty for only a few hours on two or three consecutive days." Isenbiel believed that his prosecutors were diligent "almost without exception" (a ministerial reader underlined the "almost"); but the long work days, eight hours of "hard mental labor," ten to twelve hours for some who were "intellectually less nimble," explained the "numerous mistakes and oversights, misplacement of documents, wastage and losses, which to my liveliest regret continue to occur here."[72]

Of all the elements of the Moabit culture it was the Berlin press, boisterous and mostly left-liberal in orientation, which complicated the lives of public sector jurists. In his closing address in the Sternberg trial late in 1900, Isenbiel lamented, "The press must be counted among the factors which have made it difficult for the Justice Department to do its difficult office." Looking back on a trial he conducted in 1892, Fritz Friedmann remembered how "the presiding judge visibly ... inclined more and more to my view; public opinion visibly turned more and more in favor of the defendants, through the ... reports which the highly regarded reporter Oskar Thiele sent to his papers." And in 1908, the president of the *Kammergericht* told the justice minister that the press, "which in Berlin watches closely over all events in court and engages in merciless criticisms, places particularly great demands on the peace and calm, the objectivity, the prudence and quick-wit, as well as the tact of the presiding judges." Under such circumstances "the presiding judge cannot do his office in the desired manner," and so from time to time "the official interest is seriously damaged."[73]

Yet much of the reporting on Moabit, especially that dealing with broad systemic factors, was not only agreeable to judges and prosecutors, it was probably inspired by them—a confirmation of how they recognized and sought to use its influence. The overcrowding of Berlin's courts and the overworking of its judges was a journalistic staple of this sort. The *National Zeitung*, for instance, reported in November 1898 that the fourth fourteen-day jury court session was about to begin, with another scheduled for early December. "The prolongation," it continued, "of jury court and often also of criminal chamber sittings into the late evening seems to be the usual thing; at least seven or eight hours daily without a break, but frequently even twelve hours and longer." And the judicial day did not end with the end of the sitting. "Even when the judge returns home from the sitting in the late evening, more work is waiting for him, brought to his house by the document wagon."[74]

In 1913, a minor journalistic flurry over an adjourned case provided a particularly revealing picture of the daily life of a Berlin criminal chamber. On 7 May the *Berliner Morgenpost* reported that on the previous day, the Fourth Criminal Chamber of Superior Court I had not been able to get through its docket; at 5:00 P.M., after eight hours without a break, the exhausted judges had adjourned the last three cases. One of these cases, against a man named Lindow, was a serious matter: Lindow was alleged to have attacked officials with a knife in one of the hearing rooms of the Moabit courthouse itself. Lindow's case had been set down for 1:30 P.M., but at 5:00 P.M., when the chamber adjourned for the day, it had still not been heard. A few days later, a lawyer by the name of Carl Loewenthal wrote in *Das Kleine Journal* that no one who was familiar with conditions in Moabit would be surprised by this story of chaos and delay. Appointments for hearings in the criminal chambers were, said Loewenthal, usually set at half-hour intervals. This scheduling was entirely inadequate, and the result was that anyone—parties, lawyers, or witnesses—whose case was not first on the list was condemned to wait, sometimes for hours.[75]

As was so often the case in Wilhelmine Berlin, the negative publicity led to a flurry of official reports. The presiding judge of the Fourth Chamber, Superior Court Director Hofmeister, was obliged to report to the president of the *Kammergericht,* who in turn had to report to the minister. That the incident could at least potentially derail the judges' careers can be inferred from the *Kammergericht* president's comment, "there is no occasion for . . . administrative measures." Hofmeister's report gives a rare glimpse of how the daily life of a criminal chamber looked from the bench. He pointed out several errors in the *Morgenpost* story, among them that the court had sat until 7 P.M. and not until 5 P.M. on 6 May, and included his court's docket for that day:

1. Nickel et al. for theft (two defendants, five witnesses)—finished 10:15 A.M.
2. Pape et al. for abortion (two defendants, two witnesses, one expert witness)—finished 1:50 P.M.
3. Nanjocks et al. for professional gambling (nine defendants, two witnesses)—finished 3:25 P.M.
4. Steinweh et al. for serious theft (three defendants, ten witnesses)—finished 5:20 P.M.
5. Schrieber et al. for a negligently falsely sworn declaration (two defendants, three witnesses)—finished 7:00 P.M.
6. Lehmann for embezzlement (one defendant, one witness).
7. Lindow for resistance to state authority, uttering threats, etc. (one defendant, seven witnesses, one expert witness).[76]

After such a day it would not be difficult to imagine the onset of judicial fatigue.

Berlin's defense counsel were no less subject to long hours, stress, and fatigue. Fritz Friedmann started a trend among Berlin lawyers when he began traveling extensively to other parts of Germany and even abroad to argue cases. As Friedmann's colleague Franz Hoeniger wrote in 1906: "Today in Breslau, tomorrow in Cologne, the day after tomorrow in Königsberg, now entrusted with a London matter, now with an Austrian criminal case . . . Today our great ones plead, so to speak, with one foot on the train." Friedmann himself left this memorable passage, capturing the

He knew how to hit the big "C" in "Common": Fritz Friedmann.

new spirit of movement that the technology of the nineteenth century had brought to Berlin's self-confident advocates:

> Once in all the long years I managed to plead cases in two different cities on the same day, and nonetheless hold my office hours again in the afternoon. It went like this: At 9:00 A.M. I pleaded before the Imperial Supreme Court in Leipzig; at 10:00 I traveled to Magdeburg, arrived there at 12:30 . . . defended the Deputy Gräf for libeling the noncommissioned officers of the German Army (acquittal); was back at the Magdeburg station at 3:00 P.M., and two hours later in Berlin.[77]

The best-known defense counsel were in high demand. Friedmann claimed that in the nearly sixteen years of his practice he had defended approximately 22,000 people, and that in the 1890s fifty to sixty clients or potential clients would visit his office hours every afternoon. Another famous lawyer, Karl Schwindt, wrote that in 1902 he conducted defenses in 565 criminal cases, and 543 in 1903.[78]

It was probably the stress of the work, together with the necessity of long hours spent in the cramped and airless, but very public, Moabit courtrooms, which explained the strikingly bad health of seemingly everyone in the criminal justice system. Karl Schwindt sought an adjournment of a discipline hearing in 1904 by submitting a doctor's note attesting to his neurasthenia, which was "a result of the piling-up of his professional work." Schwindt had also recently suffered from appendicitis, a tonsil infection, and high fever, "which has left a considerable general weakness in the patient." In 1896, the president of Superior Court I reported to the justice minister that an influenza epidemic among the criminal judges of his court had played havoc with the work schedule in the last months of 1895; many trials had been delayed or adjourned, as it was so difficult to find replacement personnel. A few years later the *National Zeitung* reported that "anyone in touch with judicial circles" would know that the Berlin judges could only get through their allotted workload at the cost of sacrificing their health. The number of judges who had to be given sick leave increased every year, and "even soundly healthy, productive personnel, who have come to Berlin from the provinces, exhaust themselves in a few years."

The sickness of key personnel could color whole trials. Early in 1908, reporting on the second round of the lengthy battle between Maximilian Harden and Count Kuno von Moltke, the *Berliner Börsen-Courier* wrote that "a unique and characteristic quality of this trial was that it was a trial between sick people . . . the courtroom looked like a sick-bay." And in the celebrated Heinze trial of 1891, three of the four principal legal personnel, along with one of the two defendants, were in poor health during the proceedings: Superior Court Director Rieck had just returned from a rest-cure; defense counsel Richard Cossmann had to drink on the job to calm his nerves; the other defender, Alfred Ballien, had been partially paralyzed by a stroke while still in his mid-twenties, and eventually died aged only fifty-three.[79]

In the end, everything—the crush of business in the courtrooms, the shortage of personnel, the pressures on prosecutors and judges—came down to money. The Prussian justice department was notoriously miserly, a point brought home again and again by the harried requests for more personnel that fill the archived files from the trial courts and the prosecutor's offices. Anyone familiar with the situation in Prussia was in for a surprise when he traveled and found that funds were not always so tight elsewhere. Maximilian Harden, while a plaintiff in a libel case in Munich, was amazed at the creature comforts of a Bavarian courtroom. His description stands in marked contrast to those we have seen of the cramped and airless hearing rooms in Moabit: "Nothing wanting here in the way of space, air, light . . . Room 5. Bright, large, simple. On the court table a crucifix: opposite the King of Bavaria. Not one item of cleaning equipment. (Coat hooks. Couldn't Prussia's justice budget finally afford them?)" Berlin police detective Hans von Tresckow, in London to enlist the aid of Scotland Yard with a case, found that his English counterparts "have money richly at their disposal and they need not, like German police officials, account precisely for every mark spent." The left-liberal *Vossische Zeitung* complained in 1892 that in Berlin's courts "a chamber without supernumerary judges is a rare exception, a Director is listed as being with several chambers, and a great number of standing courts must be staffed with Assessors instead of tenured judges." The responsible party for the situation was, in the first place, Justice Minister Ludwig von Schelling, but behind Schelling was perhaps the real villain of the piece, the notoriously frugal Prussian Finance Minister Johannes von Miquel. Schelling, said the *Vossische,* could be certain that if he acted forcefully to get Miquel to "open his hand" he would have the support of public opinion. It was not just the liberal papers that complained. In 1895 the conservative *Kreuzzeitung* criticized "the 'frugality' which the Herr Finance Minister has imposed on the Justice Department," without regard for the "especially difficult" conditions of Berlin's courts.[80]

What is striking about the evidence from all sides is the unanimity with which the themes of Isenbiel's irritable memo and of scores of journalistic critiques are repeated: Berlin was unique in the onerous demands it placed on everyone in the criminal justice system. Time and resources were always short, and the officials, whether judges, prosecutors, or police officers, felt overwhelmed and overmatched. The result was that the system could never operate as these authorities wished, and the picture of an over-mighty prosecutor's office, coupled with a judiciary compliant to the state's every whim, should be seen for what it was: an oppositional political myth.

The Lore of Moabit

Moabit itself came to have a folkloric position in the life of Berlin, indeed in Germany as a whole; it became one of those designations for a district of a city—like Wall Street or the Left Bank—which transcended its physical location to become a metaphor. There were many hundreds of criminal courts in Germany, wrote Franz Hoeniger, but none of them could claim to be the center and subject of a whole genre of literature. "Indeed, there is a Moabit novel, and it is practiced not only by Berlin authors," he claimed. Nor was the novel the only artistic genre in which the life of Moabit was depicted. There were even Moabit folk songs and Moabit poems. Some of the practitioners of Moabit literature were very well-known writers; the famous journalist and cabaret performer Hans Hyan, for instance, attracted favorable notices for his "Berlin Criminal Lyrics." Hyan knew the turf: he had an extensive criminal record and could speak—and sing—with authority on the culture and speech of the underworld.[81]

There is no mistaking the tone of hucksterism and bumptious civic pride that emerges from many contemporary accounts of Moabit. When Hoeniger described a typical crowd of spectators at a great criminal trial, he broke into a kind of society-column gush, praising the "real carriages," the "dresses, uniforms, the stars of orders, the thoughtful countenance of the scholar, the jewelry of the famous actress, the heroes of the press, and the corphyries of the bar." It was, he concluded, "the great international world which has one of its meeting places here, like in Nice or Cairo." This was the kind of tone that Alfred Kerr mocked when he wrote of the enthusiasm for a recent murder trial and romantic suicide in wealthy Berlin West: "One is unconsciously happy that such super things happen in Berlin. They are so 'big city.'"[82]

Such self-satisfaction and boosterism were shared by Berlin's press. Berlin, said the *Berliner Tageblatt* in 1904, was "the newspaper city par excellence." The development of the modern newspaper industry lay, to be sure, only some thirty years in the past (in other words, implied though not stated, when the *Berliner Tageblatt* itself came into being); but the development since that time had taken a form which no one in the early 1870s would have thought possible. The press was "the seventh great power," and Berlin's press was certainly not the least of contributors to the media's collective might. In 1904, 1,500 newspapers and periodicals were being published in Berlin, a third of all titles in Germany. About 50 of these were "political dailies," and there were a further 32 weekly, bimonthly, or monthly journals that also followed "a political or social-political purpose."[83]

The last quarter of the nineteenth century saw a huge expansion in the circulation of newspapers in Germany. What this meant was that a new kind of newspaper emerged, typified in Berlin by the offerings of three great media empires. August Scherl had been the first of the new-style press barons with his *Berliner Lokal-Anzeiger*. What made the *Lokal-Anzeiger* different from older papers of right or left, such as the conservative *Kreuzzeitung* or the liberal *Vossische Zeitung*, was a much greater reliance on advertising to cover the printing costs (hence the name—*Anzeiger* means "advertiser"). This made the newspaper much cheaper than its predecessors and put it in reach of a new mass audience. Scherl's paper was correspondingly less high-minded than its competitors and devoted itself to previously neglected subjects, such as local news—and especially crime.

Scherl's formula was emulated by two other publishers, whose support for left-liberal politics nonetheless distinguished them from the conservative-monarchist Scherl. These were Leopold Ullstein, with his flagship *Berliner Morgenpost* and racier *BZ am Mittag*, and Rudolf Mosse, proprietor of the *Berliner Tageblatt*. By the beginning of the twentieth century, these papers together were selling many hundreds of thousands of copies every day. Numerous contemporary accounts, from novelists, memoirists, even child-artists, bring home the centrality of newspapers to the city's culture. In Theodor Fontane's late novel *Die Poggenpuhls*, for instance, the mother of an aristocratic family down on its luck says she would rather stay home to read the *Tageblatt* than go to the theater; her brother-in-law, in a heartfelt tribute to urban pleasures, includes among them reading the newspaper in Café Josty, and the way in which "in all the noise and confusion all at once comes the call 'extra editions,' like a cry of 'fire' in the old days . . . as if at least the world were ending."[84]

Stories about criminal trials (almost never the much less sensational civil cases) made up a considerable portion of the new mass papers. Most journals ran a regular column headed *Gerichtliches* or *Aus dem Gerichtssaal* ("From the Courtroom"). When a major trial was in progress, these one or two paragraph synopses gave way to full transcripts, which could spread across several closely printed pages. The reporters were always a conspicuous part of the Moabit scene. In images that capture the striking modernity of Wilhelmine Moabit, Hoeniger described the press photographers rushing to capture the "famous judge or prosecutor" for the illustrated papers, and noted that "In front of the building stand a dozen motorcycles of the great Berlin newspapers, which are supposed to carry the fresh reports in sections at rush speed to the editors."[85]

Pictures from the Berlin Palace of Justice in Moabit, from the 1880s. The defense lawyer, bottom left facing the viewer, bears a striking resemblance to Fritz Friedmann.

Newspaper accounts (along with folk songs and poems) were not the only forms of popular media through which Moabit stories circulated. There was also the genre of the "Moabit pamphlet." Hoeniger's own account was only one of many in Hans Ostwald's *Grossstadt Dokumente* series, which demonstrated a particular interest in stories of Berlin underground and after dark. In the wake of any "sensational trial" one could expect a flood of pamphlets, often written by participants, including the lawyers. Walter Bahn wrote a pamphlet for Ostwald's *Grossstadt Dokumente* series entitled "My Clients," giving an inside account of three of his most famous cases, including those of Theodor Berger and Wilhelm Voigt (see Chapters 2 and 5). Elsewhere he wrote about his client Frau v. Schoenebeck-Weber, who in 1910 stood trial for the murder of her husband. Defense lawyer David Halpert published a pamphlet on the statutory rape trial of the banker August Sternberg in 1900, while the trial was still in progress, for which breach of propriety he was obliged to face the lawyers' discipline tribunal. Erich Sello wrote widely about trials, his own and those of others.[86]

Another genre of pamphlet, as a rule of much lesser quality, might be characterized as "self-justifications of witnesses or defendants." Works of this sort bore titles such as *My Credibility in the Metternich Trial,* by Gertrud Wertheim, or *A Judicial Murder and the Herr Superior Court Director Brausewetter in Berlin,* the latter written by a sleazy newspaper publisher named Wilhelm Friedenstein, who had been convicted of blackmail and whose own defense seemed only to confirm his guilt.[87] Pamphlets that sought to use a sensational trial to support a political argument made up a third category. Such writings came commonly from the political extremes, those who saw, or at least wished to depict, conspiracy behind any and all events: Social Democrats and anti-Semites.[88]

The great criminal trials became shared events, reflecting the sense of community that the new press could create in the impersonal space of the big city. Maximilian Harden, writing about the murder trial of Theodor Berger in 1904, noted that for eight days the case had been "almost the only subject of conversation at the commercial counselor's place and in the shoemaker's cellar"; no one had been so curious about the Moabit "penal factory" since—well, since the last sensational trial. When the *Berliner Tageblatt* first announced the discovery of Berger's victim, it noted that the excitement caused by a similar discovery of the previous week had not yet died down. In this atmosphere, "news of the terrible discovery spread across Friedrichstadt and to the other parts of the city with lightning speed." A few days later the *Tageblatt* reported that there were many rumors about the case, "easily believed by the agitated populace." And when a suspect in the case emerged, the *Tageblatt* thought it particularly suspicious that he claimed not to have heard of the murder until Sunday, when "all Berlin was speaking of it" on Saturday night.[89]

In such an atmosphere, it is not surprising to find that there was a substantial Moabit oral tradition running alongside the information disseminated by the press and the pamphlet industry. The keepers of the oral tradition were often those people who were fixtures on the Moabit scene but not jurists; they were guards or bailiffs, secretaries in the lawyers' robing room, or regular Moabit reporters. "A bailiff, for instance," said the *8 Uhr Abendblatt*, "is a very important person in Moabit: defendants, witnesses, and visitors to the court are in great part dependant on his good will."

One such man was *Justizwachtmeister* Ferdinand Beate, known as "Nande" to initiates, who guarded the criminal court for a quarter-century until his retirement in 1925. Nande saw everything: he was offered bribes of up to 200 marks to secure places in the gallery for celebrated trials; he managed the correspondence of the Kaiser's friend Prince Eulenburg during the prince's 1908 perjury trial; he even defended the court's cash box during the revolution of 1918. He knew what was going on in every courtroom and kept the reporters informed of where they would likely find the best story.

The attendants in the lawyers' lounge played an absolutely central role in lawyers' lives. Probably the most celebrated was Willy Naatz, who began working in the lawyers' lounge as a boy of fourteen in the early 1890s and kept at it until his death in 1955. Naatz's duties would not have been easy to enumerate. They included shepherding lawyers from chess matches to trials, or seeing to it that Erich Frey was suitably groomed and robed for a trial when he appeared at court in the morning, still dressed in tuxedo and top hat after a night of carousing. During the Nazi years, Naatz had the subtle task of engaging new arrivals in the lawyers' lounge in careful conversation to determine whether the strength of their National Socialist feelings was "hot," "lukewarm," or "cold." And he stayed in touch with many of Berlin's Jewish lawyers after they had been deported to concentration and death camps; cards and letters to him from places like Theresienstadt are in many cases the last traces of these victims of Nazi lawlessness.[90]

Some of the oral tradition eventually found its way into print. A popular genre of the printed oral tradition was the "humor in court" book, of which there was a great flowering around the turn of the century. These books were collections of anecdotes, never attributed to a particular court at a particular time, which either mocked the speech and habits of working-class Berliners (with a heavy reliance on phonetic renderings of the Berlin accent), or alternatively celebrated the mother-wit of the true Berliner when confronted with authority figures.

Fritz Friedmann's memoirs were another great repository of the Moabit oral tradition. One story he retold concerned a lawyer named Vincenz Deycks, one of the grand old men of the criminal defense bar when Friedmann entered practice in 1880, who was something of a figure of fun to the younger lawyers. On one occasion Deycks was late for the hearing of a fraud case. The prosecutor laconically asked for a sentence of three months, and the judges were retreating to their deliberating room when Deycks appeared, still carrying his robe in his hands. He called only two words after the judges—"civil claim." Then he put on his robe and confidently clapped the defendant on the shoulder. "You will be acquitted," he said. When the court returned, the presiding judge nodded to Deycks and announced, "The court has accepted in every respect the enlightening presentation of the defense counsel. The witness indeed has a simple civil claim against the defendant. The latter is therefore acquitted." It perhaps says something about the nature of an oral tradition that the Berlin chronicler and Moabit reporter Walther Kiaulehn—who came on the Moabit scene about four decades after Deycks had left it—tells this story as if it were about the star lawyer of the 1920s, Max Alsberg.[91]

Judges, too, could come in for this sort of treatment. Hoeniger wrote with a mixture of condescension and nostalgia of the folksy and not especially diligent judges of Moabit's early years. These judges could be especially annoyed by any effort to lengthen their work day through appeals from lower court decisions. On one such occasion, according to Hoeniger, a judge saw the defense counsel enter the court and called out to him, "You don't need to say anything at all, it is just an appeal of the prosecutor, it will be turned down one way or the other." When the prosecutor complained that he would have to make a motion to reject the judge for bias, the judge replied, "Oh, don't hold up business, I am really not at all biased."[92]

But, writing in 1906, Hoeniger acknowledged that "this nice time is past." The notion that Moabit had once been a kinder and gentler, if less professional, place was shared by most observers around the turn of the century. Such claims and wishes sound like a normal exercise in nostalgia, the evocation of a golden age that always lies two or three decades in the past. But they had a sound basis; the changes in culture could be traced in large part to the changing structural conditions of legal practice. And few lawyers coming to the profession in the 1890s gave any sign that they really hankered after a lost age of cozy relations with judges and prosecutors. With the beginning of the 1890s, a significantly more conflictual spirit came to Moabit. Why this should be so, and how the conflict played out, is the subject of the next two chapters.

CHAPTER

2

The Berlin of Surrogates

Nightwatchman Friedrich Braun was murdered in the yard of St. Elizabeth's Church early in the morning of 27 September 1887.

Braun was a representative of a very old tradition. There had been municipal nightwatchmen in Berlin since 1677. Administratively separate from the regular police, who came under the authority of the Prussian Interior Ministry, the institution of the nightwatchman was redolent of the proud town culture of the early modern era. The image was cozy and reassuring: a jovial man with a whistle and a set of keys who went on duty between 10 P.M. and 5 A.M. (11 P.M. to 3 A.M. in the summer) to arrest "beggars or lewd persons," or report those who went about with "naked light or coals." The watchmen kept keys of the buildings in their territory; for a tip they would open the doors for revelers returning home late. Or they would provide a wake-up call for those who had to go to work early.[1]

But in the Berlin of the 1880s this quaint figure seemed increasingly obsolescent. The city was growing, industrializing; migrants poured in from Pomerania and Silesia and West Prussia to fill the shops and the factories, and the suburbs rolled out to meet them over the flat markish landscape. When Prussia went to war with Austria in 1866 Berlin was a city of 665,000; at German unification only four years later the population stood at 824,000; by 1887 it was just short of a million and a half. Entrepreneurs responded by building a ring of new tenement housing districts, "from Wedding to Kreuzberg, from Moabit to Friedrichshain." Berlin's strict building regulations required that the tenements be built around a courtyard of at least five-and-a-half square meters—just wide enough to allow a fire wagon to turn around. Facing the street and usually containing the best apartments was the *Vorderhaus;* parallel to the *Vorderhaus,* behind the courtyard, was the *Hinterhaus;* joining them were the wings, the *Seitenflügel*. Some of the larger complexes repeated the pattern with a succession of courtyards, *Seitenflügel* and *Hinterhäuser* reaching back from the street; one building on Ackerstrasse had six such courtyards and was home to a thousand people. Berlin argot soon came up with a name for these tenements: they were *Mietskaserne,* "rental barracks." Especially in the north and east the rental barracks ranged for miles, street after street, around Alexanderplatz and the Scheunenviertel, north to Wedding and Reinickendorf, east to Pankow and Weissensee.[2]

Most everyone found this cityscape dispiriting: "Everywhere . . . the same boring streets, big-city apartment blocks and sooty factories, the same barracks-like quality and falseness," wrote Karl Scheffler, self-educated but high-minded art critic; "one can live for ten years in Berlin and still get hopelessly lost in the northern or eastern parts of the city." Around Alexanderplatz or in Steglitz, Tempelhof, or Pankow, one found everywhere "the same suffocating proletarian colonial milieu." Scheffler just had to look at these districts. Others had to live there. Berlin's conscientious statisticians reported in 1910 that 48 percent of all dwellings were in *Hinterhäuser*. Four hundred thousand dwellings, in which a million and a half people lived, had only one heated room; 600,000 Berliners lived five or more to a room. At a meeting of the *Verein für Sozialpolitik* in 1901, Carl Johann Fuchs said that between 1880 and 1895 the number of persons living as lodgers in Berlin in dwellings owned or rented by others had increased from 59,000 to 95,000.[3]

The basic facts of life were unpleasant enough for those on the other side of the tracks—or on the other side of the Weidendamm Bridge, as Berliners would put it.[4] But the facts were embroidered in the literature and the imagination of more prosperous Berliners to form a new kind of narrative of urban, indeed of national, decline. As Andrew Lees has written, at the turn of the twentieth century a period of optimism about the possibilities of overcoming urban poverty began to give way to a new middle-class pessimism and fear of the underclasses. Some German urban critics, with their eyes ultimately on national defense, worried about the impact of urban growth on mortality rates and on the health of those yet living. Cultural critics feared that the modern city dissolved healthy traditions and poisoned artistic creativity. Berlin was the natural subject and primary target for German urban critics of whatever stripe. Not only the crime and moral decay of the capital, but also the nervous degeneration of an accelerated age, hereditary defects, alcohol abuse, poor sanitation and hygiene, and (perhaps as compensation) a certain *frisson* of danger and glamour were tropes of the new Berlin narrative. Hugo Friedlaender's description of the Ackerstrasse, the proverbial street of working-class Berlin North, was typical. It was "an endlessly long, thickly populated street," in which "criminals, pimps, and prostitutes have also set up their dwellings." Thus there were "a great number of 'dives' *(Kaschemmen)* in this area, that is, bars of the lowest rung . . . The better citizens avoid, as far as possible, passing Ackerstrasse by night, since it is supposed to be a little creepy *(nicht ganz geheuer)*."[5]

Bourgeois and upper-class Berliners, regardless of political affiliation, spoke of Berlin North as if it were another world and its inhabitants another species—or at least another race. It was a standard rhetorical device for defense lawyers and prosecutors to address a jury as if the jurors would know nothing of the world of "control girls" and sleazy bars. The same conventions applied in journalism. According to the author of a 1904 *Feuilleton* article in the left-liberal *Berliner Tageblatt*, it was "the 'other' Berlin, the Berlin of surrogates," that one found in Berlin North. "Oxygen, butter, sausage, jewelry, clothes, love—everything here seems to be a surrogate. And also the people seem more surrogates than real, living people: they run about without physiognomy, with faces that . . . seem painted with the gray color of misery." The writer, Thomas Schäfer, closed his article with hope that society would take action so that "our home-grown Berlin Hottentots will get used to real culture and the poor, physiognomy-less surrogate people out there on the periphery will some day become real people."[6]

This "'other' Berlin, the Berlin of surrogates" was the Berlin that nightwatchman Friedrich Braun knew. His patch lay in one of its most dismal precincts, around the Stettin Railway Station, the area of the Ackerstrasse and the Invalidenstrasse, enlivened only by architect Karl Friedrich Schinkel's fine St. Elizabeth's Church. The area was sometimes called the "Latin Quarter," as it was populated to a considerable extent by students at the nearby Friedrich Wilhelm University. It was in part because of the students' presence that the area played host to many "bars of the lowest rung," and to a great number of prostitutes as well. The prostitutes in turn drew pimps after them, and thus this part of the city became "one of the most infamous in Berlin."[7]

If Berlin had a criminal underworld, this was where it lived. But can one really speak of such a thing? A myriad of political, professional, and scientific interests lay behind the rhetorical and statistical construction of the underworld of Wilhelmine Berlin. Such an idea was a useful tool in the hands of state authorities seeking to extend their reach, for police officers looking to defend or extend their empires, for a bourgeois society seeking a mirror image of its own worthiness, and for the burgeoning field of nineteenth-century criminology, which naturally sought to define the parameters of its subject and to assert its own usefulness.

Some of the more skeptically minded of Berlin's citizens saw reasons for suspicion. When pimp and alleged murderer Theodor Berger faced the jury court in 1904, Maximilian Harden wrote dismissively of "the legend of the nightly connections between an organized union of pimps and the guild of prostitutes." All Berlin could offer, he said, was "a transient *Lumpenproletariat*, that at most forms into little groups." And certainly there was no sharp line between a class of persons who did nothing for a living but break the law, on the one hand, and the class of "honest" working people on the other. Habitual criminals who appeared in Berlin's courtrooms almost always had another trade by which they could be identified; often the trade formed their nickname—Sailor-Albert, Waiter-Hugo. And yet the underworld was not altogether a construct. Its borders were porous, and its members were not "organized" in the manner of their descendants, the notorious *Ringvereine* of the Weimar years.[8] Nevertheless, the evidence, statistical and anecdotal, of a set of illegal trades with a common culture and terrain in Wilhelmine Berlin is strong.

The copious statistics assembled by the Reich Office of Justice suggest the life of the underworld revolved around theft and prostitution. The ranks of professional thieves formed a hierarchy: at the top the "bold break-and-enter artists," the so-called "heavy boys" *(schwere Jungs)*; at the bottom the much more numerous pickpockets and purse-snatchers. In 1887, 34,563 persons were tried for criminal code offenses in the Berlin Court of Appeal district; of these, 8,030 faced charges for the various forms of theft, another 4,931 for related offenses such as robbery, disposal of stolen goods, embezzlement, and fraud. The same year, 679 persons were charged with "encouraging immorality through mediation, or provision or creation of opportunity"—in other words, functioning as a procurer or brothel-keeper, an offense under section 180 of the Reich Criminal Code, and another 246 with causing a public annoyance through immoral conduct or by disseminating immoral writings. It was in fact not illegal to be a prostitute *per se* in Wilhelmine Berlin. But the oldest profession was hemmed in on all sides by the state's police power. Apart from the penalties for procuring in section 180 (and especially severe penalties in the event that the procurer was the husband or the parent of the prostitute), section 361 of the Reich Criminal Code gave the Berlin police authority to regulate the prostitute's conduct of her business. A prostitute was supposed to register with the police, whereupon she became what was known as a *Kontrolmädchen*—a "control girl." It was illegal to practice the profession without registering; breaches of the regulations were prosecuted as petty offenses *(Übertretungen)* and thus were not reflected in the Reich crime statistics. The registered prostitute was under a strict regime of medical checks and precise regulation of her public behavior. Her clothing was supposed to be "decent and simple," there were parts of the city where she was not supposed to be seen, and in other places she could not be too demonstrative in attracting the attention of potential clients.[9]

Estimating the numbers of prostitutes in Wilhelmine Berlin is a necessarily imprecise task, although determining the number of control girls is straightforward. On 1 January 1898, for instance, 4,754 women were registered as prostitutes; in the course of the year 846 women were added to this group, and 1,056 left the regulatory system, 511 to take on "legitimate" work, 304 to leave Berlin, 163 for "the serving of a longer prison sentence," and a comparatively small number of 23 for marriage (as against 36 who died). But, as a Berlin prostitute told an American researcher, "only the stupid ones get registered," and there may have been as many as 50,000 prostitutes operating outside of the regulatory system.[10]

Many contemporary observers—chief among them Hans Ostwald, editor of the *Grossstadt-Dokumente* series of pamphlets and a zealous chronicler of Berlin's underworld—stressed how the world of prostitution was integrated into the criminal underworld. This integration came partly through the agency of the *Luden* (pimps in Berlin street argot), but prostitutes also frequented the same bars as the "heavy boys," and often were involved in theft, blackmail, and other professional criminal activities. Women were underrepresented among those convicted for violent crimes in Wilhelmine Berlin. In 1901, for instance, only 10.7 percent of those convicted of bodily harm were women. On the other hand, 25.0 percent of persons convicted of receiving stolen goods, or otherwise assisting in the commission of a property crime, were women. It is a reasonable hypothesis that most of these female fences were prostitutes who knew the thieves through underworld connections, or who had conspired with their pimp to rob a client. Certainly there was a strikingly businesslike quality to female criminality. The categories of crime in which women were most strongly represented were "crimes against morality" (44.9 percent of convicts in 1901); an offense called "Verletzung fremden Gebrauchsrechts," which could arise if a person reclaimed a pawned object without paying off the loan (35.7 percent of convicts in 1901); theft (26.5 percent); violations of the trade regulations (21.7 percent); and embezzlement (20.9 percent). Indeed, among offenses in which women formed more than 20 percent of the convict pool, only libel and slander (29.7 percent) falls outside the realm of getting and spending.[11]

It was this loose network of control girls and *Luden,* heavy boys and hangers-on, that nightwatchman Friedrich Braun knew from the neighborhood of St. Elizabeth's, and he was determined to run them out, despite (or perhaps because of) his own less-than-unimpeachable character. The nightwatchman's superior said that Braun drank and visited pubs while on duty, contrary to regulations, although he allowed that "the thing had not gone so far that Braun would have had to fear his dismissal." But a policeman who knew Braun, Constable Strehlow, said that Braun had a "particularly watchful eye" for the prostitutes who "made the streets unsafe" after Randel's Pub at Invalidenstrasse 1 closed for the night; another acquaintance, parkwatchman Schulz, said that Braun often rousted people who were looking to spend the night in the yard of St. Elizabeth's, and that he never had any fear of the "rabble." Braun was "powerfully built and muscular," which no doubt contributed to his confidence in confronting "the rabble," and perhaps a little Dutch courage did no harm either. But on 27 September 1887 Braun should have been more careful.

Later the police did their best to reconstruct his movements. He was seen leaving a bar on Bergstrasse, near St. Elizabeth's, at 3:00 A.M. Two street cleaners spoke to him between 3:30 and 3:45 on Ackerstrasse, and saw him head in the direction of St. Elizabeth's. Perhaps he had heard something, or seen the light of a lantern by the door to the sacristy. Probably no one but his killers saw him alive after 3:45. Braun always visited two household servants in the neighborhood at 5:00 A.M. to give them a wake-up call, but on 27 September they slept late. Thus Braun probably died between 3:45 and 5:00 A.M.[12]

St. Elizabeth's, though it faced Invalidenstrasse, was set well back from the street, and actually lay closer to Elizabethkirchstrasse a block further north. A path connecting the two streets ran across the churchyard. Along the path were a number of trees and benches. There were street lamps on Invalidenstrasse, but toward Elizabethkirchstrasse the churchyard was very dark. It was here that parkwatchman Schulz found Braun's body, hanging from a tree near the door to the sacristy, shortly after 6:00 A.M. Braun had suffered two stab wounds to his throat, one apparently administered by a crowbar that lay, covered in blood, near the sacristy steps. There were bloodstains on the steps, and a great amount of snuff tobacco, which, according to the police, "professional criminals habitually carry with them as a weapon." Braun's face was also covered with snuff. His saber, found on the ground near the tree, was not only bloodstained, it also had hairs stuck to the blade, evidence that the struggle had been fierce and that Braun had managed to inflict a serious head wound on one of his attackers.[13]

How was this evidence to be interpreted? Criminal-Commissar Alexander Braun—no relation to the victim—thought the facts pointed to a failed robbery: nightwatchman Braun had caught a gang of thieves as they attempted to break into the church. Commissar Braun believed that the attack had taken place by the sacristy steps, and that the nightwatchman had recognized the thieves, so that for the latter the only way out was to kill him. A second theory was that Braun's murder was a revenge killing perpetrated by those who had borne the brunt of his crusade to clean up the neighborhood: the local pimps. On this theory, the killers had thrown in the evidence of a robbery only to lead the police off the trail. In fact, the police leaned originally to the revenge killing theory and, according to the first newspaper reports, also did not rule out the possibility that Braun had committed suicide and staged his death to look like a murder in the line of duty. But in time Commissar Braun came to favor the robbery-gone-wrong scenario, and this was the case the authorities eventually brought to court.[14]

The police investigations of the killing were not especially efficient or sophisticated. In 1887, and for a decade and a half afterwards, Berlin had no specialized homicide detectives or squads. Berlin's criminal police had been reorganized in 1885, as the result of a public outcry following a bungled murder investigation. The revamped force was divided into three "Inspections," designated A, B, and C. Inspection A's assignment was geographic, its personnel divided among the twelve criminal districts *(Kriminal-Bezirke)* of Berlin. Inspections B and C were designed, ironically, to mirror the presumed organization of Berlin's criminal underworld.

Inspection B formed the bureaucratic counterpart to Berlin's hierarchy of thieves; its specialty was professional theft in all of its variations, including "break-ins, store, pocket, sleeping-place thefts . . . coat thefts, coal thefts [especially common, and viewed as especially serious], bicycle thefts, thefts during sex [this invariably meant the robbing of clients by prostitutes], muggings." The guiding philosophy of Inspection B was that the officers should develop an expertise in dealing with these offenses and with the milieu of career criminals, since the Alexanderplatz believed that "according to experience, this kind of criminal as rule does not change his trade once selected." Also attached to Inspection B was a branch of the criminal police, which perhaps above all others required scientific training and a certain progressive cast of mind: the *Erkennungsdienst*, or identification service, which was spearheading all of the novel techniques of forensic science—bodily measurement according to the Bertillon system, chemical analysis, photography, and soon, fingerprints.

Inspection C was for investigations requiring a particular legal or business expertise, mostly commercial crimes: professional fraud, fraudulent and simple bankruptcy, felonies and misdemeanors against the Bankruptcy Code, forgery of documents (in particular forgery of bills of exchange), usury, offenses against the Trade Mark Act, patent infringement, lottery offenses, and breaches of the Securities Act. That Inspection C's jurisdiction also included dueling suggests that its real point was to investigate crimes where the defendant could be presumed a gentleman.[15]

In practice this system was cumbersome and inefficient, as Inspector Leopold von Meerscheidt-Hüllessem, one of the Alexanderplatz's most important officers, argued a few years after the Braun murder. The different geographic and subject-matter jurisdictions caused "a lack of clarity and uncertainty" in investigations, while in complex cases, the district commissar of Inspection A was often "not equal to the work." In 1887 there were not even any standardized investigatory procedures for homicides. Instructions that the Alexanderplatz issued in 1901 suggested a need to remedy a startling degree of carelessness: officers at a murder scene were advised to call a doctor if they were not sure that the victim was dead, and were ordered not to leave their coats lying on any items of evidence. Errors resulting from disorganization or negligence were in fact common. In one case, officers at a murder scene overlooked an overcoat which, when found the following day, proved to be the decisive piece of evidence. In the 1898 murder of prostitute Bertha Singer, the police managed to ignore a number of bloodstained newspapers in the room in which they found the body.[16]

At the time of nightwatchman Braun's murder, the natural sciences could offer the police little support. The development of fingerprints as a workable method of identification began only in the early 1890s, and in most jurisdictions two more decades went by before it came into widespread use. Around 1890 chemical tests to identify blood type were unknown; tests to distinguish human from animal blood were new. The medical evidence that was available to the police investigating the Braun murder yielded as much uncertainty as precision. *Medizinalrat* Dr. Long, who performed the autopsy, could say that Braun had sustained injuries to his head, throat, chest, and abdomen, with only the stab wound to the throat being necessarily fatal. But he could say little about the time of death. When Braun's body had been found it had not yet been fully cold, and rigor mortis had not set in, but Dr. Long said that no conclusions could be drawn from this observation. "The cooling of the body," he said, "depends on the more or less thin layer of fat with which the body is covered, and rigor mortis sometimes does not appear for eight to twelve hours. On the latter point, science is altogether still unclear."[17]

So as the police investigated the murder of nightwatchman Braun they were forced to rely on local knowledge and personal connections—which meant relying on their network of informers, or *Vigilanten*. This practice cast a revealing light on the nature of relations within the community of professional criminals, on the one hand, and between this community and the police, on the other. By the underworld's code of honor, informing on one's colleagues was the worst possible offense; but inevitably, this code was often honored in the breach. Hans von Tresckow, one of Berlin's best known police detectives during the Wilhelmine years, wrote in his memoirs that career criminals "despised no one so much as the *Vigilanten* . . . They called these people . . . 'eight-penny boys.'" From the other side of the street, an old heavy boy named "Sailor-Albert" complained that the younger generation knew nothing of "a sticking together among brothers" when nowadays "one sells the other to the gripper [policeman], brother is worth a mark to brother!" But relations between habitual criminals and police officers were an often complex mixture of natural enmity and calculated collaboration, with a dash of mutual respect and freemasonry. Tresckow recorded that he always approached his subjects in an effort to "find the human being in the criminal," and on one occasion a veteran break-and-enter artist told him, "I don't have anything at all against you. My business is stealing, yours is to catch me at it." Defense counsel Erich Frey recalled how in the 1920s the incorruptible but frequently reprimanded police detective Albert Dettmann was the butt of good-natured ribbing from the pimps and thieves in an underworld bar: "They knew that Albert Dettmann, in spite of his competence, would never make commissar. They found that unjust . . . They thought, I believe, that he was on the wrong side, that really he belonged to them." And nearly twenty-five years after the Braun murder, the *Vossische Zeitung* reported on a well-wisher at the celebration of (by then *Inspektor*) Alexander Braun's 50th service anniversary at the Alexanderplatz. An old man whom Braun's investigations had sent to jail fifty years before, and who had since compiled an extensive criminal record, had seen a newspaper announcement of the upcoming celebration. He made a point of attending to congratulate the inspector personally, because, he said, Braun "had always treated him humanely."[18]

And so, in the case of nightwatchman Braun, it was due solely to the Alexanderplatz's old-fashioned and low-tech informer network that a pair of suspects soon emerged. Hermann and Anna Heinze lived two blocks from St. Elizabeth's, in a basement apartment at Veteranenstrasse 13. Hermann was 23 years old in 1887. Born in the town of Driesen in the Neumark (now Drezdenko), he came to Berlin with his parents as a boy. He trained as a potter, and "worked at this profession, at least in the summers, while during the winter months I found employment as a laborer." In February 1887 he met Anna Will, a native Berliner. At 38 Anna was a good deal older than Hermann, and she had a "past." Anna and Hermann married within a few days of meeting, but the marriage was turbulent from the beginning. "I knew that [Anna] gave herself to prostitution," Hermann claimed, "but believed she would later stop. I also tried repeatedly to get her away from this shameful trade, but always in vain. On these occasions a row always developed between us which would finally end up in violence, and so our family life was completely destroyed." He maintained that before he married Anna he had worked at his trade "without interruption." For her part, Anna admitted working as a prostitute, but claimed she had been obliged to do so because her husband was lazy and refused to do any work himself.[19]

The police came to focus their attention on this unhappy couple through a strange set of circumstances. Anna had long supplemented her income by serving as a police informer. Shortly after the St. Elizabeth's murder she called on Commissar Braun at the Alexanderplatz and asked to see the "Criminal Album," the volumes of photographs of past convicts, claiming she had seen three men and a woman near St. Elizabeth's on the night of the killing. Anna described the woman in particularly striking detail—"but later it turned out," said Commissar Braun, "that she had given an exact description of herself." Anna claimed to be able to identify a man she had seen and spoken to by the church, but the man turned out to have a sound alibi. Her behavior made Commissar Braun suspicious, especially after he found a man who had spoken to her near St. Elizabeth's on the night in question, whose account of the conversation "made [Anna] appear very suspicious." Other evidence began to pile up as well. Braun learned that while the day before the murder the Heinzes had been broke, the day after they appeared to be flush. Other witnesses had heard them speaking of the murder before they could have known of it in any way other than through direct participation. Some had seen Hermann coming home with torn clothing shortly after the time of the killing. On the strength of this information, both Anna and Hermann were eventually taken into investigatory custody between March and May of 1888. They were released again after several months, as the authorities judged the evidence insufficient for a conviction.

But Commissar Braun remained convinced that the Heinzes were guilty. For over two years he kept them under investigation. Late in 1890 they were arrested once again, and the following summer the motions chamber of Berlin's Superior Court I ordered the opening of a full trial against them.[20]

The trial began on 28 September 1891 in the Great Jury Hall of the criminal court building at Alt-Moabit 11. After the years of investigation the event was eagerly anticipated. Berlin's papers reported "a lively hustle and bustle" and an "absolutely enormous" crowd in front of the courtroom long before the doors opened. The *Berliner Tageblatt* reported that this was a "mixed" crowd, "invited and uninvited persons, court attendants, defense lawyers, etc." When the doors of the courtroom were opened the officials had difficulty holding the people back. Only the lucky few who had obtained entry cards beforehand were allowed in. The *Tageblatt* noted that those admitted "were recruited exclusively from the better circles," and that "the fairer sex" was less strongly represented than was usual in murder trials of this sort. The next day, however, the *Tageblatt* was writing archly that "fine, or better said, finely-dressed ladies were rather strongly represented" among the spectators, and they "felt no scruples" about staying for the evidence of the "filthy scenes."[21]

The Great Jury Hall was as much a theater as a judicial arena. It was a large room: 229 square meters, well over 2,000 square feet, with 12-meter ceilings and space for 250 spectators, along with two loges for "reserved" seats, occupied for the Heinze trial by a few higher court and police officials. Everything about the room was grand, solemn, and high-minded, particularly the quotations that were painted into the wall: "to impress upon the judges their duty," and "to hold up to the eyes of the witnesses and the defendants the serious dignity of the judges and the might of the law."

> Every judge sits in the Kaiser's place. The law punishes, not the judge. The deed kills the man. In a strong court one feels the Kaiser's justice. Better one who saw than ten who heard. Do not rush the verdict, hear both sides. God judges when no one speaks. Drunken joy, sober pain. Disloyalty strikes her own man. Confession is half of atonement. Judgment binds and releases. Where there is a court, there is peace.

At the front of the room stood the high judges' bench. Here were the places for the three judges and the prosecutor, all dressed in the black robe, the *Talar,* and small round cap, the *Barrett.* On the wall behind them was a portrait of the first Kaiser Wilhelm in the uniform of a general. To the left of the judges sat the jurors, to their right the defendants and their lawyers.[22]

The defense lawyers also wore the *Talar* and the *Barrett.* This was important: their attire demonstrated that despite their lower seat, they too were *Organe der Rechtspflege*—organs of the administration of justice. Lawyers had not always dressed like this for court. The *Talar* and *Barrett* were, like so much in the life of Berlin's bar, innovations of 1879. Some veterans were not happy with the new style: old *Justizrat* Deycks called the new robe "the ape jacket," and "did not see why he should impress the jurors more in a toga" than in his accustomed frock coat.[23] The change of attire may have reflected the growing seriousness and professionalism of legal argument in Moabit, but it may also have stimulated it. Perhaps one *did* impress the jurors more in a "toga"; perhaps, too, in such a solemn room as the Great Jury Hall, with lawyers wearing robes instead of frock coats, deviations from the norms of seriousness would become all the more glaring.

The manners and mood of the Wilhelmine courtroom are indeed the most intangible and elusive element for the historian to recover. Perhaps the lawyers' robes and the sayings painted on the wall of the Great Jury Hall provide a convenient shorthand: it seems that the life of the criminal courtroom, like the life of Wilhelmine society in general, was marked by a

The Great Jury Court Hall at Alt-Moabit 11, where the Heinzes, Guthmann, Berger, and countless others were tried. (Ullstein Bilderdienst)

rigid code of manners coupled with a punctilious sense of personal honor. Historians of Germany have often invoked such qualities in the service of arguments stressing the "feudalization of the bourgeoisie" or the overmilitarization of German society.[24] But these were pan-European phenomena involving all social classes. Ruth Harris, in a study of French murder trials of the *fin de siècle*, has stressed the sense of honor among members of all classes, which came to light especially in trials of *crimes passionelles*. And Benjamin Martin has written evocatively of the heaviness in the daily life of the bourgeois of the Third Republic. In clothing: "a man in a suit, overcoat, top hat (later bowler), all in black, with beard, mustache, and pincenez . . . His wife and daughters were armored against nature and the natural with ankle boots, garters, complicated and oppressive underwear, long dresses, veils, and multiple accessories." In food: "endless courses of heavy meals"; and even in furniture: "heavy, graceless, durable enough to pass on to heirs, but designed for a crushing comfort."[25] This heaviness mirrored, or perhaps stimulated, a rigidity in personal interaction. In the novels of Theodor Fontane, one of the greatest observers and chroniclers of Imperial Germany, Major Crampas kissing Effi Briest's hand in a carriage can represent adultery, and Effi's husband Innstetten, automaton-like, must challenge Crampas to a duel when he learns of the affair.[26] These mores carried into the courtroom, and, as we shall see, decisively shaped the Heinze trial and its aftermath.

Unusually for a Wilhelmine case, the protocol, or procedural record of the Heinze trial, has survived. Among other things the protocol gives us a rare glimpse of the social composition of a Wilhelmine jury. For this case there were twelve jurors and two alternates. They came from diverse social backgrounds, ranging from "Lucas, master mason" and "Lange, pensioner," to "Steinbeck, government counselor (retired)" and even "Count v. Pfeil, Kapitan-Leutnant (retired)." One of the members was identified as Professor Dr. Lamprecht—but presumably not the famous historian, who would have been in Leipzig at this time.

As always in jury court proceedings there were three professional judges. The two assistant judges were Superior Court Counselor Dr. Pollack and Court Assessor Dr. Ramien. Presiding over the entire affair was Superior Court Director Otto Rieck. Rieck was an experienced judge, with a quarter-century of legal experience; he was also one of the deputy presidents of Superior Court I. He was one of the most respected trial judges in Berlin, drawing praise even from defense counsel such as Fritz Friedmann. Next to the judges sat the two prosecutors: State Advocate Wilhelm Unger, assisted by a young assessor named Fiedler. Unger was a senior prosecutor, a department supervisor with responsibility for the work of five other prosecutors and all of the cases in the First Criminal Chamber along with Divisions 130–132 of the Lay Judge Court.[27]

More conspicuous than the judges and prosecutors were the flamboyant young defense counsel. Hermann Heinze was represented by a court-appointed lawyer named Alfred Ballien. Ballien, from the nearby town of Brandenburg on the Havel, was thirty years old and had been practicing law only as long as Anna and Hermann had been in investigatory custody—since December 1890. Anna Heinze had hired her own lawyer,

Richard Cossmann. Born in 1858 in Greifswald, Cossmann was little more experienced than Ballien, having been at the Berlin bar only since 1886.[28]

Of course the two defendants occupied the center of attention. Reporters tended to view Hermann Heinze with some sympathy and save their condescension or scorn for Anna. To Hugo Friedlaender, Hermann was "a handsome, upright guy *(Bursche)* with curly blond hair, from a very decent family," a "skillful and diligent worker." But Anna, "a 36-year-old [*sic*] prostitute" who despite her age "could still be called pretty" had led him astray by promising a life of ease. The *Berliner Tageblatt's* correspondent wrote that Anna formed a "striking contrast" to Hermann. Her face was "sharply cut" and "yellow," her eyes "sinister"; her "pitch-black hair is tied in a simple knot, her black dress completes the gloomy picture." If this were not enough, Anna's face showed "the traces of the vice she had engaged in."[29]

Shortly before ten o'clock, after the formalities of jury selection and the initial calling forward of all witnesses, the defendants took their places in the dock. President Rieck began with an announcement that he would later regret. The court had met with the prosecutor, he said, to consider whether or not the public should be excluded from the trial. There was some official concern that "various points will emerge, the open discussion of which could endanger public morality." But the court and the prosecution had agreed that the court should not make use of its right under the Judicial Code to restrict access to the courtroom, as "it appears desirable that especially these proceedings be conducted in the full light of publicity." The court and the prosecution alike believed that "the damage to the general feeling for the law and the public administration of justice which would result from proceedings behind closed doors would be greater than any threatened damage to morality." Rieck asked that the representatives of the press report "in the most decent possible fashion" on those aspects of the case that might have given rise to an exclusion of the public. The transcript notes that none of the ladies present in the courtroom left after this announcement.[30]

Rieck then turned to questioning Anna and Hermann on their life stories, and the court was treated to the colorful details of their criminal records. Anna had no fewer than forty-four previous convictions for contraventions of the regulations of the morals police, along with seventeen convictions for theft, embezzlement, procuring, and currency offenses. As she admitted all this "such a loud cry of astonishment" came from the spectators' benches that Rieck felt himself obliged to forbid "most strenuously" any sign of approval or disapproval from the gallery. Cossmann, on Anna's behalf, pointed out that none of the previous convictions had been for violence, while Anna insisted that in all previous cases she had confessed and never lied. Soon it emerged that Hermann was not exactly "an unwritten page" either, with altogether thirteen prior convictions for theft, procuring, embezzlement, receiving stolen goods, and breaking and entering.[31]

All of this was entertaining for the spectators and the newspaper readers, but what came next was much more important. "Now, defendant," said President Rieck to Hermann, "we want to go into the matter itself." Rieck asked Hermann a few questions about the circumstances of the murder, all of which Hermann answered with a simple "no." But as Rieck pressed, "Were you not in the park after the murder of Braun, and did you not see the situation there?" Hermann replied, "Herr President, I must explain that on the advice of my lawyer I decline to give any further answer." Ballien stepped in to explain: "I know very well," he said, "that the defendant's position will be made more difficult in the eyes of the jurors, but we are well aware of the consequences of the advice and stand by the position that the prosecution must prove the claims in the indictment." Rieck gave no sign that he was particularly surprised or annoyed by this development:

Rieck: Defendant Heinze, you therefore do not want to answer my questions?
Heinze: No!
Rieck: Fine, that is all right with me.
Ballien: I would like to note, however, that the defendant reserves the right to say something in response to the testimony of the individual witnesses.
Rieck: That is totally self-evident, because it is my duty to ask the defendants if they have something to say after the testimony of the witnesses.

Later in the trial Cossmann offered a more detailed explanation for this advice, which said much about the culture of trials in the 1890s. The lawyers, said Cossmann, felt obliged to tell their clients not to testify because of the extensive publicity the trial was receiving. The newspapers carried detailed transcripts every day. Therefore witnesses who had not yet testified (and who were excluded from the courtroom so that their evidence would not be influenced by what others said) could nonetheless read all the details, thereby undoing a central protective provision of the law. Many of the witnesses, said Cossmann, were "less respectable people." Many were police informers; their honesty and good faith could not be presumed. Ballien joined in Cossmann's explanation.[32]

It was unusual for defense counsel in Berlin in 1891 to give such advice to their clients, still more to make such emphatic declarations in a highly publicized jury trial. And the young lawyers did not stop there. Throughout the trial, their relations with State-Advocate Unger and President Rieck were marked by a rare and striking degree of confrontation. The arguments between bench and bar in fact demonstrated the emerging fault lines in courtroom politics.

One argument involved Cossmann's pre-trial preparations. He had gone to President Rieck's house in August to see the official dossier on the case. Rieck was away at the time, and so his wife gave Cossmann the documents. State Advocate Unger declared that Cossmann's actions were improper. Cossmann replied indignantly that Unger was not entitled to make any such declaration: "He is but a party in this proceeding. He represents one party, the defense the other party."

This was a critical, and contested, point. It was far from clear in German law that the prosecution was a "party"; as we saw in Chapter 1, the orthodox view was that the prosecutor served something closer to a judicial function, with the responsibility of neutrally presenting evidence of the suspect's innocence as well as guilt. Yet Cossmann asserted the partisan quality of the prosecution as if it were self-evident, and no one in the courtroom contradicted him. Still, the defense did not take a consistent line. Later in the trial, Ballien asked the court to call a new witness to testify to a minor point. Rieck objected that the defense had known about this evidence for a long time and could have called the witness earlier.[33] Cossmann replied that the witness was mentioned in the documents and thus "the prosecutor has a duty also to consider all evidence that speaks for the innocence of the defendant." He added "You, Herr President, could also have summoned [the witness]." Some accounts held that Cossmann used a striking metaphor, common among Wilhelmine jurists: he insisted that it was President Rieck's duty to "divide the light and shadow equally."[34]

Another quarrel showed how Cossmann, like many lawyers coming to practice in the early Wilhelmine years, was loath to accept the inferior position in which everything in German law, down to the architecture of the courtroom, placed the defense counsel. Older lawyers like Fritz Friedmann complained of this inferiority often enough but did not actively challenge it. Cossmann and Ballien were more aggressive. Cossmann believed that State Advocate Unger had laughed derisively while Cossmann was making an argument. He complained of this to Rieck, who replied that he could not forbid the prosecutor to laugh. Cossmann would not let the point go. "As an appointed member of the public administration of justice," he said, "I must most decidedly protest that during a serious application on my part the prosecutor laughed. And now I demand of you, Herr President . . . ." This was as far as he got. Rieck interrupted him firmly: "The defense may absolutely not make a 'demand' in this manner to the president of the jury court. I reject the expression as improper!"[35]

These tense exchanges between counsel and bench, involving both questions of legal procedure and personal honor, would take on a fuller significance in the months after the trial. But the most colorful moment in the Heinze trial was not about a legal question; it was about champagne. Early on the third day of the trial Cossmann requested a fifteen-minute break, explaining that from time to time he required refreshment. On the previous days the court attendants had brought the refreshment to the lawyers in the courtroom; on the third day this was forbidden. "I would only like to ask," said Rieck, "that no disturbance be caused by the delivery." Cossmann replied, "I doubt it, it is simply champagne *(Sekt)* that we have ordered." Rieck replied, "Then I have nothing against it." The transcript notes that a moment later a glass of *Sekt* appeared before each defender.[36] But as it turned out these glasses could hardly be reduced to "simple Sekt." The champagne represented a challenge on several levels: to the somber, ceremonial tone of the Great Jury Hall; to the stifling manners of Wilhelmine society; and to the second-class position of the defense in the courtroom. Certainly it captured the symbolism of the trial. Afterwards it would be central to the public discussions of the case, and it would form one count in the indictment of Ballien and Cossmann in the discipline courts of their profession.

If relations between the defense lawyers and the court were generally tense, President Rieck could be remarkably solicitous of the defendants themselves. Throughout the hearing Rieck worried whether Anna Heinze was well enough to follow the proceedings. She took morphium in the courtroom and often had to ask for pauses, although it was noticeable that her ill-health moved in tandem with the seriousness of the evidence against her. Still, Rieck was concerned that she not miss anything important. On the second day he summoned the prison doctor *Medizinalrat* Dr. Levin to give an opinion on Anna Heinze's physical and mental condition. Levin said that her health was poor as a result of her "chronic gynecological ailments *(Unterleibsleiden),*" but mentally she was fully normal and had said that her greatest wish was to continue with the hearing. On the third day Rieck once again asked Anna Heinze if she was certain she was well enough to continue. Anna replied that she would "pull herself together":

> *Rieck:* I must have complete certainty that you can follow the proceedings with full clarity; otherwise, I have to adjourn the case against you and proceed only against your husband.
> *Anna Heinze:* But that would be too difficult, to go through the case twice.
> *Rieck:* It is by no means too difficult. If you can't follow . . . then your case will be dealt with in a later jury court session; when that can be will depend on your mental and physical condition.

But Anna insisted that she could continue.[37]

In between moments of conflict and the consumption of morphium and champagne, the evidence of the case, such as it was, emerged. Rieck had attempted to impose some order by hearing the evidence in segments according to subject matter, beginning with the "objective circumstances" of the finding of the body. This evidence came from parkwatchman Schulz, Commissar Strehlow, and a few others. *Medizinalrat* Dr. Long testified about the autopsy; Commissar Braun spoke of his investigations.[38] Then the proceedings turned to the testimony of witnesses who implicated the Heinzes in the murder. If the words "better one who saw than ten who heard" were painted into the wall of the Great Jury Hall, in this case no one appeared to have seen, while many more than ten had heard. All of the evidence that was damaging to the Heinzes was in the form of hearsay.

The star witness was one Frau Bertha Uthes, who had been the Heinzes' landlady in 1887. Her evidence was fatal—if it could be believed. At the time of the murder, she had lived at Veteranenstrasse 13 in a basement apartment. Her apartment consisted of a kitchen, a sitting room, and a bedroom. The Heinzes lived in the kitchen; Uthes lived in the sitting room; and a half-sister of Anna Heinze's, Marie Hahn, lived in the bedroom, along with her "relationship," a worker named Carl Piester. Uthes said that she had been out with Anna and Hermann on the evening of 26 September 1887. The three of them, along with a man Uthes picked up named Wilhelm Henkel, returned to the apartment about midnight. Although Uthes was presumably occupied with Henkel, she found the time to observe the Heinzes through a crack in the door, lying fully clothed on their bed. Hermann was wearing a balloon-cap which he had borrowed from Uthes, saying that he planned to go for a walk and did not want to be recognizable. Around 2:00 A.M. Uthes noticed that the Heinzes went out; then she fell asleep. She woke up around 7:00 and found that the Heinzes were back. Uthes brought them coffee, and saw Anna Heinze busy mending Hermann's shirt. His coat, which was lying on the bed, was also torn, "as if by violence." There were "cat scratches" on Hermann's face, which Anna explained away by saying she had hit him. That afternoon Uthes changed the Heinzes' bed, and found a bloodstained shirt between the mattress and the bed frame. The climax of her testimony was a remark she claimed to have heard Anna make:

> *Uthes:* Even before Frau Heinze had left the house, she said to me: "Just imagine, tonight they murdered the nightwatchman Braun."
> *Rieck:* Madame witness, this is a very serious claim. Do you know with certainty that Frau Heinze said this before she went out?
> [The witness maintained firmly that she did.]
> *Rieck:* Why then did you not report your very important observations earlier?
> *Uthes:* I was afraid because I was all alone.[39]

Electing to testify on this point, Hermann admitted that he, Anna, and Frau Uthes had gone out on the evening of the 26th, that they returned in the company of Wilhelm Henkel, and that Anna Heinze had gone out again after that. But he denied that *he* had gone out again. Henkel, on the other hand, confirmed Uthes's testimony. Later in the trial, Anna gave her version of these events. She too said that she, Hermann, and Uthes had gone to the Zionskirchplatz around 10:30 P.M. on the 26th. Uthes picked up Henkel, and they all returned to the apartment. Later Piester came to see Marie Hahn and Hermann let him in through the window. Anna said that she had stayed in bed until 3:30 A.M. and had then gone out. In the Invalidenstrasse near St. Elizabeth's she saw "two guys" and a woman whom she "took to be a Jewess." The woman complained to her, "There is nothing more to be earned here," whereupon the two women walked to the Brunnenstrasse and Anna met a man who claimed to be a landowner

(*Gutsbesitzer*). This man accompanied Anna back to the apartment, and left at about 4:45 A.M.[40]

The following day the court heard from a police officer who already had a colorful career behind him, and who would play a role in other dramatic criminal stories in Berlin in the decade to come. Criminal-Inspector Leopold v. Meerscheidt-Hüllessem treated the spectators to the titillating information that he had known Anna Heinze for years: "She was my informer." Meerscheidt-Hüllessem had met Anna at the courthouse on the day after the murder. She told him the story of having seen "suspicious persons" around St. Elizabeth's. Meerscheidt-Hüllessem took Anna immediately to the Alexanderplatz, "where she gave further evidence, and she was also used for a little while in this matter as an informer."[41]

Evidence that the eventual principal suspect had been used as an informer did not cast the police investigation in the most flattering light. Indeed, in cross-examining police witnesses, the defense strategy was to suggest that there had been wrong turns in the investigation, leads which had not been followed once the investigation settled on the Heinzes. In particular, the defense wished to establish that the police had considered the possibility of a suicide, or that there was evidence which suggested the robbery had been carried out by specialists in church robberies, which Anna and Hermann Heinze clearly were not. But the lawyers had little luck in soliciting favorable testimony from the officers. In questioning Meerscheidt-Hüllessem, for instance, Ballien brought out that human excrement had been found on the steps of the sacristy. "Is the witness aware," he asked the Inspector, "that there is a special species of break-and-enter artist which always concerns itself purely with robberies of churches, and is in the habit of soiling the scene of the crime?" Meerscheidt-Hüllessem replied smoothly, "I am not aware of the last fact, and in general there are certainly church-robbers, but they do not only commit this species of theft." Ballien returned to this theme with the next witness, Criminal Commissar Kessmann:

> *Ballien:* I would also like to ask this witness whether it is known to him that only old, experienced felons and ex-cons (*Zuchthäusler*) are in the habit of using snuff-tobacco.
> *Kessmann:* No, that is not limited merely to old, experienced felons. Anyway, old, experienced felons are not in the habit of carrying out church robberies.
> *Ballien:* Why not?

Kessmann: Because precisely old, experienced felons know very well that there is not much to be got in churches.

And as if to rub salt into Ballien's wounds, President Rieck added, "I suspected that, too. A cashbox is more tempting for old, experienced break-and-enter artists than the sacristy of a church." Kessmann drove in the final nail by adding that in the last ten years the police were only aware of three church robberies in Berlin, and in two cases the culprits had been found.[42]

The nature of the evidence in the case, and the problems it raised, were well illustrated by the three most important of the remaining witnesses. Carl Piester was a "friend" of Anna's half-sister, Marie Hahn. Piester claimed he had heard Anna yell at Hermann on the day after the murder, "You murderer, you nightwatchman-murderer!" Later, when Anna repeated the "nightwatchman-murderer" accusation, Hermann had replied "Hey, if you say anything, then you're also finished. You were there too," and added, "It is all the same to me now, even if they cut off my turnip!" The effect of this hearsay was blunted, however, when Piester grudgingly admitted under strong cross-examination from Cossmann that he too was a paid police informer.[43]

There was more hearsay to come. Marie Hahn had originally taken advantage of her relationship to Anna (the law did not compel relatives of the defendant to testify) to decline to give evidence. But Anna was foolish enough to make some insulting remarks about Hahn in open court, and Hahn was goaded into reversing her decision. Hahn's testimony confirmed what Uthes and Piester had said: that the Heinzes had gone out in the early morning of the 27th; that Anna had later spoken of the murder before she could have heard of it innocently; and that Anna had called her husband a "watchman-murderer." Under Rieck's questioning, however, it emerged that Hahn was not at all clear about particular dates, and that there were contradictions with the testimony she had given in 1888. "Sometimes my thoughts are totally gone!" she protested.

On the third day of the trial the court heard from a man named Emil Bellevue, who had lived with Anna Heinze for ten to twelve years before her marriage, "apart from the time he had had to spend in jail." A little while after the murder, Anna Heinze had sent her mother to Bellevue with the request that he come and visit her. Bellevue found Anna in tears. She told him that she knew about the murder of Braun, and gave an account of the night. Bellevue asked if Braun had defended himself, to which Anna replied, "He couldn't; he had enough to do with the snuff." Then Anna pulled herself together and said "I could tell you a few things, but what you don't know, you can't betray." Bellevue said that Anna was a violent person who was capable of doing anything when she was in a rage. When they were together she had come home one night with a pocket watch, which she said she had stolen from a man after putting snuff in his eyes; in fact, Bellevue said that Anna always carried snuff with her for use in robberies.[44]

The court heard from two witnesses who had been with Hermann Heinze in Plötzensee prison in early 1890. A man named Scheib reported that Hermann had told his fellow prisoners: "Kids, you wouldn't believe how difficult it is to hang a dead body." Another named Strey said that Hermann was worried that a button from his shirt would be found near St. Elizabeth's. But, as with all the Heinzes' underworld colleagues, the most obvious quality of these witnesses was their unreliability. Strey gave his evidence with such uncertainty that Rieck repeatedly warned him of the penalties for perjury; several other prisoners from Plötzensee testified that they had heard Heinze say that he was innocent of Braun's murder.[45]

But however unreliable the prosecution witnesses might be, the tide seemed to be running very much against the defense when, on the fourth day, the trial came to a sudden end. The issue was a prosaic one of scheduling. The court had originally estimated that the trial would take only three days. Rieck clearly believed the reason for the lengthy hearing lay in Ballien and Cossmann's many motions to hear new witnesses. "The Code of Criminal Procedure provides no means to stipulate how the defense is to do its job," said Rieck, but "on the other hand, the court is not just here for this case. Other people who are waiting in investigatory custody for their trial before the jury court are suffering under this prolongation." But Ballien and Cossmann refused point blank to estimate how many more motions they wished to bring or how much time they would need, leading to another acrimonious exchange between judge and counsel.

Rieck tried gamely to keep the trial going, but soon the question of additional witnesses arose again. Ballien asked that eighteen more witnesses be called. Among them was a shoemaker named Bernhard Just, who in 1887 had lived near St. Elizabeth's. Just had since emigrated to America, but had written to the investigating magistrate to say that he knew who Braun's killers were, and that Heinze was not one of them. Hermann Heinze insisted on calling Just to testify, or at least on having Just's evidence recorded through consular authorities in Chicago. Ballien made a show of warning

Hermann in open court that summoning Just would only mean a lengthening of Hermann's stay in investigatory custody. The transcript faithfully renders Hermann's *berlinisch* reply: "Is mir janz ejal"—"It's all the same to me, if I have to sit for ten years!"[46]

The judges withdrew to consider Ballien's motion. The transcript records that their deliberations were lengthy. When they returned, Rieck announced a decision in three parts: the trial was to be adjourned; the witness Just was to be questioned through the German consulate in Chicago; and the defendants were to remain in custody. "With this surprising conclusion," noted the *Norddeutsche Allgemeine Zeitung*, "the Heinze murder trial ends for now."[47]

But in the most important respects it was just beginning.

Moral Panic

In the following months, Germans seemed to forget that the crucial question of the Heinze case—whether or not Anna and Hermann Heinze had killed nightwatchman Friedrich Braun—remained unanswered. They seemed even to forget that the trial was not over. But they did not forget that the trial had happened. The case became the occasion for wide ranging debates on the evils of prostitution, the place of the criminal law in the moral life of the nation, and proper style and manners in conducting a criminal defense.

For the Heinze trial to become a political matter it had first to be a public matter, and reactions from all quarters showed how tightly Wilhelmine Germany was knit together by its press. In the previous chapter we saw that the mass press, with its focus on local events, was something new in the late nineteenth century. Contemporaries were alert to this novelty: the *Vossische Zeitung* observed that it was the *public* nature of the Heinze controversy that was truly something new: "Fifty years ago the Heinze trial would have been conducted behind closed doors; the public would not have learned the slightest thing about the beginning or the outcome of it."[48]

This new media culture was a product of late nineteenth-century urbanization; for virtually all observers of the Heinze trial, on right and left, the trial was fundamentally a story about the modern big city. Anxieties about modern urban life were everywhere in the 1890s. The eminent sociologist Ferdinand Tönnies coined a phrase with his 1887 book *Gemeinschaft und*

Gesellschaft ("Community and Society"), in which the big city was equated with the decline of religion and the rise of selfishness. The year of the Heinze trial was also the year of the *Rembrandt als Erzieher* ("Rembrandt as Educator") phenomenon—the stunning commercial success of Julius Langbehn's exercise in cultural pessimism. Shortly after the Heinze trial, Max Nordau would publish his famous *Degeneration,* a quintessentially fin de siècle lament of cultural, social and human-physical decline, tellingly dedicated to the pioneering Italian criminologist Cesare Lombroso. Observers from all social and political camps were looking to the big city as the scene and source of all modern troubles. For liberal, conservative, and Social Democratic commentators alike, the Heinzes represented all that was worrisome about the frightening precincts of Berlin North and East, those neighborhoods of mushrooming rental barracks with their populations of "surrogate people" voting for the Social Democratic Party (SPD) in ever greater numbers (as middle class commentators feared) or turning to anarchy and petty crime (as even the SPD feared).[49]

That the Heinzes were the exhibits in a lesson about the modern city was the burden of an editorial reflection in the liberal *Vossische Zeitung* the day after the trial ended. The *Vossische* put to one side the question of whether Anna and Hermann were guilty—"no one may make such a judgment, since arriving at one with the best knowledge and conscience is a matter for the jurors who will be summoned when the trial commences again." But the editors showed no such hesitation in judging that the trial had "revealed a gloomy, virtually gruesome picture of the life of a big city," a picture of a "light-shy rabble" whose members "only take up their activity in the dark of night, while during the day they slink into their dwellings or quench their eternally burning thirst in a saloon." It was too easy simply to vent one's moral outrage on the trial's dramatis personae. It was big-city living conditions—"three parties in a cramped kitchen, parlor, and bedroom"—that "demoralize[d] and choke[d] any feeling for decency." The *Vossische* concluded that "Effective help is needed here more than preaching: the provision of well-paid work, consideration of weaknesses and errors, genuine love of one's neighbor. From these must grow the counterweight to the lowering tendencies of the big city."[50]

Two days later the *Vossische* had altogether forgotten neighborly love and was taking a sterner tone, but the point remained the dangers of big city life. "So is the ground beneath our feet constructed," lamented the editors in an editorial called "The Scum" *(Die Hefe);* "The preconditions for a bloody deed like the murder of nightwatchman Braun are always present." The editorial spoke of the Heinzes and their circle in the language of racist anthropology and hereditary degeneracy. They "belong to the bottom level of our society," standing "so far from the circle of our ideas as ever the members of a tribe from the darkest corner of the darkest part of the world could do." "Vice is hereditary," the *Vossische* went on; "It must come to pass that children who begin to run wild under their parents' care are brought into institutions in which their sinful desires can be powerfully counteracted." It was a mistake simply to wait for the child to fall into the hands of the criminal justice system; rather "one must keep an eye open for cases in which conditions at home are such that remaining there will necessarily poison the child." The public schools of the big city posed another kind of danger. It was a good thing that in the parochial schools the children of honest workers "sit next to those of the better situated," but it was cause for alarm that "children of criminals sit next to those of honest workers." The editors concluded that only "in the careful formation of institutions of compulsory reform *(Zwangserziehung)* lies the possibility of preventing the infection of the coming generation." As for people like the Heinzes—"those who have become accustomed to the path of vice"—nothing more could be done. "One must content oneself with rendering them harmless."[51]

Social Democrats were torn between their contempt for the *Vossische Zeitung's* editorials and their contempt for the Heinzes and their ilk. On the one hand, *Vorwärts,* the flagship Social Democratic newspaper, vented more rage on the twists and turns of the *Vossische's* editors than on the starkly authoritarian pronouncements of the conservative press. On 3 October, *Vorwärts* responded to the *Vossische's* initial call for social action by denouncing the sentimentality of this "weepy" editorial; for the Social Democrats, of course, only a scientifically informed social revolution could change the living conditions of the people of Berlin North. When the *Vossische's* tone hardened, *Vorwärts* printed a sarcastic reply also entitled "The Scum." But *Vorwärts* was eager to distinguish the underworld of Berlin North from the world of "honest" workers: noting that the *Berliner Börsen-Courier* had described one of the underworld witnesses as typical of Berlin workers, the editors wrote, "The Berlin worker will know how to give thanks for that." *Vorwärts* was in fact as strident as the bourgeois papers in its denunciations of the Heinzes' milieu. On 4 October it claimed that anyone who saw the "gallery of pimps and prostitutes, who sat in choice examples on the witnesses benches, must have been surprised how little intelligence all of these faces betrayed." But for *Vorwärts* the real culprit was bourgeois society, and thus for Social Democrats the trial formed "an inexhaustible arsenal," revealing "in an unclean but accurate mirror a true reflection of today's social organization, with its repugnant excresences mocking all morality and reason." The Heinzes, along with "the crowd of pimps, prostitutes, and the whole vulgar household of 'free love' and theft—they are all products of capitalist society." That was why *Vorwärts* saw the Heinze trial as "of the highest cultural-historical interest," predicting that "future generations will stand astonished and incredulous before this abyss of filth and depravity."[52]

Given the manner in which Anna and Hermann Heinze made their living, it was perhaps inevitable that the press would dwell on prostitution and especially on pimps. Here the conservative papers rose to a flood of authoritarian rhetoric. The *Kreuzzeitung* called for tougher penalties for pimps and featured an article by a Berlin judge who decried the "false humanity" which "dominates our circumstances." The *Tägliche Rundschau* suggested that prison sentences were unlikely to be effective in protecting society from pimps; a way should be found to send them to the workhouse along with beggars and tramps. The National-Liberal *Norddeutsche Allgemeine Zeitung* preached "the fastest conceivable clearing out" of "the so-called pimps, who not only scorn all humanity and morality, but also constitute a steady danger for state and society to a degree which can not be emphasized strongly enough." Left-liberal papers tended to be more flexible. The *Vossische Zeitung* thought that focusing on the problem of pimps amounted to treating a symptom rather than the disease; for the sake of the decency and safety of streets and dwellings, it recommended a return to government-controlled brothels *(kasernierte Prostitution)*. Without street prostitution, so the argument went, there would be no pimps. Gunning as ever for the *Vossische*, *Vorwärts* responded sarcastically that "in her heartfelt anguish . . . Aunt Voss flies to the bordello."[53]

Some of the polemics on the safety of Berlin's streets were implicitly, and occasionally explicitly, critical of the police. The *Kreuzzeitung* complained that "a great part of the Berlin population" could now "only reach its home at night in a state of mortal danger." The Social Democratic weekly *Die Neue Zeit* growled that the police were so intent on pursuing their masters' political opponents that they let common criminals slip by; of every six murders in which the culprit was not found within sight of his victim, five remained unsolved. Privately, some police officers agreed; a few years later Inspector von Meerscheidt-Hüllessem wrote that "a murder case in which the identity of the culprit is not known in three days can, as a rule, be regarded as hopeless." The fear of violence and the modus operandi of the robbers of St. Elizabeth's generated an echo in the fiction of Theodor Fontane, who was at work on his novella *Die Poggenpuhls* as the Heinze trial unfolded. The novella contains a passage in which Frau Poggenpuhl warns her servant Frederike to be careful when opening the door: "Another widow has just been killed, and if you just opened up without thinking, it could happen to you too, or they could throw snuff tobacco in your eyes ... And then they will rob us of everything."[54]

The other large question for public debate was the manner in which Alfred Ballien and Richard Cossmann had argued their case. Their flamboyant style touched a nerve in the legal profession at a time when the cozy German world of the liberal professions seemed threatened by a society growing ever more mercantile and ever less deferential. This, too, was a subject which became part of the narrative of the modern city. A few years later the sociologist Georg Simmel would write that the big city necessarily broke down social ties of personal familiarity and custom and replaced them with the twin engines of money and rational calculation: "Money economy and the domination of the intellect stand in the closest relationship to one another." One consequence of the dissolving of personal bonds was a necessary increase in personal self-promotion. The need to attract attention led to "the strangest of eccentricities, to specifically metropolitan extravagances of self-distanciation, of caprice, of fastidiousness, the meaning of which is no longer to be found in the content of such activity itself but rather in its being a form of 'being different'—of making oneself noticeable." Simmel might as well have been writing about Ballien and Cossmann and their champagne, their confrontational style and controversial advice.[55]

Criticism of the lawyers reached across party lines. The National Liberal *Norddeutsche Allgemeine Zeitung* believed that Ballien and Cossmann had gone beyond the bounds of ethical professional conduct by identifying with their clients and by working against the "investigation of the truth." The lawyers could even have made themselves "accessories after the fact" to the murder (the offense of *Begünstigung*) by advising their clients not to testify. For the *Norddeutsche Allgemeine* there was a generational factor at work: the young lawyers had acted "in contradiction to the conception of older gentlemen of the same profession." In the advice they had given their clients, in their stagy confrontations with the judge and prosecutor, certainly in their flamboyant consumption of champagne during a jury trial, Ballien and Cossmann had shaken "the traditions of an honorable profession and the limits set upon it—a distressing symptom of our time." *Vorwärts* was no more sympathetic, writing of Cossmann that "if [he] does not impress with [his] juristic ability, perhaps the fact that he can drink champagne will spread an aura about him." The *Berliner Tageblatt* wrote sarcastically that "The *Herren* defense counsel worked with such great effort that they needed 'simple Sekt' to pep themselves up." Two days after the end of the trial, Theodor Fontane wrote to his friend, the judge Georg Friedlaender, to ask what he thought about "the Heintze [sic] trial and the conduct of the defense counsel, with and without champagne?" Fontane added, "This side of the trial has ultimately interested people more than the whole murder and Louis affair." Even the jurors got involved. During the trial they had asked Superior Court Director Rieck if the two defenders could be replaced; afterwards, they addressed a petition to Justice Minister Schelling, demanding that stricter limits be put on what lawyers could do in court.[56]

Many within the legal profession were just as critical. Dr. Ludwig Fuld of Mainz argued in the legal trade paper, the *Juristische Wochenschrift*, that "it cannot and may not be endured that the defense counsel considers it his profession and his task, under all circumstances—one will permit us just this once the rather coarse expression—to 'get the accused off.'" Fuld too thought that younger lawyers, at least in "particular cases," were deviating from the bar's proper ethical standards. Like many German lawyers, Fuld was glad to use the laws and legal practices of Great Britain for rhetorical comparison, and like many he misunderstood the British example. His misunderstanding was especially significant because of the gulf that separated the British and German conceptions of a proper criminal defense. Fuld claimed that in England, "the defense is filled with the consciousness that it is not there to serve the defendant, but rather the true law and justice." Therefore "It would simply be impossible for a defense counsel to go to the barricades against his better convictions for the acquittal of a client he believed to be guilty." In fact, British barristers, then as now, cultivated a proud detachment from the guilt or innocence of their clients. All of the practices of the British bar, including the "cab rank" rule by which a barrister could not decline a brief, were designed to insulate the advocate from the taint of his client's actions, rather than to force him to judge them. The attitude of the British barrister to his client's guilt was classically formulated by Baron Bramwell in an Exchequer Court decision of 1871: "A client is entitled to say to his counsel, 'I want your advocacy, not your judgment. I prefer that of the court.'" This was, and is, emphatically not the German attitude; perhaps because of the common education and training of lawyers and judges, German lawyers were much more likely to consider themselves their client's first judge. The Wilhelmine bar's own historian, Adolf Weissler, wrote that "a profession could be imagined whose task it would be solely to present the claims and allegations of the parties before the court . . . without examining their accordance with the law," but the German legal profession was not like this. Maximilian Harden's brother, the lawyer Julian Witting, wrote in 1900 that the proper role for a defense counsel was to remain silent if nothing could be said on behalf of his client, but that there were a few defense counsel "so rigorous . . . that they believe they should proceed in the *Defension* 'no differently than a judge.' Thus one can sometimes observe a defense counsel limiting himself to the words 'I, too, think the guilt of the accused is unquestionable, and I can bring forth no mitigating circumstances.'"[57]

It is this kind of defense that would be unthinkable in Britain. But Ballien and Cossmann were in Berlin, and their conduct, both in advising their clients not to testify and in quaffing champagne, offended the norms of German practice. Their colleagues worried about the damage the publicity of the Heinze case could cause. Fritz Friedmann wrote, "The bar . . . has [Ballien and Cossmann] to thank, that in the 'fin de siècle counsel' with champagne glass in hand, a new comic figure has been created." A leading article in the *Berliner Tageblatt* "from juristic circles" complained that criticisms of the Heinze defense were being generalized to the profession as a whole, and worried that the case was provoking demands to scale back the rights of the defense. Here again the critical issue was publicity. The "deregulation" *(Freigebung)* of the profession had contributed to an increase in self-promotion and advertising among lawyers. The conduct of a criminal defense, especially in a cause célèbre, was one of the most effective means of advertising because the extensive press coverage of these cases could make a lawyer's name overnight. The publicity tempted defense counsel to act in ways contrary to the sound administration of justice in order to attract the respect (and the business) of the ill-informed general public through all possible attacks on the prosecutor and the judge.[58]

This was not a baseless argument. Self-promotion was becoming ever more essential for the economic survival of Berlin's trial lawyers. From the introduction in 1879 of *freie Advokatur*—the freeing of access to the private legal profession in contrast to the older regime of tight state control—Berlin's private bar grew by leaps and bounds. Between 1880 and 1895 the number of lawyers in the city increased by nearly 400 percent. On 1 January 1897 there were 869 members of the Berlin Lawyers' Chamber; in the course of 1899 membership broke the 1,000 barrier; at the end of 1905 there were 1,246, and on the eve of the First World War nearly 2,000 lawyers in Berlin. In this crowded and competitive market lawyers could be both resourceful and unscrupulous in attracting clients. One of the best known Berlin lawyers in the early 1880s was Bruno Saul, who thrived through his mastery of the promotional gimmick. When Saul left his office, his brother would walk on the opposite side of the street to stop passersby "sufficiently stupid in appearance" and point across the street to Bruno: "Do you know, sir, who that is over there? That is the famous defender Bruno Saul, who wins every case!" On one occasion Saul was to be visited by the editor of the *Berliner Börsen-Courier*. For the occasion he tripled the number of clerks laboring in his office and hired extras to sit in his waiting room impersonating clients, to convince the "influential journalist" that he was in the office "of the most sought-after lawyer in all Berlin."[59]

An outpouring of popular sentiment on a large scale, hostile to a despised class of criminal and to the aggressive conduct of courtroom defenses, was both a spur and an opportunity for the Imperial and Prussian Governments to take the offensive on a wide legal front. The aftermath of the Heinze trial illustrated the complicated interactions of private and governmental opinions and designs in Wilhelmine public life. The trial had come at a critical political moment. In 1890 the young and impetuous Wilhelm II had dismissed the "Iron Chancellor," Otto von Bismarck. In the wake of Bismarck's fall the Reichstag allowed his notorious Anti-Socialist Law, which since 1878 had allowed the extensive persecution of Social Democratic activists, to lapse. In 1891, the resurgent Social Democratic Party—buoyed not only by the lapse of the Anti-Socialist law the previous September, but by dramatic gains in the Reichstag elections of 1890—had issued its Erfurt Program, a strongly revolutionary call to arms which struck terror into the hearts of bourgeois and upper-class Germans, however much it might have belied the party's growing reformism. What was to be done? With the direct prosecution of political dissidents for political offenses suddenly more difficult, it seems that the Prussian and German governments turned to the general criminal law as a means of political repression and control. The young Kaiser was feeling restless and looking for ways to become more involved in policy making; the Prussian Ministers of Justice and the Interior, Ludwig von Schelling and Ernst Ludwig Herrfurth, were considered to be "the Kaiser's men."[60]

On 22 October the Kaiser issued a decree on the Heinze trial. Because of its importance to what followed, it is worth quoting at length:

> The lamentable circumstances, which the trial of the Heinzes has brought to light, continue to trouble my paternal heart . . . The Heinze trial has shown in an alarming way that pimpdom, along with extensive prostitution in the great cities, especially in Berlin, has developed into a common danger for state and society. The call for an energetic struggle against this problem will in the first place bring into question how far emphatic steps against pimps can be taken on the basis of the already existing laws . . . [with which] it will be immediately effected [*hinzuwirken*] that the courts in their judgments not be led by a false humanity, and accordingly with the earliest cases pronounce the highest possible sentences. In connection with this, it will be discussed whether and how there may be an amendment or extension of the existing laws. Also, criminal procedure will be subjected to a close examination, and rules will be discussed which will prevent defense counsel from forgetting their duty to contribute to the determination of truth and prevent them from making it their task to help injustice to victory even through frivolous means . . . Finally, it appears to be required that publicity be curtailed in cases in which the most serious moral crimes form the substance of the proceedings. Regarding the gloomy appearances of the Heinze trial, it is a pleasing perception for me that the great danger and disgrace, which this trial has laid bare, is recognized by all classes of the population in its full extent, and that public opinion is at one in raising the necessity of effective defense.[61]

The Kaiser's decree is a complete guide to the events that followed. He called for combating prostitution with the existing laws. As we have already seen in Chapter 1, there was a dramatic jump in trials and convictions for procuring in 1891 and 1892, a jump which cannot be explained by any change in the formal laws at that time. Indeed, contemporaries soon began noticing a new tone in trials of pimps. On 4 November, the

Kölnische Zeitung reported a case in Berlin in which a young man, not yet twenty, was convicted of procuring. Despite his age and his lack of a previous record, the prosecution asked for the maximum sentence of five years and the court gave him the still-heavy sentence of two years in prison. By comparison, the highest sentence Hermann Heinze himself had received prior to the 1891 trial was six months.[62]

Secondly, the Kaiser proposed new vice legislation. The Prussian justice and interior ministers were soon grappling with this project as well. Directly after the trial the Kaiser had cabled Schelling from his hunting lodge to ask for a report on the case. Schelling in turn wrote to Interior Minister Herrfurth to discuss "the possibility of sharper penalizing of the pimps in Berlin." Schelling's letter has the tone of the careful professional attempting to find a way to carry out the whims of an arbitrary master. He thought that the dangerous extent of pimpdom was a result of allowing prostitutes to operate as individuals, and that if prostitution were confined to state-supervised brothels the pimps would disappear. Since there was little prospect of such sweeping legislative changes in the near future, for the time being the pimps would have to be fought more directly. Introducing criminal punishments for "the cohabitation of a male person with a prostitute for the purpose of her protection" was unworkable, however, because of "indeterminacy of the concept of 'protection.'" "It also seems to me to be wrong," said Schelling, "that the separation of this kind of relationship should be directly forced by the criminal law." Using the law to break up a marriage like that of Anna and Hermann Heinze, whose point was to cloak a business relationship, was "completely out of the question." Schelling added that he did not know if the "outrage" called forth by such abuses of the marriage tie could be "managed in other ways," since "the definitive principles for the tolerance of prostitution of married women are not known to me."[63]

It says something about Schelling, and about how things got done at the top of the Wilhelmine power structure, that these well-founded doubts about the Kaiser's proposals were of no avail. In early 1892, the Prussian cabinet sent a draft bill to the upper house of the German Parliament. The draft, responding precisely to the concerns raised in the Kaiser's decree, was entitled "A Bill for a Law Amending Regulations of the Criminal Code, the Judicial Code, and the Law of 5 April 1888 Concerning Court Proceedings in the Exclusion of the Public." It broadened the definition of procuring by creating a new criminal offense of a male person living from the "immoral earnings" of a prostitute, or "protecting" her in the conduct of her trade, and raised the sentence for a conviction. The bill also extended the reach of the obscenity provisions and raised the penalties for the publication of court proceedings from which the public had been excluded. Finally, it empowered the courts to impose particularly rigorous sentences on the most "depraved" offenders: they could be made to sleep on bare boards and survive on a reduced diet of bread and water. Such provisions were a necessary deterrent, claimed the preamble to the bill, when prison conditions were often better than life on the outside for the poorest people.[64]

This new bill soon acquired a nickname: the *lex Heinze*. When it reached committee stage in the Reichstag, the Catholic Center Party and the anti-Semites brought forward amendments which substantially changed the bill's character and the nature of the political debate it would arouse. These parties had a wider conception than the Prussian cabinet of the kinds of vice which needed to be suppressed. Their amendments raised the age of consent for girls from 14 to 16, prohibited the advertising and display of contraceptives, and made sexual harassment by employers a criminal offense. After eight years of on-again, off-again parliamentary maneuvering and debate, the bill finally passed in much weakened form on 25 June 1900. By this time its origins had been largely forgotten, and the debate over its passage revolved around issues of artistic freedom and anticlericalism; a pamphlet writer of 1900 felt the need to remind readers that "Heinze" was not a Catholic Reichstag deputy. The final version of the legislation had been shorn of many of the elements for which its supporters had most yearned, and which its opponents feared. The law introduced only the so-called "pimp paragraph," section 181a of the Criminal Code, and a somewhat broader definition of culpable obscenity in section 184a.[65]

The Kaiser's decree had also referred to the duties of defense counsel, and Schelling began to take an interest in how courts appointed lawyers for indigent defendants (as Ballien had been appointed to represent Hermann Heinze). The files of the Prussian Justice Ministry contain a clipping from the *Berliner Tageblatt* mailed to Schelling by a concerned citizen. It was a leading article suggesting that Berlin courts misused their authority to appoint "official defenders." The problem was that judges drew from too narrow a pool of lawyers. Official defenders were usually young criminal specialists; neither their youth nor their specialty were in the best interests of the administration of justice. In the busy and competitive legal environment of Berlin, where young lawyers had to scramble to build up a practice, the temptation to abuse the defense position for self-promotion was too high for precisely that class of lawyers most likely to be called upon to fill it. The general public was too ill-informed to see the difference between a skillfully conducted defense and mere sensationalism: "It is a very understandable and excusable mistaken belief of the public that those defense counsel who deal as heedlessly as possible with the prosecutor and the president of the court show particular courage and outstanding shrewdness." But all would be well if criminal defenses were more often conducted by "men . . . who enjoy a long-standing personal reputation, and were raised in the traditions of the civil service *(Beamtentum)*." In general, "the judiciary does not see the defense as an equally valid factor in deciding cases; it is frequently of the view that the defense does not see its task in protecting the law, but rather in obscuring it." Defense counsel selected by the parties themselves raised other problems. Here the court could not play a direct role, but perhaps the practice of lower court officials recommending certain lawyers to defendants could be forbidden; and the press, which had so unanimously condemned the defense in the Heinze case, could do its part by simply not mentioning the names of defense counsel, and thereby at one stroke undoing the problem of defenses conducted solely for the purposes of self-promotion.[66]

This article clearly worried Schelling, but its tone matched his own presumptions. The ministry had a clear interest in clamping down on the aggressive conduct of defenses and in preventing as far as possible the growth of a specialized criminal defense bar; curtailing the bar would make attaining convictions easier, reinforcing the general sharpening of the criminal law as a political tool. In November Schelling demanded a report from the president of the *Kammergericht* on the accuracy of the *Tageblatt* story; at the end of January he wrote again to demand a list of all defense lawyers who had been commissioned as official defenders for 1891. He was not pleased with the results. It seemed that of the 600 lawyers in Berlin, ten sufficed to handle all the official defenses. Schelling's agenda came through clearly in his observation that that "It can only contribute to the raising of the reputation of the defense if respected older lawyers also take part" in criminal defenses. Otherwise, "the less desirable training of one-sided criminal defense counsel from out of the circle of younger lawyers" received official encouragement. Schelling asked the *Kammergericht* president to report to him annually on how many lawyers were commissioned with more than one official defense. Early in 1894, the *Kammergericht* president reported that in the previous year the number of such cases "had lessened considerably," and that the current arrangements "had furthered the equal recruiting of all lawyers." A report from President Angern of Superior Court I for the same year noted that the number of lawyers on the list of official defenders who were admitted to practice at the *Kammergericht* had significantly increased; the importance of this observation was that a lawyer admitted to the *Kammergericht* was likely to be both senior and a civil law specialist. Schelling also stressed that court officials were forbidden to recommend defense counsel to accused persons and their families. It was not difficult to see why: quite apart from the concern for corruption in the form of kickbacks, the recommendations of the court attendants and jail guards would tend to go to the criminal lawyers whom they knew, reinforcing the specialization in criminal practice.[67]

But Schelling could not hope to revive the deferential courtroom culture of the 1870s by spreading out the contracts for official defenses. The reason lay partly in resistance from judges, a resistance that came to light in some of the correspondence on this question between Schelling and the senior Berlin judicial officials. In response to Schelling's November request for information on the *Tageblatt* story, for instance, President Angern had stressed that trial judges had sound reasons for seeking experienced criminal lawyers for serious cases. "Many in-and-of-themselves very capable lawyers," he wrote, "concern themselves exclusively with civil cases and occupy themselves with criminal cases only unwillingly, and therefore from lack of experience and practice as defense counsel cannot achieve very much."[68]

Opposition also came from the bar itself, or to be precise, from the resentments that criminal practitioners increasingly felt toward their civil colleagues. In the bar's internal debate on the conduct of the Heinzes' defense the more conservative arguments came from prominent civil lawyers; the most strenuous defense of Ballien and Cossmann, at least on the important procedural questions, came from the pen of star defense counsel Fritz Friedmann. The criminal bar was decidedly more left-leaning than the civil bar. Its grand old men and a few of its younger leaders in the 1890s—Friedmann, August Munckel—were active in left-liberal politics, and the few Social Democratic lawyers, such as Artur Stadthagen and, later, Karl Liebknecht, were also criminal specialists (largely out of political necessity in the age of the Anti-Socialist Law and the lèse majesté epidemic).

These criminal-procedural and political tendencies were mutually reinforcing. More narrowly professional resentments added a certain *frisson* to the ideological tensions between civil and criminal lawyers. Criminal practice always carried less prestige than civil practice; this was true not only for lawyers but also for judges, who often longed for a transfer from the criminal to the civil bench. In his memoirs, Fritz Friedmann wrote with acid resentment of civil lawyers, the "hypocritical knights of the Commercial Code and the Bankruptcy Code." He argued that criminal specialists were better and more learned lawyers, because they all knew some civil law—"I myself had a great civil practice," he wrote with typical vanity—but civil lawyers seldom knew anything about what they contemptuously dismissed as "the little criminal codelet." Defense counsel *Justizrat* Erich Sello struck a similar tone when he complained about the vanity of "Assessors who had passed the exam with the best predicate" and who possessed "the most exact knowledge of all subtleties of the Civil Code," yet were still "far from being even tolerable criminal judges."[69]

It was in fact the prosecution of Ballien and Cossmann themselves by the bar's own discipline tribunals that showed how all of these factors could combine to curb ministerial efforts to rule through the criminal law.

Fin de Siècle Counsel

After the legal reforms of 1879, the private bar's own Lawyers' Chambers *(Anwaltskammern)*, to which every lawyer had to belong, controlled the professional discipline of private lawyers. Paragraph 28 of the Lawyers' Code required that a lawyer "take up his professional duties conscientiously," and "in his conduct in the practice of his profession, as well as outside of it" show "the proper respect which his profession requires." When a lawyer failed to "show the proper respect," either the Lawyers' Chamber *or* the state prosecutor could bring a complaint before the bar's Honor Court *(Ehrengericht)* for the district in which the lawyer practiced. In either case, once a proceeding was opened, the prosecution was in the hands of the regular state prosecutor's office, a situation which could and did lead to conflicts of interest when complaints were raised against a member of the criminal defense bar. The bench of the Honor Court was composed of five members of the Lawyers' Chamber for that district; these colleagues could impose penalties ranging from a statement of disapproval to expulsion from the profession. Either side could appeal the decision to the Supreme Honor Court *(Ehrengerichtshof)* in Leipzig. Here decisions were rendered by a mixed panel of four regular judges of the Imperial Supreme Court and three senior lawyers who had been specially admitted to practice before the Imperial Supreme Court.[70]

In the case of Ballien and Cossmann, both Minister Schelling and the Berlin Lawyers' Chamber quickly agreed on the necessity of a discipline proceeding. The trial was held on 29 October at the *Kammergericht.* There were six counts in the chief prosecutor's indictment. The most serious were that Ballien and Cossmann had committed a breach of duty by advising the Heinzes not to testify and by accusing judge Rieck of bias. The most colorful involved the ordering of champagne in court and Ballien's open friendliness to his client.

These issues were more questions of manners and deportment than of law. Neither side doubted that a defendant had the right to decline to testify at trial. The procedure for the examination of a defendant was set out in §§136 and 242 of the Code of Criminal Procedure. Paragraph 136 governed the pre-trial judicial examination of a suspect; it provided that "the suspect *(Beschuldigte)* is to be advised of what criminal action he is suspected" and "asked if he wishes to make any response to the accusation." The examination was to "afford the suspect an opportunity to explain away the grounds of suspicion against him, and give him an opportunity to raise facts which speak in his favor." Paragraph 242 specified that the examination of the defendant at *trial* was to proceed according to the terms of §136. Certainly §136 did not explicitly say the suspect had a right to decline to answer the magistrate's questions, but both the prosecution and the defense accepted that such a right was implicit in the provision's wording and procedural history. This was nothing more than mainstream legal opinion: the Imperial Supreme Court Senate President Löwe, author of the definitive commentary on the Code of Criminal Procedure, wrote that this provision arose out of the "doctrine . . . (incidentally highly contestable) that no one is obliged to reply to an accusation raised against him and that accordingly an examination of the suspect . . . may only be a tool *(Mittel)* for the defense, but not for the conviction of the suspect." Therefore the prosecution based its case against Ballien and Cossmann on a distinction between conduct that was acceptable from a *criminal suspect* and conduct that was acceptable from a *lawyer*. The prosecution argued that for a lawyer to give such advice to a defendant was a breach of a lawyer's duty "to the preservation of the legal order and the clearing up of the facts of the case or the investigation of the truth."[71]

The Honor Court rejected this argument, ruling that it was impossible for anything a defense counsel did by legal means in a court of law to amount to a breach of duty. The truth of the case did not consist only of the evidence of guilt; emphasizing facts and arguments that spoke for the prisoner's innocence also contributed to the search for truth, and neither the relevant statutes nor the general concept of criminal defense supported the view that the defense counsel had to contribute to the objective evaluation of evidence of guilt. Yet there were qualifications. It was the task of the defense to bring out the truth of any and all exculpatory evidence, but *not* to work for an acquittal of the defendant for its own sake. Thus it was legitimate to ask if the defense counsel gave the impugned advice on inadmissible grounds. The indictment against Ballien and Cossmann outlined two such grounds: that they had sought only self-promotion, and that they had wished to prevent the court from doing its job. The Honor Court (perhaps surprisingly) found that no evidence at the hearing supported the first ground. Evidence for the second came from the testimony of Judge Rieck himself. Rieck claimed that in twenty-five years of judicial experience, he had never encountered such advice from a defense lawyer. The failure of Anna and Hermann Heinze to testify, said Rieck, had made impossible their orderly and exhaustive examination, which he considered essential to the determination of the truth of the matter.[72]

This evidence from Rieck was puzzling. There were trial judges in Berlin, even in the 1880s, who themselves made a habit of advising defendants at the outset of a trial that they were not obliged to testify. Rieck must have known this. Furthermore, he had seemed neither surprised nor annoyed during the trial by Anna and Hermann Heinze's refusal to testify, nor by their lawyers' explanations for this refusal. Finally, he was one of the Berlin trial judges who enjoyed a good reputation among defense lawyers for fairness. Why, then, his seeming shift in attitude? The answer is that Rieck had also become a victim of the Heinze case. The *Berliner Lokal-Anzeiger* had reported that there were rumors of an official discipline proceeding being launched against Rieck; Rieck brought a successful libel action against the paper's editor. But there was some fire under the smoke. On 29 October, Schelling and Interior Minister Herrfurth had written to the Prussian Ministry of State to say that Rieck "cannot be spared the reproach that he should have responded with greater emphasis to the outrages of the defense counsel." He should have penalized Ballien and Cossmann for contempt of court *(Ungebühr)*; and he should certainly not have permitted "the offensive taking of refreshment." The President of the *Kammergericht* had given Rieck a "disclosure in these terms." Thus, a chastened Superior Court director had a motive to make amends and restore his reputation with his superiors.[73]

Yet the Honor Court did not accept Rieck's interpretation of the case. The court ruled that a procedural right instituted for the defendant's advantage, and which the defendant could waive, could never form the foundation of a trial. The motive for the advice which Ballien and Cossmann had expressed at trial—the concern for the honesty of the other witnesses—was a reasonable one. Therefore, the advice did not amount to a breach of professional duty.[74]

The other vital question in the case was the accusation of bias. As we have seen, Ballien had asked that Rieck pay more attention to the exculpatory evidence, and Cossmann had (by some accounts) said that Rieck had a duty "to divide the light and shadow evenly." Here, too, the Honor Court was inclined to be merciful. It was possible that a judge who was convinced of the guilt of the defendant might, even unintentionally, emphasize the inculpatory more than the exculpatory evidence. In such circumstances it would not only be justifiable, but necessary, for the defense to suggest that he "divide the light and shadow" more evenly.[75]

The remaining issues were less important for the procedural quality of the administration of justice, but they had everything to do with its symbolism and public image. Here Ballien and Cossmann had clearly sinned, and the Honor Court responded accordingly. It found that "the consumption of champagne stands in contradiction to the seriousness of any judicial proceeding, and especially to that of any proceeding in a jury court." The court's reasoning paid homage to the symbolism of the courtroom and the power of the public sphere: the "seriousness of the crime of which the Heinzes were accused, as well as the moral heedlessness and waywardness of [their] lives . . . filled the spectators as well as public opinion with revulsion. The contradiction [between the consumption of champagne and the seriousness of the proceeding] thus appears all the more glaring and the behavior of the defense counsel all the more egregious." It only aggravated the offense that in a jury trial, in the presence of the public, Cossmann had given the explanation that the trial would not be disturbed because "it is simply a glass of *Sekt* that we have ordered." This explanation "could only appear to the spectators as a mockery of the proceedings."[76]

This concern for public image was also at the heart of the accusation that Ballien had been too friendly to Hermann Heinze. Ballien had shaken hands with Heinze, and had greeted his client in the morning with words like "How's it going, Heinze? Did you sleep well?" and seen him off in the evening with a cheery "Sleep well, Heinze." It was in part this conduct which had so disturbed the jurors and motivated their petition to the minister. The Honor Court was equally disturbed. "The cordial behavior of the defendant Ballien to the Heinzes, especially the . . . handshake . . . along with friendly words in the presence of the public, was unworthy of a lawyer." The Heinzes were accused of the most serious crime, and Ballien and Cossmann knew well that Anna was a prostitute and Hermann a pimp. Thus Ballien, "if he wanted to uphold the honor of the estate," should not have "afforded the display to the numerous spectators and to the assembled press" that "a lawyer could deal with Heinze as with a good friend. The two defendants [i.e. Ballien and Cossmann] were responsible to their estate not to forget for a moment that between them and the Heinzes, even should they hold the latter innocent of the charge, stood an unbridgeable chasm."[77]

By drinking champagne in court and being friendly to their clients, the lawyers had committed "a serious breach of the tact required of a lawyer." But there were mitigating factors. They had done their job "with great zeal" and had tried to be "useful to their clients." There was no evidence that they intentionally tried to delay the trial with frivolous arguments and evidence; rather, the court accepted that "the scale of the trial was beyond the capability of the two defenders, so that they lost perspective on the material; perhaps they did not have the capacity to differentiate between what was important and unimportant." In a statement that was perhaps one part protesting too much and one part declaration of independence from official and unofficial authorities, the Honor Court held that it could take no consideration "of the sharp criticisms which the papers of all parties, with rare unanimity, directed at the conduct of the defense, or of the annoyance which appeared beyond the press." As Ballien and Cossmann were still young, there was hope for improvement in their skill and deportment. Ballien was given a reprimand; Cossmann, whose sins were greater (he had been found guilty of both a statutory breach as well as an offense against "decency and custom" in taking the official documents of the case from Rieck without permission) got a reprimand and a fine of 500 marks.[78]

Few were pleased with the decision. Ballien, Cossmann, and the prosecutor appealed to the Supreme Honor Court at Leipzig. The *Berliner Tageblatt* claimed in its leading article of 5 November that the judgment "will certainly cause unease in certain circles and raise the question of whether the court has done its duty in this case," although the *Tageblatt* believed it "must answer the question affirmatively." Minister Schelling was perhaps least pleased of all. On 29 October—the very day of the hearing—Schelling and Interior Minister Herrfurth reported jointly to the Prussian Ministry of State that they would appeal the outcome, and that Schelling had ordered the chief prosecutor to press for the expulsion of Ballien and Cossmann from the legal profession. On 28 November the chief prosecutor wrote to the prosecutor who would have carriage of the trial before the Supreme Honor Court to say that the minister "lays great weight on a final judgment in the case being reached as quickly as possible."[79]

Probably as a result of Schelling's desire for speed, the Supreme Honor Court heard the appeals early in January, 1892. The young lawyers fared somewhat worse in Leipzig than they had in Berlin. Cossmann's fine was raised from 500 to 1,000 marks, while Ballien was given a 500-mark fine along with his reprimand, as the Leipzig court found that both Ballien and Cossmann had indeed improperly accused Judge Rieck of bias. But the critical question was that of the advice to remain silent, and here, while the Supreme Honor Court shaded the question more finely than Berlin, it did not alter the result. The higher court held that just because the defendant had the right to decline to answer questions at trial it did not follow that the defense counsel had the right to advise him to do so. To hold otherwise would mean that the interests of lawyer and client were identical. But this was not so. It was, for instance, permissible for an accused person to lie to the court (the defendant was never sworn as a witness), whereas a lawyer could not do so on the accused's behalf. A defense counsel was, in effect, obliged to be his client's first judge. He had to determine how much he should tell the client, according to the lawyer's conscience and conception of professional duty. Thus the decision whether to give this advice or not could only be made on a case-by-case basis. But in the end the Supreme Honor Court found that Ballien and Cossmann had given the advice in good faith, with a view to aiding the pursuit of truth rather than hindering it. So despite Schelling's hot pursuit of Ballien and Cossmann through the honor courts, the lawyers survived to fight another day.[80]

The Second Trial

By the summer of 1892 nightwatchman Braun was nearly five years dead, Anna and Hermann Heinze had been sitting in investigatory custody continuously for a year and a half, there had been one inconclusive edition of their murder trial, a law bearing their name had been introduced in the Reichstag, the discipline proceedings against their counsel had gone through two instances, Judge Rieck had cleared his name in a libel trial—and yet the question of who killed the nightwatchman remained unresolved. But in late June the Heinzes came before the jurors for the second time.

The second trial began as a replay of the first. Once more Rieck presided, while State-Advocates Unger and Fiedler (Fielder had been promoted to a regular position in the interim) represented the prosecution. Ballien and Cossmann were back in their places; the *Vossische Zeitung* even reported that Hermann wore the same suit he had at the previous trial. Only the jurors were different. Rieck had in fact tried to secure another defense counsel for Hermann Heinze, a lawyer named Traeger who was even junior to Ballien. But Traeger resigned and Rieck must have felt compelled to go back to Ballien, no doubt grudgingly after all the bad blood between bench and defense.[81]

But there was one significant difference. In October Schelling had ordered the chief prosecutors in each Prussian province to apply for the exclusion of the public in all cases in which the evidence might constitute a "danger to public order or morality." President Rieck had already begun questioning Anna on her personal data when State Advocate Unger put Schelling's directive to use and requested that the public be excluded from the courtroom for the duration of the proceedings. Ballien argued that "the defendants have an interest in having their claimed innocence made clear before all the world," to which Unger replied that any public interest had been taken care of by the airing of issues in the first trial, and that it was impossible to predict when offensive subjects would arise in the evidence. The court accepted both branches of Unger's argument, ruling that "the grounds which moved the court to allow the earlier proceedings to take place with open doors are today no longer at hand." The trial was to be held in camera.[82]

The *Vossische Zeitung* told its readers that it would inform them of the events of the trial in a few days when it was over, but the paper did not take the exclusion lying down. Its reporter petitioned the court to admit selected representatives of the press, who would report carefully on the proceedings, avoiding any offensive words. The petition provocatively cited Rieck's words from the first trial, that the harm to public confidence in the administration of justice from any exclusion of the public would outweigh any moral dangers in the evidence. Nonetheless it was rejected. A complaint to Rieck from the "citizens of the Rosenthaler suburb" (the district of St. Elizabeth's), in which the good burghers argued that they, more than anyone, needed to know what had happened in the case, met the same fate. In fact the *Vossische* reported that the exclusion of the public was being carried out so strictly that even court employees and members of the prosecutor's office who did not absolutely need to be in the courtroom were kept out.[83]

With so strict an exclusion of public and press, we are left with only rumors about how the case unfolded the second time around. But according to these rumors there were considerable differences. An anonymous pamphlet author claimed that the proceedings were calm, with none of the conflicts between bench and defense that had marred the first trial in September and October. Perhaps there was some truth in the view that fractious defenses were largely publicity stunts. The evidence against the Heinzes was said to be stronger than in the previous autumn. The police had found a fellow prisoner of Anna's named Cohn, who claimed that Anna had described the murder of nightwatchman Braun to her in detail and named Hermann Heinze and another person as the culprits; the other culprit was said to be interned in a mental institution.[84]

On 2 July the long saga came to an end. State Advocate Unger conceded in a two-hour closing speech that he could not ask the jurors to find the Heinzes guilty of premeditated murder; he left them only the question of whether or not the Heinzes were guilty of *Totschlag*—unpremeditated murder. State Advocate Fiedler also delivered a closing address which dealt especially with Hermann Heinze's incriminating statements from his time in prison. Ballien and Cossmann relied on the trial's sustaining metaphor, arguing that "The darkness, which has surrounded the gruesome deed for so long, has not been lifted even through repeated careful proceedings, and the grounds for suspicion which tell against the defendants do not suffice to bring the jurors to the positive conviction of their guilt." The defense speeches ran until 7:00 P.M. Rieck gave the jurors their instructions and the questions they were to answer. The jurors cannot have deliberated for very long; the *Vossische Zeitung* records that they returned a verdict at 9:00 P.M. They found the Heinzes guilty, not of premeditated or even unpremeditated murder, but of "bodily harm with deadly outcome" *(Körperverletzung mit tödlichem Ausgang)*. State Advocate Unger asked for hard labor sentences of fifteen years against Hermann and ten years against Anna. Evidently Rieck and his two colleagues did not need much time to consider the punishment; at 10:00 P.M. they announced that they had agreed to the prosecutors' request. Rieck read out the reasons for the court's decision, and with them, the end of the legal saga of Anna and Hermann Heinze:

> The crime over which the gentlemen of the jury have given their verdict is, in the view of the court, one so dastardly as rarely appears in the annals of the big city. A watchman of the public order, who is called upon every night to care for the security of the citizens, is killed, is physically so grievously injured, that death comes. The legislature must have thought of just such a case when it considered when the highest sentence would be justified.

Hermann Heinze took the judgment with apparent calm; Anna, on the other hand, who before the jurors retired to deliberate had said that while she was innocent she would accept a hard labor sentence calmly, became agitated, protesting her innocence and refusing to accept the sentence. With more solemn finality Rieck declared that the sitting of the court was closed and that the condemned were to be led away.[85]

The Age of Epilogues

A few months after the first Heinze trial, a few weeks after Ballien and Cossmann had been partially vindicated in the Supreme Honor Court, a columnist in the conservative *Berliner Lokal-Anzeiger* lamented: "We live now in the age of epilogues. That is especially true for our sensational trials ... The Heinze trial gave birth to a flood of excitement: planned and executed measures of discipline, the legislation machine began to creak and snort, the "affair" Cossmann-Ballien saw the light of day. And now?"[86]

"Now" came another such case, the Prager-Schweitzer attempted-murder trial (see Chapter 3), which also seemed destined to generate a number of sequels. The point was that trials no longer disappeared from public view, slipping mercifully into the trough of forgetfulness; they went on forever. This observation was both perceptive and prophetic. To adapt a phrase from intellectual history, the history of criminal law in Wilhelmine Berlin after 1891 consisted of nothing but "footnotes to Heinze." The Heinze affair owed its significance to a coincidence of content and timing. In the issues it raised and in the scale of public response it evoked, it was the most important legal event since the lapse of the Anti-Socialist Law in late 1890. It therefore defined what the issues of criminal justice were going to be in this very different political-legal climate. What was to be done about the urban underclass? This was a question which would excite a great deal of public debate and legislative activity in the years that followed, with criminal trials forming the focal points for the discussion. How much scope would the defense be permitted in the criminal courtroom? Defense lawyers, prosecutors, and judges would do battle over this question continuously throughout the near-quarter-century before the First World War. How should the police do their job in capital cases, and on what kinds of evidence could they rely? The importance of hearsay evidence would progressively decline in the coming years, as scientists began to deliver innovations such as the use of fingerprints and the chemical analysis of blood, along with other tools that appear a good deal less reliable to us but seemed promising then: intricate anthropometric measurements of suspects according to the Bertillon system, and the analysis of handwriting. The relationship between public opinion and the administration of justice would continue to be complex. Wilhelmine officials often behaved as if public opinion were irrelevant to them; in fact, nothing could have been further from the truth. Outpourings of public sentiment (or at least of editorial opinion) often pushed higher officials to take particular administrative or legislative measures; and everyone involved in the criminal justice system tailored their every move and gesture to the assumed audience of newspaper readers.

That the Heinze trial gave a set of themes and rhetorical directions to the criminal law in Wilhelmine Berlin is not merely the retrospective judgment of an historian; contemporaries knew it too. The Prager-Schweitzer case of 1892 was far from the last in which journalists, lawyers, judges, or politicians invoked the Heinze trial as a precedent. Nearly seven years after the end of the Heinze trial, another pimp named Hugo Guthmann appeared before the jury of Superior Court I. Guthmann was charged with the murder of a prostitute, a woman named Bertha Singer, who was found in her apartment in June 1898, dead of a brutal slash to the throat. When Guthmann's trial opened the following April, the facts of the case and the milieu of the witnesses brought forth memories of 1891 and 1892—and the police detective who headed up the investigation was the same Alexander Braun, since promoted to Inspector, who had brought the Heinzes to book. Even before the trial began, the *Lokal-Anzeiger* predicted that it "will be a second edition of the Heinze trial," because "the milieu is the darkest Berlin, the dives, criminal-pubs, and other places where vice and depravity celebrate their orgies." Yet the tone had changed since 1891; if the Guthmann case was still a story about Berlin's night side, no one seemed able to muster the apocalyptic rhetoric of the Heinze case. Maximilian Harden, the most skeptical and original of Wilhelmine journalists, criticized Inspector Braun "and his people" for their belief in "the nightly connections between a guild of prostitutes and an organized league of pimps," while "the reality in Berlin is that these transient elements of the *Lumpenproletariat* at the most come together in little groups." But when Guthmann's trial was over—he was acquitted—even the conservative *Lokal-Anzeiger* felt the case had fallen a little flat. In a Sunday "Berlin Observer" column devoted to a comparison of the Heinze and Guthman trials, the *Lokal-Anzeiger* explained why there would be no *lex Guthmann* to match the *lex Heinze*. In 1891, as it claimed, the feeling had penetrated "far and wide in the people, in all classes of society: something must happen here!" But Hugo Guthmann was "not enough of an interesting type to stimulate sociologically fruitful studies," and the whole atmosphere that surrounded him was more "that of the dissolute, man-of-the-world scene of the socially and morally lowest level, than a near-tragic combination of the most violent, well-organized criminal world, and the most fearful prostitute and pimp world, which formed the appalling background to the Heinze trial." The "Berlin Observer" concluded, almost with a sigh, that "Anyone who experienced the latter unforgettable days in the courtroom, as I did, from beginning to end, will understand well how to make the distinction."[87]

In 1904, yet another trial called forth memories of the Heinzes. Once again it was a murder; the victim was an eight-year-old girl named Lucie Berlin, who lived in one of the notorious "rental barracks" of the Ackerstrasse—just a few blocks from St. Elizabeth's. Lucie disappeared one afternoon as her family was preparing to eat its midday meal. A few days later her dismembered body was found in a basket in the River Spree. A pimp named Theodor Berger, who lived in the same building, was charged with her killing. In what had by now become a ritual, voices from the right called for a *lex Berger* to bring in the draconian penalties which the *lex Heinze* had failed to deliver. The *Deutsche Tageszeitung,* editorial voice of the far-right Agrarian League, claimed "even those papers who earlier joined in wild protest against the *lex Heinze* now call for a *lex Berger,*" in other words, for "measures by which it can be effected that the shameless activity of the prostitutes and their pimps is removed from the sight of the growing generation."[88]

Maximilian Harden weighed in, as he had in the Guthmann case, with a screed against the social biases of the justice system and the hypocrisy of middle class newspaper readers. Only in trial reports, he complained, could the facts of life on Berlin's meaner streets be discussed; "when nothing sexual stands immediately on the jury court program, the softest mention of prostitution and its evil accompanying phenomena is strictly frowned upon." But when a criminal trial had some sexual content, then the shock and righteous indignation grew loud—for a time. "Always the same horrified astonishment," he observed cynically. "Fourteen years ago the Heinze trial, five years ago the Guthmann trial." Harden's essay was titled for the third in the sequence: "The Berger Trial."[89]

But there was a large space between the fulminations of the far right and Harden's characteristic stance of *épater le bourgeois.* For a wide range of contemporary observers the significance of the Berger trial was not the question of who murdered Lucie Berlin, nor of Berger's "immoral" life. The point of the story was the Ackerstrasse. It was Berlin North; it was poverty. In 1891 only *Vorwärts* and other Social Democratic journals had given much thought to the idea that there could be broad social causes of crime. By the end of 1904 this possibility had spread itself across much of the spectrum of Berlin's and Germany's journalistic opinion. Of course the new social gospel was more pronounced on the left. The day after the verdict on Berger—he was found guilty of unpremeditated murder and sentenced to fifteen years of hard labor—the *Tageblatt's* leading article bore the title "Big City Misery." The *Tageblatt* thought that Berger and his guilt (of which it was mildly skeptical) were not the important questions, and there was certainly nothing new in "revelations" of what Berlin got up to at night. "Prostitutes and pimps are only symptoms of a sickness of the social body," said the *Tageblatt;* "but it was always the sign of a quack to want to cure the symptom instead of going to the seat of the evil." Still, "the social side of the Berger trial" required serious consideration. The trial had revealed the dangers of Berlin's rental barracks, and thus "it is the duty of all organs of the state and the community to improve the housing stock in particular and thereby to close off one of the most dangerous sources of vice." The *Tageblatt* hoped that "the miserable fate of little Lucie Berlin" would "contribute to causing the necessity of social reforms to be recognized in the widest circles!"[90]

More surprising reflections on the Berger trial came from the far-right papers that thundered for *lex Heinzes* and *lex Bergers* and yet accepted that environmental causes of crime might mitigate the moral taint of those caught in the underworld. The *Deutsche Tageszeitung* made this argument in its Saturday supplement, in an essay entitled "Berlin, City of Two Million," a collage of all the themes that had grown out of the Heinze, Guthmann, and Berger trials:

> What a stony waste, these streets of Berlin rental barracks! And how dreadfully the miserable living conditions destroy all family life in the property-less classes! Without interruption, the Jury Court Hall of the Moabit Palace of Justice unrolls for us a gruesome picture of the goings-on in the dark courtyards of Berlin North and East, in which prostitutes with their pimps, honest craftsmen with their families, and the honest poor live all thrown together. What a dreadful fate strikes the little innocent children, who must grow up with this filth all around them ... Is it any wonder if their young souls get caught in this morass and go the way of their appalling role-models?[91]

The gloomy tenement at Ackerstrasse 130, where Lucie Berlin was murdered, was only a few blocks from St. Elizabeth's, where nightwatchman Braun was killed. But the public reception of criminal law had come a long way. A wide segment of society was beginning to accept that the tragedy that struck Lucie and her family could be the tragedy of a social environment, of a city and its institutions, rather than of wayward and degenerate souls who needed the harshest punishments. The tendency to look at crime in an ameliorative and sociological light would only increase in the late Wilhelmine years. In the meantime, as we shall see in the next chapter, the kinds of battles fought by Ballien, Cossmann and Rieck—battles over how lawyers, judges, and prosecutors should work together and do battle together—would continue.

And eight years after Friedrich Braun's murder, as part of the movement to the professionalization of urban policing, the city of Berlin abolished the nightwatchmen.

CHAPTER

3

Honorable Men

In the last age before the coming of a mass entertainment industry, law, like politics, often served as popular entertainment. The exorbitant prices that scalpers could charge for tickets to the public gallery of the Reichstag[1] had their counterpart in the prices for tickets to Moabit's trials. In Chapter 1 we saw Franz Hoeniger's description of the dispatch riders' motorcycles lined up outside the courthouse. There can be no better symbol of the omnipresence of publicity in Moabit, and everyone who played a part in criminal justice had to be highly conscious of it.

It has become a cliché to say that everything is constructed through discourse. But in a justice system in which the most fundamental procedures and institutions lacked the aura of long tradition, and thus were subject to debate, all of the juristic professions had to work hard at establishing a desired public image. At the same time, the ever-present media sought to stamp the courts and their personnel with various characteristics, according to political stance: "good" and "bad" judges, harsh and humane prosecutors, honorable and disreputable lawyers. It was not all just a matter of rhetoric. The images of lawyers, judges, and prosecutors were worked out in relation to each other, often as not in battle. The results mattered. How lawyers thought of themselves affected how they did their jobs; how they did their jobs affected the quality of justice the courts delivered. Conflicts between lawyers on the one hand, prosecutors and judges on the other—above all those conflicts that led to trials in the Honor Courts—were the ultimate motor of change in the self-conception of lawyers, and of a gradual shift in the balance of power in the courtroom between private and public sector jurists.

Few people of any kind in Imperial Germany would admit to holding "commercial" values in high esteem, and this was certainly true of those with academic legal training. As much recent literature has shown, one need not slip into old arguments regarding the "feudalization of the German bourgeoisie" to recognize that, by European standards, the German middle classes generally held conceptions of prestige more dependent on the primacy of "cultivation" and the honor of state service than did their counterparts elsewhere. In Theodor Fontane's late novella *Die Poggenpuhls,* a dissolute young officer from an aristocratic family lists the important names of the day: "Pear's Soap, Blooker's Cacao, malt extract from Johann Hoff," and laments "chivalry and heroism stand far behind." Such views were not confined to frustrated aristocrats. The liberal Alfred Kerr could complain that "the fundamental quality of the German people today is mercantile, not political," while a Weimar-era novelist put into the mouth of a conservative judge the cry "What a crazy time . . . in which one wants to force superior court directors to think like businessmen!" Honor, not money, was the currency in Moabit; or at least its denizens spoke as if this were so. Their discipline courts were "honor courts," and German lawyers instinctively felt that the professions most analogous to theirs were those far removed from commercial concerns, the civil service and the officer corps. Historian Ute Frevert has argued that from today's perspective it is "almost impossible" to grasp "the prominence of the role played by notions of honor in the consciousness and behavior of middle class men in late nineteenth-and early twentieth-century Germany."[2]

Judges and prosecutors (to a very high degree), and private lawyers (to almost as high a degree), lived under a quasi-military regime of discipline and expectations of behavior. A reference manual on the Prussian justice service published in 1909 could still cite as valid a royal ordnance from 1816 stating that "officials belong exclusively to the administration," along with an 1851 gloss that "only genuine sickness or unavoidable hindrance can serve as the basis for a release from service." Officials were obliged to "observe those social forms which the subordinate relationship requires." It was a breach of duty for an official to fail to rise when his superior entered the office, or to fail to greet his superior in the appropriate manner, including by avoiding him. The lawyers' Supreme Honor Court applied the same obligation to lawyers vis á vis the president of the court at which they practiced. If a justice official got married he was supposed to supply details of the date of his wedding, the name of his wife, and the profession of her parents, although at least by 1909 he no longer needed official permission to marry. An official could not belong to "political parties hostile to the state," or even so much as rent an apartment to a Social Democrat. On the brighter side, the official who made it through a moderately successful career could look forward to being honored with the Order of the Red Eagle (fourth class), and if he were especially distinguished, even the third class.[3]

The questions of honor and publicity were closely related. Beyond the world where bureaucrats rose and bowed and said "Your Excellency," there loomed the increasingly unruly public sphere of Wilhelmine Germany. How were these worlds to be combined? The *Berliner Börsen-Zeitung* observed in 1907, "It is difficult to say how far the rights of the press and of public opinion to pry into the private lives of ruling personalities go. In fact it is not at all clear whether there is such a thing as a private life of official men. An officer, a diplomat, stands under the control of official discipline even in shirt sleeves in his parlor." A small innovation of the year 1907 demonstrated how increasingly difficult it was becoming for Moabit's jurists to combine their notions of a *standesgemäss* fulfillment of their duty with the demands of the publicity machine. The innovation was the practice of the journalistic "interview" with the officials involved in a trial— a technique taken from the American press, or so at least conservative Germans complained, to whom the very foreignness of the word showed how it did not fit "German feelings." In the course of the trials following Maximilian Harden's allegations that key members of the Kaiser's entourage were homosexually inclined, officials like the judge Superior Court Director Lehmann and First Prosecutor Isenbiel took to granting these new-fangled interviews. The *Deutsche Tageszeitung* thought this might be all right for senior statesmen, but for most public servants it was inappropriate to discuss matters lying "within the field of their official activities." It was self-evident that any official would simply do his duty, but "one should not say certain self-evident things, because from the fact that they have been said at all, people of bad will could draw the conclusion that it is actually not a matter of self-evident things." In short, the problem was how to do one's duty in the eyes of the public. Honor was inherently a public quality, and in a society with such a rigorous social code and uncommercial scale of values, every public encounter and every courtroom battle placed honor in question.[4]

Just as complicated as relations with the public were the problems jurists from the judiciary, prosecutor's offices, and private bar faced in their relations with each other, at least once they became set in their professional positions. The training was common to all. Wherever the young jurist hoped to make a career, the first steps were legal study at a university, followed by the first of two state-administered examinations. This first examination was known as the *Referendar* exam because those who passed it could apply to become *Referendare* at a court. The Referendar period lasted, at various times, three or four years; the duties involved assisting judges in hearing cases, doing legal research, or writing judgments. Normally the Referendar would do a rotation at the state prosecutor's office, and the Referendar who so desired could also gain experience working with a private lawyer. At the end of the *Referendarzeit*, the young jurist took the second state-administered exam, the *Assessor* Exam, which had both a written and oral component; as with the Referendar exam, the candidate received a one-word *Predikat*, or grade, ranging from "not sufficient" to "good." Upon successful completion of this exam the jurist acquired the title of *Assessor*, and only at this point did career paths diverge. An Assessor could apply to any court he wanted for admission as a private lawyer, or he could apply for a position as a prosecutor or a judge. Around 1900 the wait for a permanent position as a judge could be six to seven years, and nearly half of all Assessors, who generally spent their time going from court to court as relief judges or dogsbodies in the prosecutor's office, drew no salary. Those who were in financial need opted to become lawyers right away, along with most Jews—there was a clear, albeit unofficial, discrimination against Jews in the judicial service, with correspondingly high levels of Jews in the private bar. In 1904 9.4 percent (578) of Prussian Referendars were Jewish, as measured by formal religious affiliation, compared to 4.2 percent (191) of judges and 27.4 percent (1287) of private lawyers. In Berlin, throughout the Wilhelmine and Weimar periods, approximately half of the members of the Berlin Lawyers' Chamber recorded a Jewish religious affiliation on their personnel documents. No Wilhelmine working jurists were women; it was not until 1922 that national legislation opened up legal careers to women graduates.[5]

Thus there were obvious social and ideological differences between bench and bar. Yet a marked coolness in their relations was held to be a recent development in Wilhelmine Berlin. In the middle of the nineteenth century, it was said, a host of factors had tended to unify jurists. The community was small and its members were often related. No one needed to travel very far to do his job, and the workloads were moderate. Jurists were politically liberal almost without exception; the *Kammergericht* lawyer

Franz Hoeniger wrote that "religious variety was beginning to play a political, but not a social role." Even after the turn of the century there were smaller centers where things were still kind and gentle. In smaller cities, wrote Hoeniger in 1906, "Judges, lawyers, and prosecutors feel themselves with pride to be one profession, in spite of all dividing details." But not in Berlin. Though it had "countless jurists," the capital had no "specifically legal society," or rather "it had lost it since it became a world-city." In particular, said Hoeniger, the reforms of 1879 had played a role in the fragmentation of the legal professions. Fritz Friedmann, like Hoeniger, lamented the decline of collegiality among all of Moabit's jurists. On the one hand, with the advent of *freie Advokatur,* lawyers who had been in practice before 1879 generally viewed the new arrivals (Friedmann settled as a lawyer in Berlin in January 1880) with hostility. But prosecutors and judges were even more hostile. Before the introduction of *freie Advokatur* all jurists had addressed each other as "Herr Colleague." But in the new system Friedmann felt that private lawyers, who as free professionals in the market no longer enjoyed the cachet of royal service, were systematically belittled. Perhaps judges "did not have the courage" to insult the veterans of the bar; but towards the young, the new "un-royal lawyers, to whom one gave all the duties but almost none of the rights of civil servants," all was fair.[6]

The new conflicts were partly a product of the sheer growth in numbers, multiplied by the geographic dispersal of Berlin's courts, and the separation of the criminal and civil trial courts; and partly they were about money. The growth and dispersal of the legal professions only exacerbated those elements of conflict that were almost inevitable by-products of the system. In the German inquisitorial system, as defense counsel like Friedmann never tired of insisting, judges could easily become mental prisoners of the pre-trial brief and come to court confident that it was "their task to defeat [the defendant] with all of the weapons of higher intelligence and dialectic." The defense counsel was thus only the "accomplice," who had to be "rendered as harmless as possible." But it was not just the differing procedural perspectives of judges and defense counsel that explained the often startling hostility that could erupt between them in the Wilhelmine courtroom. There were also, as Friedmann wrote, "political and racial questions": the lawyers were often Jewish and belonged almost exclusively to the liberal, if not the Social Democratic parties; judges were overwhelmingly conservative and almost never Jewish. "Sometimes a baptized Jew loses himself among them," said Friedmann, "but then he is more Catholic than the Pope, in order to have his origins forgiven." Money was perhaps an even more bitter question. In addition to "deep political and religious differences," Hoeniger cited the "income, which has grown gigantic, of a segment of the bar," and the "search for luxury and pomp which is everywhere on the increase, even among the wealthy officials." Friedmann claimed that the annual income of a busy defense counsel could be twenty times that of a Superior Court director, and certainly judges were not paid well in comparison to other professionals with equivalent training. The pay of a judge at a Local or Superior Court ranged from 3000 to 7200 marks per year; senate presidents at a Court of Appeal and presidents of Superior Courts made up to 11,500; the presidents of Courts of Appeal up to 15,000. On top of this there were housing allowances of 560–2000 marks per year, depending on rank. Jurists in the rest of the civil service earned more—while a Local Court judge in 1900 started at 240 marks per month, a jurist who worked in the civil service began at 400. The earnings of defense counsel, however, could be much higher. A tariff was set for lawyers' fees at the time of the justice reforms, and its levels were certainly low—12 to 18 marks for a local court trial and 20 marks for a criminal chamber trial regardless of length, 40 marks for the first day of a jury trial and 20 each day thereafter—but the Fees Ordnance *(Gebührenordnung)* allowed a lawyer to charge any fee that could be agreed on with the client, so long as the agreement was in writing. This provision opened the door to riches for the best lawyers. Fritz Friedmann claimed to make 25,000 marks in a *month*; it is impossible to verify this claim, and in any event he was far from typical of lawyers, but the figure at least suggests a range inaccessible to any judge or prosecutor. Although Hoeniger praised the restraint of judges in the face of their relatively poor pay—"The Berlin judge has no newspaper, no union that can raise its voice in these matters . . . silently this profession goes its conscientious way in the service of the law"—in 1908, two Berlin judges, Superior Court Counselor Kade and Local Court Counselor Jastrow, spearheaded the formation of a Berlin Judges' Union. Just a few months later there followed the formation of a national judges' association, the *Deutsche Richterverein,* and a few months after that a Prussian equivalent, the *Preussische Richterverein.* The chief motivation behind all of this organizing was the growing annoyance among judges with their comparatively meager salaries. But the *Deutsche Richterverein,* considerably to the right of its Prussian cousin, was soon engaging in startlingly bitter anti-lawyer polemics in its *Deutsche Richterzeitung.*[7]

In taking this step, the judges bowed to the inexorable logic of a media culture: if honor is a public quality, battles over honor have to be fought in public. In this chapter we will look at how these battles defined and redefined Moabit's jurists.

The Very Model of a Prussian Judge

Judges in criminal courts were major public figures, indeed celebrities. Unlike their colleagues in the civil courts, their activities in the "sounding board of the criminal chambers or the jury court hall" found "the loudest echo in the public."[8]

In the oral tradition of Wilhelmine Moabit there was one preeminent "good judge" and one preeminent "bad judge." The "good judge," Superior Court Director Alexander Schmidt, was respected by all who knew and worked with him, including those not normally given to speaking well of judges. Fritz Friedmann called him "my dear old Schmidt . . . of whom I always think with the deepest reverence and merriest heart;" Maximilian Harden wrote that Schmidt was "widely respected for his competence." In the early 1890s, Schmidt presided over the 1st Criminal Chamber of Superior Court I. He became one of the most talked-about of German judges when, in 1893, Maximilian Harden appeared before his chamber on a charge of lèse majesté.[9]

Harden was prosecuted for an article entitled "Monarch's Education," in which he had the temerity to suggest that Wilhelm II might yet have a few things to learn about the business of being Kaiser. Even the prosecutor thought that a conviction was only "probable," not "certain." The prospects for acquittal were improved by a resourceful defense from Fritz Friedmann, who knew Schmidt well enough to send him the text of a popular play of the time which bore similarities to Harden's article; the obvious intention was to make Harden's piece seem commonplace. Although First Prosecutor Drescher, the chief of the prosecutors' office at Superior Court I, argued the case himself, Schmidt's chamber acquitted Harden in a closed-door hearing on 7 April on the grounds that "respect for a prince does not show itself in lying at his feet in Byzantine fashion and flattering him."[10]

The authorities were not pleased with this result. Schelling ordered his prosecutor to appeal the decision; but on 9 May Drescher advised the minister that although the chamber's interpretation of Harden's article was "fully mistaken and in a few places virtually naive," he could find no errors of law or procedure in the judgment or the trial protocol that would promise success on appeal. The state withdrew its appeal and Schelling tried a second tack. In a manner entirely characteristic of his efforts to sharpen the political effectiveness of the criminal courts, he moved to have Schmidt transferred to a civil chamber. But the results of Schelling's efforts were also typical of the period. Under the terms of the Judicial Code, it was the presidium of a court, a committee of the senior judges, which assigned judges to chambers. The presidium of Superior Court I refused Schelling's "request" to transfer Schmidt to civil duty. Then in November Schmidt's chamber decided a second case in a manner that displeased the minister. Again Schelling asked that Schmidt be transferred; again the presidium refused. By this time Schmidt was growing weary of the constant pressure, and in what he later called a "weak moment" he agreed to a voluntary transfer to a civil chamber. Soon after the transfer took effect Schmidt became ashamed of his acquiescence, and decided that the only honorable course was to resign altogether. He left the justice service in June of 1894.[11]

Schmidt's resignation, caught up as it was in issues of high political significance, sparked a journalistic flurry. When a Munich newspaper broke the story, the *Vossische Zeitung*, sympathetic to the Caprivi administration and the "new course," claimed that transfers to the civil side of the court were generally desired by judges, and that only a judge with an "excess of sensitivity or a large private income" could find in one an occasion to resign. Schmidt himself replied the next day, writing rather cryptically that his transfer was "for reasons which lay completely beyond my person and therefore are not to be publicly discussed." He added that whether he had "betrayed an 'excess of sensitivity'" by resigning over the issue "is a matter of subjective feeling. I possess a 'private income' to such a limited extent that my retirement, in connection with other very grave blows of fate which have recently struck my family, has placed me in a highly unfavorable financial position."[12]

For Harden, the Schmidt affair was a propagandistic godsend. Founder and editor of the lively *Die Zukunft*, Harden was an admirer and protégé of Bismarck and a sworn opponent of Wilhelm II and his ministers, a Social Democratic sympathizer who maintained a burning hatred of liberals. If he had a consistent creed, it was *épater le bourgeois*. Professing outrage at the *Vossische's* toadying to the Caprivi administration, Harden castigated the paper that "always keeps some white paper free for the praise of the new course."[13] Along with a number of Social Democratic politicians, he recycled the Schmidt story throughout the Wilhelmine years as a symbol of the evils of political justice in Imperial Germany. Generally lost in such retellings was the striking fact that Schmidt's fellow judges had twice refused to bow to ministerial pressure, and that Schmidt could have gone on leading a criminal chamber if he had not relented. Thus the story of the good judge martyred for principle becomes more complex and ambiguous the more it is examined; what remains clear is the centrality of honor. Honor dictated Schmidt's every step: he was insulted by the requests to transfer him to a civil chamber, and it was shame at giving in—or, as the *Vossische* put it, an excess of sensitivity, a different moral evaluation of the same thing—that prompted his resignation.

In the lore of Moabit, Schmidt's main function after 1894 was to serve as a rhetorical foil to the "bad judge," Superior Court Director Georg Robert Brausewetter. Brausewetter was a character with a larger-than-life quality, the most notorious and controversial judge of Wilhelmine Berlin. Lawyers called his chamber the *Totenkammer*—"the chamber of the dead;" whether they were referring to the defendants or to themselves was less clear. Brausewetter spent his brief career locked in mortal combat with Berlin's defense lawyers. These incessant battles were all about slighted honor: the insults Brausewetter believed lawyers had inflicted on him, and those the bar felt it had suffered at his hands.

Brausewetter's career provided another illustration of how, in matters of criminal law, the Wilhelmine era was "the age of epilogues." As we saw in the previous chapter, this phrase was the striking coinage of the *Berliner Lokal-Anzeiger* in an editorial on the Schweitzer-Prager attempted murder trial. In this case, heard in January 1892, Eugenie Prager and her brother Max Schweitzer were sentenced to six and five years' hard labor respectively for the attempted murder of Prager's husband.[14] The case became the "Brausewetter Case," as the *Lokal-Anzeiger* put it, chiefly because of Brausewetter's address to the jury at the close of the evidence:

> I envy the defense lawyers, who every time ask for the "not guilty" verdict with complete certainty. If the honored defense counsel sat at the judges' table there would probably be no more convictions. I envy them their benevolence, and yet it is strange that if jurists such as they are so strongly convinced of the innocence of the defendants, not all jurists are of the same view, but rather such poor innocents are still brought to the dock.

Let the facts that have appeared before your eyes influence you, and be man enough to judge by your own convictions.[15]

Even the conservative *Lokal-Anzeiger* thought that this remark would "be met with doubtful head-shaking." To make matters worse, at the close of a trial on the very next day Brausewetter summed up: "I subscribe to every word the prosecutor has said." These comments were blatant breaches of the procedural rules. According to §300 of the Code of Criminal Procedure, the presiding judge was supposed to "instruct" the jurors, "*without going into an evaluation of the evidence,* on the legal points which they must take into consideration in resolving the question which has been put to them."

Brausewetter's conduct angered Berlin's lawyers and goaded their organizations—the official Lawyers' Chamber which governed the bar, and the unofficial Lawyers' Association—into a flurry of meetings and resolution-drafting. Only two days after the end of the Prager-Schweitzer trial, the Lawyers' Association met to discuss its outrage over Brausewetter's remarks. A week later it held a heavily attended general meeting, at which 300 lawyers from Berlin and environs decided that the Board of Directors of the Lawyers' Chamber should complain formally to Justice Minister Schelling. The lawyers not only objected that Brausewetter's jury instructions contravened §300, they also believed that his remarks "insulted the entire legal profession." Schelling eventually replied that "he was not able to approve" of Brausewetter's conduct. It seems that there were no further consequences for Brausewetter, but the public statement of disapproval by the Minister was remarkable enough to satisfy the lawyers for the time being. At a meeting on 13 May the assembled lawyers of Berlin and Brandenburg passed a unanimous resolution expressing their satisfaction that "the Herr Justice Minister has corrected the conduct of Herr Superior Court Director Brausewetter and . . . that the Board of Directors of the Lawyers' Chamber has defended the dignity of the legal profession in writing, and referred to the serious conditions that can arise for the administration of justice through the impugned practices of a few jury court presidents." The incident marked a change in the organizational culture of Berlin's lawyers, and in their relations with other components of the justice system. Private lawyers were increasingly willing to make claims for equal consideration in the courtroom and in the shaping of criminal-legal policy. According to the *Vossische Zeitung,* the Brausewetter affair of 1892 was the first time the

Lawyers' Chamber had concerned itself with general questions of the administration of justice, rather than with the bar's purely internal affairs. On the other hand, the language of the Chamber's resolution betrayed an almost pathetic satisfaction with the barest ministerial recognition of the bar's claims; perhaps this satisfaction shows most clearly how questions of honor and image were always paramount in the struggles between private lawyers and judges.[16]

If the primacy of honor needed any further illustration, it got it later in 1892 in the next installment of the struggle between Brausewetter and Berlin's defense bar. The contending parties this time were Brausewetter and the lawyer Artur Stadthagen. Brausewetter and Stadthagen had in fact spent much of their careers fighting each other. Stadthagen was one of Berlin's small band of Social Democratic lawyers. He set up his practice in 1884 at the comparatively young age of 26, and soon became one of the lawyers on whom Social Democrats could rely to defend them in the many petty and not-so-petty prosecutions to which they were vulnerable. On 3 December 1886, one such case brought him before the 1st Criminal Chamber of Superior Court I, under the presidency of Superior Court Counselor (not yet promoted to Director) Brausewetter. Stadthagen's clients were four women from the board of directors of the Association for the Protection of the Interests of Women Workers. They were charged with having discussed political subjects at their meetings, and having contacted other organizations to carry out common purposes—for women, these were offenses under the highly restrictive Prussian Law of Association. After a two-day trial, all four women were convicted of having carried on politics at their meetings (but acquitted on the charges of attempting to strike up contacts with other associations) and given modest fines of 60 to 100 marks.[17]

The epilogues to this trial kept Brausewetter and Stadthagen occupied for six years. Stadthagen appealed his clients' convictions to the Imperial Supreme Court. In his written appeal he argued that the criminal chamber could not have come to the verdict that it had on the basis of the evidence presented in court. The Berlin bar's Honor Court construed this claim as an insult to Brausewetter's honor and the honor of his chamber, and punished Stadthagen with a reprimand. Both Stadthagen and the chief prosecutor appealed this decision to the Supreme Honor Court in Leipzig; this kept the case going until 1889, at which point both appeals were rejected and Stadthagen was left with a reprimand. Between 1886 and 1889 Stadthagen made a point of refusing any cases in Brausewetter's chamber. However, in the summer and fall of 1889 he felt obliged to take on three different cases involving Social Democrats before Brausewetter in his new capacity as president of the 2nd Chamber. For various reasons Stadthagen now felt himself "obliged" *(verpflichtet)* to bring motions to reject Brausewetter and the other judges for apprehension of bias (for which the Code made clear provision) in all three of the cases. The three motions all raised the same nineteen grounds, two of which were ultimately singled out for special attention by the chief prosecutor and the Honor Courts. Stadthagen alleged that Brausewetter and the other judges of his chamber had submitted a falsified protocol in one of the cases; second, he claimed that it was "common knowledge in legal circles" that Brausewetter had displayed an unseemly degree of gratitude to then-Prussian Justice Minister Friedberg when the minister promoted Brausewetter to director in 1889.[18]

Meanwhile, Stadthagen had given other hostages to fortune. He delivered speeches at Social Democratic election rallies in Friedrichsberg, Hohen-Neuendorf, and Berlin in July and August of 1889, in which he unfavorably contrasted the impartiality of professional judges with that of jurors and lay-judges, and on one occasion led a cheer for Social Democracy. He also took a few shortcuts in conducting the business of his practice. A client named Lindner left some money and commercial paper in trust with Stadthagen, who then took most of the money—some 5,000 marks—to settle his own bill. The prosecution saw two possible explanations for this transaction, both of them bad. Stadthagen and Lindner might have arranged the transaction to keep assets away from Lindner's creditors. Even if this were not so, Stadthagen's taking of his client's money, despite Lindner's (eventual) consent, amounted to unethically self-interested behavior, and violated the principle of the Lawyers' Code that fees should be "moderate."[19]

On 27 April 1892 the Berlin Honor Court found that there was "no doubt" that Stadthagen's motions against Brausewetter's chamber had "abused the position of a defense counsel," and destroyed the "good relations which must exist between the various factors involved in the administration of justice" in order for the system to work. The allegations that Stadthagen brought forward were "impassioned and hateful"; they could not, said the Honor Court, in any way demonstrate bias on the part of Brausewetter or his chamber, but rather served only to "belittle the Director Brausewetter and the other judges in the eyes of others." On the other hand, the Honor Court acquitted Stadthagen of the charges in connection with his political activity, finding that the Lawyers' Code was not intended to deprive the lawyer of his right to act publicly on his political convictions, so long as he did so within the law. On the financial matter, it found that Stadthagen had not assisted Lindner in dodging his creditors, but that Stadthagen had acted unacceptably in helping himself to Lindner's money. The Honor Court sentenced Stadthagen to a reprimand and a fine of 2000 marks.[20]

Both Stadthagen and the chief prosecutor appealed this decision to the Supreme Honor Court. As in the case of Ballien and Cossmann, the fundamental issue was whether a norm of professional ethical conduct would be allowed to negate a defendant's statutory rights. In his written defense, Stadthagen argued forcefully:

> Does it damage the respect of the judiciary if I reject a judge who is considered by the defendant to be partisan? Is the respect of the judiciary damaged by my doing my duty in the manner prescribed by the Code of Criminal Procedure? Then let the law be cursed, not me. Then let it be legally determined that judges may not be rejected for apprehension of bias.[21]

Stadthagen also relied on Brausewetter's growing notoriety. "Is it then a coincidence," he continued, "that complaints have frequently been brought against Herr Superior Court Director Brausewetter—by *non*-Social Democratic lawyers—because of disparagement of the legal profession and insults to lawyers?" Here Stadthagen called on the evidence of several Berlin lawyers, as well as of the president of the *Kammergericht* and the board of directors of the Lawyers' Chamber, concerning the latter's 1892 complaint to the justice minister about Brausewetter, and the "emphatic disapproval" of Brausewetter's conduct that the president of the *Kammergericht* had expressed on the instructions of the minister.[22]

But this time the prosecution won. Reversing the Berlin Honor Court on the basis of new evidence, the Supreme Honor Court found Stadthagen guilty not only of helping himself to Lindner's money but also of seeking to help Lindner dodge his creditors, and ruled that these transgressions alone would be enough to expel Stadthagen from the profession. The Supreme Honor Court also found a breach of lawyerly duty in the bias motions against Brausewetter. There was "not the slightest ground" for Stadthagen's claim that Brausewetter's chamber had falsified a trial protocol; therefore "a conscious attempt by [Stadthagen] to insult the honor of Director Brausewetter must be assumed." The same went for Stadthagen's allegations of Brausewetter's effusive gratitude to Minister Friedberg, which, as they "could not serve as a foundation of the motion of rejection," must have been made "only to insult the Director Brausewetter." The court came to a mixed result on the questions involving Stadthagen's political activity. There was no general breach of duty, said the court, in a lawyer speaking at a Social Democratic gathering or leading cheers for Social Democracy. On the other hand, his speech of 17 July 1889, entitled "People's Law and Jurist's Law," went too far. Stadthagen had accused professional judges of being careerists, and of having a dependent relationship to the government. When such accusations were raised in a speech meant for "a great crowd of ordinary people," they constituted a breach of a lawyer's duty to his profession. Stadthagen should have considered that he was insulting the "estate" alongside of which he was supposed to work as an "organ of the administration of justice," and that such an insult would make successful cooperation in the future impossible. For the Supreme Honor Court, such behavior, on top of Stadthagen's financial irregularities, only made him all the more deserving of expulsion from the profession.[23]

Stadthagen never practiced law again. He made a career as an editor of *Vorwärts,* as a Berlin city counselor, and as a member of the SPD delegation in the Reichstag, where he stood on the uncompromising, non-revisionist left. He was frequently in trouble with the law and had to make constant use of his parliamentary immunity. He died in 1917.[24]

If Stadthagen's experience with Brausewetter seemed to substantiate Brausewetter's reputation as a scourge of Social Democrats, the trial of the anti-Semitic activist Hermann Ahlwardt late in 1892 complicated the judge's image. That spring Ahlwardt had published two pamphlets, "New Revelations: Jew-Rifles," and "Jew-Rifles Part II," in which he claimed that a rifle manufacturer named Isidor Löwe had endangered Germany and its soldiers by selling defective rifles to the army, and that the military authorities had covered up the defects. Ahlwardt was charged with libeling Löwe and a number of officials.

Brausewetter conducted Ahlwardt's trial much as he conducted any other—making clear his presumption of the defendant's guilt and feuding with the defense counsel. On 9 December the chamber convicted Ahlwardt of the lesser of the Code's two forms of libel, denying him the defense in §193 of the Reich Criminal Code of "defending . . . or representing a justified interest," but at the same time finding that he had not printed his allegations "against better knowledge." Ahlwardt was sentenced to five months' imprisonment. The prosecutor had asked for eighteen months; the maximum was two years.[25]

With this verdict, Brausewetter demonstrated an ability to arouse antagonism across the political spectrum. He drew ferocious criticism from the right for his evident hostility to Ahlwardt. At an anti-Semitic rally in Dresden, one speaker claimed that "our judiciary is no longer in touch with the people's sense of justice;" another praised Ahlwardt's lawyer, who "had not learned to creep into a mouse hole in the face of court presidents." The *Kreuzzeitung* quoted with approval a characterization of Brausewetter and First Prosecutor Drescher as "the most unpopular people in Germany." In an article that received much favorable attention from the right-wing and anti-Semitic press, an Imperial Supreme Court judge wrote that he hoped Brausewetter's handling of the trial would not attract imitators. Brausewetter's new-found detractors on the right were not balanced, however, by any thinning of the ranks of his liberal and Social Democratic critics. The left-liberal *Berliner Zeitung* complained that Brausewetter's evident presumption of Ahlwardt's guilt served only "the continued growth of the web of lies," while "the unexpectedly mild sentence will save Herr Brausewetter just as little from suspicions of his official honor as will his statement during the trial about the justified side of anti-Semitism."[26]

Once again, Justice Minister Schelling felt the need to intervene. In a decree on the conduct of trials sent to all Prussian Court of Appeal districts on 21 December, Schelling ordered that judges, especially in "criminal cases which are connected to the political and social party struggles of the present time," should "avoid any appearance of prejudice," "clothe their conduct in a form appropriate to the seriousness of the matter," and "avoid critical comments of any sort of sarcastic coloring."[27]

Eighteen months later, in what would become his most notorious trial, Brausewetter showed how little he had taken these words to heart. The case arose out of an altercation between police and a crowd of several hundred unemployed workers at a demonstration at Berlin's Friedrichshain park in January 1894. Newspapers of all political stripes—from the conservative *Kreuzzeitung* to the Social Democratic *Vorwärts*—reported that the police had used an excessive degree of violence in dispersing the crowd, wielding, in addition to their sabers, "rubber hoses" *(Gummischläuche)*. The prosecutor's office, on behalf of the police, raised libel indictments against the editors of a selection of these newspapers—a selection drawn only from the left, from the *Berliner Tageblatt* to *Vorwärts*.[28]

Brausewetter's handling of what became known as the "Rubber Hose" trial was egregious even by his standards. He hardly let the defendants speak; rather he delivered sermons on the goodness of the police and the evils of Social Democracy, to which the defendants could only respond with comments such as "I am of a different view." He answered the editors' accounts of the events of 18 January by saying, "No, it wasn't like that." Throughout the proceedings there were signs that Brausewetter was alienated not just from the liberals and the left but from the whole spectrum of Wilhelmine opinion. He pressed one defendant to "admit" that all journalism was politically tendentious by insisting "The *Kreuzzeitung* writes differently than *Vorwärts*. In this way the truth very seldom comes to light." The most celebrated moment in the trial came when defense counsel Mosse asked if the Alexanderplatz would give a statement on its use of informers or *agents provocateurs:*

Brausewetter: To whom, then?
Mosse: To the public.
Brausewetter: Oh, come on, "the public" doesn't exist.[29]

All of the defendants were convicted; yet the sentences were not as heavy as State Advocate Benedix had requested, nor as one might have expected from Brausewetter's conduct of the trial. Against Schmidt, the editor of *Vorwärts,* Benedix asked for a sentence of one year; the court gave him five months. Of the other defendants, four received sentences of two or three months' imprisonment, while three received fines ranging from 150 to 500 marks. If to a modern North American sensibility it is an outrage to punish journalists who did nothing but report facts they reasonably believed to be true, we must also recognize that even here Brausewetter's bark was worse than his bite. And his bite struck all but one of these left-leaning defendants less severely than it had the anti-Semite Ahlwardt.[30]

But once again Brausewetter had mightily annoyed the press of all parties. In view of the facts and outcome of the trial, the most striking press reactions to Brausewetter's conduct came from the far right. The *Kreuzzeitung* referred to Justice Minister Schelling's decree on proper trial conduct from late 1892, and allowed that "it would certainly have been best if the well-known decree . . . had found the respect that it obviously deserves." The anti-Semitic *Volk,* whose editor, Heinrich Oberwinder, probably recalled his own encounters with the courts, wrote "The conduct of the presiding judge of the court seems to us to give much occasion for criticism." From Cologne, the semi-official National Liberal *Kölnische Zeitung,* which in late 1891 had been one of the papers joining in the criticisms of Ballien and Cossmann, wrote that it was "disturbing" that "the two-day proceeding took the form of an uninterrupted exchange of words between the presiding judge and the defense counsel." It blamed Brausewetter for the atmosphere, adding that the public, the press, and all jurists would urgently wish "that this modern manner of the conduct of a court proceeding not attract imitators." The *Berliner Tageblatt* thought that Brausewetter's conduct "did not contribute to raising the level of respect for German justice"; or, as the *Vossische Zeitung* added, "of German judges."[31]

It was the irony of Brausewetter's career that he had a knack for creating opposition where there had been none before. From his manner of conducting trials it often seemed that he wished for nothing so much as a world without defense counsel (to say nothing of a world without Social Democrats, especially if they were Jewish); a remark often attributed to him in Berlin legal circles was "when I have a Social Democrat in front of me, who is defended by a little Jewish lawyer, then I just see red and I lose all self-control." But his conduct toward defense counsel helped to foster professional solidarity among lawyers and to drive them to an unprecedented degree of public activity. It was the same with the press. Press outrage over his remark "the public doesn't exist," as even the *Kreuzzeitung* put it, drove the "entire German press" to a unanimity that "one otherwise seeks in vain." Here was the public for which Brausewetter had such contempt, ever growing in size and influence. For, as in 1892, this public reaction stimulated a measure of ministerial annoyance with Brausewetter. The surviving archival record is tantalizingly incomplete, but it is clear that four days after the trial the Justice Minister demanded a report from Brausewetter on his conduct of the trial.[32]

One more sensational episode remained in the career of the president of the *Totenkammer:* his own death. On 22 December 1895, the *Berliner Tageblatt* carried a terse notice that "Director Brausewetter has suddenly been taken ill." The story grew more dramatic on 11 January, when the *Tageblatt* reported on the rumors flying about Berlin that Brausewetter had tried to kill himself. It was clear that Brausewetter was afflicted by a mental illness. His assistant judges reported that he had lately been unusually suspicious of them, and had seemed unable to follow the proceedings in his chamber. A few days later the *Berliner Tageblatt* reported a grave diagnosis. Brausewetter was said to suffer from "progressive paralysis," which struck "particularly intellectually active people" and claimed as its victims predominately "businessmen, scholars and officers." Once the disease reached its crisis there could be no hope of improvement. And for Brausewetter there was none: four days later he was dead.[33]

When the news of Brausewetter's illness broke, the non-existent public took its revenge. Gingerbread cookies in his likeness were sold at the Christmas markets. Alfred Kerr compared the concurrent scandal involving lawyer Fritz Friedmann, who had fled Berlin and his creditors in the company of a 17-year-old girl, to Brausewetter's fall: "In any case [Brausewetter], the most unpopular of all Berlin jurists, is having a gray Christmas, like the other, who for years was the most popular." Many of the people whom Brausewetter had sentenced in 1895 sought to have their cases reopened. A "Brausewetter debate" occupied the Reichstag on 1 February 1896; among the deputies who spoke was Artur Stadthagen. The Social Democratic deputy Singer touched on one of the tropes of the "Age of Epilogues" when he asked if the Reich secretary of state for justice would bring forward a "lex Brausewetter" to allow *Revisionen* in Brausewetter's recent cases. The government refused, and Germans discovered with amazement that their laws made no provision for a retrial or an appeal on the basis that the presiding judge had been mentally incompetent.[34]

Some members of the public took up another question after Brausewetter's death: to what extent was he typical of Prussian judges? Stadthagen argued in the Reichstag, "When a man acts like this one, always brusque to those below and obsequious to those above . . . and when this manner and style did not attract attention and gave no occasion for doubt, that is proof that the danger is no singular one." Arguments like Stadthagen's have been followed by some historians, but in their time they were very far from representing a consensus, even among critics of German judicial institutions. Richard Grelling wrote in the *Berliner Tageblatt* that Brausewetter's image as a tyrant was unwarranted. When he said "the public doesn't exist," he used the same quiet tone of voice in which he invited witnesses to take a seat; and when he told a jury that he did not see how they could come to any other conclusion than a finding of guilt, what impressed the hearer was Brausewetter's tone of naive sincerity. Some even claimed that Brausewetter was neither consistently friendly to the prosecution nor hostile to defendants and defense counsel. The *Tageblatt*, whose editor had been a defendant in the "Rubber Hose" trial, claimed that while "in certain circles, because of his hard judgments in political trials, there were attempts to present Brausewetter as the 'model of a Prussian judge' . . . the draconian strictness of Herr Brausewetter's judgments in political matters seemed to stand in striking contrast to his occasionally observed mildness in non-political trials." The *Tageblatt* was not alone. Maximilian Harden wrote that Brausewetter was "never one of the worst judges, one of the cool and correct, who seem externally well-meaning and secretly summon up their influence in order to arrive at the hardest possible sentence." Fritz Friedmann made an equally surprising comment about Brausewetter's attitude to the fair conduct of a defense. Brausewetter, said Friedmann, unlike many judges, always appointed experienced defense lawyers to be duty counsel for impecunious defendants. "With his unchangeable sad-serious face," wrote Friedmann, "the poor man, recognized too late as mentally ill, would say: 'The defendant has a right to be well defended.'" Even his frequent anti-Semitic utterances could sometimes be qualified. In the Ahlwardt trial, Brausewetter lectured the defendant on the errors of racial anti-Semitism: "Either someone is a Jew, then he's a Jew; or he's become a Christian, then he's a Christian." Did these contradictory images add up to a picture of a typical Prussian judge? Grelling concluded that Brausewetter was only a "model in the negative sense," through which one could study the shortcomings of a presiding judge "in the same way as in an anatomical museum one shows prepared slides with all conceivable afflictions on them so that the students can learn the disease."[35]

Brausewetter's career, like Schmidt's, has much to tell about the culture of the Wilhelmine courtroom: the overriding concern with honor, the centrality of publicity, the inescapable politicization, and the manner in which politics drove the debates about judges. The received images of both men, the "good" judge and the "bad" judge, were stereotypes, considerably at variance with much of what we can know of how they actually performed on the bench. Probably neither was "typical" of a Wilhelmine judge, not in their outspokenness, nor in the manner in which they left the bench, nor indeed in their enduring roles as rhetorical markers. But their puzzles and contradictions, both within themselves and toward each other, are altogether representative of a justice system marked by the conflict of an authoritarianism ill at ease with a deepening concern for procedural justice, and by a cult of honor always torn between conflict and accommodation with the demands of a new, mass public. In this sense Schmidt and Brausewetter really were what many said: the very models of a Prussian judge.

The Honor of the Estate

There were very few lawyers in Imperial Germany who made their living exclusively or even predominantly as criminal defense counsel. Most lawyers were civilists, for whom criminal law was at most an occasional diversion. Only in a few big cities—above all in Berlin—were there concentrations of criminal specialists. "Their total number is difficult to estimate," wrote lawyer Julian Witting in 1900, "but for all of Germany it might be scarcely over fifty."[36] With such a small bar, even in a big city like Berlin, the influence of a few dominant personalities could determine the professional culture and style of practice of criminal lawyers. This culture and style changed significantly during the Wilhelmine years. The changes were largely a matter of how lawyers presented themselves to the public.

In the last years before the justice reforms of 1879, the principal defense lawyers in Berlin were "the big three," Vincenz Deycks, Aurel Holthoff, and August Munckel. Deycks, born in 1805, was the eldest of the trio. Though he had had a distinguished career, appearing in many of the most celebrated cases of the mid-nineteenth century, in old age he became a figure of fun to younger lawyers. "He pleaded totally *ad hominem*," said Fritz Friedmann, "without especially emphasizing the points of law . . . He operated with old tricks, weeping and joking, not far from a preacher or a popular tribune." Aurel Holthoff was, according to the Wilhelmine bar's contemporary historian, "of a much finer nature." Three years younger than Deycks, he was probably best remembered for Ferdinand Lassalle's high treason trial, although Lassalle, "defending himself in a long and brilliant speech, left his lawyer little to do." Not that Holthoff was without lawyerly skills. Friedmann remembered him as a "master of questioning witnesses and of the courteous, impressive handling of the judges . . . [His] penetrating gaze forced anyone to whom he spoke to share his point of view," and Erich Sello thought that Holthoff was the most effective of the big three at securing acquittals. August Munckel was thirty years younger than the others. Lawyers generally allowed that his pleadings lacked the pathos of Deyck's and perhaps the irresistible persuasiveness of Holthoff's. Yet among his peers he was the most extravagantly admired of advocates. Weissler said Munckel brought the defense to "high artistic fulfillment."

"For years I looked up to him with limitless admiration," said Friedmann, not a notably generous judge of his colleagues, while Sello claimed that no one else came close to Munckel's blend of juristic brilliance and eloquence.[37]

Deycks, Holthoff and Munckel were products of a milieu that had disappeared by the beginning of the twentieth century, and they shared certain characteristics that their heirs would not seek to emulate. Friedmann was on the mark when he likened Deycks to a popular tribune. The grand old men of the bar were politicians, cultivating a distinctly "out of doors" courtroom style. The big three had all become famous representing liberal or Social Democratic causes in major political trials; Munckel was also, at various times, a left-liberal member of the Reichstag, the Prussian House of Representatives, and the Charlottenburg City Council. The lawyers who came to dominate the bar in the 1890s and after were different. In 1906, Franz Hoeniger wrote of the two claimants to Munckel's mantle, Erich Sello and Max Wronker, that "they distinguish themselves from their predecessors above all in that they do not have their origins in the political arena." Sello himself gave a clue to the new attitude in his obituary for Munckel in the *Vossische Zeitung*. "I do not think here of the parliamentarian," he said, after asking rhetorically who could replace Munckel. "Many have lamented with me that already at the beginning of the 'eighties Munckel took himself away from the field that he ruled, to chase after meager and fruitless laurels in the political realm." By the turn of the century the representative defense counsel was a pure jurist, accustomed to speaking in the cramped hearing rooms of Moabit rather than at political rallies. This shift in venue had stylistic consequences. Hoeniger wrote that "today one is weary" of the "pathos and elegance" of the earlier days. Modern lawyers were "much more sober, matter-of-fact, and above all more juristic."[38]

There was certainly a degree of self-congratulation, even wishful thinking, in the talk of a new style. Comments like Hoeniger's are the kind of thing that each generation of lawyers says of its elders. Still, the self-depiction was itself revealing and the new style was underpinned by institutional factors. The reforms of 1879 had shifted the bulk of criminal cases from the jury courts to the criminal chambers. "The criminal chamber," wrote Hoeniger, "in its purely juristic composition, is the most unsuitable sounding board that the defense counsel of great style could wish for." Thus lawyers toned down their rhetoric to suit the audience of cold-eyed judges they now most often faced. Professional authorities buttressed the change. In a 1912 manual for the instruction of young lawyers, Richard Finger wrote that the purpose of modern court proceedings "is not the victory of the beautiful, but the victory of the truth," and he cited a decision of the Supreme Honor Court from 1893 that had held that it was the duty of the defense counsel to bring out the truth to the advantage of the defendant, not to "obscure any truth disadvantageous to his client through rhetorical floods of emotion and pathetic appeals to the affections, especially of the lay judges."[39]

The judges of the Supreme Honor Court were not the only jurists who sought to distinguish their cool calculation from the passion of lay judges. In the next chapter we will see that, around the turn of the twentieth century, liberal lawyers began to fear that unenlightened mass opinion was a greater threat to the integrity of judicial decision-making than official fiat. It is probably no coincidence that this new attitude to the public set in at the same time lawyers began to cultivate a more austere professional demeanor and to retreat from formal political engagement. Some historians have criticized the bar for this turn.[40] But as we shall see in the next chapter, Berlin's criminal lawyers hardly absented themselves from the public sphere. Rather, they chose to address it from a more specifically juristic platform, and on matters closely related to their professional competence —matters that were, after all, of vital public interest.

Certainly the changes in professional style were gradual, and younger lawyers could not always live up to the desired image of cool detachment. Sello himself had a formidable reputation as a speaker of pathos: the *Berliner Morgenpost* recorded that he had been known to "shed tears of inner emotion" in the course of his pleadings, something characteristic of "speakers of Latin countries" but unknown among "defense counsel in a German courtroom" (an observation that suggested memories of Vincenz Deycks were growing dim). The next generation of lawyers, those who came into practice in the last Wilhelmine years, carried the *neue Sachlichkeit* a step farther. The new ideal for courtroom style was embodied by Max Alsberg, who came to the Berlin bar in 1906. Although his hearers often spoke of Alsberg's gifts as a speaker, the tears of a Deycks or a Sello were not for him. Alsberg's closing addresses were always painstakingly prepared down to the finest detail, displaying a complete mastery of the case, replete with references to "psychological and juristic academic literature," and often of astonishing duration—hours, sometimes days.[41]

Not all lawyers could be Munckel or Sello or Alsberg, and not all lawyers tried. In his 1905 history of the German legal profession, Adolf Weissler wrote that practicing law amounted to a "difficult, incessant struggle with sins," and that "our profession corrupts the character." He saw a serious decline of professional and ethical standards in the private bar since the institution of *freie Advokatur* in 1879.[42] He was not alone. Throughout the Wilhelmine years German lawyers worried about the moral health of their profession, and even more about the public perception of its health. Those who lost the battle with financial, sexual, or legal-procedural temptation could be assured of the attention of the honor courts; and such proceedings repeatedly demonstrated the centrality of honor for lawyers, both on an individual and at a corporate level.

Probably no lawyer of Wilhelmine Berlin was as regular a customer of the Honor Courts as Alfred Ballien. After the proceedings that grew out of the Heinze case, Ballien appeared before the Honor Court again at the end of 1892, and in 1895, 1897, 1898, 1902, 1904, 1906, and 1908.[43] Two of the cases involved Ballien's relations with prostitutes. In 1897 the charge was that Ballien had disgraced his profession, not only by being seen with a prostitute in a notorious Berlin dance hall called the *Blumensäle,* but by threatening her with denunciation to the morals police in the hope that she would return 100 marks Ballien believed she had stolen from him. The Berlin Honor Court found all of this unforgivable, and expelled Ballien from the profession. Ballien retained the eminent Adolf von Gordon to argue his appeal, and Gordon played skillfully on the questions of image in his written defense:

> The very elegant big-city ballroom in question is notoriously visited by the most eminent parties of gentlemen in Berlin; it is frequented not only by officers from the most eminent and socially high-standing aristocratic families—albeit in civilian clothes—but also by officials, judges, Reichstag deputies etc., and certainly by no means anxiously incognito, but rather completely openly. Even married women from the social classes indicated are not afraid to have a look at this place in the company of their husbands—evidence that, at least outwardly, decent forms are preserved. If, therefore, an unmarried younger lawyer seeks out this sort of place, it is impossible to find anything incriminating in this.[44]

The impact of this argument can be seen in the prehearing report written for the judges of the Supreme Honor Court:

According to the custom of big cities, visits to such places even by an unmarried *lawyer* may not be so seriously condemned. That good-time girls are admitted and seek opportunities for their trade is well known. So long as such connections are carried out *inconspicuously* in a great crowd of people, no occasion will arise to lift the veil, even for a lawyer . . . For the acceptance of an *open*, conspicuous interaction of the accused in the *Blumensäle* there is no *sufficient* evidence.

This conclusion, with all of its carefully worded concern for what was "conspicuous" or not, was incorporated in the final judgment. With appearances apparently satisfied, the Supreme Honor Court reversed the decision to expel Ballien and let him off with a reprimand and a 2000 mark fine.[45]

Five years later the Berlin Honor Court decided once again to expel Ballien from the profession. This time the most serious finding was that Ballien had arranged, and profited from, prostitution. Ballien had a client named Steuben, a pimp, who was in a mental hospital and unable to pay Ballien's bill. Ballien arranged for Steuben's prostitute, a woman named Badek—also Ballien's client—to visit Steuben at the mental hospital. While there, Badek evidently practiced her profession with some patients, the patients paid Steuben, and Steuben paid Ballien. In the eyes of the Berlin Honor Court, Ballien confounded his offense in that he "later went to a public bar with this prostitute . . . and was her guest there."[46]

The Supreme Honor Court agreed that Ballien had a bad record, and that in this case he deserved a severe punishment. But the Leipzig judges still did not believe that Ballien was incorrigible and they held back from expelling him from the profession, citing as evidence his marriage in 1901 to "a lady from a respectable family." "It may be assumed from this," said the court, "that the duties which he has taken on with his marriage will remind him of the duties that his profession imposes on him."[47]

The Berlin Lawyers' Chamber had now twice tried to exclude Ballien from its midst for breaches of lawyerly decorum, and twice been foiled by Leipzig. At the end of the year, the chairman of the Chamber's Board of Directors wrote in frustration to the justice minister that the colleagues believed the "mildness" of Leipzig's decisions did not "help our profession." He had repeatedly received complaints from members of the bar that "the Lawyers' Chamber has not succeeded in cleansing itself or keeping itself free of the isolated elements which do not do it honor." Furthermore, experience suggested that the Supreme Honor Court's indulgences did not lead to "the turn-around of those who have been mildly punished, but rather that these persons, mostly within a short time, had to appear before the Honor Court again." Ballien did little to dispel the chairman's concerns. He appeared three more times before the Honor Court, on charges of paying kickbacks to "agents" who had referred clients to him, and for pressing an opposing lawyer for the prorogation of a case in an "undignified" and "self-interested" manner. He received fines in all cases. In 1908 he appealed a conviction to Leipzig once more, promising rather pathetically "to be a proper and careful as well as conscientious lawyer in the future," and asking "that my many transgressions be forgiven." Although the Supreme Honor Court rejected his appeal, this time Ballien managed to make good on his promise. In the brief time left to him he never again became the subject of a discipline proceeding. He died in 1914, aged only 53; Berlin's newspapers seemed not to notice.[48]

In his memoirs, Fritz Friedmann remembered coming to the bar in 1880 along with two other young lawyers "who then for a decade and a half would conduct along side of me the greatest and most numerous defenses, Erich Sello and Max Wronker." These men were the new big three; by 1906 Hoeniger could write that Munckel's mantel fell either on Sello or Wronker (by then Friedmann had been expelled from the bar for a combination of financial and sexual scandals).[49] Wronker was to be the longest-lived: born in 1853, he practiced law in Berlin until his death in 1935. With his younger partner Ludwig Chodziesner, Wronker acted in many of the most celebrated Wilhelmine trials, including the defense of the Countess Kwilecka (see Chapter 4), and the even more notorious perjury trial of the Kaiser's close friend Prince Phillipp Eulenburg in 1909.[50] But for the culture and image of Berlin's bar Sello was the more important figure, for Sello redefined how a trial lawyer would approach his work, the judicial system, and the broad public.

The crucial element of this redefinition was Sello's growing refusal to accept the subservient position that everything from the laws of procedure to the architecture of the courtroom forced on the defense counsel. Lawyers of the pre-1879 generation had tended to be carefully deferential to judges. Fritz Friedmann praised Aurel Holthoff's tactful handling of judges, and referred to his own "diplomatic, although never servile style" of arguing a case, and his desire never to "provoke the human being in the judge." He wrote of the vexation that arrogant and overbearing judges could cause defense lawyers, insisting that it had driven lawyers like Stadthagen and the gifted *Justizrat* Kleinholz from the bar.[51] The shift on the part of younger lawyers away from older habits of deference was the subtext, if not surtext, of the discipline cases against Ballien, Cossmann, and Stadthagen. But whereas Ballien and the others could at best hope to survive their battles with their license to practice still in hand, the revered *Justizrat* Dr. Sello had the prestige to force a reevaluation of the status of criminal defense.

In 1900, Sello was engaged to defend the millionaire banker August Sternberg, who stood accused of having had sexual relations with girls under the consenting age of fourteen. With its eye-catching allegations of corruption on all sides, and the distension of the proceedings through eight full weeks of hearings, Sternberg's trial provided a lesson in the procedural weaknesses of Wilhelmine Berlin's criminal justice. We will return to this theme in Chapter 4. Like the Heinze trial, the case also raised important questions of the role and status of the defense counsel.

For Sello, the critical moment of the trial came on the third day. The first witness was a determined constable named Stierstädter, whose investigations had brought Sternberg to trial. The constable's evidence contained a bomb: he said that his superior officer, Commissar Thiel, had offered Stierstädter large amounts of money if he would get the star prosecution witness, a thirteen-year-old girl named Frieda Woyda, to change her story. The money, along with a promise not to ask Stierstädter "any uncomfortable questions" at trial, was supposed to have come from Sello. In response, Sello declared that "he could not decide whether it was a matter of perjury by Stierstädter or crimes in office by Thiel, but he confirmed most solemnly that not a word of this story was true, so far as it touched his person."[52] In early December, Thiel told an examining magistrate that he had gone to Sello for legal advice the previous March, and had admitted taking Sternberg's bribes. This revelation lead to a long courtroom exchange on 7 December between Sello and the presiding judge, Director Müller. Müller said that Sello's "outrage" over Stierstädter's testimony was inconsistent with the fact that he knew in March that Sternberg had bribed Thiel. Sello insisted that he had been outraged solely by the allegation that he had offered Stierstädter money; the duty of confidentiality he owed Thiel had made any further comment impossible. State Advocate Braut objected that Sello had formally denied any knowledge of Thiel's illegal activity. The exchange culminated in the following words:

> *Müller* [to Sello]: It would at least have been your duty to refer somehow to the requirement of confidentiality. The particularly

solemn manner [of Sello's earlier statement] gave the impression that the defense counsel was convinced of Thiel's innocence, and perhaps the prosecutor abstained from Thiel's immediate arrest in consideration of this very certainty.

Braut: I must just say that more or less solemn declarations of the defense make no impression on me when it comes to the question of whether I should arrest somebody.[53]

Sello saw a personal insult in Braut's words, as well as an insult to his "estate and profession." No one ever claimed Sello was the most pacific of lawyers. He had earned an Iron Cross in the Franco-Prussian war; watching him in court in 1897, Alfred Kerr noted that when Sello began to speak, or "even when he yanks his pencil out of the desk upon the dismissal of a notion," one saw "that he is hot-tempered *(ein Choleriker)*." Sello showed his temper now. He dispatched a friend, one Major Wagner, to Braut to demand a public retraction. Braut refused. So on 9 June Sello sent Wagner back to Braut—this time with a challenge to a duel with pistols. Braut refused to meet Sello on these terms as well, with the explanation that his statement had been "purely official."[54]

This challenge is one of those gestures in the life of Berlin's criminal courts, like Ballien and Cossmann drinking their glasses of champagne, that captures in an instant the essence of a complex set of relationships. Ute Frevert, the historian of the duel in German middle class life, writes that the point of a duel was less to seek to inflict harm on one's opponent than it was to demonstrate that one valued honor more than life itself—and in so doing, to restore whatever damage the insult had done to that honor. For a lawyer like Sello there were further levels of significance. The duel "placed in question the state's physical monopoly of violence," and thereby raised serious issues of the relationship of the legal order to societal norms. As a *Rechtsanwalt*, an advocate of the law, Sello was expressly called upon not only to respect but to serve the legal order. He did not take this task lightly; Sello was a prolific and serious writer on questions of morality and justice.[55] It was all the more telling, then, that when it came to a perceived insult to himself and to his "estate," he placed honor above fidelity to the law and sought "satisfaction."

This was not the only conflict between the defense and the court during the Sternberg trial. There were other allegations, of varying degrees of credibility, of unethical defense conduct. The anti-Semitic *Staatsbürger*

"When he begins to speak . . . even when at the dismissal of a motion he yanks his pencil out of the desk, one sees that he is hot-tempered": *Justizrat* Erich Sello. (Ullstein Bilderdienst)

Zeitung claimed that Sello's co-counsel Johannes Werthauer had been involved in an elaborate scheme to bribe First Prosecutor Isenbiel and the judges of the Imperial Supreme Court. The defense team had engaged a private detective named Schulz to investigate the credibility of prosecution witnesses, above all that of Constable Stierstädter. These inquiries proved fruitful. Schulz found that the fanatical Stierstädter (who was said to have told his colleagues repeatedly "the Jew must go to prison," in the erroneous belief that Sternberg was Jewish) had had sexual relations with two prostitutes he was investigating. However, it appeared likely that Schulz himself had arranged to entrap Stierstädter; and it was certain that Schulz had doled out liberal quantities of Sternberg's money to bribe witnesses and to fabricate evidence. If in the wake of the Heinze trial it had seemed improper to many professional and lay observers for a lawyer to advise a client not to testify, now the same people questioned whether a defense lawyer should ever hire a detective. The reason was the same: striving for an acquittal at all costs would triumph over the search for truth. In light of all the allegations, Sello and Werthauer withdrew from Sternberg's defense.[56]

The conflicts between defense, prosecution and bench dominated the closing speeches of the trial, often at the cost of the facts of the case. State Advocate Braut was moved to say, "one considers: two lawyers have had to leave the defense table, a third must just as well expect a discipline proceeding." Braut's superior, First Prosecutor Isenbiel, struck the same tone in defending Braut from press criticisms that a "young, inexperienced prosecutor" was sent to plead against "six of the most experienced Berlin lawyers." Isenbiel wondered if the paper he quoted would still maintain this criticism, as "in the course of the trial two lawyers have stepped down, and the prosecutor has just given a closing speech of an excellence that could not have been expected from anyone else." Isenbiel was goaded into stronger words by criticisms of the prosecution from the last of Sternberg's three counsel, *Rechtsanwalt* Fuchs. In words that would be endlessly if not always accurately quoted, Isenbiel claimed "the prosecution is the most objective authority up to the raising of the indictment." Then, with much show of being reluctant to name names, Isenbiel delivered a more focused attack on Sello. Sello had admitted that he knew Commissar Thiel had been bribed, yet still met with him. It was implausible for Sello to claim that he thought Thiel would turn away from his criminal conduct; even more implausible to say that he did not know if Thiel had made himself guilty of perjury or offences in office. As a lawyer, said Isenbiel, Sello would have to know it was the latter.[57]

Sternberg was convicted and sentenced to two-and-a-half years in the penitentiary on Lehrterstrasse. But after all the scandal this outcome seemed almost beside the point. The press devoted much ink to "the honor of the lawyers' estate." The *Tageblatt* criticized Braut's failure to grasp that the defense, like the prosecution and the judges, "wore the black robe of honor," while Isenbiel's speech sounded as if he saw the forensic search for truth in the courtroom as a medieval tournament, in which it did a prosecutor particular honor to have fought against six defense counsel and left two of them in the dust.

The honor of the estate came up most directly for discussion when Sello was prosecuted criminally for challenging Braut to a duel. The trial took place on 1 June 1901 before the 1st Criminal Chamber of Superior Court II. Sello explained that the "pointed accusation of conscious professional dishonesty," as he interpreted Braut's comment, "was the most serious criticism that one could make of him." He was not a "young student who dashed around with a pistol in hand." But hundreds of people in the courtroom had head Braut's remark; a purely personal and private explanation from Braut (which Braut had offered) could not undo the damage. "If Herr Braut had been misunderstood by me," Sello explained, "he was also misunderstood by the broad public." Here, of course, lay the rub. Only a public expiation would do; "therefore nothing was left for me but the challenge to pistols."[58]

Braut himself was the only witness, and his evidence was surprisingly emollient. Although he maintained his own statement had been "purely official" and correct, he acknowledged that Sello had been entirely in the right in making his "solemn declaration." The court itself also showed Sello a good measure of sympathy. The prosecutor argued in his closing speech that a duel between a lawyer and a prosecutor would be "understandable in the case of a serious insult to personal honor"; he claimed only that this was not such a case. The court found that:

> *Justizrat* Sello is to be believed that he—like many others—saw [Braut's] statement as being directed against his person, and if this were so, certainly it would be a serious insult to his honor, because then the sense would lie in the words that the statement of a defense counsel meant nothing at all to a prosecutor. This, and the fact that State Advocate Braut denied the request of Major Wagner to give a public correction of the statement, are to be seen as mitigating circumstances.

On the other hand, the judges held that Braut had been acting in the line of duty, and Sello was *objectively* wrong to assume the remark was directed at him. The court gave Sello a mild sentence of one month open custody *(Festungshaft);* Major Wagner got four days.[59]

In a further effort to retrieve his honor, Sello himself requested that the Lawyers' Chamber investigate and prosecute him for all of his alleged misconduct in the Sternberg trial. The result was full acquittal on all charges. To be sure, the Berlin Honor Court found Sello's challenge to Braut a breach of professional discipline, but thought the criminal penalty to which he had been subject was an adequate punishment. When the prosecution appealed, the Supreme Honor Court in Leipzig held that Sello's challenge was unjustified *because Braut's statement was official.* The implication was clear: an unofficial insult by a prosecutor to the honor of a lawyer would justify a challenge to a duel. Furthermore, the court chose not to impose a penalty on Sello because "the content of [Braut's] statement was . . . of such a kind that the defendant could very well take it as an intentional insult directed at him," and Sello only issued the challenge when Braut refused to deny publicly that he had intended such an insult.[60]

The validation of lawyerly honor in these criminal chamber and Honor Court decisions heralded a kind of arrival: official certification that defense lawyers had come within the magic circle of those whose claims of honor, like officers and higher servants of the state, had to be taken seriously. And lawyers like Sello, perhaps with the laughable figure of old Vincenz Deycks in the backs of their minds, wanted nothing more than to be taken seriously. This quest lay behind the more sober presentation of cases and the more scholarly *habitus* which many criminal lawyers began to adopt. In the next chapter we will look at another kind of claim-staking, the literary activity in which Sello and colleagues like Johannes Werthauer and Max Alsberg engaged in the last Wilhelmine years. Pick up one of Sello's many books and turn to the title page: "By Dr. Sello, Berlin. *Justizrat*." The pride in the double title, with its claims both to profound professional knowledge and royal favor, seems to shine from the page.

We will conclude this chapter with a look at how the "arrival" of the defense counsel changed the practices of late-Wilhelmine courts.

The Defendant Is a Fanatic

Karl Liebknecht, fiery spokesman of the Social Democratic Party's radical left, leader of the Spartacus uprising of 1919 and, with Rosa Luxemburg, one of the victims of that uprising's brutal suppression, is by a wide margin the best known of the criminal defense lawyers of Wilhelmine Berlin. The son of one of the early heroes of the Social Democratic movement, Wilhelm Liebknecht, Karl showed his legal talents early by receiving the rare predicate "good" on the Assessor exam. He entered practice at Berlin's Superior Court II in 1899.[61] Liebknecht soon proved himself a skillful and effective advocate who earned the respect of peers, clients, and—grudgingly—judges and prosecutors. Herein lies an important element of the culture of late-Wilhelmine criminal law. Even a radical like Karl Liebknecht came within the world of lawyerly honor. He claimed his share of it and lived by its codes, and his claim was recognized by colleagues and opponents alike.

Even Liebknecht's trial in 1907 for high treason paradoxically demonstrated his high degree of professional integration. He was prosecuted for publishing a pamphlet entitled "Militarism and Anti-Militarism with Special Consideration of the International Youth Movement." No one, certainly not Liebknecht, was surprised that the Imperial Supreme Court in Leipzig found him guilty of the charge. The significance of the case lay in the sentencing. The prosecutor asked for a prison sentence of two years and suspension of civil rights—called in German "rights of honor" *(Ehrenrechte)*. The latter request seemed to be the one event at the trial that angered Liebknecht. The judges were not impressed either and refused to grant it, just as they did not grant the request for a prison sentence. Instead, Liebknecht was sentenced to eighteen months' open custody *(Festungshaft)*, the typical sentence for crimes in which there was no element of dishonor, such as dueling or political offenses. Loss of civil rights could not be combined with a sentence of open custody.[62]

Liebknecht also faced a professional discipline trial arising out of his treason conviction, significantly at the insistence of the prosecutors' office and not of the Lawyers' Chamber. Even the prosecution seemed ambivalent about its case. At the trial on 29 April 1908, General Prosecutor Wachler asked that Liebknecht be expelled from the profession, as in his view a man who had been convicted of high treason could not be called upon to play a role in the administration of justice. Yet at the same time Wachler emphasized "not only the personal integrity of the defendant," but also his "great juristic knowledge" and his "unimpeachable position in the Berlin bar." Liebknecht pointed out the Imperial Supreme Court's finding that he had not acted dishonorably. Only a conviction for a dishonorable criminal act, said Liebknecht, could bring in its train a disciplinary penalty.[63]

The Honor Court agreed with Liebknecht and acquitted him completely, ruling that a breach of professional duty "cannot be assumed especially when the unlawful conduct . . . is not attributable to dishonorable sentiment *(Gesinnung)*." There was nothing inherently wrong, said the court, even with a lawyer belonging to a political party hostile to the state. Furthermore, since "there can be no doubt about his love of truth" and there was "no stain on his character," Liebknecht's personality and position in the bar gave "no cause to believe that he has lost the respect which his profession requires." The *Berliner Tageblatt* thought this decision would be "accepted with satisfaction in wide circles," and indeed the Leipzig court rejected the prosecution's appeal, an outcome all the more interesting as it was effectively a branch of the court that had convicted Liebknecht of treason in 1907. As in the case against Sello, the Supreme Honor Court held that not every criminal conviction necessitated an additional professional sanction, and found, like the Imperial Supreme Court, that Liebknecht had acted honorably. More remarkable was the court's finding that although a lawyer had a duty to help maintain the justice system, it did not follow that he might not "fight against individual components of the prevailing legal order."[64]

Three years later Liebknecht had a second encounter with the discipline process. At the 1910 Social Democratic Party convention in Magdeburg, he made a speech denouncing the visit of the Russian Czar to Germany, and criticizing the Prussian and Hessian governments that had invited him. Liebknecht called the Czar a "crowned criminal" and charged "that the tax-pennies of German taxpayers were squandered" to pay for his visit, thus bringing disgrace upon the German people. The governments involved "had trampled the laws of Germany without mercy" and thereby established in Germany "a barbaric, arbitrary rule." As in 1908, the state prosecutor sought a disciplinary penalty against Liebknecht for this speech despite the refusal of the Lawyers' Chamber to bring a case. In October 1911 the Berlin Honor Court found that Liebknecht had libeled the Czar, but that his remarks lay within the bounds of permissible free speech for a lawyer. Liebknecht's attacks on the Prussian and Hessian governments were a different matter. Taking a less tolerant stance than three years before, the court found that sincere belief was not a defense to such a "measureless attack on the authorities of his fatherland," in which Liebknecht had used "grievously insulting" expressions that were "unworthy of a man who is called upon to be an organ of the administration of justice." Yet if sincere belief could not negate liability, it could mitigate severity of sentence. In assessing the penalty, the Honor Court considered as mitigating circumstances "that the defendant may have been convinced of the correctness of his exposition, and that he is a fanatic." The penalty was light: a reprimand without a fine.[65]

The story had a curious epilogue. Both Liebknecht and the general prosecutor appealed to Leipzig, but the hearing was delayed until after the outbreak of the First World War. By this time, as the chief Reich prosecutor wrote with some understatement, "the political situation [had] . . . considerably changed," such that high places judged it expedient to abandon the prosecutor's appeal. Liebknecht refused to win this way, and wrote indignantly to the chief Reich prosecutor to ask "that you kindly inform me of the reason for this withdrawal" and to demand "the earliest possible trial date." He added,

> I should like to point out that I find the present propaganda against the Russian Czar, which has broken out in Germany under official toleration and promotion, thoroughly reprehensible. I have absolutely no intention of making this mood, which has been artificially created to inflame the chauvinistic passions of the German people, useful to me in the present case. On the contrary, I will refuse absolutely to allow myself to be borne by the comfortable semi-official wind which is now blowing in Germany.

Liebknecht's own appeal was duly heard on 7 November 1914, and dismissed. The whole process was one more ironic indication of the extent to which the radical, "fanatic" Liebknecht and the highest authorities belonged to the same world of professional honor.[66]

Max Alsberg has one thing in common with Karl Liebknecht: he is the only other criminal lawyer of Wilhelmine Berlin who has been the subject of a biography. Born in 1877 in Bonn, Alsberg studied law there, in Leipzig and in Berlin, and flirted with a university career, before deciding to settle as a lawyer in Berlin in 1906. He quickly acquired a reputation as an extraordinarily competent but also fiercely combative advocate.[67] In 1912 and 1913 he and a colleague named Walther Jaffé became involved in a discipline proceeding that, along with Liebknecht's cases, formed the late-Wilhelmine bookend to the earlier cases against Ballien, Cossmann, and Stadthagen.

The Alsberg-Jaffé case involved the classic issue of the Wilhelmine court: the etiquette of disagreement. The case grew out of two trials. The first was a fraud trial in the autumn of 1910, in which Alsberg was one of several lawyers representing the main defendant, Glaser, while also acting for one of the many codefendants, a woman named Werner. The case was in the chamber of Superior Court Director Lieber, a tough judge about whom there was an underworld pun: "Lieber—lieber nicht" ("Lieber—rather not"). At the end of the trial the prosecutor asked for a stiff sentence against Glaser of nine years' hard labor. Alsberg responded with the observation, "If the court were to agree with the prosecutor's exorbitant request, it would constitute a record in comparison to other judgments in similar matters." When Lieber and the other judges insisted on treating this re-

The man in the black robe: the great advocate Max Alsberg. (Ullstein Bilderdienst)

mark as contempt of court *(Ungebühr)*, Alsberg withdrew from the case, claiming that his advocacy could no longer help his clients. The court adjourned the trial against Frau Werner and continued the hearing against Glaser und the others. Afterwards, the general prosecutor argued that Alsberg's withdrawal was really a bad-faith effort to delay the Glaser trial.[68] But by the time the Honor Court could hear this case, the facts and the issues had become complicated by the sensational trial of Count Gisbert von Wolff-Metternich.

Count Wolff-Metternich, a nephew of the German ambassador in London, was a walking literary cliché, a Fontanian stereotype of a dissolute aristocrat. A younger son with little prospect of inheritance, he devoted himself to finding a wealthy bride, and at the same time obtained credit from various sources on the strength of assurances that he was about to marry well. Two days before Christmas, 1910, the Count was installed in the holding cells in Berlin-Moabit, under suspicion of belonging to a ring of international card sharks. In the early months of 1911 the investigation was steadily extended to include 33 counts of credit fraud. Wolff-Metternich's trial opened in July 1911, with Walther Jaffé as his defense counsel, but after a few days of evidence the case had to be adjourned. During the summer Wolff-Metternich added Alsberg to his defense. When the trial reopened on 3 October, Alsberg and Jaffé brought a motion to reject the presiding judge, Superior Court Director Crüger, and his chamber, for apprehension of bias. Their motion had two grounds. Both lawyers claimed that Director Crüger had demonstrated partisanship with an improper ultimatum to the defense: that they either had to abandon calling evidence to dent the credibility of a prosecution witness (Gertrud Wertheim, wife of the department store magnate Wolff Wertheim and mother of one of the Count's putative marriage prospects), or else accept an adjournment of the trial until Frau Wertheim could return from Italy to defend herself. The second ground of the motion was even more incendiary. Only Jaffé argued in support of it; Alsberg refused to do so. Jaffé claimed to have learned from examining magistrate Dr. Dreist that Prussian Justice Minister Max von Beseler had intervened in the prosecution to Wolff-Metternich's disadvantage, by insisting that Dreist keep the investigation going to uncover new material. Normally one might expect that official intervention in a case against a privileged person would be to the advantage of the prisoner. But Jaffé claimed that precisely *because* the Count was so well connected, the minister was afraid of the consequences of having held him in custody for ten months without grounds, and so he urged Dreist to do whatever he could to build a case.[69]

At the reopening of the trial on 3 October, all of the judges declared formally that they were unbiased and the trial went ahead. But the conflicts in the court mounted. Jaffé was forced to admit having had conversations with a witness before the adjournment. The prosecutor claimed that Jaffé had intentionally misled the court. This allegation drove Jaffé to say that the conviction of the defendant, even with a very minor sentence, would be an unprecedented miscarriage of Prussian justice; that the indictment in the case was so poorly drafted that any prosecutor's *Referendar* who wrote such a thing would be certain to fail the Assessor exam; and that the German ambassador in London had been asked whether he wanted to get involved in the case. It was almost an anticlimax when on 12 October the Count was convicted on only three counts of credit fraud and sentenced to nine months' imprisonment, six of which were counted as served in investigatory custody.[70]

Just like Ballien and Cossmann twenty years before, the conduct of the two defense counsel "aroused strong indignation" among Berlin lawyers. In 1911 as in 1891, the bar was defined by its conflicts and cleavages, between younger and older lawyers and between civil and criminal specialists; the central concern in all conflicts remained the bar's public image. At the regular monthly meeting of the Berlin Lawyers' Association on 19 October, a discussion of limiting lawyers' self-promotion in the press degenerated into a storm of criticism of Jaffé and Alsberg. This was another case of the elders of the bar dressing down two brash novices; *Justizrat* Leonhard Friedmann's "forbidding" Alsberg and Jaffé from associating themselves with Berlin's bar was typical. The meeting ran until two in the morning, and by then it was clear that a majority of the lawyers opposed Alsberg and Jaffé.

Jaffé wrote to the *Vossische Zeitung* on 24 October to say that the behavior of Berlin's lawyers at the meeting was "fully unworthy of the profession," and hinted that other motives (his implication was jealousy) must be in play. One reason for the bar's concern lay in the special commission that the Reich secretary of state for justice had struck to consider wide-ranging reforms to the laws of criminal procedure. Private lawyers wished to see an easing of the restrictions on their access to pretrial proceedings, documents, and defendants in custody. The publicity given to Jaffé and Alsberg could only add "considerable difficulties" to this cause. In fact, Leonhard Friedmann himself was a member of the commission.[71]

In such an atmosphere it was inevitable that the case should make its way to the Honor Court, and when it did, the allegations against both Alsberg and Jaffé arising out of the Wolff-Metternich trial were joined to the case against Alsberg going back to the Glaser trial. On 27 November 1912, the Honor Court acquitted Alsberg of abandoning Glaser's defense in bad faith. On the other hand, it found that the claims that Alsberg and Jaffé had made in their motion against Crüger's chamber were "enormous insults to the judges, the prosecutors, and the justice minister." There was no evidence that the investigations of Count Wolff-Metternich had been handled "any differently than if they had been about a business apprentice Wolff or worker Wolff." That a powerful person could pressure the justice system either to the advantage or disadvantage of a defendant was "a condition that scarcely exists in uncultivated states"; still less could it exist "in a state like Prussia where the rule of law prevails." Since a baseless motion to reject a judge could "weaken the pillars" of the independence and impartiality of justice, the Honor Court ruled that a lawyer had to be certain of the facts he alleged and that there was a "need" to bring the motion. Alsberg and Jaffé had fallen short of this standard. The court gave Alsberg a reprimand. Jaffé's allegations regarding the justice minister were "so grave" that they alone would have warranted expulsion from the bar for a senior lawyer, or one with a prior record of disciplinary infractions. But as Jaffé had only been in practice for four years when he took on Wolff-Metternich as a client, and the trial had admittedly been a tense proceeding, the Honor Court settled for a reprimand and a fine of 1000 marks.[72]

Both Jaffé and Alsberg appealed to Leipzig. Alsberg's appeal was allowed on the basis that Director Crüger had committed a breach of the Code of Criminal Procedure when he forced the defense to choose between abandoning its attack on Frau Wertheim's credibility or accepting a delay in the trial. Such conduct by a trial judge was enough to ground a motion of rejection. The court's analysis of Jaffé's situation was more complicated. It found that Jaffé's allegations of the machinations of the justice minister constituted "a serious violation of the duty of conscientious professional practice." Paragraph 24 of the Code of Criminal Procedure, which permitted a motion to remove a judge "because of apprehension of bias," did not permit such a motion on the basis of a "subjective, undefined, and in its justification untestable feeling." The lawyer who did not carefully evaluate the justification of his client's wish to reject a judge committed a breach of his professional obligation as surely as if he brought the motion for an improper purpose, such as causing a sensation, or insulting the judge. Once again, just as when Ballien and Cossmann told the Heinzes not to testify, it was not the objective commission of the act itself that the discipline court would examine; rather, it was the lawyer's motive in committing that act. Once again the court obliged the lawyer to be his client's first judge. The lawyer had to consider whether the facts alleged in the motion were true; and he owed a higher duty of care if he were alleging "an attack by the justice ministry on judicial activity," and "when it is a matter . . . in which the general public is interested, over which detailed newspaper reports may be expected to appear." On this basis the Supreme Honor Court rejected Jaffé's appeal and left his sentence from the first instance unchanged.[73]

Yet beneath the parallels between the Alsberg-Jaffé case and the earlier lawyerly scandals around Ballien, Cossmann, and Stadthagen, there lurked a quiet transformation. The future belonged to Alsberg and Jaffé and others like them coming into practice just at the time of the First World War, including the flamboyant Erich Frey, who with Alsberg would dominate Berlin's criminal bar in the 1920s. The editor of an edition of Alsberg's writings claims "Alsberg can be seen as the founder of an independent criminal defense, as the prototype of the defense counsel who insists determinedly on upholding the legal requirements that the state . . . has set itself."[74] This is an overstatement; as we have seen, Alsberg was neither alone nor without precedent. But if we expand the claim to add the names of Liebknecht, Sello, and many others, then the point is valid. Berlin's lawyers were in the aggregate more independent-minded and aggressive in their tactics by 1913 than they had been in 1891. In 1913 Maximilian Harden could stereotype the typical appearance of a Berlin defense counsel:

> He would, in order never to be overlooked by the newspapers, demand to be heard ten times a day; scrap with the court and the prosecutor; spray his annoyance all over the protocol; brandish the client like a lousy piece of junk; romp about the courtroom waving his right to complain; behind the specter of an unavoidable appeal flaunt the decision [to abandon the defense] at the next insult and leave the accused defenseless; finally, when all rockets had been fired, plunge into psychology and squeeze the official performance out of his tear ducts.[75]

Harden's caricature comprises nothing less than a complete list of the forms of defense-court conflict we have seen in this chapter. In the Glaser case in 1910 Alsberg could court a discipline proceeding by withdrawing from a case. By the 1920s Erich Frey would make a habit of withdrawing, for frankly tactical reasons, without disciplinary consequences.[76] Stadthagen had been disbarred in 1892, among other reasons, for daring to suggest that Brausewetter would bend the rules of procedure. In 1913 the Supreme Honor Court accepted without qualm that Director Crüger had breached the rules with his ultimatum to Alsberg and Jaffé, and that the lawyers were justified in using this breach as the foundation of a motion to reject Crüger and his chamber. Perhaps even more striking is that the discipline courts, which in one case acquitted Liebknecht and in another gave him a light sentence for public political statements, relied for authority on the principle articulated in the decision to disbar Stadthagen: that a lawyer might speak publicly on legal and political matters like any other citizen. Thus do legal precedents often take on a life unintended by their authors.

Finally, Liebknecht and Alsberg differed from their predecessors simply in that they were better lawyers: they knew how to pick their battles and to argue them so that their own position was protected from disciplinary consequences. That they were better lawyers than their predecessors of twenty years before is in itself part of the story of the increasing professionalism of the bar; it was with some justice that a lawyer speaking at the XXI German Lawyers' Convention in 1913 claimed that "in serious work as well as scholarly or practical achievements in legal service," the profession of 1913 was superior to that of 1879.[77]

There were many signs of the rising status of criminal defense in the last years before the First World War. One of them was a 1912 book by Bremen lawyer Richard Finger, entitled *Die Kunst des Rechtsanwalts* ("The Art of the Lawyer"), intended as a "how to" manual for young lawyers. Finger took as uncontroversial a more aggressive conception of the role of the defense than the consensus position of 1891. He argued that while the Code of Criminal Procedure obliged the prosecutor to weigh equally the evidence for and against guilt, there was no such requirement for the defense. And he cited the Berlin law professor Franz von Liszt for the even stronger proposition that a defense counsel was entitled to plead for "not guilty" even when he was convinced of his client's guilt. Finger's treatment of the rights of a lawyer in the public sphere also confirmed that much had changed from Stadthagen to Liebknecht. "Lawyerly criticism of the administration of justice is precisely faithfulness to the law," he said; and fidelity to the law was the lawyer's highest duty—the theme of the first third of Finger's book.[78]

A curious incident in 1909 cast a sharp light on the shifting balance of power between lawyers and judges. At the German Lawyers' Convention in Rostock, a Berlin defense lawyer gave a speech criticizing judges for ignoring oral evidence in trials in favor of what they learned from the documents. "We as lawyers know," he told his colleagues, to enthusiastic applause, "that it is totally irrelevant [to judges] what is brought forward in the oral proceeding, that is only decoration." This remark caused great annoyance in the judiciary but no disciplinary consequences for the lawyer. The left-liberal representative and Berlin judge, Martin Peltasohn, struck a petulant tone when he complained about the speech in the Prussian House: "Gentlemen, the speaker is a respected lawyer, well known as a defense counsel in Berlin . . . He made this remark to the applause of his colleagues, and no disagreement was voiced in the most honorable assembly; not a single lawyer could be found to make any kind of protest against this statement." The petulant tone of Peltasohn's remarks would become altogether typical of judges in the Weimar Republic. As an example of the kind of protest that the relatively powerless make about insults to their dignity, it bears comparison with the complaints of Berlin's defense lawyers about Brausewetter in 1892. A more lurid sign of shifting power was the propaganda war which the new Association of German Judges carried on in its newspaper, the *Deutsche Richter-Zeitung*, after 1909. Beginning with petty resentments—that lawyers, unlike judges, were almost never attacked in the press, or that a representative of the Reich Office of Justice had been present at the Lawyers' Convention in 1909 but not at the Judges' Convention—by 1911 the judges had worked themselves up to a campaign against the lawyer as "the born enemy of the judiciary." Judges complained that lawyers could never be equal factors in the administration of justice when they were subject to less stringent discipline than judges, and even claimed the right to lie on their clients' behalf. Tellingly, the lawyers' *Juristische Wochenschrift* struck the calm, measured tone of the winner in its responses to these attacks.[79]

Aside from this blood feud, there were many signs in the last Wilhelmine years that lawyers were beginning to get more respect from the highest levels of officialdom. When August Munckel died in 1903, among the organizations that sent a wreath was the prosecutor's office at Superior Court I. From time to time lawyers and parliamentarians raised the question of appointing lawyers to judgeships. In the last year of peacetime these efforts began to bear fruit. On 5 February 1914, Justice Minister Beseler gave a declaration in the Prussian House of Representatives that the justice ministry was going to make efforts to recruit more private lawyers to the bench. On 21 February he wrote to all presidents of Prussian Courts of Appeal asking for the names of "a few especially capable lawyers from your district," who "by their qualifications and achievements, as well as by their conduct in and out of their profession, would be suitable for judicial positions, especially those on Courts of Appeal."[80]

If the line "conduct in and out of their profession" pointed to the continuity of concern with personal behavior and personal honor, in every other respect the minister's letter marked a watershed. It showed how far things had come since the days in which Stadthagen lost his long battle with Brausewetter's *Totenkammer*. It marked the Wilhelmine conclusion of that complicated dance in which lawyers, judges, and prosecutors worked out who they were and how they would function, with one eye always fixed on the reporters and one eye—metaphorically and sometimes literally—on their dueling pistols.

CHAPTER

4

Justice Is Blind

Early in 1901, Berlin lawyer Ludwig Flatau published a pamphlet demanding in its title "More Protection for the Administration of Justice!" In many respects it was a typical performance for a lawyer with literary inclinations. The tone was learned and (despite the exclamation mark) sober, the author easily conversant with the laws and legal history of all European countries, and capable of the literary allusions one could expect of an academically trained professional. Flatau also displayed many of the prejudices of such a professional: against the cultural level of eastern Europeans, even of Germans in the eastern regions, where "the general cultural work began about a hundred years later than in the other parts of Germany," and "the level of cultivation closely approaches the Slavic regions of Austria"; against women: it was "very characteristic" that a "passionately excited" crowd watching a miserably unjust trial was composed, "as in the time of the jacobin knitters in the 'Hall of Freedom,' in large part of female persons"; and against the great majority of the population, by any description: "The hope that the broad masses will ever acquire such a desirable level of enlightenment . . . is the slimmest imaginable."[1]

If these attitudes were normal for a liberal professional in Wilhelmine Berlin, the thesis that Flatau built on them was surprising indeed, for it was not the kind of argument liberals usually made about the law and its afflictions. By 1901, a triumphal narrative of the progress of justice in nineteenth-century Germany was well established, and Flatau gave this narrative its due. Public trials and the legally stipulated independence of judges had rolled back the old vices of "cabinet justice." "One can say," said Flatau, that "the course of justice in Germany today, so far as legislative provisions allow, has been made safe from any influence from above." In fact he cited the case of Superior Court Director Schmidt to show how difficult it was for a minister to effect even the transfer—let alone the removal—of an awkward judge. But new times brought new dangers. The institutions of German justice now resembled nothing so much as "a fortress whose strong works are all set out in one direction." Two new threats to the integrity of justice were inherent in a "modern, democratic society," apparently for Flatau an appropriate characterization of Imperial Germany: "Below the masses, above the strong financial powers." These were forces against which the courts as presently constituted stood utterly defenseless, yet Flatau believed proletarians and plutocrats were now as capable of perverting justice as ever Frederick the Great had been. Flatau built the core of his argument around two recent German trials. The trial of a Jewish man for perjury in the West Prussian town of Konitz had demonstrated the baleful influence of "popular currents led astray by agitators," while the trial of the millionaire August Sternberg in Berlin exemplified the American-style danger of "a giant fortune concentrated in one hand."[2]

How did these baleful influences work? Demagogic activists and press campaigns could induce prosecutors to bring charges against someone they believed to be innocent, *ut aliquid fieri videatur*—to give the impression that something was being done. The general public could influence the courts both passively as newspaper readers and actively as spectators and jurors: "Far from providing an effective guaranty for the strict application of the laws," said Flatau, Germany's "fundamentally flawed continental imitation of the English jury" coupled with the publicity of trials raised the danger that when passion collided with law, "passion rather than law carries away the victory." Flatau was not alone in his opinions. Reviewing his book, the *Berliner Tageblatt* found that "in view of the events in Konitz and similar trials abroad . . . we must agree with the author when he sees a serious danger for the administration of justice in popular currents mislead by agitators."[3]

At the turn of the twentieth century, traditional liberal concerns with the integrity of judicial decision-making and the capacities of ordinary people began to melt together into a new fear that Germany's liberalized legal structure was buckling under the weight of its own optimism. Such fears were in part a response to the democratic surge of the new century. "The masses have come of age," wrote a radical nationalist politician, "through elementary schooling, mass conscription, universal suffrage and the cheap oil lamp." In the years after 1890, a complex of mutually reinforcing technological, social, and political factors went together to create an entirely new kind of mass involvement in public life in general and politics in particular. Newspapers became less expensive to print; by virtue of the railways, easier to distribute; and with "elementary schooling . . . and the cheap oil lamp," more widely read. Popular participation in politics, measured not only by voting but by membership in a plethora of political organizations and lobby groups on right and left, increased dramatically. This democratic surge represented both a crisis and an opportunity for the cozy elite of German politics.[4]

Related to the democratic surge was the notorious mood of revolt or *Aufbruchstimmung* in German-speaking Europe. This mood took many forms: the Nietzsche cult; the various movements of secession in the visual, literary and performing arts; and social movements for feminism, gay rights (especially conspicuous in Germany), and many other causes. There were secessionists in the legal world as well. Flatau wrote of secessionist trial lawyers who did not respect the older traditions of the bar; he could easily have been thinking of Ballien and Cossmann.[5] Legal secession could be characterized as a rejection of sober rationality in thought and behavior, and by 1900 the rationality of outcomes in criminal trials appeared to be under two kinds of threats. The first threat was to the rationality of factual determination. German lawyers were becoming increasingly afraid that their procedural structures were defenseless against the seeming tide of superstition and ignorance from "below." The second and in some respects more insidious threat was to the rationality of legal conclusions: that is to say, in cases where the facts were not disputed, German lawyers were increasingly coming to believe that even exhaustively codified law could offer no final, indisputable resolution. Such a notion was heresy to the formalism of late nineteenth century legal thought, which held law to be a closed system of logical concepts, cleanly separable from morals, politics, or history, and abundantly capable of logically correct and incorrect answers. Some scholars were beginning to argue that rather than clinging to the Olympian mantle of formalism, law should seek closer ties with the natural feelings of "the people;" judges should decide individual cases freely on such an intuitive basis.[6]

Thus a three-cornered struggle emerged, which would become characteristic of the predicament of German criminal law until the Nazi period. The state was forced to defend its stake in the rational administration of justice against anti-rationalist currents from the political left as well as right. Lawyers of a rationalist bent contributed by formulating a new literature on the sources of judicial error. This literature was assembled from the observation of many cases in which the court system, through its openness to public opinion and the broad scope it gave for the gathering of evidence and the extensions of appeals, seemed to have been blown badly off course.

The Struggle against Stupidity

In the late 19th century, the medieval legend of Jewish "ritual murder"— the Christian folk belief that Jews required the blood of a Christian child, usually a boy, for the making of Passover *Mazze*—underwent a revival in central and eastern Europe. Perhaps the dissemination of old folk tales by *Germanisten* like the brothers Grimm helped spark this revival; certainly the growth in political and racial anti-Semitism after the 1870s gave it wings. There were also economic factors. Ritual murder accusations invariably arose in small and isolated rural communities hard hit by the great depression of the 1870s to the 1890s.[7]

Xanten, a village on the lower Rhine, was one such community. In 1891 a small boy named Johann Hegmann was murdered there. Soon local opinion, fanned by anti-Semitic activists and journalists who flocked to Xanten, began to attribute the killing to a Jewish butcher named Adolf Buschoff. Prussian administrative and judicial authorities were torn by conflicting desires to cater to anti-Semitic opinion while preserving the authority of the state. Local prosecutors brought Buschoff to trial, but promised the jurors *in their opening statement* that the evidence would exonerate him (as it did). An anti-Semitic publisher named Heinrich Oberwinder brought out a pamphlet on the case alleging that high authorities including Justice Minister Schelling had given way to a Jewish conspiracy in their handling of the case. This was too much for the justice department. Oberwinder was brought to trial in Berlin for libel, but for the government the trial was hardly a success. One of the judges clearly sympathized with Oberwinder; the evidence exposed the official ambivalence about the Hegmann murder; and though he was convicted, Oberwinder soon received royal clemency. The implication of the state's indecision was that the integrity of judicial decision-making was vulnerable to any current of public opinion vocal enough to worry the men at the ministerial green tables. Thus the Xanten case and its aftermath formed the foundation of a new narrative of the baleful influence of mob opinion on the courts. But the full flowering of this narrative came eight years later with the notorious Konitz case.[8]

The Town of Konitz (today Chojnice in Poland) had approximately 11,000 inhabitants, a few hundred of them Jewish, the rest evenly divided between Catholics and Protestants. The town's principal claim to fame was its *Gymnasium,* which like most small town high schools attracted not only young men from the surrounding region but considerable numbers of prostitutes as well. One of the pupils at the Gymnasium was an eighteen-year-old named Ernst Winter, who enjoyed a precocious reputation as a ladies' man. On Sunday, 11 March 1900, Winter disappeared after he had left his *Pension* hinting at a rendezvous. Two days later his body was found in Konitz's Mönchsee, sans head and limbs. At first, suspicion for the killing centered on the non-Jewish butcher Gustav Hoffmann, whose teenaged daughter had been receiving Winter's attentions; it was a plausible theory that Hoffmann had caught the couple *in flagrante* and killed Winter in rage. The case against Hoffmann was bolstered by evidence that the dismemberment of Winter's body had been carried out by a skilled hand, and that "certain spots" on Winter's clothing suggested that shortly before his death he had had "intercourse with a female person." But, inspired in part by previous "ritual murder" cases, and in part by the claims of a notoriously weak-minded Jewish rag dealer named Alexander Prinz (known in Konitz as "dumb Alex"), stories began to circulate that "the Jews" were responsible, that here was another ritual murder. The evidence: Winter's body had been found near the Synagogue and the home of the Jewish butcher Adolf Levy; the body seemed not to contain any blood; and the murder occurred at a time suspiciously close to Passover. These rumors led to a wave of anti-Semitic disturbances in Konitz and across West and East Prussia, Posen, and Pomerania. Jews were jeered on the streets; the windows of Jewish shops and homes were broken. The climax came on 10 June, when the Synagogue in Konitz was robbed and then threatened with arson.[9]

Once again, Prussian officialdom tried to contain all shades of opinion by partially catering to them. Troops were dispatched to maintain order in Konitz, closely followed by the Berlin police detectives Inspector Braun (the same one who had investigated the Heinzes and Hugo Guthmann) and Commissar Wehn (who would soon do the same for Theodor Berger). The detectives were less than impressed with what they found in Konitz.

Inspector Braun said later, "The investigations were dreadfully difficult because the people were so uncommonly agitated. Either one heard, 'I will testify only against the Jews,' or else 'leave me in peace, I don't want to know anything about the case.'" In his reports he complained of "the accusations of ritual murder against the Jews, which mock all Christian feeling," and insisted that these accusations "be kept out of the discussion." The chief prosecutor for the Marienwerder Court of Appeal district, which included Konitz, agreed. He reported to Justice Minister Karl von Schönstedt on 24 April that he had ordered officials to abstain from all steps "not absolutely necessary for the investigation" that might "give nourishment to the starkly apparent arousal of the population against the Jews." Still, he betrayed the characteristic desire of Prussian prosecutors to have it all ways when he added "I do not exclude the possibility that the murder was committed by Jews, and in particular by butchers, for revenge or out of jealousy." A few days later he wrote that "the Jews" had "occasionally contributed to the suspicions by their statements and their behavior."[10]

Certainly the "arousal of the population" found its way into the legal processing of the case. Part of the reason, as in Xanten, lay in the vulnerability of judicial institutions to surges in popular opinion, especially when a case had to be built largely on witness testimony. In the days and weeks after the discovery of Winter's body, the burghers of Konitz came forward with all manner of fantastically contrived stories that implicated Jewish families in the killing, especially the butcher Adolf Levy and his son Moritz (who in the end received a stiff sentence for perjury for denying an acquaintance with Ernst Winter). Communal resentments or hatreds played a role in the witnesses' attitudes, but so did money. Anti-Semitic activists offered a reward for information on the killing, which the Prussian government gradually topped up until it reached a staggering 32,000 marks. Many in Konitz were willing to risk a perjury prosecution for this kind of sum. Furthermore, Konitz's First Prosecutor Settegast and his successor Schweigger did not share Inspector Braun's aversion to the anti-Semites. The prosecutors seemed at times to be working hand in glove with the agitators and journalists who descended on Konitz after the murder. In a report to Schönstedt that fiercely criticized Settegast's handling of the case, Settegast's superior Chief Prosecutor Wulff complained that "[Settegast] has not kept himself sufficiently independent of the influence of the press."[11]

No one was ever convicted of Winter's murder, but the authorities busied themselves with a remarkable number of incidental prosecutions of Jewish and non-Jewish citizens of Konitz for perjury or for being an accessory to the killing. Like the Xanten case, the Konitz murder also found its way to Berlin's courtrooms. Reporters from the Berlin-based *Staatsbürger Zeitung,* the preeminent anti-Semitic newspaper of Wilhelmine Germany, had been prominent among the agitators in Konitz in the spring of 1900. On 28 July, First Prosecutor Isenbiel advised Schönstedt that he had raised an indictment against the *Staatsbürger Zeitung*'s editor and publisher, Paul Bötticher and Wilhelm Bruhn. The indictment charged them with the libel not only of a number of officials but also of several Jewish private citizens as well—including the Konitz butchers Adolf and Moritz Levy. Certainly Isenbiel did not display any excess of sympathy for the Jews of Konitz; he showed himself to be as ready to make gestures toward anti-Semitic opinion as had earlier prosecutors. "It might not appear desirable," he wrote to the minister, "to bring a prosecution solely because of the libel of a few Jewish citizens"; the police and judicial authorities in Konitz, Marienwerder, and Berlin should also be involved as private prosecutors *(Nebenkläger).* On the other hand, Isenbiel made gestures in other directions: referring to a libel prosecution of the Catholic Center Party's flagship newspaper *Germania,* he said it was important that *Germania* not be prosecuted alone while the *Staatsbürger Zeitung* was overlooked.[12]

Whether it was wise for the state to fight the battle of Konitz in a Berlin courtroom was another question. It was clear from the beginning that the *Staatsbürger Zeitung* would use its trial to make propaganda. Shortly before the appointed trial date of 16 October 1900, the defense raised a series of motions to summon testimony showing that the investigations in Konitz had been carried out incompetently, that public confidence in the administration of justice had thereby been severely shaken, and that the Levys and the businessmen Gustav Caspari in Konitz and Grossmann in Lütow were "more or less suspected of having participated in the murder of Ernst Winter." Isenbiel conceded that the libel of the persons involved made the third ground relevant to the case, but he argued that evidence on the first two points was inadmissible, as it could only involve the judgment of poorly informed and partisan individuals. And yet the logic of the case drew him inexorably into fighting on these "inadmissible" grounds. He wrote to Schönstedt that he wanted to call the Konitz officials and the Berlin police officers as witnesses, to establish that these officials "acted in a thoroughly dutiful and legal manner . . . and in no way committed a perversion of justice, and that none of them issued any kind of instruction to work in a definite pattern of sheltering the Jews." Isenbiel wanted the court to be able to assess the demeanor and credibility of these witnesses from personal observation. The chamber decided instead, to Isenbiel's vexation, to have depositions taken before trial, and then introduce into evidence those which seemed valuable. No trial date could be set until all the depositions had been taken.[13]

After these depositions (and yet more delays resulting from Ernst Winter's father's insistence that the Levys were truly guilty, revealing again how procedural generosity left the justice system vulnerable to sufficiently motivated interests), the trial of Bötticher and Bruhn opened on 30 September 1902. Bötticher was charged with twenty-six counts of libel, Bruhn with two, under the terms of sections 185 and 186 of the Reich Criminal Code. For the authorities, the trial was an exercise in public relations. Isenbiel's correspondence with the minister showed that this had been his concern all along; presiding judge Superior Court Director Opitz announced early in the trial that all official witnesses had been released from their duty of confidentiality, "in order to document that from the state or from any official side there is nothing to hide." The defense was also playing to the gallery, and its stubborn insistence that the Levys had killed Winter and that authorities had sought to protect "the Jews" forced the prosecution to counter these allegations. Defense attorney Hahn claimed, for instance, that reports by First Prosecutor Settegast in Konitz and Chief Prosecutor Wulff in Marienwerder from March to June 1900 showed that these officials recommended against prosecuting Moritz Levy for fear of further agitating the crowds in Konitz. Settegast denied that he had said any such thing. Yet Wulff's evidence came close to substantiating the claim. He had "advised First Prosecutor Settegast that the investigation must be extended in all directions," and that "if it took only a one-sided direction against the Jews a great excitement could, and would be bound to, arise *(könne und müsse... entstehen)*." Settegast admitted "the chief prosecutor asked me to leave these investigations to the police, since so sharp a procedure on my part could perhaps create bad blood, as I was already suspected of anti-Semitic inclinations." He denied that he had been told simply to drop investigations of Jews, but he admitted that people in Konitz could have got a different impression from him in casual conversations at the time. Indeed, Settegast's own anti-Semitism emerged clearly from the record. He admitted that on the very first day of the investigation he had requested the official documents from the Xanten case, along with those of an 1884 "ritual murder" case from the nearby town of Skurz. Not a single day had gone by, he said, in which he did not interrogate a Jewish person: "He had even investigated anonymous denunciations, had not even scorned to question people who claimed to be able to find the culprit by spiritualist means, in short, he had not neglected a single clue against the Jews."[14]

After eight days of evidence the chamber gave its verdict. The defense failed to persuade the court that Winter's death had been a ritual murder and that the authorities were sheltering "the Jews." After deliberating for several hours, the judges convicted both defendants and denied them the protection of section 193 of the Criminal Code, the justification of acting in defense of a public interest. Bötticher was sentenced to a year, Bruhn to six months in prison. Their applications for royal clemency were stubbornly resisted by Isenbiel and eventually rejected; word of the rejection came on the very day that Moritz Levy was granted clemency and released from his hard labor sentence for perjury.

In a demonstration of how alienated the anti-Semitic movement had become from the symbols of the Wilhelmine state, the *Staatsbürger Zeitung* vowed that it would carry on the struggle against "everything un-German, and the unpatriotic rabble, without concern for whether higher places approve or not."[15] But like the Xanten case, if the long trail of prosecutions arising out of the Winter murder demonstrated anything, it was the rudderlessness of German criminal justice. The system was driven from pillar to post by its efforts to harness and contain public opinion, while fighting forlornly to preserve the state's authority.

We began with Ludwig Flatau, who showed how the Xanten and Konitz cases dramatized the new threat from below. This kind of argument became increasingly common after 1900 as its props multiplied. The threat from below could appear not only in the form of recirculated medieval anti-Semitic legends; other forms of popular "stupidity" and "superstition" could also confound the modern court. One example was the spiritualist Anna Rothe, the "flower medium," so named for her supposed ability to pull flowers out of thin air. Rothe was brought to trial in 1903 for defrauding the credulous patrons of her seances. As in the cases of Xanten and Konitz, the defense strategy and the scope that the laws of procedure allowed defendants forced the prosecution to fight on ground that was less than congenial. In a manner analogous to the Xanten and Konitz libel cases, Rothe's defense argued that she had not committed fraud because her claims about her seances were *true*. The court itself summoned 40 witnesses requested by the defense: Rothe's satisfied customers, convinced that through her they had heard their dead aunts' counsel on back pain, or departed spouses' revelations of a son's secret lover. The judges nonetheless found that Rothe had committed fraud. Their reasoning was simple. The scientific experts said there was no room in the scientific world view for the existence of spirits; therefore, Rothe had promised something to her patrons that she could not deliver, and taken money from them to do so. These actions fulfilled the legal definition of fraud. The court sentenced her to eighteen months' imprisonment.[16]

This judgment provoked widespread criticism in three distinct forms. The first was that the law should not seek to protect the credulous; the second was that it was undignified to use a courtroom as a forum to debate the merits of spiritualism. The third came from lawyers who argued that the court had erred in law. What was striking about all criticisms from the liberal press, and from jurists, was how they joined the Rothe case with Xanten and Konitz to form a narrative of the baleful influence of the masses on the courts, a narrative of liberal despair. Court journalist Hugo Friedlaender lamented that despite all of the progress of modern science, "when one looks more closely at the life of the people, one comes to the recognition that we are still stuck in the middle ages." Maximilian Harden complained that the "modern world view" had not yet penetrated from the heights to the "dark quarters of the masses." Erich Sello linked the Rothe case not only to the murder of Ernst Winter but also to another case which had grown out of anti-Semitic riots: the burning of the synagogue in Neustettin in the 1880s, in which, as a young lawyer, he had made his name by securing acquittals for several Jewish defendants. "How desperately thin," Sello wrote, "even in our much-praised days, is the veneer of culture that covers the age-old swamp of moral and intellectual barbarity":

> The evil spirits of hatred, of horror, of superstition still lurk under this surface, as they did a thousand years ago, ready to break their weak chains at any moment . . . Anyone who thinks back on the frenzy of persecution, which the fire at the Neustettin Synagogue, and fifteen years later the murder of the Gymnasiast Winter, unleashed, even in classes of the population which counted themselves with pride among the cultivated, will no longer hold the horrors of the witch persecutions for a popular plague

which for us is only a sinister legend from the past, and whose return in our golden age of enlightenment and tolerance is no longer to be feared.[17]

Sello also wrote the most penetrating legal analysis of the case, an analysis that put a specifically legal-doctrinal spin on the vulnerability of German legal institutions to popular opinion. There were two branches to Sello's argument. The first was that the judges had given time to arguments and evidence that insulted a courtroom by their very presence in it. "Did it have to be?" Sello asked. "I know that I am not the only one who found the serious discussion of this tomfoolery *(Possen)* a kind of demeaning of the administration of justice, and who felt a little ashamed as a jurist." But the court had also let the barbarians through the gate by an error of legal interpretation. It held that "those who went to the defendant to see appearances from the spirit world, and instead received conjurers' tricks, have been materially injured; they did not receive that which they could claim contractually." Sello disagreed. The laws of fraud protected only *legitimate* contractual interests. Contracts that were either immoral or impossible of performance fell outside of this protection. The Imperial Supreme Court, for instance, had ruled that a prostitute who did not receive payment for her services could not claim to have been defrauded; the leading criminal law expert Franz von Liszt held that "if the 'claim' in which the disappointed party is injured is not recognized by the law, the possibility of fraud is excluded." Therefore, Sello concluded, so long as no one wished to claim that the summoning of spirits was a legally protected interest, Rothe had been unjustly condemned. The court's decision amounted to a statement that it would enforce the expectation of *genuine* appearances from the spirit world.[18] And so, as with the Xanten and Konitz cases, the court had been hijacked, forced to give a platform to views better left in obscurity, forced even, as in some of the Konitz prosecutions, to legitimate those views.

Filthy Squalor Is Now Much in Fashion

"The law's delay" had been a trope of literature and social criticism from Shakespeare to Kleist to Dickens, so it was hardly novel that at the beginning of the twentieth century many well-informed observers thought German courts were succumbing to gridlock. What was new was the reason they offered. Just as in the "stupidity" cases, there was an element of "liberal despair" in this diagnosis, for the problems arose out of the liberality of the reformed justice system of 1879. The Code of Criminal Procedure and the Judicial Code gave defendants wide latitude to summon witnesses and launch appeals; by 1900 these rights were beginning to show their weaknesses. Two Berlin cases of the first years of the twentieth century dramatized these problems. They were the trial of August Sternberg in 1900, and a 1902 case involving a naughty book.

Sternberg, it will be remembered, was the millionaire banker charged with having had sexual relations with girls below the consenting age of 14. The star witness against him was a girl named Frieda Woyda, who told the police that as a foster child at the house of one Margarethe Fischer, a friend of Sternberg's, she had been forced to have sex with Sternberg on three occasions in 1899. Sternberg was found guilty in the spring of 1900 and sentenced to two years' imprisonment. But the Imperial Supreme Court allowed his appeal on the basis that the trial court had excessively restricted his defense, and sent the case back to Berlin for a re-trial.[19]

At the second trial it was not just Sternberg who sat in the dock. He was joined by three codefendants: Fischer and another woman who had procured girls for him, and an employee who had helped Sternberg cover his tracks and suppress evidence. We saw in Chapter 1 the complaint of the superior court president that the prosecutor's office too often put "various offenses of various defendants in one indictment" when "separate proceedings would perhaps be managed more quickly and coherently." Sternberg's trial was a case in point. At first only 50 witnesses were summoned, "so that the evidence does not appear as extensive as earlier assumed." But this would change. The trial would run for nine weeks; and with almost every day of the proceedings the case would become more complicated, the allegations and counter-allegations more Byzantine, the list of witnesses longer. Maximilian Harden mocked the eager interest of the newspaper-reading public in the case by pointing out that Sternberg had even managed to push Konitz off the front page. "Filthy squalor is now much in fashion," he concluded.[20]

Frieda Woyda recanted her earlier testimony and now stubbornly maintained that Sternberg had done nothing to her. In response, the prosecution called witness after witness in a sustained assault on her credibility. Ever more lurid evidence emerged concerning Sternberg's efforts to bribe police officers, witnesses, prosecutors, even Imperial Supreme Court judges. The *Staatsbürger Zeitung,* wrongly convinced that Sternberg was Jewish, alleged that he had employed his defense counsel as agents in the bribery campaign. More witnesses had to be called to support and rebut these claims. "For days on end," wrote Harden with his usual acuity, "witnesses were heard only to support or discredit the testimony of other witnesses . . . anonymous letters led to the summoning of new witnesses; often one could believe that not Sternberg et al., but rather their defense counsel, sat in the dock." And yet, as Hamburg lawyer (and Harden's brother) Julian Witting wrote, "The core [of the case] was formed by the most simple set of facts that one could imagine: the question whether the defendant had carried out certain actions with two specific girls, knowing that their age was under fourteen." Where did the blame lie for the prolongation of this simple case? Harden thought the rule of "free evaluation of the evidence" (which, as we have seen, was fundamental to the German conception of the judicial office) had given Sternberg's judges too much scope to expand the trial and to believe what they chose about the witnesses, rather than what the evidence logically proved. Without Frieda Woyda's testimony, there was no direct evidence before the court that Sternberg had had sexual relations with her. But "the court decided according to its free conviction, pronounced Woyda's testimony [exculpating Sternberg] false . . . and sent the defendant to the penitentiary." Julian Witting added that it was clear to "every well-informed person" that any criminal case could receive the Sternberg treatment if the court were willing to delve so deeply into the lives of defendants and witnesses alike, and to reveal everything that went on "behind the scenes." Admittedly, "no orderly system of justice could be carried on that way in the long run."[21]

The myriad sequels to the Sternberg trial were still working their way through the courts in the spring of 1902 when another case arose to dramatize the state of Wilhelmine judicial gridlock. This time the subject was a slim novel in letters which had found a ready market among the teenage girls of Berlin.

The book was called *Nixchen* ("Little Nymph"), rather more grandly subtitled "A Contribution to the Psychology of the Upper-Class Girl." The author, "Hans von Kahlenberg," was in fact a well-to-do Steglitz lady named Helene von Monbart. The story involves two friends, a high minded, good natured, and very dense idealist named Achim von Wustrow, and a jaded man-about-town named Herbert Gröndahl, and their relationship to a young woman known to Achim as Mathilde and to Herbert as Isolde. Achim courts "Mathilde" in the most proper form, little realizing that her entire family is conniving at a marriage in order to save their finances. Meanwhile, "Isolde" carries on an affair with Herbert. The friends write to each other of their experiences. Achim is too dim to catch the obvious resemblance between his girlfriend and Herbert's; more surprisingly, the point evades Herbert also. Eventually Achim marries Mathilde. Herbert is a guest at the wedding, but he and Mathilde manage to contain their mutual surprise at meeting under these circumstances, and all is well.[22]

The novella's point was really a conservative one. Like Fontane's *Frau Jenny Treibel* (though with more sex and less literary skill) it condemned the materialism and lack of principle of young urbanites, especially of young women. Only one paragraph in the book described a sexual encounter, and that in less than graphic language;[23] *Nixchen* had been in print for several years and had gone through six editions before Prussian officialdom found it posed a threat to the social order. What in the end disturbed the official mind was less the tale's sexual content than its lack of uplift: the scheming "Nixchen" gets exactly what she wants, rather than having the decency to die in the last chapter like more conventional adventurous heroines. The manner and target of *Nixchen*'s distribution—at low cost in a department store, to a youthful and impressionable market—only compounded the problem in official eyes.[24]

The slow response of the authorities to *Nixchen*'s publication proved typical of the course of the prosecution, marked throughout by official error and delay. The first error was Isenbiel's: he took jurisdiction of the case for Superior Court I when it properly belonged to Superior Court II. The authorities remained ambivalent about the merits of the case. Berlin's chief prosecutor thought Isenbiel's conclusion about the book's obscenity was not "absolutely correct"; the motions chamber of Superior Court II refused the prosecution's request to open a trial against Monbart and her publisher, Karl Reissner, accepting the defense that the book had a serious purpose and was conceived as a "warning to mothers." The *Kammergericht* reversed this decision and ordered the opening of a trial for "spreading immoral writings"—which the state then lost. "The tendency of the novel consists solely of depicting the character of a morally degenerate and hypocritical girl," said the criminal chamber, "a subject which is thoroughly suitable for literary treatment." Admittedly, passages of the letters taken in isolation could be seen as injurious to morality, but the work had to be seen as a whole; and as a whole it counted as art, and could not "on the average" injure the sense of decency of adult readers, male or female.[25]

The prosecutors had better luck on appeal to the Imperial Supreme Court. In May 1903 the high court overturned the trial decision. The criminal chamber had failed to consider that if the book could injure the morals of "immature, morally still not yet settled" people, then it was "objectively obscene," and the only question was whether author and publisher had been conscious of this possibility. Leipzig sent the case back to Berlin for a retrial. Still Berlin judges showed no great enthusiasm for punishing Monbart and Reissner. On 22 September 1903, the 9th Chamber of Superior Court I ordered the confiscation of all copies of the text, while acquitting Monbart and Reissner on the subjective ground that they had not been conscious of any danger to the morals of the young. Isenbiel launched another appeal to Leipzig, but a month later notified the minister that the appeal was hopeless and withdrew it. Monbart and Reissner also appealed to Leipzig, and there the 2nd Criminal Senate concluded in January 1904 that once again the lower court had erred in law, though not in the sense the appellants had wished. The 9th Chamber had not considered whether the obscenity of one part of the book could color the whole. This time the case was sent for retrial to the Superior Court in the provincial Brandenburg town of Neu-Ruppin.[26]

The judges in Neu-Ruppin were harder on *Nixchen* than their Berlin colleagues had been. The Neu-Ruppin chamber thought that more than one passage of the book was obscene, and objected to Herbert's "realism" triumphing over Achim's "bright and pleasant" world view (an over-literal reading suggesting that these judges were at least as thick as Achim). But as the withdrawal of Isenbiel's appeal meant that the *personal* acquittal of Monbart and Reissner had become legally binding *(rechtskräftig)*, the chamber could only order that the plates and forms for printing the book be rendered unusable. Still the long court battle was not over. Monbart launched another appeal to Leipzig, which was predictably dismissed on 24 June 1904. But after the appeals were finally over, the state realized that the Neu-Ruppin prosecutor had forgotten to ask for confiscation of copies of the book, and thus the court forgot to order it. At the minister's urging, the prosecutors wrestled with the problem of how the judgment could be amended. In September, the chief prosecutor and the president of the *Kammergericht* reported jointly that it would be "impermissible" to try to vary the existing judgment. There could be no objection to beginning a new prosecution, if the author or publisher took further steps to disseminate the book, but the outcome of such a case was "certainly not free from doubt." In 1904 *Nixchen* was published in Vienna, and copies soon went on sale again in Berlin. Isenbiel "saw occasion to intervene in the way of an objective proceeding," with the aim of confiscating the book rather than trying once more to penalize author and publisher. In late 1905 he succeeded in getting such an order from Superior Court I. This time the order included both confiscation of the copies and destroying the forms and plates for its printing, although the latter was a technicality, as the place of publication lay beyond the court's jurisdiction. And so, eight years after its initial publication, nearly four years after the Berlin authorities first intervened, the legal saga of *Nixchen* came to an end. It had been a frustration for all concerned. Harden, summing up the case in late 1904, criticized both the unconscionable length of the process and the multiplicity of legal opinions that the courts had generated:

> And if we only had the chance to recognize clearly the opinion of the judges! That we do not have this chance is the lesson of a comparison of the eight judgments . . . What is permitted in Berlin is frowned upon in Ruppin, and the longer the courts concerned themselves with the evil book, naturally the greater became the number of incriminating passages. Wasn't it really enough that in October 1902 a Berlin criminal chamber declared that the novel did not have the character of an immoral writing? Did one really have to fill official documents and plague persons for years with this inconsequentiality? The eight judgments are hardly distinguishable from the first in practical effect: the book is no longer confiscated and can once again be sold in Germany. In the meantime it has been published in Austria and nearly one hundred thousand copies distributed. And that is the humor of it.[27]

Cases that served only to expose the paralysis of the courts became increasingly frequent in the last Wilhelmine years. Many of them had a definite political *brisance*. In 1905, the prosecutor's office brought several Social Democratic journalists to trial on charges of libeling the doctors at Plötzensee prison. Articles strongly critical of the medical care of prisoners had appeared in 1904 in both *Vorwärts* and *Die Zeit am Montag*. The prosecutors had every advantage; by artfully renaming the case, they brought it before a judge who was clearly biased against the defendants. Nonetheless, after a three-week proceeding that did no one's reputation any good, the prosecution and the doctors gave up and agreed to an out-of-court settlement. The press greeted this outcome by criticizing the squandering of public resources. In 1910 and 1911 Berlin's courts took up a string of prosecutions arising out the famous "Moabit riots." Again observers were struck by the vision of juridical impotence: Harden wrote "one must accustom oneself to the certainty that criminal trials of something more than every-day extent have become unmanageable in Prussia. Mostly the end brings losses to the state's treasury and reputation." And in 1912, a man named A. O. Weber complained sarcastically of the delay in processing his appeal against his wife's committal to a mental institution (the appeal was filed in January 1911 had not yet been heard by the end of the year): "No hurry, after all it isn't the Moabit riot-trial!" Many officials agreed with the criticisms. In late 1912, the chief prosecutor at the *Kammergericht* told the minister he sought reductions in the length of trials "in the unusually extensive criminal matters which are so frequent here." The Berlin area first prosecutors had agreed that reductions were "urgently to be wished."[28]

Liberals might have seen a silver lining in this cloud. In 1896 Numerius Negidius had rebutted Aulus Agerius by arguing that the courts were chaotic rather than systematically biased. When Harden complained about the multiplicity of judicial opinions in the *Nixchen* case, he was (unintentionally) pointing out that the courts were engaged in a real dispute in which there was no consistent, ruling position. In other words, judges were grappling with the law, with all of the attendant inconsistencies and contradictions to which mortals are subject, rather than exercising justice by ministerial fiat. Set against the criticisms of contemporaries like Agerius or Karl Liebknecht, this was progress; it spoke of a mature, perhaps even democratic legal system. But few lawyers in Wilhelmine Berlin spoke up for the civilizing virtues of disorder. Instead, they began to think about reform.

The Errors of Justice and Their Causes

In the last decade before the First World War, the cases we have surveyed in this chapter, and others like them, began to be pulled together into a composite narrative of judicial error and delay. This narrative appeared in a new kind of literature. German legal academics had always tended to be hostile to the study of individual trials; Franz von Liszt, professor of criminal law at Berlin University, wrote in 1906 that "appeals to the many 'individual cases' prove nothing at all." Practitioners increasingly complained of this scholarly short-sightedness. "We lack a science of the application of law," wrote Bremen lawyer Richard Finger in 1912, "as a sub-genre of legal science; and we especially lack a literature of the application of law." Some were working to fill the gap. A number of Berlin writers, lawyers and journalists began producing a body of work that proceeded from an observation of the defects in individual trials, to broad diagnoses of defects in the system, to various recommendations for reform. Their writings spoke with remarkable unanimity on the nature of the justice system. The problem with the courts was not that they were too harsh, or indeed too lenient. It was not that their practice betrayed a consistent bias, at least in political or social terms. The problem was that outcomes were random; that, as Richard Finger put it, Justitia was truly blind, wielding her sword carelessly and—in every sense—without judgment.[29]

This new literature of judicial error began with the wellspring of all criminal cases, human perceptions, and opinions; it was in its strongly negative assessment of the capacities of ordinary people as informants, witnesses, and consumers of newspapers that it showed its roots in the fin de siècle European discourse on the degeneracy of the masses.[30] But the new lawyers' literature differed in one respect from the books of Tarde, Le Bon, Nordau, or Lombroso. Sociological, criminological, and conventional legal discourse saw the "dangerous classes" as the raw material or subject matter of scientific inquiry and legal processing, entirely distinct from the institutions of justice. The new literature of judicial error raised the alarm level a notch precisely because it saw that this distinction was vanishing.

Erich Sello, for instance, devoted a 1910 pamphlet to "The Psychology of the *Cause Célèbre*," a critique of the effects of public opinion on the courts. The phenomenon of mass suggestion characteristic of the *cause célèbre* was, he said, "a sickness of the entire population, just one of the many symptoms of a general illness of our social organism, a symptom of that general neurasthenic disposition of our time that grabs for ever newer and greater sensations." Sello believed the courts caught this disease from the press. When crimes were especially bloody, or when they caused serious damage to the economic, political, or religious interests of a community, irresponsible journalists had an easy time stirring up public hysteria. Then "it [is] all the worse for the objective determination of the truth," Sello wrote; "the springs from which the judge is supposed to shape his verdict will run all the cloudier." If it sounded as though Sello was writing of Xanten or Konitz, he was. In a rhetorical illustration entirely typical of the genre, he told his readers that they did not need to travel back in time to early modern witch persecutions to see such hysteria at work: "Have we not ourselves experienced them with a shudder: . . . the trial concerning the

Xanten child-murder, the Konitz and Polna ritual-murder trials, haunted by the horror story of Jewish ritual murder, as in ages past?" The cultural stereotypes typical of liberal gentlemen also shaped Sello's assessment of public opinion. Those who were less educated, along with women and children, shared a "general mental disposition, in which the power of imagination is uppermost," making them "more commonly victims of mass suggestion than are grown-ups and men." One had then to be "shaken to the core" by the inexhaustible sources of error that rendered truth-finding "difficult to the point of impossibility."[31]

Once ill-formed public opinion had set the investigatory machinery in gear—through denunciations or the evidence of witnesses in police or judicial investigations—the machinery could all too easily run off in its own directions. Julian Witting explained the bureaucratic realities in an article inspired by the Sternberg trial and Isenbiel's much-quoted claim that the prosecutor's office was the "most objective authority." The legality principle, Witting reminded his readers, was one of the cornerstones of liberalized criminal law. It obliged the prosecutor to investigate any case that was brought to his attention. Often enough, the prosecutor wished to "kill the case" at this stage, but was reluctant to face the victim's or complainant's official protest to the chief prosecutor (as happened in the Winter case), and the long reports such a complaint would require of him. So instead the prosecutor raised the indictment and told himself "the motions chamber can always turn it down." But the motions chamber judges—like the prosecutor—might easily conclude "the case is legally or factually uncertain, let's bring it before the proper judge." Witting pointed to the dangerous desire to cater to public opinion that could drive such decision: "Cases even occur in which an indictment is raised and a trial opened, even though not one of the officials involved seeks a conviction." His examples were Xanten and Konitz. The authorities often brought such a prosecution out of a laudable desire to educate the public. But then to achieve the necessary "clarification," the limits on admissible evidence had to be set as widely as possible, leading to the distended proceedings characteristic of the Konitz cases; and "this latitude is easily transferred to other 'sensational' trials."[32]

What was most surprising about the new literature of judicial error was that it contained critiques of institutions that had represented benevolent progress to earlier generations of liberal lawyers. Trial by jury had long been a classic liberal *desideratum* in the criminal courtroom. But if ordinary people were ill-fitted to be witnesses, were they not all the more unsuitable to be judges? In view of the acquittal statistics for Wilhelmine jurors (see Chapter 1), it was not surprising that a judge like Otto Schwarz might insert an editorial favoring the abolition of juries into his outline of the laws of criminal procedure. Nor was it very surprising that a police officer like Hans von Tresckow should look at juries with disdain, quoting in his memoirs "the words of a high justice official" who told him "juries are good for a guilty person, they mostly get acquitted. But if a really innocent person ever comes before the jury, they will convict him sure as death." What *was* surprising was the ambivalence, ranging to hostility, with which defense counsel regarded juries. Sello was prominent among the critics, calling himself "a fundamental opponent of the jury court, at least in the form obtaining in Germany." He hoped indeed that his position would counter the "vulgar prejudice" that a lawyer supported amendments to the criminal law only in so far as they would help his clients be acquitted, as the probability of acquittal was "by long experience greatest in the jury courts." In *Cause Célèbre,* he contrasted the credulous vulnerability of the juror to press and community opinion with the professional judge, who had "daily experience of dutiful practice in seeking and pronouncing the law." Sello wished to see incorporation of a lay element in all courts of first instance, including the criminal chambers, but with the lay elements joined with the professional judges in one unit instead of sitting separately as a jury. Fritz Friedmann believed that juries were more likely to convict wrongly than to acquit wrongly; he recommended that juries be sequestered for the entire length of the trial to insulate them from public and press opinion. Max Alsberg supported the general notion of a jury court—"there are some professions that do not lend themselves to being carried out professionally"—but he could not avoid reservations. In 1911, he wrote a pamphlet about a pornography trial he had conducted in Bavaria. With the condescension of the big city lawyer stuck in the provinces, Alsberg poked fun at the jurors' complete lack of interest in the proceedings, their desire to be finished as soon as possible so that they could get back to their fields, and their efforts to bribe him so that he would reject them. His assessment of the weaknesses of jurors, especially in such a case as a prosecution for "spreading immoral writings," said much about the attitudes of judicial insiders: "The juror who comes from enlightened circles would likely want nothing to do with stamping out the distribution of pictures with fire and sword," he wrote. But jurors were unequal in their understanding of literature and art, an inequality that was "certainly not to be found among professional judges. The academic education which the professional judge has enjoyed always creates a certain common foundation. The lay judges completely lack a comparable equal foundation." Alsberg thought that the remedy was to appoint lay judges especially selected to be social and professional equals *(Standesgenossen)* of a given defendant. In other words, the cultivated had to be insulated from the opinions of the great unwashed.[33]

At first, the literature of judicial error was a scattered and piecemeal one, a composite of newspaper editorials and articles in legal journals and highbrow periodicals like *Die Zukunft*. But in the last Wilhelmine years several Berlin lawyers began assembling the strands of the new narrative into broadly synthetic accounts. The most prominent among them were the trio Johannes Werthauer, Erich Sello, and Max Alsberg. Their works, though widely different in style, were strikingly similar in their fundamental message: that the danger facing the courts was not consistent political bias but rather randomness of outcomes—a product of human and procedural weaknesses, a product of irrationality.

Werthauer was first into the field with a pamphlet entitled *Moabitrium: Scenes from the Administration of Justice in the Big City*. It took the form of an account of a day's business in a busy Berlin criminal chamber. The fictionality of the account was telegraphed, at least to initiates, by the fact that the chamber was designated the 21st—Superior Court I, the largest Berlin trial court, had no more than twelve criminal chambers in the Wilhelmine years. But Werthauer's stories were only barely fiction. In later years he wrote that, as a young lawyer, he had been shaken by how frequently the innocent were convicted; even when he succeeded in securing acquittals, "I recognized that this was actually a matter of chance, that the system was so flawed that even correct judgments actually rested on erroneous functioning." Thus in *Moabitrium,* Werthauer's theme was the frightening arbitrariness of justice.

The first chapter, "Proceeding I against Müller et al. for theft," tells the story of husband and wife greengrocers, August and Mieze Müller. The Müllers become the innocent victims of a fraud artist who sells them stolen shirts for resale. Things go badly for the Müllers from the start. Their lawyer tells them their reputation as honest business people, carefully cultivated over ten years and well known in their street, counts for nothing; big city judges do not know the defendants, and character evidence is irrelevant. The lawyer warns them they should make arrangements for someone to take over their shop in the event that they are convicted, "because one can really never know how it will come out, justice is not only blind in the sense that it should judge with no respect for persons, but also in that it cannot know the right thing to do on its own, as it wasn't there and thus can only rely on third persons." The Müllers are indeed convicted and sentenced to one-and-one-half years hard labor—a half-year over the minimum for receiving stolen goods—largely because their failure to confess angers the presiding judge. The young con man who sold them the goods confesses and receives a milder sentence.[34]

If the Müllers are innocents who do not know how to work the system, the second chapter presents their foil. It concerns the trial of "heavy boy" Adam Schoppach. Schoppach is arrested the day after he has committed a robbery from a shop in the Potsdamer Strasse—but the arrest is not for the robbery, it is for an assault on a school teacher in the Rosenthaler Strasse. A search through the "criminal album" suggests him as a suspect, and the police know that one of his girlfriends lives near the scene of the assault. As Schoppach is waiting to be interrogated at the police station, he overhears that he is also being sought for the Potsdamer Strasse robbery. Thinking quickly, he realizes that if he confesses to the assault, he will have an alibi for the robbery, which would carry a much more serious penalty. He maintains this "confession" at trial. After some pressure from the presiding judge, Schoppach "admits" that he carried out the assault with a knife and not a brass knuckle as he had previously claimed. The judge is pleased with Schoppach's willingness to confess and gives him a light sentence of four months in jail.[35]

The pattern is repeated in case after case. Hardened criminals know how to work the system, are cunning enough to lie, even to their apparent disadvantage, when they recognize that they will be better off in the long run. Innocent and inexperienced people fall victim to their naiveté, the prejudices of the court, the dishonesty of more calculating witnesses, and the inadequacies of the evidence. The lessons of the chapters are summarized in the table of contents. The point of the Müllers' case is "limited possibility for individual judgment of the inhabitants of the big city." The lesson of Adam Schoppach is "big city alibi. Dependence of the criminal law on the statements of people involved. Limitation of proof of recognition. Exaggeration of the importance of confession." Other dangers include an inadequate recognition of the importance of psychology, and the inability of judges to understand the daily life of social classes remote from themselves.[36]

Werthauer returned to these themes throughout his career; the titles of his later books convey the message. In 1912 he published *Wie leicht man sich strafbar machen kann (How Easy it is to become Indicted)*, which warned the nonjurist of the many traps the criminal law can set for the unwary. Werthauer followed this book in 1919 with *Strafunrecht (The Injustice of Criminal Law)*, which set out both a critique and an ambitious program of criminal law reform.[37]

Erich Sello was the next practicing lawyer to publish a synthetic treatment of judicial errors. His book, *Die Irrtümer der Strafjustiz und ihre Ursachen (The Errors of Criminal Justice and Their Causes)*, was conceived as a magnum opus. Published in 1911, though Sello had been at work on it since 1897, it was supposed to be the first in a multi-volume study. It rested squarely on the belief that the positivistic, scientific spirit of the time could be turned to account in the reform of the courts. "My book," said Sello, "should, if it is just to its task, present a collection of practical examples of the lessons of judicial errors taken from experience, and in this sense supplement the material derived from modern experimental research." It consisted of a collection of brief narratives of criminal cases drawn not only from Germany but from across Europe and North America. Each one, Sello believed, was a case of a judicial error. It was his conviction that the courts were prone to errors to a degree that, when thoroughly studied, could only arouse "disquiet and horror." Many of the themes of Sello's collection had been raised by Werthauer: above all, the dangers of false confessions and the overemphasis the system placed on them. It made little difference, said Sello, that confessions—"the pride of every inquisitor"—could no longer be extracted from prisoners under torture. "Months of investigatory custody, the reference to a milder judgment in return for a confession, the spiritual torture of the eternal interrogations, are able even today to tempt confessions especially from weaker defendants." Errors of medical evidence were another of Sello's themes, especially the frequent failure of experts and courts alike to recognize when a prisoner was mentally ill. But significantly, again like Werthauer, Sello did not believe the errors of justice worked *only* to convict the innocent. Though he had presented only such cases in his book, he went so far as to say that "their number would be considerably outweighed by faulty verdicts in favor of the defendant." Fixing the sources of the one problem would fix those of the other. "The effort that we apply to this task, if it helps us to a deeper insight into the nature of the sources of error in this field . . . will teach us to avoid frivolous acquittals no less than frivolous convictions." The best remedy was science. In his conclusion, Sello wrote "I am not of the despairing opinion that the administration of justice is damned for all time to remain the prey of error to the dreadful extent that it has up to now." Salvation lay with "the microscope and the photographic apparatus," with blood tests and fingerprints, and with psychology, that would "more and more become the common property of the criminalist." Indeed, for Sello, psychology was the queen of the criminalistic sciences. Earlier he had written that anyone who thought he could make a career in criminal law without studying psychology would be better off to "simply hang up the trade . . . He might, as paradoxical as it sounds, rather dispense with the study of law than with that of psychology."[38]

Max Alsberg was Sello's heir in the combination of skill and combativeness he brought to the courtroom; and he soon showed himself to be Sello's heir as a practical scholar as well. In May 1913, a few months after Sello's death, Alsberg published a collection of cases with a title and method strikingly similar to Sello's *Errors of Criminal Justice*. Although Alsberg did not seek to imitate Sello's "grandly conceived and grandly carried out, though sadly uncompleted work"—indeed Alsberg thought that one lesson of Sello's collection was that there was insufficient data for a comprehensive, scientific explanation of judicial errors—yet justice could still be "approached scientifically," and Alsberg's goal was to throw the spotlight on the inadequacy of remedies for error. Thus his book—*Justizirrtum und Wiederaufnahme (Judicial Error and Retrial)*—focused on the remedy of *Wiederaufnahme*: the application to open a new trial on the basis of new evidence.

The book had two parts. The first was an extended essay by Alsberg, addressing in turn "the dangers of the criminal trial," "the inadequacy of the remedy of revision" for jury and criminal chamber decisions, and "the limited value of the application for a retrial for the elimination of judicial errors." The second part of the book comprised a collection of cases designed to illustrate the systemic weaknesses. Some of them were trials Alsberg himself had conducted; some of them were submitted by eminent lawyers from all over Germany, among them Alsberg's Berlin colleagues Karl Liebknecht, Siegfried Löwenstein, and Johannes Werthauer. Thus the book reflected the new literature's enthusiasm for learning from experience. As Alsberg wrote, "the life of the law thus gets its say in the second part of this book" (and here the American lawyer cannot help thinking of Holmes' famous epigram, "The life of the law has not been logic: it has been experience").[39]

While Sello had concentrated on psychology, Alsberg emphasized legal-procedural shortcomings. His view of the principle of orality (*Mündlichkeit,* another cornerstone of the Code of Criminal Procedure and key demand of nineteenth century legal reformers) was typical. For Alsberg, requiring the oral presentation of all evidence placed excessive demands on the power of the judge to grasp quickly the essential point of a proceeding. It was too easy for the judge to overlook a critical factor in the heat of the moment. More extensive use of documentary evidence, as in civil trials, was the remedy. Ironically, this reform would mean a return to the documentary trials of the *ancien regime,* against which an earlier generation of liberals had struggled. Similarly, Alsberg saw it as a weakness that there was no procedural mechanism to ensure that the presiding judge brought out exculpatory evidence in his interrogation of the defendant. But this "defect" could be seen as the flip side of the defendant's right to decline to testify. Like many, Alsberg believed that the laws of procedure placed too much emphasis on the principle of "free evaluation of the evidence." Criminal procedure went farther in this point than did the civil laws. The Code of Civil Procedure *(Zivilprozessordnung)* required the court to state the evidentiary basis for its decision, and the Imperial Supreme Court regularly overturned civil judgments that lacked such a foundation. The Code of Criminal Procedure said only that the grounds "should" be given where the court's decision rested on circumstantial evidence; the lack of such grounds did not render a decision invalid. Too many judges took the principle of free evaluation to mean the freedom to write vague or unsupported judgments. Finally, like many Wilhelmine legal commentators, Alsberg was alarmed at the courts' vulnerability to biased or perjurious witnesses, or to the inability of honest witnesses to render an accurate account of what they knew. "Through the scientific study of witness testimony," he wrote, "it becomes ever more strikingly revealed how easily a precise functioning of perception and memory can be disturbed."[40]

The writings of Werthauer, Sello, and Alsberg, for all their differences in points of detail, taught one basic lesson: the procedures of German justice were inadequate to protect the courts from a wide array of human failings. The result was that judicial decisions were frighteningly arbitrary. Far too often the guilty went free, while the innocent were sent to hard labor or the scaffold. The stories these lawyers told were informed by a hard-earned pessimism, garnered in the arena, from too much experience with fumbling jurors and witnesses, arbitrary judges, and cases that dragged on interminably in the manner of *Jarndyce v. Jarndyce.* But the concern for rationality of outcomes in German courts was not limited to the world of practice. It could be found in the realm of legal theory as well.

The vital question for German legal theory in the first decade of the twentieth century was the response to codification. Codification had come in a flurry after German unification: the Reich Criminal Code in 1871, soon followed by the complex of laws of 1877 to 1879 and (after two decades of academic debate and legislative wrangling) the monumental Civil Code in 1896 (in force in 1900). These new codes represented the jurisprudential state of the art: they were modern, thorough, comprehensive, the fruits of a centuries-long tradition of serious thought about the law by some of the world's foremost thinkers. Must they not, then, provide answers to all conceivable legal questions, so that a judge need only be a "high state bureaucrat with an academic education . . . armed only with a thinking machine, admittedly of the finest sort," his only furniture a green table, able to produce on demand "with the aid of purely logical operations" and with "absolute precision" the "result predetermined by the legislator"? Very quickly, legal scholars decided that the new codes offered no such panacea. In part this decision reflected practical experience, the realization that, as Oskar Bülow wrote, the utmost of human experience, caution, and imagination could not hope to keep pace with the "the freely striving human will, the inventive desire for gain, the cunning of egoism and of crime," which would always throw up new and unanticipated legal problems. More cynically, but not implausibly, Max Weber speculated that the resentments of jurists who feared being relegated to the status of "subsumtion machine" lay behind the calls for a "free law" at the beginning of the twentieth century. Those calls came from a new generation of liberal and left-leaning lawyers and law professors, above all from the Czernowitz professor Eugen Ehrlich, the Cassel trial lawyer Ernst Fuchs, and the Freiburg *Privatdozent* (eventually law professor at Kiel) Hermann Kantorowicz. The movement sought, to varying degrees, a law that was less driven by the formalism and syllogistic logic of nineteenth-century positivism, a law in which the judge played a more critical and creative role, a law that was in closer touch with popular opinion and desires.[41]

This movement had everything to do with the perceived threats to the rationality of factual determination we have surveyed thus far, and not just because Hermann Kantorowicz cut his teeth in legal practice with a period as an associate in Erich Sello's office. Both sides of the debate over free law acknowledged that at issue were attitudes to the rationality of law and the place of popular opinion in it. Kantorowicz wrote that "the anti-rationalist outlook" went "hand in hand" with the free law movement; and he sought a jurisprudence that would "express the free law that lives in the people." Weber, for his part, had nothing but contempt for popular opinion and, logically, for juries, which he dismissed as an example of irrational "Khadi justice." For Weber the popular and the intellectual tide of irrationality were two sides of one coin; this assessment led him to some pessimistic conclusions. Looking about at his society he saw demands for substantive social and economic equalization from the propertyless classes, which "judges or administrators" could not meet without "assuming the substantively ethical and hence nonformalistic character of the Khadi," that is, giving up everything that was inherent in "lawyers' law." He saw too that "the rational course of justice and administration is interfered with not only by every form of 'popular justice' . . . but also by every type of intensive influencing of the course of administration by 'public opinion,' that is, in a mass democracy, that communal activity which is born of irrational 'feelings' and which is normally instigated or guided by party leaders or the press." To these he joined the "anti-formal tendencies [that] are being promoted by the ideologically rooted power aspirations of the legal profession itself." For Weber, these several "interferences" were "as disturbing as, or, under circumstances, even more disturbing than, those of the star chamber practices of an 'absolute' monarch." Weber also noted that the trend to utilitarianism in criminal punishments meant that "increasingly nonformal elements" were introduced into legal practice.[42]

Enlightened Measures

Was one to be pessimistic or optimistic, then, about law and criminal justice in the last years of Wilhelmine Germany? The fact that would-be reformers like Sello and Alsberg took up their pens even to complain of the ills of the system bespoke a measure of optimism. Sometimes the optimism was explicit. As determined a merchant of gloom as Sello could still write in 1910, "If progressive culture, education, and attitudes have already brought much improvement even in this field, if we may trust with confidence that certain intellectual epidemics of the past now belong to the grave and are certain never to return, so may we allow ourselves a modest hope for a still better future."[43]

But what would that future look like? Some reformers saw forensic science as a panacea that could ultimately prevent the errors of criminal justice. Certainly the evolution of forensic science and police procedures in the decades before the First World War was dramatic. Their effectiveness was another question. If the reformers showed a sturdy faith in the virtues of enlightenment rationality and its applications in science, in the courtroom those applications often seemed to raise the specter of new dangers paradoxically inherent in such rationality—as intellectuals of the Frankfurt school would soon be warning.[44]

Trials were often major spurs to the reform of police procedures. The criminal police had been extensively reorganized in 1885 in the wake of press criticisms of a bungled investigation. In 1899 the cycle was repeated after the trial of tailor and pimp Hugo Guthmann for the murder of prostitute Bertha Singer. This outcome was in one respect paradoxical: the Guthmann case was factually so reminiscent of the Heinze case that the advances in forensic science were all the more striking. As we saw, the prosecutors in the Heinze case had to rely almost exclusively on hearsay from unreliable witnesses; the little forensic evidence there was—consisting of the autopsy report and the hairs found on nightwatchman Braun's saber—was inconclusive. Eight years later, the Guthmann trial provided a forum for an impressive battery of scientific expert witnesses, among them the court chemist Dr. Jeserich, and no fewer than four handwriting experts who gave opinions on whether Guthmann had written some incriminating letters. Jeserich used photographs to explain a new kind of evidence to the jurors: "The lines of the finger, which are fundamentally different with every person."[45]

Yet after a nine-day trial the jurors needed only forty-five minutes to decide to acquit the defendant. Skepticism about the competence of the police investigation and the good faith of the prosecution was widespread in the Berlin press, including its conservative wing. While the trial was still in progress, the *Lokal-Anzeiger* ran a leading article entitled "Traces of Criminals" by Conrad Alberti, which criticized the police for failing to secure some vital evidence that contained bloody fingerprints: an "experienced and capable criminalist" would, as "Professor Hans Gross . . . insists, pay attention to everything." The extensive evidence from the handwriting experts seemed dangerously flaky to many, even including one of these experts, who took to the pages of *Die Zukunft* to criticize his colleagues. He wrote that "It had never occurred to any reasonable expert before now to want to parade in the courtroom with the actual or presumed results of graphological research . . . only the most banal truths belong in the courtroom, just as in the daily press."[46]

Such criticisms met with substantial agreement from one of the most important officials at the Alexanderplatz, the notorious *Intrigant* Inspector Leopold von Meerscheidt-Hüllessem. Meerscheidt-Hüllessem was head of Inspection B, which included the *Erkennungsdienst*—the office that dealt with matters of criminal identification. Soon after the Guthmann case was over, Meerscheidt-Hüllessem wrote a memo on the procedures he believed should be followed in the investigations of capital crimes. The memo dealt with some of Meerscheidt-Hüllessem's longstanding concerns, but he had, he said, held off circulating his memo until the Guthmann trial was over: "So far as I knew the material, I was not convinced of Guthmann's guilt, and I said to myself that a trial which ended with an acquittal might . . . more than one which ended with a conviction, draw attention to present defects and contribute to the further avoidance of mistakes." Meerscheidt-Hüllesem was concerned both with recent failures of the criminal police and with the bad public relations that followed. The public and the press judged the competence of the criminal police by their success or failure in capital cases, "certainly incorrectly." The "many failures" in capital cases were not to be attributed to any lack of ability on the part of the officials. They were due in part to big city conditions, where murders often occurred that "did not offer the slightest clue for investigation," and in part to the lack of sufficient preparation and the failure to have "the already designated man in the right place at the right time." Years ago he had suggested reforms to the procedures in capital cases, but "the failures have remained the same."[47]

Now Meerscheidt-Hüllessem proposed a thorough overhaul of police procedures, beginning with the investigation at the crime scene. "The first and most important work," he said, "is taking down the facts to the smallest detail, because from this above all, the clues should emerge which will lead to the identification of the culprit if one does not wish to rely on chance and accidents." Witnesses should not be questioned at the scene, but taken to the police presidium and interviewed later. Nowhere did Meerscheidt-Hüllessem's attachment to the cult of professionalism show itself more than in his exhaustive list of the equipment a detective should bring to a crime scene: a specialized waterproof case packed with a bewildering array of supplies, including "a 12-meter tape measure, a compass, a box of matches, a magnifying glass . . . a house-apothecary containing

Cholera-Hoffmann's drops, vinegar, ether, colodium, liquid amonia, carbolic acid, Anthyprin, Dowersche-Bromkali powder and citric acid tablets . . . a Criminal Code along with the most useful Reich criminal laws . . . a cigarette case, containing 5 cigars . . . chemical equipment including glass beakers . . . a booklet on first aid, little glass plates for taking fingerprints and blood spots; a spatula; a ruler." The detective should also have with him a railway map of Europe and railway information including emergency points; a telegraph book with carbon paper; maps of Berlin, including its police districts; an alphabetical notebook for taking down the names of suspects and witnesses; and a writing case with various kinds of writing paper, blotting paper, and envelopes. He should carry preprinted forms to remind him of various tasks in the investigation, as "in the excitement of investigating a capital case" it was easy to forget things. Thus equipped, "the commissar is in the position to meet all eventualities at the scene of the crime."[48]

Beyond matters of supply, Meerscheidt-Hüllessem's principal recommendation was that murder cases should be investigated by specialists, assembled into "murder commissions," consisting of experienced detectives assisted by medical experts and subordinate officials. In 1901, the Alexanderplatz followed his advice and established these commissions. Meerscheidt-Hüllessem himself negotiated a contract with a number of Berlin's practitioners of forensic medicine by which the physicians agreed "to place ourselves at the disposal of the police presidium, and be called upon in capital cases." Each time one of the "Herren doctors" was called upon, he would be paid an honorarium of 50 marks.[49]

This was not the first time Meerscheidt-Hüllessem had succeeded in setting the investigatory techniques of the Alexanderplatz on a more systematic footing. He had begun a personal collection of photographs of criminals in 1876, which eventually grew into the *Verbrecheralbum*—the Criminal Album, or mug book. By 1892 the "Album" actually consisted of twelve volumes with 8,000 photographs. Each photograph was accompanied by a detailed physical description: height, hair color, eye color, shape of nose, shape of lips, shape of head, and color of facial hair. Among policemen, Meerscheidt-Hüllessem was also famous for his confidential index of homosexuals, which Hans von Tresckow credited as an especially useful resource in blackmail cases. Meerscheidt-Hüllessem had traveled to Paris in 1895 to study the Bertillon system of identification of criminals through anthropometric measurements. The brainchild of Alphonse Bertillon, a clerk at the Paris prefecture of police, this system was a complicated procedure in which a specially trained official took eleven different measurements of a prisoner's body: height, head length, head breadth, arm span, sitting height, left middle finger length, left little finger length, left foot length, left forearm length, right ear length, and cheek width, all in the course of a carefully choreographed routine. Bertillon determined that these measurements would be the least affected by age. The results were recorded on a card and filed in a complex classificatory system beginning with sex and head length, so that an official with a new set of measurements could begin looking for a match. Although the Paris police began using Bertillon's system in 1882, it was not until the early- and mid-1890s that German police forces began introducing a version of *Bertillonage*, beginning with the Hamburg force in 1893. Meerscheidt-Hüllessem was impressed with the system, and it was his enthusiastic advocacy that led to its adoption and the creation of the *Erkennungsdienst* at the Alexanderplatz, which maintained Bertillon measurements from all over Germany. By June 1901, the Alexanderplatz had measurements of 24,796 persons; it claimed that successful identifications of criminals through the use of the system had risen from three in 1896 to 214 in 1900. In 1902 all prisoners in Prussian penitentiaries were measured according to the Bertillon system.[50]

A strange trial in 1903 illustrated some of the implications of *Bertillonage*, and with it the tendencies of the new criminology. In 1896 the Count Kwilecki and Countess Kwilecka, owners of the estate Wroblewo in Posen, found they needed a male heir to secure a mortgage. As things stood, they had only daughters, and their age and the state of their marriage did not auger well for further procreation. Then, as if by a miracle, the 51-year-old countess gave birth to a son on 27 January 1897, in a Berlin apartment she had rented for the occasion. Relatives who stood to inherit the Kwilecki estate if the couple remained without an heir were understandably suspicious and hired a private detective to investigate. The detective found a servant girl from Krakow who claimed to have sold a son, born out of wedlock in January 1897, to a count and countess from Posen. The Krakow servant, now married to a Bohemian railway official, wished to reclaim the child. In January 1903, the Count and Countess were arrested and charged with the peculiar criminal offense of "passing off a child" *(Kindesunterschiebung)*. Their trial opened before the jury of Superior Court I in October.[51]

Proof of parentage was naturally the critical question. But how was it to be established? The putative biological mother, Cäcilie Meyer, had another son by the same putative father as the child in dispute. *Medizinalrat* Dr. Störmer suggested that a commission consisting of himself, his colleague Professor Dr. Strassmann, and a portrait painter should investigate the similarity between the alleged brothers. The court agreed. The commission also called on the services of the officer in charge of *Bertillonage* at the Alexanderplatz, Inspector Klatt. On one of the last days of the long trial, Dr. Störmer delivered the commission's report comparing the bodily details of the two boys:

> The form of the head, the form of the face, the behavior of the cheek bone, the shape of the ears, arch, course and hairiness of the eyebrows, behavior of the irises, shape and hairiness of the bridge of the nose, the form of the nose, the line and fullness of the lips, the form of the corners of the mouth, the course of the oral fissure, the formation of the teeth, shape of the hard and soft gums, the configuration and direction of the chin. Then the shape of the hands, form and length of the fingers and the nails, the course of the lines in the palms of the hands, the arch of the feet, and finally also the walk, were investigated.

The results of the comparison were inconclusive. While the commission found that the young Count's moderately long facial formation and ears resembled the Kwilecki family (the painter thought that the Kwileckis' ears had a decided "racial" quality), the bridge of his nose and the lines of his hands looked more like the servant's son. Both boys had the same kind of "genital abnormality," although the commission put little weight on this factor. The members concluded that they could not answer the question definitively one way or the other. The jury acquitted the Kwileckis of the charge.[52]

It is impossible for the modern reader not to see the disturbing implications of all of this measuring and classification of human beings. Beginning with the pioneering work of Cesare Lombroso, inventor of the idea of a genetically determined "born criminal" representing an anthropological throwback to more "primitive races," much of turn-of-the-century criminology had plainly illiberal affinities with the racial anthropology and "social" and "racial" hygiene then so much in vogue. Bertillon's system bore a close resemblance to Lombroso's criminal anthropology (Lombroso indeed welcomed *Bertillonage* with enthusiasm). Francis Galton, pioneer of the practical use of fingerprints, whose other principal scientific interests were evolutionary biology and eugenics, hoped to find racial patterns in fingerprints: he sought, for instance, "a more monkey-like pattern" in the fingerprints of Indians. In his recent book on the history of fingerprints, Simon A. Cole has shown the degree to which the racial typologies that British colonial officials brought home from India influenced their ideas about their domestic "criminal classes"—and indeed, influenced Lombroso himself. Hans Gross, the foremost expert on forensic science at the time, believed criminals to be such a threat to society that in 1913 he advocated the castration of all sex offenders and all young men in prison for violent crimes and the sterilization of alcoholics and those with a criminal disposition.[53] As the twentieth century would teach again and again, the effort to enlist science to rescue justice from human error and irrationality—the dearest wish, as we saw, of people like Werthauer, Sello, and Alsberg, as well as scientifically inclined police officers—was a classically "enlightened" project that yet harbored dangers of an unprecedented darkness.

Before the Kwilecki trial, however the career of the Alexanderplatz's principal reformer came to a lurid end. It is tempting to draw a symbolic parallel between the nature of the man and the nature of his work. In his commitment to professionalism and reform, coupled with his comfort with arbitrary measures, Meerscheidt-Hüllessem was virtually a stereotype of the vices and virtues of Prussian officialdom. If one thinks of the implications of all the measuring and classifying, the search for organization and control and secret knowledge in the "Criminal Album," the index of gay men, *Bertillonage*, and the elaborate plans for the detective's carrying case, perhaps it does not come as a great surprise that Meerscheidt-Hüllessem's subordinate Hans von Tresckow said that he "possessed the character of an intriguer." Early in his career Meerscheidt-Hüllessem had played an almost comically devious role as an undercover investigator of the villagers of Marpingen, who, in the context of the repression of Catholics of the 1870s, caused a nationwide sensation by their claim to have spoken to the Virgin Mary. Later he was almost fired when Police President von Richtofen caught him trying to assemble evidence of Richtofen's homosexual activity. Tresckow wrote that Meerscheidt-Hüllessem's income did not suffice to support his large family, and "he was obliged again and again to incur debts with people who were not irreproachable."[54] In the Sternberg trial, Meerscheidt-Hüllessem was exposed as one of several officers who had attempted to divert the investigation under the influence of Sternberg's hefty bribes. Perhaps for this reason, or perhaps out of grief from the death of his wife the same year, Meerscheidt-Hüllessem took his own life on 21 December 1900. He had already hinted at plans to do so in a letter to his (highly improbable) close friend, the campaigner for gay rights Magnus Hirschfeld. He left behind a testament, which, however self-serving, underscores the seriousness with which he took his enlightened measures:

> You know that I was a criminalist with body and soul, but in the decent sense, not one of those who find their joy in putting people away; it seemed much nicer to me to help, where I could combine this with the office. For my profession as such, in the good sense, have I lived; for it I want to die. The voice of the living man will achieve nothing, that of the dead man will sound like thunder . . . and so force the government to act.[55]

CHAPTER 5

"Were People More Pitiless Fifteen Years Ago?"

On the first day of 1910, the *Berliner Morgenpost* ran a feature expressing wonder at the transformation of Berlin in the past decade. "If one recalls the picture of our traditionless city as it offered itself ten years ago, it is almost like a vision out of old, old times." The article described those things in the Berlin of 1900 that would seem amusing to the reader of 1910: *Droschke* carriages and horse drawn streetcars (the *Pferdebahn*); the ungainly and awkward automobiles that had "certainly not been made for the transportation of the masses"; the electric bus "whose continuous accidents the Berliner greeted with only a contemptuous 'Aha!'"; and the scaffolding around Hallesches Tor and Potsdamer Strasse for the newfangled elevated trains. Germans were still laughing at Count Zeppelin in 1900; there was no radio; Madame Curie had not yet made her great discoveries. Who in 1910 could imagine such ignorance and deprivation? That the pace of life was growing faster was more than a cliché. In 1901 the German Post Office introduced the first form of teletype machine. It was capable of producing 24,000 words per hour. Five years later it could reach 100,000 per hour. In 1913 Germany had five times as many telephone subscribers as did France; a French observer noticed that Germans were too pressed for time to bother articulating whole words, but would say "m.w." instead of "machen wir" ("let's do it") to close a business agreement.[1]

Some items in the daily papers gave less conscious, if no less important, testimony to the changes in Berlin. Advertisements for department stores became ever more ubiquitous. The opening of Hermann Tietz's department store on Leipziger Strasse in 1900, near the former home of the Reichstag, had prompted Alfred Kerr to complain that the German people had given up politics for commerce; by 1910, Tietz had expanded to Alexanderplatz and the Frankfurter Allee. The Wertheim empire was even more extensive. Alexander Wertheim had his flagship store on Leipziger Strasse, with other branches on Oranienstrasse and Rosenthaler Strasse. Wolf Wertheim was on Potsdamer Strasse and Friedrichstrasse. The *Berliner Tageblatt* could run a feature entitled "Shopping: A new custom in Berlin"—using the *English* word "shopping." Berliners could get around from store to store with ever greater ease and speed. On 11 January 1910 it was reported that the electric underground and elevated trains had carried 54 million people in 1909. Perhaps it was this blur of commerce and rapid transit that led a Yale professor to claim in a lecture that Berliners were the typical Americans.[2]

Amid all the bustle there were victims. Transportation disasters—the fall of an elevated train from the tracks near Gleisdreieck station, or the remarkable number of plane crashes the *BZ am Mittag* managed to find and report—were common. Hardly a day went by without headlines like "Lovers' Double Suicide" in the Berlin papers. Suicide was also on the mind of the Hoteliers' Association of Germany, which addressed a request to those contemplating it, not that they not do it, but that they not do it in a hotel. But there was compassion in the air nonetheless. Berlin's police president was concerned about the abuse of horses that were made to pull overloaded wagons. "This sort of torment of animals," he said, "will in the future be particularly severely punished."[3]

This was Berlin at the end of the twentieth century's first decade: bursting with novelty, be it in science, in commerce, in engineering; be it in ethics or public administration. At the same time, the losers and the victims of the urban struggle were also ever-present, in the headlines about rail disasters and lovers' suicides, in naturalist fiction and theater, and not least in the hearing rooms of Moabit. The relationship between news, art, and life was complicated. Did the newspapers take up the stories of lovers' suicides so readily because they could be easily assimilated to the sensibilities of a nation that read (according to taste) the *Sorrows of Young Werther* or *Frühlings Erwachen?* Or did urbanites, frustrated in love, pattern their behavior on literary heroes? What was clear was that the ever-wider circulation of cheap newspapers, phonograph records, motion pictures, postcards, and a host of other forms of popular media was creating, for the first time, one national public from the German patchwork of class, religious, and geographic milieus. The new media and their new public created, in turn, a new kind of celebrity—and a new kind of culture war. The criminal justice system was at the center of it all.

A number of factors combined in the last peacetime years to cause German courts to treat offenders more mildly than they had ten and twenty years before. The most important was politics. The Social Democrats and (to a lesser extent) the Left-Liberals were in the ascendant in the last Wilhelmine elections. These parties were increasingly likely to view an individual lawbreaker as a morally blameless victim of social or medical circumstances, and they were increasingly likely to oppose the death penalty. Their growing political clout meant not only that their views on crime got a thorough hearing in parliaments and in the press, but that the conservative Prussian and Reich governments were concerned to appease them by liberalizing the criminal law. The Reich government, responsible for the major legislation, launched serious efforts at law reform; meanwhile, those in the Prussian government responsible for the day-to-day administration of justice—from ministers to judges and prosecutors—tried to present themselves to the public in a more moderate light. At the same time, new ideas about the uses of psychology in criminal law were being injected into the justice system—without any formal change in the laws governing, for instance, the defense of insanity. Bismarck's social insurance schemes had had the unintended effect of bringing the mental health of the working classes to medical attention; and the new criminology was spearheading a move away from traditional conceptions of personal responsibility, especially through such influential teachers and writers as criminologist and law professor Franz von Liszt. The courts were highly dependent on the evidence of expert medical witnesses, and thus inevitably became susceptible to the newer views on the psychology of personal responsibility.

Tying these medical and political threads together was the burgeoning mass press. The circulation of newspapers rose dramatically in the early twentieth century, and everyone from the minister of justice to the courthouse guards had to adjust to a press that grew ever more intrusive, aggressive, and critical. Conservative papers (Berlin's press was overwhelmingly Left-Liberal or Social Democratic) could only fight a rear guard action; they were ever more chagrined at the omnipresence of what they saw as an undignified, if not downright subversive publicity machine, ever more chagrined at the patent liberalizing of the criminal justice system and the shift away from retributive concepts of justice. In this chapter we will examine how these political, legal, professional, intellectual, and cultural factors worked together to transform the criminal courts of the last Wilhelmine years.

Stone among Stones

In 1905, Hermann Sudermann, playwright and chairman of the Berlin Press Association, published a new play in four acts entitled *Stone among Stones*, a melodrama about the redemption of an ex-convict. The central figure is a stonemason named Jakob Biegler, who, as the play begins, has just been released from a prison sentence for second degree murder; he had killed a man in self-defense in a fight over a woman. The Society for the Welfare of Ex-Convicts writes to a golden-hearted stonemason named Zarncke, who often employs released prisoners, asking if he will take Biegler in. Zarncke makes Biegler his nightwatchman, telling no one of Biegler's past. But Biegler is still subject to the onerous regime of police supervision of ex-convicts. One day, a malevolent police Commissar named Reitmaier comes to Zarncke's shop and reveals that one of Zarncke's employees is a killer. The workers have little difficulty guessing who it is, and several of them, led by the braggart Göttlingk, try to force Biegler to leave. Biegler and Göttlingk get into a fight when, once again, Biegler seeks to defend a woman from Göttlingk's insults. But the other stonemasons have realized that Biegler is a highly skilled colleague, and they intervene to persuade Zarncke to keep Biegler in the shop. The story ends happily.[4]

A year after the play's premier a real-life Biegler appeared on the scene in Berlin. Once again the influences of "life" and "art" ran both ways. If the real Biegler, a man named Wilhelm Voigt, seemed to be a product of Sudermann's pen, he would in turn be immortalized by writers of the rank of Carl Zuckmayer and actors like Heinz Rühmann and Harald Juhnke. The unknown Wilhelm Voigt would become the celebrated "Captain of Köpenick."[5]

Voigt, a trained shoemaker, was a small-time hood and con man who had spent most of his life in prison. In early 1906 he finished serving a 15-year hard labor sentence for armed robbery. Upon his release from the penitentiary at Rawitsch, the Society for the Welfare of Ex-Convicts wrote on his behalf to a golden-hearted shoemaker named Hilbrecht in the Mecklenburg town of Wismar. Hilbrecht agreed to give Voigt work, and later, echoing the fictitious Zarncke, he recalled that Voigt "conducted himself superbly and was a good, dependable worker and a sober and diligent person . . . Voigt had a workroom to himself and it was as if he belonged to the family. In the evening he sat with me at the table and read to me from the newspapers, which he could do very nicely . . . Not only Voigt's diligence but also his honesty left nothing to be desired. He had repeated opportunities to take money; I even trusted him with my cashbox key." But Voigt would stay with Hilbrecht for only three months. In May he was summoned to the Wismar police station and ordered to leave town; the reason was that, as an ex-convict, he constituted a public danger. The odd thing was that, while Prussian police had the authority to make such an order under a still-valid law of 1842, the police of Mecklenburg-Strelitz did not—and so this catalyzing event in Voigt's tale of woe amounted to an unlawful abuse of authority. Voigt spent the next several months wandering from his old home of Tilsit to Marienburg, Graudenz, Berlin, and Potsdam. Everywhere he could either find no work or the work he found was too punishing for his health, weakened as it was by so many years in the penitentiary. Finally he moved in with his sister in the working-class Berlin neighborhood of Rixdorf (today's Neukölln), and he found a job in a shoe factory. But bad fortune struck again: the Alexanderplatz expelled Voigt, not just from Rixdorf and not just from Berlin, but also from a long list of the surrounding suburbs. The reason was, once again, that Voigt's criminal record made him a danger to public safety and morality.[6]

With his plans to go straight thus in disarray, Voigt reverted to old habits. He decided that a suburban town hall would make a good robbery target. He examined several of these and finally settled on the town hall of Köpenick, southeast of Berlin. He researched the regular movements of small squads of soldiers in the greater Berlin area. He bought himself the components of a captain's uniform in several second hand stores. On the afternoon of 16 October 1906, with the aid of his captain's uniform and excellent acting skills, he stopped two squads of soldiers, ten men in all, near the Putlitzstrasse railway station in Moabit. He ordered the soldiers to follow him, and took them by train to Köpenick (thoughtfully stopping on the way to buy them beer) and on to the town hall. There, claiming to be acting on "all-highest command," Voigt used his soldiers to seal off the town hall and place the mayor and other officials under arrest. He also ordered the town treasurer to hand over the cash, a sum of nearly 4,000 marks. When he was finished, Voigt sent the officials and several of the soldiers by car to the police station at Berlin's Neue Wache. Voigt himself departed with the cash in several large sacks, but he did not have long to enjoy his new wealth. He was betrayed to the police by an old accomplice and arrested on 27 October.[7]

From 1906 to today, writers, historians, filmmakers, even soldiers, have taken the point of Voigt's story to be German reverence for uniforms and unthinking readiness to obey commands (never mind that Voigt himself was of a highly militaristic disposition, and a critique of Prussian militarism was the last thing on his mind). Some even rejoiced that "the highest soldierly virtue, obedience, continues unshaken in the army."[8] But underneath the vaudeville and the easy satire of the "Köpenickiad" lay something very different. It was the public *reception* of Wilhelm Voigt's case that was important. Thousands or millions of Germans were laughing *at* the credulous soldiers and officials, which itself suggests no very great reverence for their authority. And Voigt's trial, on 1 December 1906, offered an unexpected lesson about German society and its changing criminal justice.

News of the assault on the Köpenick town hall was a worldwide sensation and there was tremendous public and official interest in the trial. Most papers ran the transcript on their front page; hundreds of people were turned away from the courtroom, where places were reserved for high personages like Prussian Justice Minister Beseler and Reich Secretary of State for Justice Rudolph Nieberding. General Prosecutor Wachler from the *Kammergericht* was there, as were celebrity writers and journalists like Paul Lindau and Maximilian Harden. All reports noted that military officers filled the first rows of the public gallery. Voigt was defended by the capable team of Karl Schwindt and the young Walter Bahn, who took the case pro bono, doubtless aware of its advertising potential.[9]

The trial was one of the first major cases to be heard in the Jury Court Hall of the new courthouse on Turmstrasse. The room itself seemed to make a difference: reporters noticed it was "brand-spanking new and clean," and perhaps for this reason:

> to anyone who has experienced the practice of the great judicial events of the last twelve years as a spectator, the Berlin courtroom seemed in this sensational trial thoroughly decent and proper. No young lawyers squatted on the floor in Turkish manner, no ballerinas surrounded the president of the court like Raphaelite angels, and the Herr President only said "I ask for quiet" from time to time in order not to deviate from the prevailing custom.[10]

Everyone acknowledged that the calm had much to do with the cool control and strong sympathy for the defendant displayed by the presiding judge, Superior Court Director Dietz. Dietz's patient questioning laid bare the harshness with which the justice system had treated Voigt in the past. After some minor theft convictions as a teenager, Voigt had been given a twelve-year hard labor sentence at the age of eighteen for forging a few checks. Then from 1879 to 1889 he managed to stay out of trouble. He moved to Bohemia, married, had children, and worked steadily as a shoemaker. But in 1889 he fell back into old habits and was sentenced to thirteen months' imprisonment for theft and forgery. In prison he met a man named Kallenberg, who convinced him to join in a robbery of the cashier's office at the courthouse in Wongrowitz. They were caught in the act. Voigt's trial, before the Superior Court in Gnesen in February 1891, lasted only twenty minutes. The court took no account of the fact that Voigt had prevented Kallenberg from killing the policeman who caught them. Furthermore, the trial was marred by serious procedural errors. Voigt wished to call witnesses; the court did not let him. Afterwards Voigt wanted to appeal, but the official who was supposed to prepare the documents did not visit him until after the deadline had passed. The court in Gnesen had given Voigt the maximum sentence—fifteen years' hard labor—and after missing the appeal deadline, he was obliged to sit it out.[11]

Voigt's testimony about these past brushes with the law, confirmed in most respects by the official documents, made a visible impression on Judge Dietz. With the protocol of Voigt's Gnesen trial before him, Dietz confirmed that Voigt had summoned six witnesses, but none were examined; nothing in the protocol recorded that Voigt had waived his right to call evidence. Thus, said Dietz, "The verdict was, in fact, challengeable." As Voigt told of being driven from town to town after his release, Dietz became even more sympathetic. Walter Bahn read aloud from an article in the *Deutsche Juristen-Zeitung* by legal scholar Robert von Hippel, a student of Franz von Liszt's. Hippel harshly criticized the police supervision of ex-convicts, calling the practice "a means of furthering the development of career criminals," and he argued that Voigt "would have become an honest man" if he had not been expelled from Wismar. Dietz asked that the journal be passed to him, and he "read the professor's words with visible interest."[12]

The prosecution's legal analysis broke Voigt's assault on the Köpenick town hall into five separate offenses. Voigt was charged with the unauthorized wearing of a uniform, the unauthorized exercise of a public office, intentional and illegal confinement of the mayor and several other Köpenick officials, defrauding the town of Köpenick of 3,557.45 marks, and issuing a false private document "with the intention of securing a pecuniary advantage"—this last because he had given the Köpenick town treasurer a receipt for the money, signed with a false name. Voigt pleaded guilty to the first three charges, but denied that his motive had been to take the money. He claimed to the end that all he had wanted was a passport, which he had been unable to get from any authority, and that he concocted the elaborate plan to commandeer the Köpenick town hall only to get a supply of passport forms. He took the money as a last resort when he found there were no such forms in the town hall.[13]

The prosecutor, Superior Court II's Chief Prosecutor Wagner, seemed to be the only person unmoved by Voigt's hard luck story. In his closing address he called Voigt's stunt "an unparalleled assault on the military authority," which "was felt in broad circles to have shaken the authority of the state." There was a quirk in the legal evaluation of the case that struck most observers as perverse. The most serious of Voigt's charges was not the illegal confinement of the Köpenick officials, nor even the impersonation of an officer, but rather the issuing of a false private document—carrying a maximum penalty of five years' hard labor. Since all five offenses with which Voigt was charged arose from the same transaction, the appropriate punishment for the whole was to be determined solely by the most serious of the five. Thus Wagner requested that the court give Voigt five years' hard labor. Voigt, exhausted by his insistence on standing through the entire proceedings, could hardly follow his own counsels' vigorous defense.[14]

The judges deliberated longer than expected; when they returned, Dietz courteously apologized to Voigt for the wait with the words, "You gave the court a hard nut to crack with your deed." The court did not believe that Voigt had sought only a passport at the Köpenick town hall, and convicted him on all five charges. But the defense had persuaded the court that Voigt's treatment, especially at the hands of the Wismar police, partially excused his actions. The oral reasons for judgment contained a remarkable statement. Voigt was to be granted mitigating circumstances on the grounds that he "became a victim of circumstances *and of the existing state order,* and without the expulsions would perhaps still today be living as a shoemaker in Wismar." (Emphasis added) Rather than five years' hard labor, the court gave Voigt four years' imprisonment, arithmetically only half as serious a punishment. And if it was remarkable enough for a Prussian judge to refer to a convict as a victim of the state, something more remarkable was to follow. Voigt described in his memoirs what happened: "The president laid his black cap aside, took off his robe, came up to me at the barrier and wished me God's blessing that I might come through my sentence in good health."[15]

However remarkable, Dietz's gesture was important precisely because it symbolized the sea change that was under way in Berlin's legal culture. The roots of this change went back a decade, to the state's failure in the early and mid-1890s to sharpen the criminal law as a political tool. But the evolution of criminal justice had remained largely subterranean and unrecognized until 1906. Voigt's trial and the public reaction to it formed one of those moments in which a social change is first recognized by great numbers of people.

Four features of the public and official reception of Voigt's case were important: (1) most observers thought the Prussian justice system had became more merciful sometime between the 1870s and 1906; (2) most were coming to accept that a lawbreaker could be a morally innocent victim of circumstances; (3) Prussian officialdom went out of its way to treat Voigt gently; and (4) in response to the first three features, a right-wing critique of Prussian justice began to evolve, with its main proposition that the criminal courts and society as a whole were becoming "soft on crime." Let us look at these four points in turn.

Criticisms of the manner in which police and courts had borne down on Voigt in the past were ubiquitous after the trial. The melodramatic parallels to Sudermann's *Stone among Stones* were too obvious to miss. The *Vossische Zeitung* pointed out that Sudermann had "depicted the fate of a criminal who is released from prison, stands under police supervision, and tries to lead an honest life," although the *Vossische* thought Voigt showed that "reality is more inventive" than the writer's imagination. The *National Zeitung* imagined Sudermann would wish he had held his play back, as it would now receive a more friendly critical and public reception. Judge Dietz, as we saw, had publicly criticized the Gnesen verdict. Walter Bahn claimed that Dietz went so far as to say "today that judgment would probably not be possible." Paul Lindau recalled that Dietz "showed discretely but unmistakably that he found the Gnesen proceedings incomprehensible." Bahn himself referred to the twelve-year hard labor sentence which Voigt garnered at age eighteen as an example of "the pitiless justice of that time";

the left-liberal *Berliner Morgenpost* called it "a judgment whose hardness no court today would understand." Even stronger evidence of a shift in attitudes came from more conservative observers. A representative of the director of the Berlin criminal police wrote that the rules of police supervision "do not in general correspond to the modern criminal-legal view." *Das kleine Journal* was said to be the favorite newspaper of the Kaiser's entourage. Two days after Voigt's trial, it surveyed his record and asked plaintively "Doesn't one get a little dizzy at these numbers? Twelve years' hard labor; fifteen years' hard labor. It is as if each time a veritable lust for, and joy in, barbaric penalties filled this man's judges. Or were people in earlier years harder and more pitiless than today, forty years ago, and even fifteen years ago?"[16]

The second theme of the post-Voigt conversation was the increasing acceptance that an offender might not be morally responsible for his actions, that he or she could be the victim of a social environment. We have seen that even Judge Dietz and his chamber believed that Voigt had been a victim of "existing circumstances and the order of the state." There was a broad consensus in the press, including, eventually and grudgingly, the *Kreuzzeitung*, that the regime of police supervision of ex-convicts was largely at fault for Voigt's predicament. The *Morgenpost* said that Voigt's fate was "largely a product of human institutions," and that police supervision was "the real cause of the Köpenick attack." Paul Lindau asked, "Is the guilt his? Is it not really the persecutors who made him mad?" As hard-headed a journal as the *Berliner Börsen-Zeitung* recorded that "Berlin's criminal history has given us two such cases this year, which give us more than a little doubt about the justice and reasonableness of our world-order." The first case was that of the ruthless killer Rudolf Hennig (see below). Voigt was the second. "Both cases ask of our anxious conscience, would these people have ended up in the same way if they had been born sons of a commercial counselor?"[17]

The cabinet ministers watching attentively from the gallery, Director Dietz's startling gesture after sentencing Voigt to yet another stretch—this is not Brausewetter's "chamber of the dead" anymore. Dietz himself provides an example of how new jurisprudential ideas could percolate down to the courtroom. Although §268 of the Reich Criminal Code, the "false private document" provision under which Voigt was sentenced, made express provision for a lesser sentence in the event of mitigating circumstances, it is unlikely in the extreme that the legislators contemplated "being a victim of the state" as one of the possible grounds. In making the finding he did for the reasons he did, Dietz was acting more in the manner of the bold, innovative judge contemplated by Kantorowicz and the other writers of the free law school. He showed the same tendency when he justified mitigating circumstances in part because the offense the statute regarded as the most serious—issuing a false private document—"played in reality a secondary role." That Liszt student Robert von Hippel's article in the *Deutsche Juristen-Zeitung* appears to have so influenced Dietz's assessment of the case supplies an empirically traceable link between the ideas of the new sociological school and the practice of the Wilhelmine courtroom. So, too, the highly subjective orientation of the court's evaluation of Voigt's record and life history owed more to Liszt than to Karl Binding's classical school. For Binding, in keeping with the nineteenth-century liberal criminal law tradition, the only possible basis for punishment was the offense itself; he would have agreed with Gilbert and Sullivan's Lord High Executioner that the punishment should fit the crime. For the modern school, however, the punishment was to fit the *criminal;* an idea which drew Binding's characteristically vituperative wrath, especially when a lessening of punishment came in question.[18]

And in the wake of Voigt's trial, Prussian and German authorities worried about their past treatment of Voigt, or at least how this treatment appeared to the public. A week after Voigt's trial, Reich Secretary of State for Justice Nieberding wrote to Prussian Justice Minister Beseler to voice concern about the press reports of Voigt's Gnesen trial, that claimed the court had prevented Voigt from calling witnesses and launching an appeal. "The president of the criminal chamber," Nieberding went on, "is supposed to have confirmed the correctness of these claims from the documents." That the root of Nieberding's concern was public relations was abundantly clear. "With the great excitement that the case has caused," he observed, "it is not unlikely that the matter will come to discussion in the Reichstag." Nieberding suggested that Beseler might wish to forward "information on the facts" in the event that "the trial has been presented incorrectly." Beseler replied on 21 December with the official line of defense. It was true, he said, that the trial documents confirmed the court had denied Voigt his witnesses. But Beseler argued that this lapse could have had little impact on the outcome or sentence; the judgment rested in all essential points on Voigt's own evidence and that of his accomplice. Furthermore, the documents contradicted Voigt's claim that he had been prevented from applying for *Revision*. A protocol prepared by the prison inspector recorded that Voigt had officially waived his right of appeal on the day of the trial, and applied instead for a retrial. Two days later Voigt withdrew this application as well. He did not make another application for a retrial until 1899.[19]

But the state did not only seek to defend itself; in time the authorities launched their own bid for public favor. From the day Voigt began his sentence at Berlin's Tegel prison, clemency petitions on his behalf filled the justice ministry's mailbag. They came from around the world; even the mayor of San Francisco sent one on official letterhead. These requests were all denied. But on 10 July 1908, Justice Minister Beseler himself wrote to the first prosecutor at Superior Court II to ask if, since Voigt had served more than eighteen months of his sentence, the prosecutor would now recommend clemency. Beseler ordered the first prosecutor to "expedite" his report. The first prosecutor replied that he believed Voigt's four year sentence had already taken full account of the mitigating circumstances. But Beseler was undeterred. A few days later he wrote to the Prussian interior minister to say that "In consideration of the hardness of [Voigt's 1891 sentence] . . . and since after serving this sentence the prisoner had tried to find a place in civil life, I am inclined to support immediate clemency." In August, Beseler wrote to the Kaiser to make the case. The archive file contains two versions of the critical passage of Beseler's letter dealing with Voigt's 1891 sentence; both are revealing of the direction of his thoughts. The first version, which is crossed out in the draft, reads: "Although he had been previously sentenced several times, especially for theft, the facts of the case [in 1891] could scarcely have justified the highest legally permissible sentence. Voigt thus served more than he deserved." These sentences were replaced with one which significantly updated the analysis: "In all probability, *in accordance with today's views,* a sentence of this length . . . would not have been pronounced." (Emphasis added) The Kaiser was said to have shared the general amusement at Voigt's stunt, and he accepted Beseler's argument, granting Voigt clemency on 15 August 1908. Voigt was released from Tegel the following day. The Prussian minister of the interior informed Prussia's police forces that "there were no objections" to "the mildest possible application of police supervision in this case," and ordered in particular that "no difficulties were to be made for Voigt through limitations of the right to stay in a particular locality."[20]

Just as Voigt's trial had brought the recognition that German society, and with it its legal system, had grown gentler in the preceding quarter-

"Were people more pitiless fifteen years ago?" Wilhelm Voigt leaves Berlin's Tegel Prison in 1908. (Ullstein Bilderdienst)

century, so his release forced conservatives to see that they were losing the culture wars. The issues in these wars were broad and hard to separate. They were partly matters of morality and public media; this was an age in which cultural conservatives were driven to despair not only by such relatively traditional menaces as avant garde paintings, plays, and novels, "dirty" postcards, and leather-bound collectors' editions of pornographic illustrations, but by newer threats like the cinema and Germany's active and highly visible gay rights movement.[21]

Such issues were close neighbors of the criminal law. It did not escape the attention of conservatives that the sentencing practices of German courts were growing ever more lenient, nor that defenses of insanity were becoming more common, and certainly not that the popular press could create a cult following around killers and thieves—to say nothing of men who donned captains' uniforms to hold up town halls. It was the mass press that had the capacity to fuse all of the threads of the culture wars together and spread them to an eager public; and it was around sensational newsmakers like Wilhelm Voigt and Count Ferdinand von Zeppelin that the press began to create a truly national "public."[22]

The parallels between the public adulation of Count Zeppelin and Wilhelm Voigt were striking and drew much commentary. Not two weeks before Voigt was released from Tegel, Zeppelin had captivated Germans with the flight of Zeppelin LZ 4 over southwestern Germany, before the ship was forced down near the village of Echterdingen. While on the ground it was destroyed by a gust of wind and a subsequent fire. There followed a remarkable public campaign to raise money for a new airship, which was so successful so quickly that it became known as "the miracle of Echterdingen." Peter Fritzsche has described the material side of the cult that grew up around the Count: ordinary Germans sent hams, liqueurs, and woolen socks to his factory; his image was sold on postcards, cigars, cheese, and boot polish.[23] The same things happened with Wilhelm Voigt. While he was in prison, several Berlin newspapers organized public collections for him, and a wealthy woman assured him a pension when he finished his sentence. After his release a permanent crowd lingered outside his sister's apartment in Rixdorf; photographers were waiting at the prison gate and chased him everywhere else he went; he was the subject of a wax display at the famous Passage-Panoptikum in the Friedrichstrasse; a gramophone company paid him 200 marks to record his story; a restaurateur in Kreuzberg offered him free meals for a month if Voigt would only grace his head table. Eventually Voigt wrote his memoirs and made his living giving lectures and selling postcards of himself, sometimes depicted in evening dress, sometimes in captain's uniform.[24]

All of this public attention lavished on a notorious criminal, coming so soon after the "miracle of Echterdingen," was bound to provoke a certain gnashing of teeth in conservative circles. The *Leipziger Neueste Nachrichten* complained on 20 August 1908 that after "Count Zeppelin had just released us from the terrible fever-dream of the Eulenburg scandal," now "a new roll of film" had been placed on the "fast-changing projector that we call public life. Rrrr . . . another picture: Wilhelm Voigt, the Captain of Köpenick." And now the same people who had cheered the Count "stormed the streetcar in Berlin, in order to run after a released prisoner." Indeed, comparisons of Zeppelin and Voigt soon became a cliché in the conservative press. On 23 August the *Deutsche Tageszeitung* carried a Sunday supplement essay with the title "Zeppelin or Voigt?" The point was that the glorification of Wilhelm Voigt made Germans ridiculous in the eyes of foreigners—and Germans, with the insecurity of the "late-comer" nation, worried incessantly about what foreigners thought of them.[25]

The themes of "Zeppelin or Voigt?" fitted smoothly into an existing pattern of *Deutsche Tageszeitung* editorials. A week before Voigt's release the *Deutsche Tageszeitung* had run a leading article entitled "Confusions and Distortions," which rested on a contrast between "feminine" and "effeminate" qualities—the first desirable, the second not. "Everything sensational is unmanly," the paper proclaimed. "Just as in the middle ages old and young women loitered around the stocks and the gallows, today it is effeminate to seek and to make sensation in the courtrooms, in the criminal dives *(Verbrecherspelunken)*, in the back tenements *(Hinterhäuser)*, and the prostitute alleys *(Dirnengassen)*." It was one thing (good) to have "genuine compassion." It was quite another (bad) to show "distorted," and therefore "effeminate," compassion. It was "distorted compassion" when "so-called public opinion in part shies away from the application of punishments that deter to a sufficient extent"; when it shied away, in other words, from "retaliation" through the "infliction of sensations of physical pain" on "beastly monsters." A litany of cases in which the public had showed "distorted compassion" for serious criminals was emerging: the *Deutsche Tageszeitung* mentioned Carl Hau and Grete Beier. Hau was a lawyer who was charged with murdering his mother-in-law. A jury convicted him and he was sentenced to death, although the Grand Duke of Baden reduced the sentence to life imprisonment. That Hau was innocent soon became an article of faith for many liberals. Grete Beier was the daughter of the mayor of the small town of Brand in Saxony; in 1908 she was convicted and beheaded for the murder of her fiancé. But despite all the hoopla for these celebrity criminals, the *Deutsche Tageszeitung* concluded "we do not need to fall into pessimism." The reason was that "these poisonous weeds thrive better, much better, on the asphalt than in the fields . . . the rural population has kept itself much freer of the effeminate degeneration than have urban people, whose nerves are assaulted by so much that is wearing and corrosive." On 18 August the *Deutsche Tageszeitung* quoted gleefully from an article in a Social Democratic journal in which the author dissented from Social Democratic orthodoxy to argue that Grete Beier and Carl Hau were guilty and one ought not to regret their execution or serious punishment. On 19 August the leading article, written by an anonymous judge, was "Weaknesses and Damages in the Life of the Law." The article dealt with opponents of the death penalty, who had "a mostly unconscious inclination to excuse everything and to judge and deal with crime as mildly as possible," a "sickness of our time" which was "increasing, not decreasing." Once again the case of Grete Beier was invoked; the article turned to a jeremiad against the "number of cases in which the mental competence of the criminal is placed in question," a practice which "within the last decade has increased by a far greater percentage than has mental illness in general." The "Zeppelin or Voigt?" article argued that Germans, as well as people abroad, had to be made aware that "the cross section of the German character does not lie in the enthusiasm for Voigt, Grete Beier, Hau . . . but rather, now as in the past, in the serious men of quiet and unremitting work," men such as "Hutten, Luther, Fichte, Kant, and Bismarck," along with—naturally—Count Zeppelin, "proud in his modesty, honest and brave."[26]

These themes became the common property of the right wing press. The *Reichsbote* complained of the "senseless glorification of crimes and criminals," which the "serious" press displayed in Voigt's case as in (inevitably) those of Beier and Hau; like the *Deutsche Tageszeitung*, it concluded "it is really a sickness of the time, which has lost all consciousness of good and evil, all respect for law and justice." The *Leipziger Neueste Nachrichten* also called the "Voigt cult" a "symptom of a social and national sickness," and linked it to "the criminal and sexual-pathological trash literature" that was available for sale to Germany's youth on every street corner—and this among what had once been "the people of writers and thinkers." Once again correct behavior was gendered: the "unripe youth who poison their imagination with the reading of filthy ten-Pfennig booklets . . . later form the contingent of female 'criminal students' who storm the spectators' gallery for a morals trial, none of whom leave the room when the presiding judge . . . leaves it to the ladies present to disappear from the courtroom before the presenting of smutty postcards."[27]

Sex and publicity were not the only things that could enrage the polemicists of the Wilhelmine right. There was also madness.

Love, Madness, and Death in the Tiergarten

The Prussian Criminal Code of 1851 provided for a defense of mental illness in blunt terms that equated it to duress: "A crime or misdemeanor is not present if the culprit at the time of the deed was insane or idiotic, or if the free formation of his will was rendered impossible by violence or threats." Already by 1871 the Reich Criminal Code had sanitized this language and severed the connection to duress. Paragraph 51 of the new Code read: "Punishable conduct is not present if the culprit at the time of the commission of the act found himself in a state of unconsciousness or disturbance of the mental processes due to illness, by which the free formation of his will was rendered impossible."[28] But despite this doctrinal progress, as a matter of practice the defense of insanity remained something of a dead letter until the turn of the twentieth century. Then it came into its own.

Part of the reason for the rise of forensic psychology lay in shifting class perceptions of mental illness. The institution of social insurance in the 1880s brought large numbers of workers to medical attention for the first time; and so, as Joachim Radkau writes, in Germany more than any other country there came a "dramatic displacement of the social classification" of "neurasthenia." What had once seemed to be an affliction only of "brain workers" was now broadly diagnosed in the working classes. Certainly there were still critical class differences in the analysis of mental illness. The Heidelberg neurologist (and future DDP presidential candidate) Willy Hellpach wrote in 1904 that "the preconditions of nervousness" lay in bourgeois culture, while in working class culture one found "the preconditions of hysteria."[29] Since most criminal defendants came from the working classes, this psychological doctrine would play an important and increasingly visible role in Germany's courtrooms.

The other powerful motor for forensic psychology was the burgeoning field of criminology. By the end of the 1890s, the lawyers, physicians, sociologists, and anthropologists who assembled in groups such as the International Criminological Association were becoming increasingly interested in the mental conditions of lawbreakers. Franz von Liszt provided a considerable stimulus with a lecture before the International Congress of Psychology in 1896 on the problem of treating mentally deficient *(minderwertige)* defendants, those who fell somewhere between full responsibility and insanity as defined by §51. Within a few years, the amount of scholarly, associational, and law-reform activity on the subject had markedly increased.[30] The psychological ideas of the new criminology—disseminated to practicing lawyers and judges not least by Liszt's teaching activity as a professor of law in Berlin—began to become more conspicuous in daily legal practice.

Some statistics give an idea of the growing concern with psychological factors in the criminal law after 1900. Under §81 of the Code of Criminal Procedure, a prosecutor had the discretion to send an accused person for a psychological evaluation as part of the pretrial investigations. Between 1895 and 1897, approximately 250 persons per year were so evaluated in Prussia; by 1904–05 the number had doubled. In 1880 there were altogether 27,000 persons in Prussian mental institutions; in 1910 the number was 143,000. Psychology began to play a particular role in the judicial treatment of young offenders. A special young offenders' court was established in Berlin in 1908. Between 1909 and 1912, it commissioned an average of 767 psychiatric examinations per year; between 1912 and 1917, the average rose to 889.[31]

A Berlin criminal case with two installments—one in 1896 and one in 1905—neatly illustrated the human reality behind these statistics. In October 1896, two teenage boys, Bruno Werner and Willy Grosse, were charged with the brutal murder of the prominent lawyer *Justizrat* Meyer Levy. Both boys confessed to all essential elements of the crime. As they were under eighteen, their maximum penalty was not death but rather fifteen years' imprisonment; even hard labor was not an option. Not only the judge and prosecutor, but virtually all of the Berlin press and even the defense counsel seemed to regret the mildness of the provisions for young offenders. One of the defense counsel concluded his final speech by saying that "he could only decently join in the prosecutor's request for the application of the highest penalty," while the other complained that no Berlin lawyer had wanted to take the case. Unsurprisingly, Werner and Grosse received the maximum sentence.[32]

Yet there were many indications that all was not medically well with Willy Grosse. He claimed to have suffered as a child from rickets; when he was twelve he had been afflicted by convulsions. Among the expert witnesses summoned for the trial was one *Medizinalrat* Dr. Menger, who was supposed to give an opinion on Grosse's mental state. But the court dispensed with Menger's evidence, and no reason for this decision appears in any of the available accounts. Certainly no one drew any legal conclusions from Grosse's medical history or disconcerting courtroom behavior. The *Berliner Tageblatt* commented after the trial that while Werner had a "highly intelligent facial expression," followed the proceedings in court alertly, and knew how to use unusual expressions for a boy of his background, Grosse "made an impression of great stupidity." And yet "none of the gentlemen who were active in the course of the trial were doubtful that the big, strong lad knew of the criminality of his conduct." The nearly universal opinion was not that Grosse required more serious medical attention, but rather that "today's proceedings will form highly significant material for an expected amendment of the privileges which benefit youthful criminals." Even Maximilian Harden, who, as ever, distanced himself from the cries for vengeance in the liberal press, based his speech for the defense on the exploitation of the boys' labor and their adolescent longing for the things of this world, rather than on Grosse's evident illness.[33]

The case disappeared from public consciousness for eight years. Then in 1904, the gadfly-liberal newspaper *Die Zeit am Montag* ran a series of articles criticizing the brutal treatment of a prisoner who seemed beyond all doubt to be mentally ill. Since his arrival at Berlin's Plötzensee prison, the prisoner had been tormented by dreams in which his victim's widow swore vengeance; he had tried to kill himself; and he often needed to be restrained. But the prison doctors treated him as a malingerer. The prisoner was Willy Grosse. Over several months in the spring of 1904 *Die Zeit am Montag,* and the Social Democratic *Vorwärts,* broadened the attack. They alleged that the hygienic condition of the cells and workrooms at Plötzensee and the provision of food and drinking water were scandalous; and more particularly, that the two prison physicians, *Obermedizinalrat* Dr. Bär and *Medizinalrat* Dr. Pfleger, were guilty in some cases of negligence and in some cases of deliberate cruelty in the performance of their duties. The most sensational allegations concerned sadistic disciplinary penalties for mentally ill and epileptic prisoners, who were, according to *Die Zeit* and *Vorwärts,* routinely thrown into the cellars, beaten with broomsticks, and sprayed with water. A prisoner who (like Willy Grosse) was deemed a discipline problem was subject to solitary confinement or *Arrest,* which in its most severe form involved being kept in total darkness for up to six weeks, with only the stone floor to sleep on and bread and water to eat and drink.[34]

As a result of these allegations the physicians brought a libel prosecution against Karl Schneidt, two editors from *Vorwärts,* Julius Kaliski and Paul Büttner, and a former Plötzensee inmate named Fritz Ahrens who was now calling himself a reporter. The trial opened in May 1905. The evidence soon left little doubt that Willy Grosse was mentally ill. Even *Medizinalrat* Dr. Leppmann, the prison physician at the Moabit holding cells, allowed that Grosse suffered from "diminished mental capacity" and was "emotionally mentally ill" *(im Affekt geisteskrank),* which meant that he was in "a state of illness which lessened the understanding for the criminality of certain conduct, or lessened the resistance to criminal conduct." Certainly Leppmann thought Grosse should remain in prison rather than be transferred to a mental hospital, but he argued that this was in Grosse's own best interest, so that he could be released when his sentence was over. A medical expert called by the defense, Dr. König, went farther. König thought there was a "high probability" that Grosse could not bear full responsibility for his crime; "Such a person does not belong in prison!"[35]

The trial was fought with extraordinary bitterness on all sides, but the outcome was a surprise. After three weeks of evidence, which ran very much against them (despite the biased judge that Isenbiel's machinations had secured; see Chapter 1), the prosecution and the prison doctors agreed to an out-of-court settlement. Few doubted that this outcome represented a moral victory for the defendants. More importantly, the case demonstrated the changes in attitudes toward mentally ill offenders since 1896. Either forgetting or wishing to forget its earlier cries for vengeance, the *Berliner Tageblatt* concluded "there could no longer be any doubt that Grosse belonged in a mental hospital. But with this proof the wings of the indictment [against Schneidt et al.] were broken." When Karl Schneidt suggested that the prison regime did not correspond to the "state of modern science," even the private plaintiff Dr. Bär testified that "he certainly had seen cases in which he regretted that there was not a middle station between prison and hospital. In such cases it was a matter of diminished mental capacity *(geistige Minderwertigkeit)* and not mental illness *(Geistesstörung).*"[36]

The Plötzensee trial was the psychiatric counterpart of Wilhelm Voigt's case: it dramatized the inroads psychology had made in the courtroom in just a few short years, and like Voigt's case, raised the question of whether the criminal justice system existed fundamentally to punish or to reform the prisoner. Eight years later a remarkable session of the jury court of Superior Court I would dramatize the broad political and cultural resonance of this question.

The session opened on 22 September 1913, under the chairmanship of Superior Court Counselor Schlichting. With what would later seem dramatic irony, Schlichting began with a speech calculated to stiffen the jurors' sinews. He feared that some of the cases—which were "almost exclusively homicides"—might lead the jurors to be too merciful, to lose "the struggle with one's own moods and feelings." Compassion, or the feeling that "the whole wretchedness of humanity is taking hold of me," could play no role in the criminal court. Hearing the cases would put great demands on the jurors, but Schlichting asked that with "their best knowledge and conscience" they "help law and justice to victory," and not "let mercy go before law in a mood of humanity."[37]

After this speech the court turned its attention to its first case, that of Josef Ritter, who stood accused of murdering thirteen-year-old Otto Klähn. Klähn had been a delivery boy in a "colonial goods" shop in the Lützowstrasse in Berlin West. On 10 May 1913, the Saturday of Pentecost, Klähn had brought some beer to the apartment where Ritter was employed as a servant; Ritter gave the boy a generous tip. Ritter claimed that he had gone for a walk and encountered the boy again on the Lützow bridge. Klähn, said Ritter, offered to bring him oranges later that evening, and Ritter gave Klähn 30 pfennig to pay for them. That evening Klähn did an unusual thing: he lied to his employer in order to get away from work early. He went to Ritter's apartment in the Hohenzollernstrasse.

Only Ritter could give an account of what happened there. He claimed that Klähn tried to blackmail him for 100 marks. Ritter had been blackmailed before, and this time lost all composure: he strangled Klähn and dismembered the body. In the standard modus operandi of killers in a time before mass automobile ownership, he left the body parts in several packages, the legs in a public lavatory in the Kaiserallee (today's Bundesallee), the trunk and head at the Potsdam railway station in Potsdamer Platz. The various packages were found the next day.[38]

The police put considerable investigative talent to work on the case, including Inspector Wehn, who had brought Theodor Berger and Wilhelm Voigt to trial, and the young Criminal Commissar Ernst Gennat, who by the 1920s would become not only a celebrated figure in Berlin, but an important reformer and innovator in police procedures.[39] From questioning the other boys who worked at the colonial goods store, the officers found that Josef Ritter had a reputation for making "immoral propositions." One boy testified that he had met Ritter on Lützowstrasse around 9:00 P.M. on the night of the murder; Ritter looked anxious and asked the boy if he knew of a paper goods shop. This was enough for an arrest. Under interrogation at the Alexanderplatz, Ritter confessed.[40]

The bank of expert witnesses at the trial was formidable. The court summoned the Medical Counselors Dr. Leppmann, Dr. Hoffmann, and Dr. Störmer; the defense called several experts of its own, among them Dr.

Magnus Hirschfeld. There were forty other witnesses: friends and classmates of Klähn's, other medical men, and police officers. Because of the sexual nature of the offense, the court excluded the public from the hearing; but as in the Sternberg case, the press and certain well-known persons were allowed to remain. Among these spectators was Karl Liebknecht, who, the *BZ am Mittag* reported, justified his desire to remain on the grounds of "criminal-psychological study."[41]

As few important facts were in dispute in the trial, the outcome would turn on the assessment of Ritter's mental condition. As a *Leichendiener* (one who attends to the dead bodies) at an Austrian military hospital, Ritter had suffered blood poisoning and since then had been susceptible to fits of rage. The illness also seemed to have caused lapses in his memory. Ritter admitted that he had been "abnormally inclined" since his youth, and had always had a particular fondness for the wearing of women's clothing. On the second day the court heard from the expert witnesses. *Medizinalrat* Dr. Leppmann read out an Austrian medical report saying that Ritter's job as a *Leichendiener* had had severe effects on his mental balance. He had complained of terrible dreams which made him jump out of bed and babble "crazy things"; he suffered fits of rage and had to be put in a straightjacket. Another report from Graz in 1897 found that he was epileptic. On the basis of his own investigations, Leppmann reported that Ritter suffered from "a strong tendency to emotional arousal"; and he was "a born homosexual" with "a feminine streak . . . which expresses itself among other ways in that he likes to wear women's clothing and tell tales *(Märchen)*." The critical question was whether or not Ritter knew what he was doing when he killed Klähn, and here Leppmann found that "the defendant was moved to commit the deed by normal motives and had not lost consciousness, but rather retained a memory of the details." Yet at the same time, although nothing spoke against "the free formation of [Ritter's] will," Leppmann believed that Ritter had a "reduced reasoning capacity *(vermindert zurechnungsfähig),*" meaning that his "inhibitions are less and the emotions greater and hold longer than with a normal person."[42]

When Leppmann referred to the state of "reduced reasoning capacity" he was invoking a construct of psychologists that had been taken up by criminal law reformers and began finding its way into jurisprudence after the turn of the century, without ever being incorporated in the Criminal Code. Formally the law knew only the binary distinction of §51, that the defendant was either mentally ill to the point that he or she was unable to form the will to commit a crime, and hence was to be acquitted, or else was to be judged as fully responsible. In the former case, the defendant went to a hospital; in the latter, a prison. The effect of Leppmann's evidence would be to send Ritter to prison for a limited time, a time probably shortened by the mitigating factor of his evidence—an ironic result indeed, as he followed the common view of the time that the criminal law should protect society against incorrigible dangerous offenders through either permanent incarceration or hospitalization.[43]

Next came the testimony of Magnus Hirschfeld, one of the most unusual medical experts of Wilhelmine and Weimar Berlin. Hirschfeld devoted his career to the research of human sexuality and was a pioneer of the gay rights movement in Germany. In 1897, he founded a group called the Scientific-Humanitarian Committee to lobby for the repeal of section 175 of the Criminal Code, which made sex between men (but not between women) a criminal offense. Despite his own brushes with the law—he was prosecuted in 1904 for circulating a petition on sexual experiences among Berlin university students—Hirschfeld was in high demand as an expert medical witness and enjoyed good, even friendly, relations with senior police officers like Meerscheidt-Hüllessem and Hans von Tresckow. In the Ritter case, Hirschfeld was at pains to point out that the defendant's sexual orientation was in and of itself no ground to limit or exclude his responsibility for his actions. Hirschfeld agreed with Leppmann that this was no case of a sexual murder *(Lustmord)* or killing out of sadism, but he disagreed on the application of section 51. He testified that "the free formation of the defendant's will cannot be affirmed with the certainty required by the Imperial Supreme Court." But like Leppmann he hedged, adding that Ritter was "a mentally ill person who is dangerous to the community, who belongs in a closed institution."[44]

State Advocate Banning argued in his closing speech that, on the basis of Leppmann's report, Ritter was responsible for his actions but was afflicted by diminished reasoning capacity. Banning asked the jurors to affirm the question of guilt for unpremeditated murder *(Totschlag)* and, despite his acceptance of diminished capacity, to reject mitigating circumstances. Defense counsel Grunspach argued that Ritter's condition was "not a hateful aberration, but rather an aberration of nature." This "aberration of nature" had to be kept in mind when judging Ritter and in considering his mental state at the time of the killing. The jurors leaned toward the defense argument, insofar as they convicted Ritter of unpremeditated murder but approved mitigating circumstances, thus bringing the maximum penalty down from fifteen years' hard labor to five years' imprisonment. Banning asked for, and got, this maximum sentence. When the judges returned from their deliberations, Superior Court Counselor Schlichting explained the dilemma in which the combination of psychological evidence and legal provisions had placed the court: "The defendant is sick, but not so sick that he was not responsible; he is certainly guilty, but not so guilty that there are no mitigating elements." Schlichting acknowledged that "from the standpoint of protecting the community, many people will find this result unsatisfactory."[45]

He was right. "Where is the protection of society?" asked the headline in the *Lokal-Anzeiger*. To be sure, the decision of the court—"Action under the effects of emotion *(Affekthandlung)*—therefore only unpremeditated murder, not premeditated; strongly reduced reasoning capacity—therefore mitigating circumstances"—was legally correct. But it was out of touch with "the people's sense of law," and dangerously unmodern, for the reasons Leppmann and Schlichting had given. The *Kreuzzeitung* agreed, saying that "one could . . . come to terms with this result, if the culprit's reduced reasoning capacity also had the consequence that after serving his sentence he would be placed under sufficient supervision. But for this, the current law offers no surety."[46]

After Ritter's trial, the jury court had several less sensational cases on its docket, but the outcomes continued to provoke a low rumble in the conservative press. A man who shot and killed his girlfriend out of jealousy—an act the *Kreuzzeitung* called "the annihilation of a blossoming young human life"—was given five years' hard labor for second degree murder. A man named Bruno Bierwagen who had killed his wife was found guilty of committing grievous bodily harm with deadly outcome and sentenced to eight years' hard labor. This was not in itself a mild sentence, but there was much about Bierwagen that might have led one to expect a worse outcome. He had an extensive criminal record. The police had found him as he sat in prison under an assumed name, serving time for counterfeiting; and he had already served an eight-year hard labor sentence for killing a watchman in 1898. A Superior Court judge complained in the *Kreuzzeitung*: "After he serves his sentence, a third human life can fall victim to him. Who can then escape the call for a better protection of the community? In such a case who can believe in the capability of criminals to be rehabilitated?"[47]

On Friday, 3 October, the jury court reached the final case on its docket.

Hedwig Müller was twenty years old, employed as a shipping clerk in a bookstore. She stood accused of luring her boyfriend, nineteen-year-old Georg Reimann, to the Tiergarten and killing him with two shots to the back of the head. The first thing reporters noticed about her when she appeared in the dock was that she was unusually good-looking. Hugo Friedlaender wrote that if Homer came back from the dead, he would see the "strikingly beautiful" young woman as a siren; the *Berliner Morgenpost* gushed that "a six-month stay in the cells of the investigatory prison has not been able to steal anything from her captivating appearance." Beauty was not all that the commentators noticed. "To her undeniable external attractions," the *Morgenpost* continued, "are added an intelligence and a mental dexterity" which, as even Judge Schlichting felt free to remark, "raise her from her surroundings and cause her to appear doubly interesting."[48]

While in custody awaiting trial, Müller had written, at the examining magistrate's request, a kind of autobiography. Schlichting read this autobiography into the record on the first day of the trial. Although it was certainly not intended to be so, this life story proved to be the master stroke of the defense. In the overwhelmingly male milieu of the court and the press it won over any whom Müller had not already conquered through her appearance.

"I, Hedwig Lucie Marie Müller, was born on 4 April 1893," she began. The theme of her story was mental illness; her own and her family's. Because of a "nervous illness" in her twelfth or thirteenth year, she was unable to remember anything of her earliest childhood. Her mother told her that she had been a lively child with an unusual talent for acting. Her father was an architect, following the traditions of the Müller family, artists and architects for many generations. Unfortunately, so Hedwig wrote, the very success of these men was fatal: "Through degeneration" and because "the extraordinary gifts and intelligence of all the men brought them a high income" and left them exposed to the temptations of "gambling away and squandering countless sums," the family had descended "from the greatest heights to the current position." This information came to Hedwig Müller through an aunt on her father's side of the family, who "herself very sensitive, had taken this blow very hard and worked seriously on herself to suppress any weak-mindedness she might have inherited." Her father had succumbed to the family "weak mindedness" when Hedwig was a child. She had two half-brothers who, despite the difficult family circumstances, had

"Beautiful sinner": Hedwig Müller.

worked their way to good positions as engineers; but "this tough energy to rise out of nothing brought the oldest brother a serious nervousness, and he longed to shake off his burden as fast as possible." Both brothers left home and Hedwig and her mother were forced to fend for themselves. She worked for a time for a dentist and then for a lawyer before finding the position with the bookstore.[49]

In the summer of 1911 she met a prosperous doctor named Leo Sternberg and eventually began an affair with him. In January of 1912, however, the picture was complicated by the arrival of a third party. Georg Reimann was hired as a messenger at the bookstore. Reimann and Müller shared a work space and soon were getting along very well. Reimann brought her candy and fruit, and, so Müller said, "read my thoughts," but the blissful interval was short-lived. Reimann was of a jealous disposition; when he learned of Müller's relationship with Sternberg he became abusive, tormenting her at work and intercepting her letters. He threatened to reveal her affair with Sternberg to the owner of the bookstore, thereby costing Müller her job. Finally, Reimann claimed from her "a one time payment for his silence," but not in money. Müller went to Reimann's apartment, and, Friedlaender wrote, "the depiction of the events [there] must be omitted for reasons of propriety."[50]

Eventually Reimann was fired from the bookstore, but things only got worse for Müller. Reimann continued to abuse her and stalk her. On one occasion he saw her entering Sternberg's apartment. He waited until she came out, and then stole her key to Sternberg's flat. Müller claimed that she became so distressed she decided to kill herself; but she also wanted to get Sternberg's keys back. She made her plans with cool deliberation. She wrote to Reimann and arranged a rendezvous for the night of 7 March 1913 in the Tiergarten, so that he could return the keys. She went to Wertheim's department store and bought a revolver; she went to another store and bought twelve rounds of ammunition. On the evening of 7 March she said goodbye to her mother, wrote a last letter to Dr. Sternberg, and went out.[51]

Reimann was nervous, and told his sister he thought it was strange that Müller had suggested they meet at 10:00 P.M. rather than 8:30. Nonetheless he met her at the appointed hour at the corner of Wullenweberstrasse and Jagowstrasse, on the north bank of the Spree in Moabit. From there Müller and Reimann walked to the Lichtenstein bridge over the Landwehrkanal, in the southwest corner of the Tiergarten near the zoo. Müller's written version of events had it that Reimann refused to return the key and demanded that she go home with him. She refused and left him; he ran after her, crying. Feeling dizzy she leaned against a tree and pulled out the revolver. Reimann lunged at her and tried to grab the revolver, yelling "For God's sake! Then I will shoot you and come after!" There was a struggle; Müller said that she heard several shots and knew nothing after that. She claimed that Reimann had killed himself. Three witnesses heard the shots and appeared seconds afterwards. They found Georg Reimann lying face down, blood trickling from his head. Next to his body lay a revolver. A foot or two away from the body Müller stood motionless; when they asked her what had happened, she fainted. Soon the police arrived.[52]

Müller was fortunate to know Dr. Sternberg. On the morning after Reimann's death Müller's mother summoned Sternberg to their apartment. When he learned what had happened, Sternberg got in touch with a lawyer named Ledermann, who in turn made inquiries with the police. The police told Ledermann that they thought Reimann's death was a suicide. Müller was visibly cheered by this news. But then Legal Physician Dr. Hoffmann's autopsy revealed that Reimann had two bullet wounds in his head, either one of which would have been instantly fatal. There was no possibility of suicide. The police turned their attentions back to Müller. Sternberg stood by her, providing her with a defense of a caliber she would otherwise have been unable to afford: she was represented in court by the distinguished *Justizrat* Leonhard Friedmann (cousin of Fritz), assisted by Ledermann.[53]

As with the Ritter case, evidence concerning Müller's physical and mental health was crucial to the outcome of the trial. On the first day, several witnesses testified to Müller's propensity to sudden fainting spells. A dentist for whom she had worked testified that without any warning signs she would sometimes pass out and lie as if dead for a few minutes. Similar testimony came from an old friend, now "Frau Superior Court Judge B." Müller's mother said that one of Hedwig's uncles had shot himself out of fear of illness, and that Müller's father had been "weak-minded" and prone to spending whole nights pacing. A Dr. Steinitz testified that he had treated Müller for St. Vitus' Dance when she was a child, and that the year before her trial she had complained to him of nervousness and sleeplessness. Her nervous condition had so struck him that he had asked, "What is with you, have you had annoyances, or worries, or have you speculated on the stock market?"[54]

The third day of the trial belonged to the expert witnesses. Müller's psychological state was the subject of a report from the neurologist Dr. Toby Cohn. Cohn testified that Müller was "a genetically strongly burdened person." He referred to her father's mental illness, her half-brothers' "nervousness," and her uncle's suicide, and added that her mother, too, had once attempted suicide. Müller showed a series of symptoms—obsessions, trembling fits, fainting spells—which together were called the "hysterical *Globus*" or *"Kugel."* "Objectively," she suffered from a disturbance of the reflexes and of the sensitivity of the skin; one side of her body was less sensitive than the other. "When one puts it all together," said Dr. Cohn, "one must assume the presence of a serious hysteria." What did this mean for her legal responsibility? Cohn thought there was "a high probability that the defendant acted in a hysterical trance *(Dämmerzustand)*." Cohn likened this condition to sleepwalking or feverish hallucinations. "In such a condition the consciousness is not excluded, but only restricted," he said. In someone as severely hysterical as Müller, the firing of a shot could certainly trigger such a trance. "The defendant therefore . . . found herself in a trance and thus in a condition of mental activity which excluded the free formation of the will." Of course, Cohn's report assumed the honesty and accuracy of Müller's testimony that she had not fired the first shot, or at least had not done so with the deliberate intention of hitting Reimann. Nonetheless, the *Berliner Morgenpost* found Cohn's testimony so significant that on the following day its headline for the trial read "The Expert Reports in the Murder Trial. Hysterical Trance."[55]

Neither the prosecutor, State Advocate Gysae, nor Superior Court Counselor Schlichting were content with Dr. Cohn's opinion. Schlichting was skeptical that a "normal" person would not have responded to the shock of events just as witnesses suggested that Müller had. And he suggested that "such a deed can . . . follow from normal motives, and if the person involved can still remember the details, a disturbance of the mental processes is not to be assumed." State Advocate Gysae wondered if "an hysterical trance does not exclude the possibility that after a short time the person involved can recount so many details of the events, as the defendant did to the three witnesses?" And he added "Is the accused, in her serious hysteria, not a public danger?" Cohn denied the first question and responded to the second that an hysteric was as such no more dangerous than an epileptic or an alcoholic.[56]

The court also heard from *Geheimer Rat* Dr. Kortum, who bore the title of Directing Physician of the Dalldorf Mental Institution. Dr. Kortum had observed Müller in July and had come to the conclusion that she was an hysteric. His opinion was a few degrees more cautious than Cohn's and correspondingly more to the liking of the judge and the prosecution. He admitted the "limited possibility" that Müller had been in an hysterical trance at the time the last two shots were fired—assuming that her account of the events was true. It was consistent with what was known about the hysterical trance that, as she awakened from the condition at the arrival of the three witnesses, her consciousness went back to the last event before the onset of the state, the firing of the first shot, and she said "he shot me!" A normal person, said Dr. Kortum, would register horror or despair in such a situation, rather than simply appearing stunned or vacant as Müller had. On the other hand, if Müller's account was not true, then there was no basis for assuming the "exclusion of the free formation of her will." But, invoking the newly-minted category, he added that she was likely afflicted by a "reduced capacity to reason." Asked by Gysae whether Müller was mentally ill to the extent of constituting a public danger, Kortum declined to give an opinion.[57]

Müller needed all the support she could get from the psychological evidence because the other evidence went very much against her. *Medizinalrat* Dr. Hoffmann gave the results of the autopsy on Georg Reimann, with the damning conclusion that "anyone who has suffered one such shot [to the back of the head] is not in a position to fire a second one." What was more, according to Hoffmann, Reimann would have had to contort himself in a difficult and unnatural manner to be able to fire even one of the shots. Also damaging was a letter Müller admitted writing to Reimann on 3 March in which she said, "You or I—one of the two of us makes too many in the world."[58]

On Tuesday the case reached the closing arguments. State Advocate Gysae began with a surprising admission. He said that the evidence would not support the contention that "we are concerned here with a planned, premeditated, treacherous murder." The Imperial Supreme Court had repeatedly ruled that the prosecution had to prove "premeditation at the moment of the deed" to sustain a charge of murder; in this case "at the moment of the deed all premeditation was absent." He asked therefore that the jury find Müller guilty of unpremeditated murder. He also asked them to find that there were mitigating circumstances. "She is hysterical and was tortured until she bled, to the point of wishing to extinguish her own life," he said, adding "in his last days Reimann was not an especially admirable member of humanity." Still Gysae carried on his feud with Dr. Cohn, whose evidence had caused him "physical pain" and was "without a doubt completely wrong *(verkehrt)*. The psychiatric gentlemen see only the sick . . . But God be thanked the majority of people are still normal." An expert witness who "like Dr. Cohn does not have the courage to face the consequences, does not deserve to be heard." Gysae suggested that Dr. Kortum had grounded his report more carefully by saying that Müller could have been in a state of "hysterical trance" at the time of the shooting only "if one holds [her] statements to be true," which Gysae certainly did not. Here he effectively turned Hedwig Müller's intelligence and self-assurance against her. "She is an extraordinarily gifted person," he said; "You have yourselves heard how she always found an answer in fabulously clever ways." He countered her own storytelling, her reliance on her own experience, with some of his own. "In my professional activity I get a look at hundreds of different situations," he told the jurors; and on this basis he could say that no mentally ill person could ever get through life as successfully as Hedwig Müller did. But he rejected the notion that following Cohn's opinion would be more merciful for Müller: "There can be no question at all that I want to send the defendant as mentally ill to an institution." Better that she get a short stretch of prison behind her.[59]

For the defense, *Justizrat* Friedmann emphasized the psychiatric evidence. "You will not be the only ones," he told the jurors, "who will be astonished that the prosecutor has requested a guilty verdict." Wide circles of the population, to say nothing of "the men on the defense bench," were similarly amazed: "Such a request, following the opinions of the psychiatric expert witnesses, is scarcely comprehensible and is irreconcilable with the whole course of the proceedings, the prehistory of the trial, and the results of the evidence." The applause with which the spectators greeted his speech suggested Friedmann was correct that sympathies were running in Müller's favor, although the report on the front page of the *Berliner Morgenpost* was a shade cooler: "It was in no way surprising that the prosecutor dropped the indictment for premeditated murder and pleaded for unpremeditated murder with approval of mitigating circumstances. After the results of the evidence, nothing else was to be expected." But the jury took longer than expected to reach a verdict, and, as the *Morgenpost* reported, "one began to feel in the room that the scales had tipped against the defendant . . . The many people who had expected a verdict of 'not guilty' became uncertain in their opinion."[60]

After two-and-a-half hours the jurors returned. They had complied with Gysae's request, finding Hedwig Müller guilty of second degree murder, with the approval of mitigating circumstances. In the sentencing hearing Gysae argued that there were two sources of mitigating circumstances: Müller had been in a state of reduced mental capacity and in a position, partly through her own fault, but partly not, from which she did not know how to extricate herself. Certainly it was a matter of a human life, "but one must consider, of which human life? Of a person who had tormented and persecuted the defendant." In consideration of Müller's youth he asked for a sentence of one year and six months' imprisonment, with at least some allowance for the time she had already served. The court imposed a more severe sentence, but one still well under the maximum: thirty months' imprisonment, of which six months could be counted as served. In its reasons for judgment the court drew on both environmental and medical arguments. Müller's story was in part an urban cautionary tale: "She came to the big city, where the temptations appeared before her, and where a particular control through reliable girlfriends would have been especially necessary. The ground was prepared for her." When Reimann showed his nastier side, Müller's "hysterical nature" drove her to drastic measures to be free of him. "In this state she committed the deed . . . Thus, the court, in the consideration that she, despite her intelligence, possessed a limited moral education and found herself in a desperate state, since she had fallen victim to a blackmailer, and in the further consideration that she was intellectually close to Dr. Sternberg but morally closer to Reimann, believes that it should impose a sentence of middling range."[61]

The mild sentence and the prominent role of the psychiatric experts, following so close upon the trials of Ritter and Bierwagen, provoked howls of mockery and contempt from the right. The headline in the Free-Conservative *Post* was clear: "Expert witness mischief." "Today," the *Post* told its readers, "we no longer have any major criminal trials in which the expert witnesses do not parade at the end of the proceedings," even if it were just to "contradict each other in full view of the public." The *Post* believed that psychiatric experts were unnecessary: the jurors in Hedwig Müller's trial "were men enough to make the decision on their own." It was scathing about Toby Cohn: "It seems that one cannot treat the nervously ill for years on end without a certain wear and tear on one's own nervous system." These views were common across the right and center of the journalistic spectrum. A judge wrote in the *Kreuzzeitung* that the Ritter, Bierwagen, and Müller trials "allowed the need for a reform of the criminal law or the law of madness to emerge particularly crassly." Although the jury did not follow Dr. Cohn's opinion and at least convicted Müller of a criminal offense, it was not impossible that another jury might give someone like Müller "a free pass" for the commission of endless future crimes. The *Tägliche Rundschau* fumed over the "bewildering deployment of the 'soul-experts,'" and "the mists" of Cohn's evidence.[62]

Hand in hand with this critique of the application of psychology to the courtroom went the sort of hostility to ostentatious learning that was and is so often an element of conservative thought. The *Post* editorialized:

Just follow sometime the explanations of the expert witnesses who let themselves be heard in court! Take a careful look at technical expressions and consider whether the normal brain of a juror is in any kind of position to take in all of that which is expected of him. In the course of a half-hour he is supposed to master all of the scientific material which the distinguished expert playfully commands! In this short space of time he is supposed to decide on mental and psychological values and grades, which can only be recognized by the initiates! "Hallucinations," "serious hysteria," "typical trance," "free formation of the will," "conditional possibility," "reduced capacity to reason"—so many concepts, so much confusion! Our jurors should be spared such chains and traps if they are supposed to find the law.[63]

The figure of Hedwig Müller herself was a source of considerable theorizing. The Berlin correspondent for the *Kölnische Zeitung* thought that Hedwig Müller's "type of woman" was so interesting because "she embodies something absolutely modern." She was modern in her readiness to give "logical" explanations, especially concerning "that which . . . in the new-Berlin style she calls her 'psyche.'" Her social striving was also modern: "Having come from low circumstances," she used her education "chiefly to make herself interesting." As much as she might aspire to the world of Dr. Sternberg, it was likely she got involved with Reimann out of a desire to return to the social circles from which she came. Naturally her love life was also an essential component of her modernity; perhaps she had two lovers because "she also held that to be a modern requirement." But the most modern thing about Hedwig Müller was her relationship to the publicity machine. The *Kreuzzeitung* vented its spleen about the "feuilletonistic depictions in which the woman charged with a grievous blood-guilt was painted thus: 'A chic hat and coat, totally the type of the sweet little thing,' and in which one chatted about the 'beautiful sinner.'" *Germania* feared that when "the revered 'beautiful sinner'" was released from prison she would, Wilhelm Voigt-style, be able to secure her future through "the promotion of the press." In light of this kind of spectacle, "the 'publicity' of trials has become virtually a farce."[64]

The right-wing press seldom missed an opportunity to score anti-Semitic points, and in the case of Hedwig Müller it saw its opportunity with Dr. Leo Sternberg. Most of the press reports had not given his full name, but rather abbreviated it to "Dr. St." In a manner reminiscent of anti-Semites at the time of August Sternberg's trial, conservative papers jumped on this practice. "While the right-wing press referred to the disconcerting exceptional position of Dr. Leo Sternberg," wrote the *Kreuzzeitung*, "the socialist press seemed to find it absolutely in order. On what grounds? We will leave the question open." The *Deutsche Tageszeitung* wondered "What public materialistic notion of life is it, that something can be 'given' to a girl through money, jewelry, visits to the theater, and travel letters, when she sells her woman's honor for it!" It wondered why "that girl's" becoming "the prostitute of a well-situated man of a foreign race," was spoken of as if it could not be changed or bettered. Did decency "depend only on the outer behavior and spending money"?[65]

Indeed, resignation was the characteristic tone of conservatives in late 1913 as they reflected on Hedwig Müller and Josef Ritter. Gone was the fire-breathing eagerness to suppress urban vice and sentence criminals to hard labor and diets of bread and water. The right now knew that it had lost, or at least was in the process of losing. In an editorial on psychoanalysis, the *Post* lamented, "The weak are cared for, the strong neglected, one turns one's attention to failure, fulfillment of duty is neglected . . . One speaks of the duty of the state to the sick criminal—but on the duty of the individual to the community one is silent." The *Kreuzzeitung*, with the motto "Forward with God for King and Fatherland" emblazoned on its masthead, complained that the sentences in the Ritter and Müller cases were not "the right atonement," but sighed that these judgments were products of the time, like "the struggle against the death penalty." The psychiatric experts, too, had risen with this current, "which more and more shrinks from measuring the punishment to the total severity of the deed."[66]

The verdicts of the jury court session of autumn 1913 were all the more remarkable in that presiding judge Counselor Schlichting himself hardly demonstrated much sympathy for the newer criminological ideas. He had urged the jurors at the outset of the session not to let "mercy" get in the way of "law," and it is clear from the transcripts of Müller's trial how firmly Schlichting believed in her guilt. He probably sympathized with the editorial positions of the *Kreuzzeitung* and the *Post*. Yet he presided over this string of mild judgments in serious cases, and given the opportunity to impose stricter sentences in several of them, including Müller's, declined to do so.

Here is the most dramatic illustration of the limits on the power of any one component of the late Wilhelmine judicial system, even a component with all of the institutional power of the president of a jury court. Other elements in the system—the growing prestige and scientific muscle of the expert witnesses; the press, which could give voice to popular sentiments; the jury, which could bring those sentiments directly to the act of judgment—were themselves simply too powerful for the state, at least as represented by the prosecution, to have things all its own way.

The Full Weight of the Law

The controversy sparked by the autumn 1913 session of the jury court did not soon fade. In January 1914 the debate reached the Prussian House of Representatives. There the Free Conservative delegate Delbrück complained that "it is certainly a very modern striving that in sentencing and punishment one speaks only of the purpose of betterment and of influencing people." That was all very nice if it worked, he said. "But as soon as you take away the element of deterrence from the punishment, it altogether ceases to be a punishment." Karl Liebknecht, as we saw, had been permitted to watch the Ritter trial for the sake of scientific study. His intervention in the Prussian House debate showed how expert testimony, especially from psychologists, had become one of the essential political divisions in criminal justice. Noting that he had often spoken in previous years of the importance of training judges to have "a political backbone and social understanding," Liebknecht argued that "the next most important thing" was to inculcate respect for "the complications of our life and the entire business of the world, the recognition that ultimately one is not, as a judge, called upon to pronounce authoritatively on everything and everyone." He denounced the "reactionary press" and the "storm" of criticism of psychiatric experts occasioned by Hedwig Müller's trial. Such criticism, he said, was short-sighted, "and in the final result, if it should go farther in judicial circles, it will only damage the judiciary itself."[67]

It was clear by 1914 that the expert witness had arrived; so too had the importance of defendants' social circumstances. But the trend to "mercy" in the late Wilhelmine courts was by no means irreconcilable with the often disturbing randomness of judicial outcomes, which we surveyed in the previous chapter. Sometimes these phenomena were two sides of the same coin. In 1910 Max Alsberg represented a young hairdresser named Hans Jünemann, who was accused of stabbing his girlfriend, Alice Rakowski, and taking 65 marks form her cash box. Jünemann claimed that Rakowski had begged him to put an end to her life and that the couple had made a suicide pact. Alsberg argued for the application of §216 of the Criminal Code, "killing on the express and serious demand" of the victim; rather than the penalty of death for premeditated murder, the section stipulated a minimum penalty of three years' imprisonment. But the jury did not believe Jünemann and he was convicted of premeditated murder and sentenced to death. Alsberg succeeded in getting the verdict overturned by the Imperial Supreme Court in Leipzig, and found some new evidence which made Jünemann's story of a suicide pact appear more plausible. At Jünemann's second trial the jurors opted for unpremeditated murder with a recommendation of mitigating circumstances, so that, as in the cases of Ritter and Müller, the maximum sentence dropped from death to five years in prison. As Superior Court Counselor Claude read the judgment, he grumbled that the court "saw no reason to go below the already disproportionately low maximum sentence set by the law." Even the *Berliner Tageblatt* thought that someone who took a life without sufficient cause should meet "the full weight of the law" so that "the feeling of responsibility remains, and the respect for the individual human life does not sink deeper than it already has in the circles of jaded young lovers of the type of Herr Jünemann."[68]

There were still defendants in murder trials who fell through all the safety nets, were convicted, sentenced to death, and executed. The best known example in late-Wilhelmine Berlin was Rudolf Hennig. In December 1905, Hennig lured a domestic servant and waiter named August Giernoth to a meeting on the pretext that Hennig could find Giernoth a good job; all Giernoth needed to do was gather up his references and pay Hennig a surety of 500 marks. As the two walked through the woods by Wannsee, Hennig shot Giernoth and took his papers. On 6 February 1906, when two police officers went to arrest him, Hennig escaped and fled over the rooftops of Prenzlauer Berg. Like Voigt's capture of the town hall, Hennig's bold flight became the subject of a cottage industry of jokes, music hall routines, and newspaper contests. He was finally arrested in March 1906, in Stettin, and went on trial in Potsdam in early summer. As far as one can tell from the surviving accounts of the case, Hennig was a defendant for whom very little could be said. The evidence of guilt was overwhelming; he showed no sign of any physical or mental illness, nor was there any obvious mitigation to be found in his personal circumstances. He was sentenced to death and executed four days after the trial of Wilhelm Voigt.[69] A similar case in 1911 led to a similar result. A man named Albert Hartmann attacked and murdered a woman in the Stölper Forest, in order to rob her of 10 marks. The jury convicted him of murder and the court sentenced him to death, finding "the defendant acted from low motives. In order to obtain a minimal sum of money, he strangled a poor, weak woman."[70] As with Hennig, there was little to say on Hartmann's behalf.

But for all the randomness—and the occasional beheading of a convicted murderer—there could be no doubt of the main trend in the criminal courts of late Wilhelmine Berlin. The great majority of archival records of late-Wilhelmine murder trials show results consistent with those in the Ritter and Müller cases. In 1907 the jury of Superior Court III heard a case strikingly similar to Jünemann's, in which a man named Waldeck was charged with killing his girlfriend. The indictment was raised for premeditated murder; the prosecutor allowed that question to go the jurors, although he recommended a conviction for unpremeditated murder. The jurors found Waldeck guilty of "killing on express demand" under section 216. The court sentenced Waldeck to five years and two weeks of imprisonment rather than the minimum sentence of three years, as "less serious cases are conceivable." In 1909 a man named Grabowski killed his wife and was convicted of second degree murder with the recommendation of mitigating circumstances; the court gave him a sentence of three years' imprisonment, less seven months for pre-trial custody—well under the maximum. The outcomes of these cases are consistent with the available statistical evidence. We discussed in Chapter 1 the findings of Franz Exner's late-1920s study of German sentencing practices, which showed a clear and steady trend toward lighter sentences after the turn of the twentieth century. A similar pattern was at work in the imposition of the most severe sentence. Richard Evans reports a dramatic drop after the succession of Wilhelm II in the percentage of homicide convictions that led to executions.[71]

Why did this trend toward leniency become so apparent in the last Wilhelmine years? It is perhaps all the more remarkable when one considers the illiberality of much of the contemporary criminology. Hans Gross, for instance, much lauded by lawyers like Erich Sello and Max Alsberg, argued that humanitarianism in criminal law was a weakness and advocated the castration of all violent offenders. Some historians have stressed the authoritarian implications of the rise of psychology, arguing that the institutionalization of so many persons designated as mentally ill could serve the goals of authoritarian rule. But in German criminal justice, the insanity provision of §51 opened a door for bourgeois professionals and not for the "old gang" of Prussia's aristocratic rulers; and it is clear from cases like those we have seen in this chapter how little the state's judges and prosecutors, at least, welcomed the ameliorative effects of the new science. We speculated in the previous chapter about the dangers for criminal law of the social Darwinism, racial anthropology, "social hygiene" and eugenics, and fears of degeneration and national decline that were common currency in Europe and North America. But the political constellation in Prussia and Germany was growing increasingly unfavorable to illiberal reforms of the criminal laws. The Social Democrats and the Left-Liberals were the chief advocates of applying sociology and psychology in the courts. By 1912 the Social Democrats had become the largest party in the Reichstag, while the Left-Liberals' vote share rose in each of the last three Imperial Reichstag elections. Although the three-class franchise kept the Conservatives in control of the Prussian House, the popular vote patterns in Prussia were similar to those in the Reich; and the Social Democrats and Left-Liberals between them had an absolute lock on Berlin (83.5 percent of the vote in the House elections of 1908, 89.0 percent in 1913). Beyond the simple numbers of parliamentary deputies, the public opinion demonstrated by voting patterns could be influential. With Wilhelm Voigt we saw the extent to which public opinion could drive cabinet ministers to ostentatious mercy. Journalist (and cabaret star) Hans Hyan's successful press campaign for clemency for several young accomplices of a notorious murderer demonstrated how public opinion could be mobilized even in support of the most serious offenders.[72]

Fictional treatments of late Wilhelmine criminal law provide another clue to public opinion and its possible impact on the administration of justice. One trope, combining elements of social criticism and liberal compensatory fantasy, emerges from this literature: the merciless prosecutor who experiences a heart-softening transformation, a kind of Scrooge of Moabit. The *Berliner Morgenpost,* for instance, printed a short story in 1910 called "Der Ankläger" ("The Accuser"), which dealt with a fierce prosecutor handling a case of a man who had killed his wife's lover. The prosecutor burns with the zeal of securing a conviction, until he find letters from his own wife to her lover. Emotional testimony about the defendant's painful lot in life buttresses the prosecutor's new-found empathy. As he rises to give what the public expects to be his familiar "brilliant" closing speech "painting the crime in lurid colors," all the prosecutor says is, "I withdraw the indictment."[73]

A novel by Hans Land, *Staatsanwalt Jordan. Ein Berliner Roman (State Advocate Jordan: A Berlin Novel)*, was written to the same formula. State Advocate Matthias Jordan is a late-Wilhelmine culture warrior of the most uncompromising sort. Early in the novel he prosecutes one Frau Hecker for acting as her daughter's procuress. It is clear to the reader that the evidence against Frau Hecker is weak, but for Jordan the case represents the decisive battle in the war against moral decay. He thinks Berlin's nightlife is "on this path to degeneration" and is appalled by "signs of a general moral and cultural wildness, whose bestial pleasure-seeking was already in such a lecherous rush today that the birth-rate of the population, especially in the cities, was beginning to sink rapidly." With his fiery determination, Jordan is able to secure Frau Hecker's conviction and a sentence of one year of hard labor. He prosecutes the case uncompromisingly despite having just received a warning from the chief prosecutor:

> "So, Herr colleague Jordan—unofficially—just man to man, you use—for my feelings—all too much severity in your office. You know very well that there has been a storm for ages in parliament and in the press against the prosecutor's office. Our office . . . enjoys little favor . . ."
> "Little," Jordan interjected, "among the followers of subversion . . ."
> "I believe, on the contrary, that these antipathies reach deep into the bourgeois classes."
> "They don't worry me!" remarked Jordan.
> "But we should pay a little attention to them, dear colleague. The prosecutor, whom we together embody, should take care that he does his accusatory duty with humanity."

Like the prosecutor in the *Morgenpost* story, Jordan eventually learns this lesson, but too late. He falls in love with Frau Hecker's daughter Herta and begins an affair with her. It all ends badly; Jordan dies when Herta Hecker abandons him and he is hit by a car, believing he has just murdered his wife. Shorn of its melodrama and mildly pornographic trappings, the novel amounts to a 249-page sermon on the hypocrisy of uncompromising cultural conservatism, and a critique of over-zealous prosecutions.[74]

Although the conversation between State Advocate Jordan and his superior was the imaginative construction of an outsider to the prosecutor's office, evidence from the late Wilhelmine period suggests that conversations very like it could have taken place on a regular basis behind the scenes in Moabit. For all his determination to win his cases, First Prosecutor Isenbiel was always conscious of the need to appear reasonable in public. Prosecuting Maximilian Harden for the libel of Kuno von Moltke early in 1908, Isenbiel referred to Harden as a "genius," and, as *Die Zeit am Montag* reported, "distinguished himself in many other ways from other persons of his profession," including by speaking well of critical writers and intellectuals like Franz Mehring and Paul Lindau. Isenbiel's remarkable 1907 memo to the Justice Minister suggests that he was so careful to present himself sympathetically in public because he knew how much public opinion could affect what went on in Moabit. Many judges seem to have come to similar conclusions. Director Dietz's gracious gesture to Wilhelm Voigt may have owed something to Dietz's consciousness of how closely the world was watching him. A few years later a reporter at another well-publicized trial, the Eulenburg perjury case, wrote of the presiding judge: "He knows that in this moment Europe has its eyes on him. And he knows that he represents the entire German judiciary to Europe. If he did not know it, a glance at the press table would stamp it into his conscience: Englishmen, Frenchmen, Russians, Italians, listen as he speaks." Whether trials should be publicized as they were was an issue that remained controversial from the Heinzes to Hedwig Müller. The *Kreuzeitung* had tried to hold itself ostentatiously aloof from the salacious details of the Müller case, covering the trial in a paragraph or two per day, in contrast to the columns and full pages of the *Morgenpost* and the *Tageblatt*. "We do not have the intention to publish details," the editors sniffed; "The political newspaper as educator of the people does not have the task of giving way to curiosity and lust for sensation." But the right had to accommodate itself to a public airing of more than Hedwig Müller's love life; not even the internal processes of the prosecutor's office were sacrosanct. We saw in Chapter 3 the consternation Isenbiel created simply by giving an interview; the situation became even worse in conservative eyes when the First Prosecutor was obliged to give interviews with good grace even on rumors of his impending dismissal. By the late Wilhelmine years there was no escaping the maw of publicity. The National Liberal *Hamburger Nachrichten* complained, "If any proof were still required that the public spirit in Germany is in rapid decline, it would be provided by the increasing number of scandal-trials and the passionate, almost exclusive interest of newspaper readers in them." And it added an apocalyptic conclusion: "We have long ceased to believe in the restoration of the public spirit through exhortations to deeply concerned friends of the Fatherland; rather, we are of the view that a thoroughly shattering internal or external catastrophe will be needed for the moral recovery of our people."[75]

By the last years before the First World War the courts could no more avoid the engines of publicity and the impact of the public opinion they brought with them than they could the phalanx of scientific experts whose power in the courtroom was so much in the ascendant.[76] The structure of the laws, especially the evolution and increasing sophistication of the insanity defense in the Reich Criminal Code, created a need for expert evidence; the scientific temper of the time and the respect paid to scientific authorities ensured that such experts got a careful hearing when they gave evidence. The receptivity of the courts to this kind of evidence had the same kind of result as did their openness to popular opinion: it meant that they were often compelled to make decisions they would rather not have made. This was the real story of criminal justice in late Wilhelmine Germany. The courts' own nature forced them to function in a way that perhaps few insiders in the system, but many outside, wished them to.

Epilogue

In 1959, at the age of seventy-eight, star Berlin lawyer Erich Frey published his memoirs. They bore the title *Ich beantrage Freispruch—I Ask for Acquittal*, the standard summation of the defense counsel. Frey wrote that the lawyer was accustomed to "watching that nothing in the trial escapes him; he poses the decisive questions, attacks and clarifies, as well as he is able."[1] Something of the same task faces the historian wishing to uncover the nature of past events, or the quality of a vanished world; the difference is that the results cannot be forced into the binary frame of "acquittal" or "conviction." The historian seeks to draw a balance, and he or she asks the reader to find that the balance is reasonable, indeed just.

In the preceding chapters we have analyzed the practice of Berlin's criminal courts over two-and-a-half decades. We have found that German criminal laws created a flexible system that could respond to different kinds of pressures and be pulled in very different directions. The Code of Criminal Procedure contained many safeguards for persons accused of crimes, including the right to be provided with counsel at state expense in the most serious cases, and the right not to testify in the pretrial investigations and in the main trial. The Judicial Code enshrined such long-standing liberal demands as public trials, jury and lay-judge courts, and the independence of the judiciary. The creation of the office of the state prosecutor and the consequent separation of the functions of raising and judging an indictment were also supposed to protect the defendant from a kangaroo court. On the other hand, defendants had few rights in the investigatory phases of a proceedings, and presiding judges had extraordinary power to control a trial. German laws of evidence did little to disallow inherently suspect sources of information (such as hearsay) and, especially in the early part of our period, the organization of the police and the state of forensic science offered few other evidentiary sources. Judges were formally independent but wholly dependant on ministerial officials for appointment and promotion; trials were to be open and public but could be closed any time a judge deemed it expedient for the sake of public or state security. The benefits of the right to counsel, to remain silent, or to reject a biased judge could be negated by a conservative private bar to which exercising these rights amounted to a breach of professional ethics. The trial of Willy Grosse and Bruno Werner demonstrated that a court-appointed lawyer was of little use if the tendency of German lawyers to act as their client's first judge prevented them from raising all possible mitigating circumstances. The limited grounds for the remedy of *Revision,* the crush of business, and the resistance of appellate judges to more liberal interpretations of the laws could all negate the theoretically extensive rights of appeal that the Code of Criminal Procedure granted the defendant.

The result was a situation in which professional culture, the impact of public opinion, the state of scientific and other scholarly advances, and (from time to time) high politics could mold the clay of the formal legal structures into a myriad of possible shapes. We have seen that in the early 1890s the Prussian and Reich authorities made a concerted effort to use the judicial system as a surrogate for the lost Anti-Socialist Law. Prosecutions for lèse majesté and other overtly political offenses climbed dramatically; the authorities also made a serious effort to make prosecutions of seemingly "unpolitical" crimes, above all those related to sex, serve a political purpose as well, in the sprit of "the more punishment, the more order in the country!" Judges who made rulings unpopular with their political masters, most famously Superior Court Director Schmidt, were sanctioned; the Prussian justice ministry, under the regime of Minister Ludwig von Schelling, embarked on a wide-ranging offensive to scale back public access to trials, restrict the scope (and even the competence) of defenses, and rid the system of turbulent barristers. This picture is the one familiar to readers of the secondary literature on law in Imperial Germany. But we have also seen that this offensive by the authorities was largely repulsed: the statistics on convictions in the lèse majesté epidemic of the early 1890s suggest that the judiciary showed a considerable resistance to ill-founded and overtly political prosecutions. The same lesson emerges from the unwillingness of the judges of Superior Court I to see their colleague Schmidt banished to a civil chamber, or the difficulty the Ministry experienced in securing discipline convictions against the lawyers it most directly targeted. With the failure in the Reichstag of punitive legislative efforts like the "Hard Labor Bill," the "Sedition Bill," and the partial failure of the *lex Heinze,* this chapter of German criminal-legal history came to a close—at least until the 1930s.[2]

In the years after the mid-1890s the potential dynamism of the criminal justice system began to work in other ways. Two professional groups in particular staked a claim to authority in the courtroom and challenged some of the more authoritarian conceptions of the goals of criminal law. The first group was the defense bar. The position of defense counsel changed dramatically between 1891 and the First World War. Through a string of confrontations the bar succeeded in widening the scope for mounting effective defenses; and private defense lawyers, once a rather disreputable fringe of the legal profession, were beginning to garner more public and official respect. Figures like Erich Sello and Max Alsberg were able to play the role of public sages of the law, active in diverse realms of advocacy and scholarship, while the justice ministry was making efforts to appoint more defense lawyers to judicial positions. The second group was the community of expert witnesses, who became increasingly indispensable to the conduct of criminal trials. They rode a wave of public esteem for the natural sciences, and profited from considerable intellectual ferment in fields such as psychology, anthropology, chemistry, and medicine, which had or were believed to have implications for the administration of justice. As we have seen, the chief impact of the ascent of defense lawyers and expert witnesses was to limit the ability of prosecutors to obtain convictions or to obtain sentences as severe as they might have wished.

Surrounding all of the players in criminal justice, fundamentally shaping how they did their work and tried to present it, were the organs of publicity, themselves in the grip of a dramatic expansion in the Wilhelmine years. The twenty-five years before the First World War were the years in which one could truly begin to speak of a mass press in Germany. Criminal justice, a subject combining sensational interest and serious political implications, was tailor-made to be a focus for the new press. The result was that everyone from cabinet ministers to medical men, from judges to criminals, lived in constant fear of bad publicity and constant hope of good. The sensitivity to public opinion of officials like the Prussian Justice Ministers Schelling, Schönstedt, and Beseler, and Reich Justice Secretary Nieberding, seems astonishing at first blush. These men were in no way democratic politicians; they were appointed by, and solely responsible to, the Kaiser and King. Yet they worried about politics. The elephant in their cabinet room was the steady rise in the electoral fortunes of the Social Democratic Party and, to a lesser extent, the recovery of the Left-Liberals in the last Wilhelmine years. These men were often forced to make connections between events in the courtroom and events in the wider political culture; their concern for public opinion often determined who was prosecuted and who received clemency. At a time when the still-new policy of *freie Advokatur* was coming under pressure from the competitive forces it had unleashed, the legal profession was refashioning its preferred public image into one more reserved and austere, its claim to authority based more specifically on professional competence than on a broader claim of political leadership.

Finally, for legal intellectuals the very question of what law was and how the stability of its meanings could be assured seemed up for debate in a way it had not been for a century. Was the criminal law to remain a fixed scheme of precisely calibrated offenses and penalties, as envisioned by a line of thinkers running from Kant and Feuerbach to Binding? Or was it time to abandon the fixed scheme of offenses to concentrate on the individual offender and his or her treatment, as Liszt and the sociological school maintained? Was the whole project of legal codification misplaced, doomed to create a sterile jurisprudence out of touch with the living law of the people, as the free lawyers argued? The questions thrown up by both the theory and practice of Wilhelmine criminal law were, in short, serious and profound. They were not to be answered in peace.

The First World War had an immediate impact on the business of Berlin's courts. Large numbers of lawyers, judges, prosecutors, police officers, and nonjudicial employees of the justice department volunteered for active service. Police Commissar Hans v. Tresckow saw combat and was seriously wounded; Hedwig Müller's judge, Superior Court Counselor Schlichting, left Superior Court I in October to go to the front; lawyer Erich Frey, who had just opened his practice in 1911 but had already begun to make his name, closed his practice for the duration and joined the navy. The Justice Ministry kept careful records of who went to the front, and, week by week, of who died. Not surprisingly, the bulk of the names were supplied by young *Referendare* and *Assessoren,* but many in senior positions were also killed in action. A first state advocate was killed in October 1914; a *Kammergericht* judge and a superior court director from Superior Court II in

November; a judge from Superior Court III the following January. When the war was over, 414 Prussian "higher justice officials," 433 lawyers and notaries, 509 *Assessoren*, and 1,222 *Referendare* had been killed in action. The number of Assessors who obtained positions as judges or prosecutors dropped sharply during the war, from 397 in 1914, to 236 in 1916, to 37 in 1916. The number of law students in Prussian universities showed a slight decline when the war broke out, from 5,376 in the winter semester of 1913–1914 to 4,560 the next year, but thereafter it climbed, reaching a new high of 7,120 in the winter semester of 1917–1918. One of the few bright spots for the justice department was that the business of the courts declined during the war years.[3]

In comparison to what would come in the 1940s, German justice in the First World War retained a startling concern for procedural niceties. In 1915 the president of the *Kammergericht* took time to upbraid the presidents of Berlin's trial courts because there had been complaints that "the generally practiced forms of courtesy" were not being used in correspondence with the "law-seeking public." In 1917, the news that two men had been left in custody for eight days when the law required that they be brought before a judge for a hearing on the merits of their arrest within twenty-four hours caused a minor bureaucratic flurry. Both the general prosecutor at the *Kammergericht* and the first prosecutor at Superior Court I believed that the men's protests about their treatment were justified. The general prosecutor wrote to the minister that "laws and regulations must always be correctly employed"; the first prosecutor noted in his report that "it is a matter of the most important legal guarantees for personal freedom."[4]

But in other respects the stresses and hatreds of wartime began to tell on the culture of Berlin's courts. The *Deutsche Richterzeitung* published an article in 1917 celebrating that "the war has, praise God, healed us from foreign influences, which foreign conceptions of the position and task of the judge wanted to transplant on our soil practically with violence." Midway through the war came a journalistic squabble over the numbers of Berlin lawyers who had been killed in action. The anti-Semitic weekly *Die Wahrheit* claimed in 1916 that twenty-eight Berlin lawyers had been killed, of whom eight were Jewish, although Jews made up 1,000 of the 1,500 lawyers in Berlin. The *Berliner Tageblatt* responded that the Lawyers' Chamber did not record the religion of the twenty-eight lawyers known to have been killed; the *Tageblatt* claimed that at least sixteen were Jewish. Furthermore, all the numbers were underreported. Figures "from the responsible source" indicated that two-thirds of Berlin's lawyers were "in the field." Between eighty and 100 of these, more than half of them Jewish, had "died a hero's death for the fatherland." In view of these numbers, said the *Tageblatt*, "it is incomprehensible to every right-thinking person" how *Die Wahrheit* "could have the nerve to dishonor the memory of the so-numerous Jewish lawyers who, in the struggle for the Fatherland, in east and west, in north and south, have lost their lives."[5]

With the human losses, the bitterness of defeat, and the legacy of the revolution, it was hardly surprising that the atmosphere of the courts in the Weimar Republic was more poisoned and politically volatile than in the last days of the peacetime *Kaiserreich*. All of the components of the system—judges and prosecutors, lawyers, the ministers and their staffs, and perhaps the press most of all—now went about their jobs with a degree of mutual suspicion and intolerance greatly surpassing the most conflictual moments of prewar Berlin. Almost all judges and prosecutors who had served the Kaiser went on serving the republic. Many on the left had wished to see a thorough housecleaning in the courts. A left-leaning Berlin lawyer and publicist named Ludwig Bendix wrote to the Prussian Ministry of State only days after the revolution to complain that the criminal court judges and prosecutors presently in office "are all persons who were raised in the old spirit of the authoritarian conception of the state and are accustomed to judging accordingly." A few years later Kurt Tucholsky would write with characteristic intemperance of what he wanted for the courts: "Revolution. Cleaning. Clearing out. Airing." In libel actions brought by Republican cabinet ministers or prosecutions of artists like Georg Grosz for blasphemy, the Weimar judiciary often vented its hostility toward much of what passed for the modern world. The brave professor of statistics Emil Julius Gumbel chronicled the severe imbalance in sentences for political killers and gave Weimar justice one of its catchphrases: "Hard on the left, easy on the right."[6]

But in many respects generally underappreciated by historians, the prewar trends toward greater consideration of the sociological and psychological explanations of the defendant's behavior, and toward liberal victory in the judicial-cultural wars, continued. Sentences grew ever lighter; the system for granting clemency was regularized and made more bureaucratic. Erich Frey remembered in the context of a 1923 case that "the jurisprudence was beginning then to pay more attention to the youth, upbringing, and milieu of defendants as mitigating circumstances." The practice of psychiatrists became ever more indispensable to the courts and ever more ubiquitous, prompting a Berlin judge to write that "earlier the psychiatrist may have been a rare figure in the courtroom; now there is hardly a significant case in which he does not play a role." An incident in 1930 provided a Weimar parallel to reactions to Wilhelm Voigt. Berlin judge Superior Court Director Steinhaus heard a case in which it emerged that the defendant had served six months' imprisonment in 1917 for breaking and entering. According to the *Deutsche Zeitung*, Steinhaus remarked: "One can hardly believe that such a thing was possible. Today we live in a more humane time." Steinhaus was certain that in 1930 the defendant would receive probation. And despite the "crisis of confidence in justice" that marked the middle 1920s, by the end of that decade the tortoise of republicanisation was beginning to catch up with the hare of nationalist and monarchist resentment. Probably no justice system could have continued to function well in the crisis conditions of the early 1930s; the complete breakdown of any kind of political and social consensus led to a growing rejection of the legitimacy of the courts from left and right alike. Still, the legacy of four decades in which the rule of law had become increasingly settled and internalized by German jurists showed itself in an occasionally bizarre concern for procedural fairness even amid the abuses of the Third Reich.[7]

This book has not sought simply to replace the familiar "Tory" narrative of the authoritarian continuities in criminal justice from Imperial Germany through the Third Reich with an optimistic "Whig" account. Every facet of change in the justice system, like the basic architecture of the system itself, brought with it malign as well as benign possibilities. The openness of the judicial system to influence by popular opinion could seem "progressive" when it pushed the authorities to pardon a man like Wilhelm Voigt or to reform the treatment of prisoners at Plötzensee. But popular opinion also drove the authorities to expedient prosecutions of Jewish suspects like Wilhelm Buschoff and Moritz Levy for crimes that few in the prosecutors' offices or the ministry believed they had committed. The bureaucratic realities of the courts—their chronic underfunding and heavy workloads—and some of the procedural advantages granted to defendants to call evidence, seek adjournments, and appeal decisions, could frustrate officials just as much as defendants, and ensure that often enough the system produced outcomes that were to the liking or benefit of no one. Most of the developments in medicine and forensic science were similarly Janus-faced. It is impossible to read without alarm of the use of anthropometry to determine the parentage of a child, as in the Kwilecki case of 1903. Much of the new criminology, like the legal scholarship of Franz von Liszt, was authoritarian in its implications, if not intent. It is in fact difficult to apply modern western notions of "liberal" and "conservative" to many of the actors in this story; the labels simply do not fit. Liszt, high priest of the progressive reformers, proceeded from the assumption that the first task of the criminal law was to protect society from the offender, and thus he believed that the regime of general deterrence through fixed sentences, a classic liberal demand of the mid-nineteenth century embodied in the Reich Criminal Code, was obsolete. On the other hand, he took a maximally liberal position on the procedural rights of accused persons, arguing for instance that there could be no objection to a defense counsel pleading for the acquittal of a prisoner he believed to be guilty—a position which few German lawyers would take then (or probably now); and unlike most jurists after the turn of the century, Liszt remained a firm supporter of the traditional jury court.[8]

If there is no cause for unbridled Whiggery in this history of German criminal justice, there is a need to introduce a degree of nuance into the existing narrative. Above all, it is important to remember how many issues of law and legal politics in Wilhelmine and Weimar Germany were fiercely, often bitterly, contested. It is simply wrong to say, as many historians have, that the idea of "the rule of law" as something transcending the rule of the state was foreign to German thought. It may be that the conservative notion of the *Rechtsstaat*—"that the state agreed voluntarily to implement its purposes by legal means"—was the prevalent one in the judiciary and in the ministries. But what judges and ministers believed did not alone determine what Germans thought about law and the state. The conservative idea of the *Rechtsstaat* was demonstrably not prevalent in the private bar or in the press, and both were crucial to the character of justice in Wilhelmine Germany. Richard Finger, in his manual for young lawyers, wrote that it was perfectly proper for the lawyer to argue that a particular *statute* was not in harmony with the *law*, and that it was inherent in the title of a lawyer—*Rechtsanwalt*—that he was an advocate of the law, not an advocate of the statute *(Gesetzanwalt)* or of the state *(Staatsanwalt)*. In 1899, First Prosecutor Isenbiel said in the course of a trial that a controversial arrest had been ordered "by a higher authority" and thus could not be criticized.

Trial lawyer David Halpert responded with outrage: "We have a right to examine judicial actions in light of the requirements of law and logic . . . There is a higher instance than the Imperial Supreme Court, and that is criticism."[9] Scientists also challenged the state's claim on the sole right to determine what was law, especially the psychiatrists, who complained of the inadequacies of the mental illness provisions of the Criminal Code. The very last thing that the public conflicts over justice suggest is that there was a great deal of journalistic deference to the state's law-making powers. Claims of superior political or moral legitimacy drove liberal and left-wing campaigns for more mercy in the justice system, whether it was in the treatment of prisoners, the imposition of the death penalty, or police treatment of ex-convicts like Wilhelm Voigt. Far-right papers like the *Staatsbürger Zeitung* would in no way allow the left to outdo them when it came to questioning the legitimacy of the state's legal policies. They claimed a rival source of authority, the "healthy popular feeling of the people," which was in all respects to be preferred to the reluctance of even the Monarch to recognize patriotic hearts when he saw them. Even the performance of Germany's much-maligned judges casts doubt on the familiar arguments about their subservience to rulers. It was the judges of the Supreme Honor Court who refused to discipline Karl Liebknecht in 1908, on the basis that criticizing the application of the laws was consistent with a lawyer's duty to the *Rechtsstaat*. The judges who twice refused to transfer Director Schmidt, who refused to disbar Ballien and Cossmann, or who became increasingly likely to acquit defendants on political charges in the early 1890s, certainly appear to have been something more than automata in the service of the powerful.

Of course, there were many continuities in individual lives reaching across the lines historians draw at 1918, 1933, and 1945. The available documents allow us to trace the fates of some of our principal characters in later years.

Anna and Hermann Heinze served their full sentences. Anna came out of the penitentiary in 1902; Friedlaender reports that she found another young man to serve as her "protector" and went right back to her previous profession. Shortly afterwards both she and her protector fell afoul of the law that now bore her name: he was convicted of pimping, and she of incitement thereto. Hermann was released from the penitentiary in Sonnenberg in the summer of 1907. As he had conducted himself well while a prisoner, he was given permission to change his name, and afterwards he found a job in a factory.[10] In October 1913, the *Tägliche Rundschau* reported the death of a man it called Karl Heinze, in Burg Hospital near Magdeburg. "Shortly before his death," it said, "he confessed to the nurse who was treating him, that now, when he would soon stand before God, he wanted to insist once again that he had been wrongly convicted. His wife . . . had also been innocent of the deed."[11]

Alfred Ballien's colleague in the defense of the Heinzes, Richard Cossmann, shared Ballien's ability to get into serious trouble. Cossmann was, in fact, disbarred in 1898, for a number of dubious financial dealings with a client. He campaigned for years for his reinstatement. In 1905 he actually succeeded—the only time the Supreme Honor Court ever reversed such a decision. The court changed his penalty from expulsion from the profession to a fine. Even then he was not satisfied, and kept up a campaign for full rehabilitation, year in and year out, and without success, until his death in 1933.[12]

Theodor Berger, the putative killer of little Lucie Berlin, did not see his fifteen-year sentence through. In 1913 the Alexanderplatz prepared a list of convicted murderers who had either been executed or died in prison. Among the names one finds "Berger, Theodor August Karl. Worker. 25.5.69 Quedlinburg." No date of death is given.[13]

Wilhelm Voigt devoted his remaining years to the systematic exploitation of his celebrity. To be sure, even after 1908 he was not entirely finished with police powers or the criminal law. From time to time, as he traveled about giving lectures and selling postcards of himself, Voigt was still run out of town by anxious or humorless police forces—in France as well as in Germany. His aggressive self-promotion after his release led to a noticeable cooling of sympathy for him on the editorial pages. He faired well financially, but was ruined by the postwar inflation. Voigt died, broke, in Luxemburg in 1922, a few days short of his seventy-third birthday.[14]

August Sternberg, perhaps predictably, faired much better. The Sternberg trial had a kind of Weimar replay, which brought back memories of the drawn-out litigation of 1900 and served to inform Berliners of what had become of its protagonist. Sternberg had moved to Paris and then to Milan, and somehow or other acquired a Spanish patent of nobility; his sexual proclivities were unchanged. A woman named Luise Knopf was tried in 1927 for having procured teenaged girls for Sternberg when he visited Berlin. Sternberg, by then seventy-five years old and retired, was himself summoned as a witness in the case, and Knopf was defended by

Johannes Werthauer, who had represented Sternberg in 1900. Although the court thought the circumstances highly suspicious, especially in light of Sternberg's past, Knopf was acquitted for lack of evidence.[15]

Maximilian Harden went on publishing *Die Zukunft* into the 1920s. His politics had evolved; the First World War had taught him the dangers of rabid nationalism, and he became a convert to republicanism and pacifism. This stance made him a target for the radical right, and in 1922 he was brutally assaulted near his home in the Grünewald. He survived the attack but could no longer keep up with the demands of putting out his weekly journal. The last issue of *Die Zukunft* appeared in the autumn of 1922; Harden died in 1927.[16]

Hugo Isenbiel, Harden's sometime nemesis, fulfilled the expectations of his superiors and was promoted to the position of General Prosecutor at the *Kammergericht* in 1909. But thereafter he disappears from the record; whether from illness, death, or sudden career change, I have not been able to discover.[17]

The fate of lawyers from Wilhelmine days who were still in practice in 1933 depended on whether the Nazi regime considered them Jewish or not, or associated them with liberal or left wing causes. Both conditions applied to the great Max Alsberg. Alsberg fled to Switzerland when Hitler came to power, but he could not accommodate himself to life in exile. He turned down offers of a position at the Sorbonne and a practice in London. His biographer writes that Alsberg would greet visiting friends by asking plaintively "How are things in Berlin . . . Don't you have any news for me? Can I go back?" But he could not go back; Alsberg committed suicide in the autumn of 1933. Johannes Werthauer, throughout the Weimar era among the lawyers most hated by the extreme right, also went into exile. More adaptable than Alsberg, Werthauer took up a position at the Sorbonne. He died in Paris later in the 1930s.[18]

One of the most eminent lawyers of the Wilhelmine age, Ludwig Chodziesner, fared much worse. Chodziesner had acted for such clients as the Countess Kwilecka and the Kaiser's close friend, Prince Eulenburg. By the 1930s a very wealthy and elderly man, he had moved into semiretirement. Due to his seniority Chodziesner was permitted to remain in the Berlin bar after the infamous "Law to Reform the Professional Civil Service" of April 1933 expelled many Jews from the private bar. But in 1936 Chodziesner resigned from practice with a two-sentence letter to the President of the

Berlin Lawyers' Chamber. In its terse eloquence the letter is a farewell, not just to a career, but to the world of old Moabit, to the world of the confident and colorful lawyers who worked there, to the world of the cultured and progressive Jewish middle classes of Berlin, a farewell to everything which in 1936 *Justizrat* Chodziesner could see being destroyed around him. "It is now 50 years since I entered the Pruss. Judicial Service as a *Referendar*," he wrote. "As I now have nothing more to do, I ask that my name be removed from the list of lawyers." It was; but Chodziesner was not to be granted a peaceful retirement. The man who had pleaded for counts and princes before the high windows of the old courthouse was deported to the Theresienstadt concentration camp in September 1942. He died there on 13 February 1943.[19]

Our last glimpse of Walter Bahn, defender of Theodor Berger and Wilhelm Voigt, tireless campaigner and pamphleteer for a more liberal and humane justice system, is scarcely less depressing. Bahn was still in practice in Berlin in 1944 when he became embroiled in a discipline proceeding. He was accused of extorting unreasonably high fees—2,500 and 2,000 reichsmarks respectively—from two clients facing prosecutions before the Berlin Special Court *(Sondergericht)* and the dreaded *Volksgerichtshof* for "treasonous" remarks. Days before the trials, Bahn had threatened to withdraw if the clients did not pay him. Bahn claimed the demands were a mistake by his office personnel, but added for good measure that one of these clients "was a lying informer with a clearly terrible reputation" who had "insulted the Führer so seriously" that in 1944 "he would probably be sentenced to a heavy hard labor sentence, if not death, for damaging the national defense, and it would be appropriate to take him into protective custody [i.e. a concentration camp]." Suggesting to a prosecutor that one's client should be sent to a concentration camp is hardly the action of a steadfast defense counsel, and if it can be taken at face value, this statement (along with Bahn's extortionate fee demands) can serve as an apt symbol of the moral collapse of the defense bar in the Third Reich. But can it be taken at face value? More even than in most periods of history, legal documents from the Third Reich pose challenges of interpretation. What were the conditions under which Bahn was interrogated? What did he have to fear? The prosecutor's memo itself offers a clue: another investigation had been launched against Bahn for "having requested the acquittal of his client in a criminal proceeding without justification." It would be difficult for most people to carry on an upright professional activity in a legal system where such things were possible. The documents do not record the outcome of this case. Probably either the Third Reich or Bahn himself ran out of time.[20]

The buildings where our stories played out have histories too. St. Elizabeth's church, where nightwatchman Braun was murdered, was heavily damaged during the Second World War. It still stands; since the fall of the Berlin wall, fitful efforts have been under way to restore it, though like all architectural matters in Berlin such plans are complicated by historico-moral questions. (Should the church be restored exactly as the great Schinkel conceived it, or is to do so to fall into the kind of search for a usable German past which errs too much in neglecting how that past turned out?). The old courthouse at Alt-Moabit 11, where the Heinzes, Guthmann, Berger, Sternberg, and many thousands more faced their judges, was also a casualty of the war. By 1945, only the towers by the entrance remained; a dramatic photograph shows them standing guard over a pile of rubble. In the 1950s the towers were pulled down to make way for an expansion of the holding cells—without doubt an architectural setback. The "new" courthouse on Turmstrasse survived the war, but the early twenty-first-century visitor will find that the mood inside remains somehow frozen in 1906. The *Tagesspiegel* complains that "behind the imperial gesture of the main entrance" the "greatest judicial institution of the republic labors in Wilhelmine wretchedness." The building is vast and gloomy, a dimly lit maze of hallways, staircases, and mezzanines, institutional green tile on the walls, all the signs ("Witness Waiting Room," "Lawyers' Lounge") in their original gothic script. The guards who search one's bags speak in rapid-fire Berlin dialect. It is easy to imagine the prosecutors and prosecuted of 1906 coming and going, or remaining.[21]

We began with Erich Frey. In another sense, the history of Wilhelmine Moabit ends with him; when he died in Santiago, Chile in 1964, Frey was among the last of those who could recall it. A flamboyant as well as skillful advocate, his memoirs also revealed him to be an eloquent writer and an engaging raconteur. He closed by listing many of the notable people he had known in Berlin: clients, prosecutors, police officers. "Here too," said Frey, speaking of himself in the third person, "he is in the first place an advocate; here too he tries to awaken understanding for his clients and to show that concealed even in the most incomprehensible criminal is a human being."[22]

The last days of Alt-Moabit 11: all that remained of the old courthouse in the 1950s. (Ullstein Bilderdienst)

Though I do not approach this subject as an advocate, I have tried to return a full measure of human complexity, of irony and paradox, of good as well as ill will, to a subject which has often been treated with the two-dimensionality of a cartoon. As Frey said, "The high court: that is now the readers of this book."

APPENDIX

ABBREVIATIONS

NOTES

ARCHIVAL AND PRIMARY SOURCES

INDEX

Appendix: Regimes and Rulers

German Regimes, 1871–1933

Imperial Germany *(Deutsches Kaiserreich)*, 1871–1918: conventionally divided into two periods: "Bismarckian Germany" (1871–1890) and "Wilhelmine Germany" (1890–1918)
Weimar Republic *(Weimarer Republik)*, 1919–1933

German Emperors, 1871–1918

Wilhelm I, 1871–1888
Friedrich III, 1888
Wilhelm II, 1888–1918

German Federal Chancellors, 1871–1917

Otto von Bismarck, 1871–1890
Leo von Caprivi, 1890–1894
Chlodwig Fürst zu Hohenlohe-Schillingsfürst, 1894–1900
Bernhard von Bülow, 1900–1909
Theobald von Bethmann Hollweg, 1909–1917

Prussian Justice Ministers, 1889–1917

Ludwig von Schelling, 1889–1894
Karl Heinrich von Schönstedt, 1894–1905
Max von Beseler, 1905–1917

Abbreviations

A	*Abend*, evening edition of a newspaper
BA-BL	*Bundesarchiv Berlin-Lichterfelde*, Federal Archives, Berlin-Lichterfelde
BLA	*Berliner Lokal-Anzeiger*, a conservative daily newspaper
BLHA	*Brandenburgishes Landeshauptarchiv*, Main Archive of the State of Brandenburg, Potsdam, and Bornim
BM	*Berliner Morgenpost*, a left-liberal daily newspaper
BT	*Berliner Tageblatt*, a left-liberal daily newspaper
DT	*Deutsche Tageszeitung*, a conservative Berlin daily newspaper
GSA	*Generalstaatsanwalt*, chief prosecutor
GStA	*Geheimes Staatsarchiv Preussischer Kulturbesitz*, The Prussian Secret State Archives, Berlin
GVG	*Gerichtsverfassungsgesetz*, Judicial Code
EG	*Ehrengericht*, Honor Court for the legal profession
EGH	*Ehrengerichtshof*, Supreme Honor Court for the legal profession
IM	*Innenminister*, minister of the interior
JM	*Justizminister*, minister of justice
JW	*Juristische Wochenschrift*, the weekly trade paper of the legal profession
KG	*Kammergericht*, Berlin Court of Appeal
KGP	*Kammergerichtspräsident*, president of the *Kammergericht*
KZ	*Kreuzzeitung*, a conservative Berlin daily newspaper
LB	*Landesarchiv Berlin*, The Archives of the City of Berlin
LG	*Landgericht*, Superior Court

LGP	*Landgerichtspräsident*, president of the Superior Court
M	*Morgen*, morning edition of a newspaper
NAZ	*Norddeutsche Allgemeine Zeitung*, a National-Liberal Berlin daily newspaper
OLG	*Oberlandesgericht*, Court of Appeal
ORA	*Oberreichsanwalt*, chief federal prosecutor
OSA	*Oberstaatsanwalt*, chief prosecutor
RGBl	*Reichsgesetzblatt*, the official gazette of new German laws
S	*Sonntag*, Sunday edition of a newspaper
STA	*Staatsanwalt*, prosecutor
StGB	*Strafgesetzbuch*, Criminal Code
StPO	*Strafprozessordnung*, Code of Criminal Procedure
SZ	*Staatsbürger Zeitung*, a radical right, anti-Semitic Berlin daily newspaper
TR	*Tägliche Rundschau*, a nonpartisan but conservatively oriented Berlin daily newspaper
VZ	*Vossische Zeitung*, a left-liberal and particularly highbrow Berlin daily newspaper

Notes

Introduction

1. Eberhard Schmidt, *Einführung in die Geschichte der deutschen Strafrechtspflege*, 3rd ed. (Göttingen, 1995).
2. Howard Zehr, *Crime and the Development of Modern Society: Patterns of Criminality in Nineteenth Century Germany and France* (London, 1976); Eric A. Johnson, *Urbanization and Crime: Germany, 1871–1914* (Cambridge, UK, 1995); Richard J. Evans, *Rituals of Retribution: Capital Punishment in Germany, 1600–1987* (London, 1997); and *Tales from the German Underworld: Crime and Punishment in the Nineteenth Century* (New Haven, CT, 1998); as editor, *The German Underworld: Deviants and Outcasts in Germany History* (London, 1988). The pioneer of social-historical research into crime in nineteenth-century Germany was Dirk Blasius; see his *Bürgerliche Gesellschaft und Kriminalität: Zur Sozialgeschichte Preussens im Vormärz* (Göttingen, 1976).
3. The classic work is by Adolf Weissler, *Die Geschichte der Rechtsanwaltschaft* (Leipzig, 1905). Weissler's book was updated on the occasion of the hundredth anniversary of the German equivalent to the American Bar Association—the *Deutsche Anwaltverein*—by a Munich lawyer named Fritz Ostler: *Die deutschen Rechtsanwälte, 1871–1971*, 2nd ed. (Essen, 1982). See also Konrad H. Jarausch, *The Unfree Professions: German Lawyers, Teachers, and Engineers, 1900–1950* (New York, 1990); "Die unfreien Professionen: Überlegungen zu den Wandlungsprozessen im deutschen Bildungsbürgertum, 1900–1950," in Jürgen Kocka, ed., *Bürgertum im 19. Jahrhundert: Deutschland im Europäischen Vergleich* (Munich, 1988), 3 vols., II: 124–146; and "Jewish Lawyers in Germany, 1848–1938: The Disintegration of a Profession," *Yearbook Leo Baeck Institute* 36 (1991); Kenneth F. Ledford, *From General Estate to Special Interest: German Lawyers 1878–1933* (Cambridge, UK, 1996); Hannes Siegrist, *Advokat, Bürger und Staat: Sozialgeschichte der Rechtsanwälte in Deutschland, Italien und der Schweiz (18-20 Jh.)* (Frankfurt/Main, 1996), 2 vols.; Eva Douma, *Deutsche*

Anwälte zwischen Demokratie und Diktatur, 1930–1955 (Frankfurt/Main, 1998); Tilmann Krach, *Jüdische Rechtsanwälte in Preussen: Über die Bedeutung der freien Advokatur und ihre Zerstörung durch den Nationalsozialismus* (Munich, 1991); Helmut Heinrichs et al., *Deutsche Juristen jüdischer Herkunft* (Munich, 1993); Simone Ladwig-Winters, ed., *Anwalt ohne Recht: Das Schicksal jüdischer Rechtsanwälte in Berlin nach 1933* (Berlin, 1998).

4. Famously in the case of "Miller Arnold." See Uwe Wesel, *Geschichte des Rechts: Von den Frühformen bis zum Vertrag von Maastricht* (Munich, 1997), 398–400.

5. See Karl Liebknecht, speech in the Abgeordnetenhaus, 5 February 1914, GStA Rep. 84a/2942, *Richter und Staatsanwälte: Allgemeine Bestimmungen über die Anstellung im höhern Justizdienst, 1913–1922*, 19–20; Erich Kuttner, *Klassenjustiz!* (Berlin, 1913); Gerd Linnemann, *Klassenjustiz und Weltfremdheit: Deutsche Justizkritik, 1890–1914*, (Ph.D. diss., University of Kiel, 1989).

6. Emil Julius Gumbel, *Vier Jahre politischer Mord* (Berlin, 1922).

7. Gumbel, *Vier Jahre*; Alfred Apfel, *Behind the Scenes of German Justice: Reminiscences of a German Barrister, 1882–1933* (London, 1935); Karl Frohme, *Politische Polizei und Justiz im monarchistischen Deutschland* (Hamburg, 1926); Theo Rasehorn, *Justizkritik in der Weimarer Republik: Das Beispiel der Zeitschrift 'Die Justiz'* (Frankfurt/Main, 1985); Robert Kuhn, *Die Vertrauenskrise der Justiz (1926–1928): Der Kampf um die Republikanisierung der Rechtspflege in der Weimarer Republik* (Cologne, 1983).

8. Gustav Radbruch, "Gesetzliches Unrecht und übergesetzliches Recht," in Radbruch, *Rechtsphilosophie*, 8th ed. (Stuttgart, 1975), 339.

9. Hubert Schorn, *Der Richter im Dritten Reich. Geschichte und Dokumente* (Frankfurt/Main, 1959); Hubert Schorn, *Die Gesetzgebung des Nationalsozialismus als Mittel der Machtpolitik* (Frankfurt/Main, 1963); Hermann Weinkauff, *Die deutsche Justiz und der Nationalsozialismus. Ein Überblick* (Stuttgart, 1968). The general tone of this historiography is discussed by Michael Stolleis and Dieter Simon, "Vorurteile und Werturteile der rechtshistorischen Forschung zum Nationalsozialismus," in Kolloquien des Instituts für Zeitgeschichte, *NS-Recht in historischer Perspektive* (Munich, 1981).

10. Heinrich Hannover and Elisabeth Hannover-Drück, *Politische Justiz*, 2nd ed. (Bornheim-Merten, 1987), 21–33. See also Rasehorn, *Justizkritik*; Kuhn, *Vertrauenskrise*; Ralph Angermund, *Deutsche Richterschaft 1919–1945. Krisenerfahrung, Illusion, politische Rechtsprechung* (Frankfurt/Main, 1990).

11. Gottfried Zarnow, *Gefesselte Justiz. Politische Bilder aus deutscher Gegenwart*, Vol. 1 (Munich 1931); *Gefesselte Justiz. Politische Bilder aus deutscher Gegenwart* Vol. 2, 2nd ed. (Munich, 1932).

12. See Geoff Eley, *Reshaping the German Right: Radical Nationalism and Political Change after Bismarck* (New Haven, CT, 1980); David Blackbourn, "The Politics of Demagogy in Imperial Germany," in *Populists and Politicians: Essays in*

Modern German History (London, 1987); Roger Chickering, *We Men Who Feel Most German: A Cultural Study of the Pan-German League* (Boston, 1984).

13. See Chapter 4, infra.
14. See *inter alia* Michael Stolleis, *Recht in Unrecht. Studien zur Rechtsgeschichte des Nationalsozialismus* (Frankfurt/Main, 1994), and *Geschichte des öffentlichen Rechts in Deutschland, Vol. 3, Staats- und Verwaltungsrechtswissenschaft in Republik und Diktatur, 1914–1945* (Munich, 1998); Lothar Gruchmann, *Justiz im Dritten Reich 1933–1940. Anpassung und Unterwerfung in der Ära Gürtner* (Munich, 1988); Stefan König, *Vom Dienst am Recht. Rechtsanwälte als Strafverteidiger im Nationalsozialismus* (Berlin, 1987); Angermund, *Richterschaft*; Bernd Rüthers, *Entartetes Recht. Rechtslehren und Kronjuristen im Dritten Reich* (Munich, 1994).
15. Jörg Friedrich, *Freispruch für die Nazi-Justiz. Die Urteile gegen NS-Richter seit 1948. Eine Dokumentation* (Berlin, 1998), 15.
16. See *inter alia* Krach, *Jüdische Rechtsanwälte*; Ladwig-Winters, *Anwalt*; and Chapter 7 infra.
17. See Evans, *Rituals*, 636–637; Johnson, *Urbanization*, 3–4.
18. H. L. A. Hart, "Positivism and the Separation of Law and Morals," 71 *Harv. L. Rev.* 593, reprinted in R. M. Dworkin, ed., *The Philosophy of Law* (Oxford, 1977), 17–37, 18.
19. See Karl Larenz, *Methodenlehre der Rechtswissenschaft*, 6th ed. (Berlin, 1991); Arthur Jacobson and Bernhard Schlink, eds., *Weimar: A Jurisprudence of Crisis* (Berkeley, CA, 2000).
20. Carl Schmitt, *Gesetz und Urteil. Eine Untersuchung zum Problem der Rechtspraxis* (Berlin, 1912); Eugen Ehrlich, *Freie Rechtsfindung und freie Rechtswissenschaft* (Leipzig, 1903); Gustav Radbruch, "Rechtswissenschaft und Rechtsschöpfung," *Archiv fur Sozialpolitik* 22 (1906): 355; Hermann Kantorowicz (Gnaeus Flavius), *Der Kampf um die Rechtswissenschaft, mit einer Einführung von Karlheinz Muscheler* (Baden-Baden, 2002).
21. Stolleis, *Recht in Unrecht*, 23–24.
22. Karl Llewellyn, *The Bramble Bush: On Our Law and Its Study* (New York, 1960), 13.
23. Richard Finger, *Die Kunst des Rechtsanwalts*, 2nd ed. (Berlin, 1912), 10.
24. See James E. Herget and Stephen Wallace, "The German Free Law Movement as the Source of American Legal Realism," 73 *Va. L. Rev.* 399 (1987); Michael Ansaldi, "The German Llewellyn," 58 *Brooklyn L. Rev.* 705 (1992).
25. The great monument of German criminal-law history remains Eberhard Schmidt's dated classic, *Einführung* (see note 1), first published in 1947. No one has yet produced a thorough update. For a more recent look at the still rather Rankean paradigm of German legal history, see Michael Stolleis's *Geschichte des öffentlichen Rechts in Deutschland*, 3 vols. (Munich, 1988–1999).

For the formalism of present-day German legal education I know of no literary citation; I am indebted to many of the German LLM students at Harvard Law School from 2001 to 2003 for a number of fascinating conversations on this point.

26. Carlo Ginzburg, *The Cheese and the Worms: The Cosmos of a Sixteenth-Century Miller*, trans. John and Anne Tedeschi (Baltimore, 1992); *Clues, Myths, and the Historical Method*, trans. John and Anne Tedeschi (Baltimore, 1992); Emmanuel Le Roy Ladurie, *Montaillou: The Promised Land of Error* (New York, 1979); Evans, *Tales*, 1.
27. Franz Exner, *Studien über die Strafzumessungspraxis der deutschen Gerichte* (Leipzig, 1931), 14.
28. Ginzburg, *The Cheese and the Worms*, xxi.
29. Eley, *Reshaping*, 194.

1. In Moabit

1. Erich Frey, *Ich beantrage Freispruch: Aus den Erinnerungen des Strafverteidigers Prof. Dr. Dr. Erich Frey* (Hamburg, 1959), 5.
2. Karl Scheffler, *Berlin: Ein Stadtschicksal* (Berlin, 1910), 267; Alfred Kerr, *Wo liegt Berlin? Briefe aus der Reichshauptstadt* (Berlin, 1999); Ruth Glatzer, ed., *Das Wilhelminische Berlin: Panorama einer Metropole* (Berlin, 1997), 36, 38, 39, 298; Walther Kiaulehn, *Berlin: Schicksal einer Weltstadt*, (Munich, 1997), 20–21.
3. Kiaulehn, *Berlin*, 222; Paul Lindenberg, *Berliner Polizei und Verbrechertum* (Leipzig, 1892), 11–12, 15, 145.
4. Glatzer, *Berlin*, 14, 66; Alfred Kerr, "Berliner Brief vom 30. September 1900," in *Wo liegt Berlin?* 615–616.
5. Glatzer, *Berlin*, 66.
6. Business Plan for 1896, GStA Rep. 84a/20442, *Landgericht Berlin I Allgemeines 1896–1901;* Karl Schwindt, *Verteidigungsschrift*, 12 April 1904, BA-BL R. 3005/671, *Ehrengerichtliches Verfahren gegen den Rechtsanwalt Dr. Karl Schwindt in Berlin*, 18; Frey, *Freispruch*, 8.
7. Johannes Werthauer, *Moabitrium: Szenen aus der Grossstadt-Strafrechtspflege*, Grossstadt-Dokumente Vol. 31 (Berlin, 1908), 6; Alsberg to EGH, 4 September 1912, BA-BL R. 3005/380, *Ehrengerichtliches Verfahren gegen den Rechtsanwalt Dr. Fritz Friedmann in Berlin*, 78.
8. KGP to JM, 5 May 1933, GStA Rep. 84a/20363, *Durchführung des Berufsbeamtengesetzes bezgl. Rechtsanwälte und Notare 1933*, 122; Frey to OSA II, 5 December 1924, LB Rep. 358/243, *Strafsache gegen Gerth*, vol. 2, unpaginated; Curt Riess, *Der Mann in der schwarzen Robe: Das Leben des Strafverteidigers Max Alsberg* (Hamburg, 1965), 163; Glatzer, *Berlin*, 305.
9. Lindenberg, *Berliner Polizei*, 146–148; Evans, *Rituals*, 417.

10. Lindenberg, *Berliner Polizei*, 131.
11. Architekten Verein zu Berlin, *Berlin und seine Bauten*, vol. 2 (Berlin,1896), 337; *Aus dem Berliner Rechtsleben: Festgabe zum XXVI. Deutschen Juristentage* (Berlin, 1902), 92.
12. Architekten Verein zu Berlin, *Berlin und seine Bauten*, 338; *Aus dem Berliner Rechtsleben*, 78.
13. Architekten Verein zu Berlin, *Berlin und seine Bauten*, 338–339, *Aus dem Berliner Rechtsleben*, 78.
14. Carl Vohl, "Das neue Kriminalgericht in Berlin-Moabit," in *Zeitschrift für das Bauwesen*, vol. 43 (1908), pp. 330–360 and 548–573, quoted in Helmet Engel et al., eds., *Geschichtslandschaft Berlin: Ort und Ereignisse*, Vol. 2: *Tiergarten* (Berlin, 1987), 217; Kiaulehn, *Berlin*, 505.
15. *Aus dem Berliner Rechtsleben*, 78–79; Franz Hoeniger, *Berliner Gerichte*, Grossstadt Dokumente vol. 24 (Berlin, 1905), 76.
16. Kiaulehn, *Berlin*, 505; *National Zeitung*, 6 November, 1898, GStA 84a/20442, *Landgericht Berlin I Allgemeines 1896–1901*, 154; Alfred Kerr, "Berliner Brief vom 30. May 1897," in *Warum Fliesst der Rhein nicht durch Berlin? Briefe eines europäischen Flaneurs* (Berlin, 1999), 110.
17. Fritz Friedmann, *Was ich erlebte!* vol. 1 (Berlin, 1911), 227–228; Maximilian Harden, "Guthmann," *Die Zukunft*, 29 April 1899, 186; Kiaulehn, *Berlin*, 506–507.
18. For an excellent brief discussion of the significance of substantive and procedural laws, see Kenneth F. Ledford, *From General Estate to Special Interest: German Lawyers 1878–1933* (Cambridge, UK, 1996).
19. Karl Binding, *Handbuch des Strafrechts* (Darmstadt, 1885), vii; Thomas Vormbaum, ed., *Strafrechtsdenker der Neuzeit* (Baden-Baden, 1998), 432; Eugen Ehrlich, *Freie Rechtsfindung und freie Rechtswissenschaft* (Leipzig, 1903); Hermann Kantorowicz, *Der Kampf um die Rechtswissenschaft* (Heidelberg, 1906); Gustav Radbruch, "Rechtswissenschaft als Rechtsschöpfung: Ein Beitrag zum juristischen Methodenstreit," *Archiv für Sozialwissenschaft und Sozialpolitik*, vol. 22, part 2 (1906), 355–370; Michael Stolleis, *Geschichte des öffentlichen Rechts in Deutschland*, vol. 3; Justus Olshausen, *Kommentar zum Strafgesetzbuch für das Deutsche Reich*, 9th ed. (Berlin, 1912), 1; Eberhard Schmidt, *Einführung in die Geschichte der deutschen Strafrechtspflege*, 3rd ed. (Göttingen, 1995), §§297–298 and §§327–338; Richard J. Evans, *Rituals of Retribution: Capital Punishment in Germany, 1600–1987*, (London, 1997), 331–347; Richard Wetzell, *Inventing the Criminal: A History of German Criminology 1880–1945* (Chapel Hill, 2000); Hans Heinrich Jescheck, "Einführung," *Strafgesetzbuch*, 33rd ed. (Munich, 1999).
20. Olshausen, *Kommentar*, 41, 90–95, 99–100, 104–112; O. G. Schwarz, *Strafrecht, Strafprozess: Ein Hilfsbuch für junge Juristen* (Berlin, 1907), 58–59.
21. GStA Rep. 84a/20255, *Akten betr. Miscellanea: Berlin Bezirks-Akten 1922–1923*,

333; Lindenberg, *Berliner Polizei*, 183, 187–1890; Olshausen, *Kommentar*, 96; Schwarz, *Strafrecht*, 64–65.
22. Franz Exner, *Studien über die Strafzumessungspraxis der deutschen Gerichte* (Leipzig, 1931), 19, 22; Olshausen, *Kommentar*, 104.
23. R. J. Delisle, *Evidence: Principles and Problems* (Toronto, 1993), 1–2.
24. Quoted by Lord Denning in *Jones v. Nat. Coal Board.*, [1957] 2 Q.B. 55, 64 (C.A.).
25. John Henry Wigmore, *Evidence in Trials at Common Law*, 4th rev. ed. (Boston, 1961).
26. See Andrew L.-T. Choo, *Hearsay and Confrontation in Criminal Trials* (Oxford, 1996); also Edmund M. Morgan, *Hearsay Dangers and the Application of the Hearsay Concept* (Cambridge, MA, 1949).
27. See John Langbein, *Torture and the Law of Proof: Europe and England in the Ancient Regime* (Chicago, 1977), especially Chapter 1; Langbein, *Prosecuting Crime in the Renaissance: England, Germany, France* (Cambridge, MA, 1974), Part II.
28. Schwarz, *Strafrecht*, 192–194.
29. E. Löwe, *Die Strafprozessordnung für das Deutsche Reich*, 12th ed. (Berlin, 1907), 632.
30. Schwarz, *Strafrecht*, 214.
31. This situation has only begun to change in recent years. The practice of plea bargaining began to work its way into German criminal law in the 1970s under the pressures of increased business, especially stemming from drug and commercial crime prosecutions. The controversy and the soul searching that have followed among German lawyers serve as an index of how utterly foreign the assumptions of such an "American" and adversarial practice are to the workings of German law; an Argentinean lawyer has called the practice of plea bargaining the "Trojan Horse" carrying the values of Anglo-Saxon common law into the civilian systems of continental Europe and Latin America. See Máximo Langer, "La dicotomía accusatorio-inquisitivo y la importación de mecanismos procesales de la tradición jurídica anglosajona. Algunas reflexiones a partir del proceedimiento abreviado," in Julio Maier and Alberto Bovino, eds., *el Procedimiento Abreviado* (Buenos Aires, 2001), 261. On the German plea bargaining debate, see Bernd Schünemann, *Absprachen im Strafverfahren? Grundlagen, Gegenstände und Grenzen. Verhandlungen des achtundfünfzigsten deutschen Juristentages* (Munich, 1990). I am very grateful to Maximo Langer for bringing these recent trends to my attention.
32. Löwe, *Strafprozessordnung*, 161; Schwarz, *Strafrecht*, 238–239; Aulus Agerius, "Der Einfluss der Staatsanwaltschaft in der preussischen Justiz," *Preussische Jahrbücher*, Bd. 81, Heft 1 (July 1895): 1–29, 13.
33. For an excellent legal analysis of the issue see Hecht, *Die Harden Prozesse*.
34. Löwe, *Strafprozessordnung*, 156–160; Chapters 2, 3 and 4, infra.

35. Schwarz, *Strafrecht*, 197–199.
36. Ibid., 230.
37. GVG, third title, Amtsgerichte, fourth title, Schöffengerichte, fifth title, Landgerichte, sixth title, Schwurgerichte, eighth title, Oberwaltungsgerichte, ninth title, Reichsgericht, Löwe, *Strafprozessordnung*, 41–105, 109–123.
38. Löwe, *Strafprozessordnung*, 43–73; Schwarz, *Strafrecht*, 174; *Justiz-Ministerial Blatt für die Preussische Gesetzgebung und Rechtspflege*, 1888, GStA Rep. 77/114/222, *Die Jahresberichte des Justizministers über die Justizverwaltung in der Preussischen Monarchie sowie die Jahrbücher der Preuss. Gerichtsverfassung*, vol. 1 1837–1899, 274–282, 524–531.
39. Löwe, *Strafprozessordnung*, 73–105; Schwarz, *Strafrecht*, 175–146.
40. Schwarz, *Strafrecht*, 237–249.
41. Martin Wiener, *Reconstructing the Criminal: Culture, Law and Policy in England, 1830–1914* (Cambridge, UK, 1990), 265.
42. Superior Court I, Overviews of Business for 1904 and 1905; GStA Rep. 84a/20443, *Landgericht Berlin I Allgemeines 1901–1906*, 183.
43. Reichs-Justizamt, *Deutsche Justiz-Statistik*, vol. 13 (Berlin, 1907), 222–223.
44. Von Klemens Klemmer, Rudolf Wassermann, and Thomas Michael Wessel, *Deutsche Gerichtsgebäude: Von der Dorflinde über den Justizpalast zum Haus des Rechts* (Munich, 1993), 107–111.
45. Erich Sello, *Die Irrtümer der Strafjustiz und ihre Ursachen* (Berlin, 1911), 461–462; Löwe, *Strafprozessordnung*, Drittes Buch, "Rechtsmittel," and Viertes Buch, "Wiederaufnahme eines durch rechtskräftiges Urteil geschlossenen Verfahrens," 742ff.
46. Schmidt, *Einführung*, 324, 327–342; GVG §1, Löwe, *Strafprozessordnung*, 21.
47. Agerius, "Einfluss," 3–4. The pseudonym was a reference that German lawyers, schooled as they were in Roman law, could be expected to understand. "Aulus Agerius" was a name like "John Doe," used for the plaintiff in a sample pleading or formulary in Gaius' *Institutes*. Charles Donahue, *Materials on Roman Law*, Privately Printed for Harvard Law Students, Fall 2002, 34, 38.
48. Schmidt, *Einführung*, 325–327, 330, 345–332; John H. Langbein, *Comparative Criminal Procedure: Germany* (St. Paul, MN, 1977), 90–92.
49. Schwarz, *Strafrecht*, 175–176.
50. Ernst Heinrich Rosenfeld, *Der Reichs-Strafprozess: Ein Lehrbuch*, 4th and 5th ed. (Berlin, 1912), 50, 101.
51. Agerius, "Einfluss," 4–5, 8, 10, 14, 16.
52. Numerius Negidius, "Aulus Agerius und die Preussische Staatsanwaltschaft," *Preussische Jahrbücher*, vol. 83, part 1 (January 1896): 97–114. Continuing the joke, Numerius Negidius is the name of the defendant in Gaius's sample formulary.
53. Ibid., 97, 99–100, 105–108.

54. Average calculated from the figures in *Statistisches Jahrbuch der Stadt Berlin*, vols. 16–27 (Berlin, 1890–1902).
55. *Frankfurter Zeitung*, 10 September 1907 M, GStA Rep. 84a/8255, *Meineid 1872–1930*, 86.
56. Figures are from *Statistisches Jahrbuch der Stadt Berlin*, vols. 15–31, 1888–1906, and the annual Reviews of Business, GStA 84a/20442, *Landgericht Berlin I Allgemeines 1896–1901* and GStA 84a/20443, *Landgericht Berlin I Allgemeines 1901–1906*.
57. Figures are in ibid.
58. *Statistisches Jahrbuch der Stadt Berlin*, vols. 16–20 (Berlin, 1890–1895).
59. Ibid.
60. BA-BL R.3001/6157, *Majestätsbeleidigung*, 11.
61. *Statistisches Jahrbuch der Stadt Berlin*, vols. 22–33 (Berlin 1897–1916).
62. LGP I to JM, 17 March 1896, GStA Rep. 84a/20442, *Landgericht I Allgemeines, 1896–1901*, 44–46; Isenbiel to JM, 22 June 1900, GStA Rep. 84a/57471, *Ermordung des Gymnasiasten Ernst Winter in Konitz*, vol. 1, 250–251; Frey, *Freispruch*, 5.
63. Theodor Liebknecht, *Beschwerde*, 8 August 1904, Isenbiel to OSA KG, 16 August 1904, GStA Rep. 84a/49721, *Kaliski-Schneidt*, 4–9, 14.
64. Ludwig Flatau, *Mehr Schutz für die Rechtspflege! Legislative Betrachtungen über einige Prozesse aus der letzten Zeit* (Berlin, 1901), 74, 55; Friedmann, *Was ich erlebte!* vol. 1, 120, 126; Maximilian Harden, "Hammerstein und Friedmann," *Die Zukunft*, 4 January 1896, 8.
65. *BM*, 20 December 1907, GStA Rep. 84a/49839, *Die Strafsache gegen den Schriftsteller Harden wegen Beleidigung des Grafen Moltke: Beiakten enthaltend Zeitungsberichte*, vol. 1, 256; OSA KG to JM, 14 February 1902, GStA Rep. 84a/20201, *Beförderung*, 52–53. On Isenbiel's conduct of the Harden-Eulenburg cases see Hans von Tresckow, *Von Fürsten und anderen Sterblichen. Erinnerungen eines Kriminalkommissars* (Berlin, 1922), 133–211; and Karsten Hecht, *Die Harden Prozesse: Strafverfahren, Öffentlichkeit und Politik im Kaiserreich* (Ph.D. diss., Ludwig-Maximilian-University, Munich, 1997); for the Sternberg case see Chapters 3 and 4.
66. 1st STA LG I to OSA KG, 18 October 1907, GStA Rep. 84a/20891, *Staatsanwaltschaft beim LG I 1905–1913*, 82 ff.
67. Ibid., 82.
68. Ibid., 83–84.
69. Ibid., 84.
70. Ibid., 85–86.
71. Report of the Vors., Strafkammer 4, to LGP, 28 May 1913, GStA Rep. 84a/20446, *Landgericht I Allgemeines, 1911–14*, 201b-c; Report of the KGP, 12 May 1908, Vorsitz der Strafkammern, GStA 84a/20444, *Landgericht I Allgemeines, 1906–08*, 163.

72. 1st STA LG I to OSA KG, 18 October 1907, GStA Rep. 84a/20891, *Staatsanwaltschaft beim LG I 1905–1913*, 85, 87.
73. *BT,* 20 December 1900; Friedmann, *Was ich erlebte!* vol. 1, 283; Report of the KGP, 12 May 1908, Vorsitz der Stafkammern, GStA Rep 84a/20444, *Landgericht I Allgemeines, 1906–1908*, 163.
74. *National Zeitung,* 6 November 1898, GStA 84a/20442, *Landgericht I Allgemeines, 1896–1901*, 154.
75. *BM,* 7 May 1913, *Das Kleine Journal,* 13 May 1913, GStA, Rep. 84a/20446, *Landgericht I Allgemeines, 1911–1914*, 198a.
76. KGP to JM, 11 June 1913, Vors. Strafkammer 4, 28 May 1913, in ibid., 201a, 201c.
77. Hoeniger, *Berliner Gerichte,* 54; Friedmann, *Was ich erlebte!* vol. 1, 144–145.
78. Friedmann, *Was ich erlebte!* vol. 2, 23, 65; Karl Schwindt to EGH, 12 April 1904, BA-BL R. 3005/671, *Ehrengerichtliches Verfahren gegen den Rechtsanwalt Dr. Karl Schwindt in Berlin,* 22. Friedmann actually wrote that sixty to seventy people would visit him during his office hours, but ten or fifteen would be creditors or bailiffs.
79. Attest des Dr. Merzbach, 18 June 1904, in BA-BL R. 3005/671, *Ehrengerichtliches Verfahren gegen den Rechtsanwalt Dr. Karl Schwindt in Berlin,* 36; LGP I to JM, 17 March 1896, *National Zeitung,* 6 November 1898, GStA Rep. 84a/20442, *Landgericht I Allgemeines 1896–1901,* 44–46, 154; *Berliner Börsen Courier,* 4 January 1908 M, GStA Rep. 84a/49840, *Die Strafsache gegen den Schriftsteller Harden wegen Beleidigung des Grafen Moltke. Beiakten enthaltend Zeitungsberichte,* vol. 2, 24. For the Heinze trial see Chapter 2 infra.
80. Maximilian Harden, *Prozesse: Köpfe III. Teil* (Berlin, 1913), 207–208; Tresckow, *Fürsten,* 94; *VZ,* 14 May 1892 A; *KZ,* 10 April 1895 A, GStA Rep. 84a/20507, *Landgericht II Allgemeines vol. I 1895–1900,* 37.
81. Hoeniger, *Berliner Gerichte,* 9–10; *BT,* 12 March 1903 M. See also Evans, *Rituals,* 472–475; Peter Jelavich, *Berlin Cabaret* (Cambridge, MA, 1996), 89–90.
82. Hoeniger, *Berliner Gerichte,* 11; Alfred Kerr, Berliner Brief vom 1. December 1895, in Kerr, *Wo liegt Berlin?* 98.
83. *BT,* 4 December 1904 S.
84. Peter Fritzsche, *Reading Berlin 1900* (Cambridge, MA, 1996), 16–18, 78; Theodor Fontane, *Die Poggenpuhls* (Stuttgart, 1969), 42, 45. On the Berlin press see also Peter de Mendelssohn, *Zeitungsstadt Berlin* (Frankfurt, 1982); Kurt Koszyk, *Deutsche Presse im 19. Jahrhundert. Geschichte der deutschen Presse Teil II* (Berlin 1966).
85. Hoeniger, *Berliner Gerichte,* 24–25.
86. Walter Bahn, *Meine Klienten: Beiträge zur modernen Inquisition,* Grossstadt-Dokumente vol. 42 (Berlin, 1908); Walter Bahn, *Der Prozess der Frau Schoenebeck-Weber* (Berlin, 1910); David Halpert, *Der Prozess Sternberg. Kriminalistische Randglossen* (Berlin, 1900); Erich Sello, *Die Hau-Prozesse und*

ihre Lehren. Auch ein Beitrag zur Strafprozessreform (Berlin, 1908); Erich Sello, *Zur Psychologie der cause célèbre: Ein Vortrag* (Berlin, 1910).

87. Gertrud Wertheim, *Meine Glaubwürdigkeit im Metternich-Prozess* (Berlin, 1911); Wilhelm Friedenstein, *Ein Justizmord und der Herr Landgerichtsdirektor Brausewetter in Berlin. Ein Beitrag zur Frage der Wiedereinführung der Berufungsinstanz in Deutschland* (Leipzig, 1892). Friedenstein's Justice Ministry file also survives: GStA Rep. 84a/16413, *Betrug, Beleidigung und Erpressung durch den Zeitungsverleger und Redakteur Wilhelm Friedenstein aus Berlin 1889–1892*.

88. Examples of the anti-Semitic variety are legion: see, e.g., *Der Konitzer Blutmord vor dem Berliner Gericht: Die Verhandlungen des Presseprozesses gegen die "Staatsbürger-Zeitung" vor der II. Strafkammer des Königl. Landgerichts I , 30. September bis 11. Oktober 1902* (Berlin, 1902). An example of the left-leaning variety is Karl Schneidt, *Der Plötzensee-Prozess und seine Bedeutung* (Berlin, 1906).

89. Maximilian Harden, "Prozess Berger," *Die Zukunft*, 24 December 1904, 412; *BT*, 11, 13, and 15 June 1904.

90. "Der Mann, der Justitia bewachte. Was 'Nande' erzählt. Aus den Erinnerungen eines Moabiter Justizwachtmeisters," *8 Uhr Abendblatt*, 28 October 1925, GStA Rep. 84a/20256, *Misc. betr. Rechtsanwälte 1923–1926*, 196; Simone Ladwig-Winters, *Anwalt ohne Recht: Das Schicksal jüdischer Rechtsanwälte in Berlin nach 1933* (Berlin, 1998), 14, 21; Dietrich Güstrow, *Tödlicher Alltag: Strafverteidiger im Dritten Reich* (Berlin, 1981), 12–13.

91. Friedmann, *Was ich erlebte!* vol. 1, 104–105; Kiaulehn, *Berlin*, 513. For a typical humor-in-court book see *Berliner Humor vor Gericht: Heitere Scenen aus den Berliner Gerichtssälen* (Berlin, 1905).

92. Hoeniger, *Berliner Gerichte*, 13.

2. The Berlin of Surrogates

1. Joachim Schlör, *Nights in the Big City: Paris, Berlin, London 1840–1930*, trans. Pierre Gottfried Imhof and Dafydd Rees Roberts (London, 1998), 77–90.

2. *Statistisches Jahrbuch der Stadt Berlin, 34. Jahrgang, enthaltend die Statistik der Jahre 1915–1919* (Berlin, 1920), 4; Ruth Glatzer, *Das Wilhelminische Berlin: Panorama einer Metropole* (Berlin, 1997), 312–313; Walther Kiaulehn, *Berlin: Schicksal einer Weltstadt* (Munich, 1997), 87; "Die Welt der Lucie Berlin," *BT*, 19 December 1904 M.

3. Karl Scheffler, *Berlin: Ein Stadtschicksal* (Berlin, 1910), 183, 86–7; Glatzer, *Berlin*, 313; Andrew Lees, *Cities Perceived: Urban Society in European and American Thought, 1820–1940* (Manchester, UK, 1985), 121.

4. Cf. *SZ* 19 March 1905 M: "The cesspool of the big city doesn't just begin across the Weidendamm Bridge—we find it already in full display in the center of town."
5. Peter Fritzsche, *Reading Berlin 1900* (Cambridge, MA, 1996); Robert A. Nye, *Crime, Madness and Politics in Modern France: The Medical Concept of Decline* (Princeton, NJ, 1984); Schlör, *Nights;* Lees, *Cities Perceived,* 106, 42–43, 85; Fritz Stern, *The Politics of Cultural Despair: A Study in the Rise of German Ideology,* (Berkeley, CA, 1961); Hugo Friedlaender, "Die Ermordung der 8-jährige Lucie Berlin. (Ein Beitrag zum Berliner Zuhälter- und Dirnenwesen)," *Interessante Kriminalprozesse von Kulturhistorischer Bedeutung,* vol. 4 (Berlin, 1911), 4.
6. Schäfer, "Die Welt der Lucie Berlin."
7. Heinrich Löwenthal, *Der goldene Galgen. Berichte über Kriminalfälle aus dem alten Berlin* (East Berlin, 1951), 126.
8. Isabella Classen, *Darstellung von Kriminalität in den deutschen Literatur, Presse, and Wissenschaft 1900 bis 1930* (Frankfurt am Main, 1988); Richard Wetzell, *Inventing the Criminal: A History of German Criminology 1880–1945* (Chapel Hill, 2000); Maximilian Harden, "Prozess Berger," *Die Zukunft,* 24 December 1904, 417; Erich Frey, *Ich beantrage Freispruch: Aus den Erinnerungen des Strafverteidigers Prof. Dr. Dr. Erich Frey* (Hamburg, 1959), especially 247–268; Artur Landsberger, *Die Unterwelt von Berlin. Nach den Aufzeichnungen eines ehemaligen Zuchthäuslers, mit einer Schlussbetrachtung von Dr. Max Alsberg* (Berlin, 1929). Patrick Wagner, *Volksgemeinschaft ohne Verbrecher: Konzeption und Praxis der Kriminalpolizei in der Zeit der Weimarer Republik und des Nationalsozialismus* (Hamburg, 1996), has an excellent discussion of the politics of criminal statistics: see "Einleitung," 9–16.
9. Paul Lindenberg, *Berliner Polizei und Verbrechertum* (Leipzig, 1892), 67–68; Reichs-Justizamt, *Kriminalstatistik für das Jahr 1887* (Berlin, 1889), 12–14; Justus Olshausen, *Kommentar zum Strafgesetzbuch für das Deutsche Reich,* 9th ed. (Berlin, 1912), 799, 809–810; Karl Lorenz et al., eds., *Justus von Olshausen's Kommentar zum Strafgesetzbuch für das Deutsche Reich,* 11th ed., vol. 2 (Berlin, 1927), 1991; Richard J. Evans, *Tales from the German Underworld: Crime and Punishment in the Nineteenth Century* (New Haven, CT, 1998), 183–184.
10. *Statistisches Jahrbuch der Stadt Berlin,* vol. 27 (1900–1902) (Berlin, 1903), 509; Evans, *Tales,* 198.
11. Peter Fritzsche, "Vagabond in the Fugitive City: Hans Ostwald, Imperial Berlin and the Grossstadt-Dokumente," *Journal of Contemporary History* 29 (1994): 385–402, 387–388; Evans, *Tales,* 171–74; §289 Reich Criminal Code, Olshausen, *Kommentar,* 11. ed., vol. 2, 1610; *Statistisches Jahrbuch der Stadt Berlin,* vol. 27, 536.
12. *NAZ,* 29 September 1891 M.

13. Police sketch of the crime scene, BLHA Rep. 30 Berlin C, Tit. 198 B/18, Polizeipräsidium Berlin Mordkommission, unpaginated; *VZ*, 27 September 1887 A; *NAZ*, 29 September 1891 M.
14. Hugo Friedlaender, *Kulturhistorische Kriminal-Prozesse der letzten vierzig Jahre* (Berlin, 1908), 72; *VZ*, 27 September 1887 A; *NAZ*, 29 September 1891 M.
15. "Die Organisation der Berliner Kriminalpolizei," undated, BLHA Rep. 30 Berlin C, Tit. 198 B/1936; Andreas Roth, *Kriminalitätsbekämpfung in deutschen Grossstädten 1850–1914: Ein Beitrag zur Geschichte des strafrechtlichen Ermittlungsverfahren* (Berlin, 1997), 52–53, 252–254.
16. Leopold von Meerscheidt-Hüllessem, "Vorbereitung und Bearbeitung von Kapitalsachen," 15 May 1899, Meerscheidt-Hüllessem, "Vorbereitung und Bearbeitung von Kapitalsachen," 7 August 1899, "Anleitung für die Bearbeitung von Kapitalverbrechen," 3 July 1902, BLHA Rep. 30 Berlin C. Tit. 198B/1933, *Vorbereitung der Polizei auf die Bearbeitung von Kapitalverbrechen,* 5, 18, 20–37.
17. *NAZ*, 29 September 1891 M.
18. Hans von Tresckow, *Von Fürsten und anderen Sterblichen: Erinnerungen eines Kriminalkommissars* (Berlin, 1922), 61; Lindenberg, *Berliner Polizei,* 58; Frey, *Freispruch,* 102; *VZ*, 2 October 1911 M.
19. *VZ*, 28 September 1891 A; Trial Protocol, 28 September 1891, BA-BL R. 3005/286, *Ehrengerichtliches Verfahren,* 41.
20. Trial Protocol, 28 September 1891, BA-BL R. 3005/286, *Ehrengerichtliches Verfahren,* 38, 41; *NAZ*, 29 September 1891 M.
21. *NAZ*, 29 September 1891 M; *BT*, 29 September 1891 M. The *NAZ*, the *VZ*, *Vorwärts* and the *BT*—despite the wide range of ideologies represented here— evidently got their coverage of the story from the same reporter, as the transcripts they carried are identical. Each paper supplemented the transcripts with its own editorial commentary, however.
22. George Weyhe, "Die Berliner Justizgebäude," in *Aus dem Berliner Rechtsleben: Festgabe zum XXVI. Deutschen Juristentage* (Berlin, 1902), 78; Lindenberg, *Berliner Polizei,* 142; Architekten Verein zu Berlin, *Berlin und seine Bauten,* vol. 2 (Berlin, 1896), 339; Von Klemmens Klemmer, Rudolf Wassermann, and Thomas Michael Wessel, *Deutsche Gerichtsgebäude: Von der Dorflinde über den Justizpalast zum Haus des Rechts* (Munich, 1993), 90.
23. Fritz Friedmann, *Was ich erlebte! Memoiren* (Berlin, 1911), vol. 1, 104.
24. David Blackbourn, *The Long Nineteenth Century: Germany 1780–1918* (London, 1997), 351–399.
25. Benjamin F. Martin, *The Hypocrisy of Justice in the Belle Époque* (Baton Rouge, LA, 1984), 3–4.
26. *Effi Briest*, in Theodor Fontane, *Romane* (Düsseldorf, 1998).
27. Trial Protocol, 28 September 1891, BA-BL R. 3005/286, *Ehrengerichtliches Ver-*

fahren, 38; Landgericht I, Business Plan for 1896, GStA Rep. 84a/20442, *Landgericht Berlin I Allgemeines 1896–1901*, 11–33; Judgment of the Berlin EG, 29 October 1891, *JW*, 22 February 1892, 117; Friedmann, *Was ich erlebte!* vol. 1, 127; OSA KG to JM, 3 May 1893, GStA Rep. 84/20890, *Staatsanwaltschaft bei dem Landgericht I Allgemeines, 1893–1905*, 1.

28. *Reichsgerichtsrat* Olshausen, Bericht, BA-BL R. 3005/286, *Ehrengerichtliches Verfahren*, 61.
29. Friedlaender, *Kulturhistorische Kriminal-Prozesse*, 73; *BT*, 29 September 1891 M; *NAZ*, 29 September 1891 M.
30. Trial Protocol, 28 September 1891, BA-BL R. 3005/286, *Ehrengerichtliches Verfahren*, 38; *NAZ*, 29 September 1891 M.
31. *NAZ*, 29 September 1891 M.
32. Ibid.
33. In fact, §245 of the StPO stated explicitly that a court could not deny a motion to call further evidence only on the grounds that the motion was brought at too late a stage of the proceedings. E. Löwe, *Die Strafprozessordnung für das Deutsche Reich*, 12th ed. (Berlin, 1907), 602–603.
34. *NAZ*, 29 September 1891 M; *JW*, 22 February 1892, 115.
35. *NAZ*, 30 September 1891 M.
36. *NAZ*, 1 October 1891 M.
37. *Vorwärts*, 1 October 1891.
38. *NAZ*, 29 September 1891 M; Trial Protocol, 28 September 1891, BA-BL R. 3005/286, *Ehrengerichtliches Verfahren*, 42–43.
39. *BT*, 29 September 1891 M; *NAZ*, 29 September 1891 M.
40. *Vorwärts*, 2 October 1891.
41. *NAZ*, 29 September 1891 A.
42. *NAZ*, 29 September 1891 A.
43. Ibid.
44. *NAZ*, 30 September 1891 M, 1 October 1891 M.
45. *Vorwärts*, 1 October 1891.
46. *VZ*, 2 October 1891 A; *NAZ*, 2 Oktober 1891 M; Trial Protocol, 28 September 1891, BA-BL R. 3005/286, *Ehrengerichtliches Verfahren*, 55.
47. *NAZ*, 2 October 1891 M.
48. *VZ*, 4 October 1891 S.
49. Andrew Lees, *Cities Perceived: Urban Society in European and American Thought, 1820–1940* (Manchester, UK, 1985), 163; Fritz Stern, *The Politics of Cultural Despair: A Study in the Rise of German Ideology* (Berkeley, CA, 1961); Max Nordau, *Degeneration* (Lincoln, NE, 1993).
50. *VZ*, 2 October 1891 M.
51. *VZ*, 4 October 1891 S.
52. *Vorwärts*, 2, 3, 4, 6 and 15 October 1891.

53. *KZ*, 7 October 1891, GStA Rep. 84a/17195, *Äusserungen der Presse betreffend Verbrechen und Vergehen wider die Sittlichkeit*, 2; *TR*, 13 October 1891; *NAZ*, 4 October 1891 M; *VZ*, 4 October 1891 S; *Vorwärts*, 15 October 1891.
54. *KZ*, 2 October 1891 A, GStA Rep. 84a/17195, *Verbrechen und Vergehen wider die Sittlichkeit*, 1; *Die Neue Zeit*, 5 October 1891, 65–66. A (presumably ministerial) reader marked the passage in Meerscheidt-Hüllessem's memo with a "?" and a "!" Meerscheidt-Hüllessem, "Vorbereitung und Bearbeitung von Kapitalsachen," 7 August 1899, BLHA Rep. 30 Berlin C. Tit. 198B/1932, *Vorbereitung*, 21. Fontane finished his novella early in 1892, though it was not published until 1896. Theodor Fontane, *Die Poggenpuhls* (East Berlin, 1980), 128, and "Afterword" by Hans-Heinrich Reuter, 51.
55. Kenneth F. Ledford, *From General Estate to Special Interest: German Lawyers 1878–1933* (Cambridge, UK, 1996), ch. 8; Tilmann Krach, *Jüdische Rechtsanwälte in Preussen: Über die Bedeutung der freien Advokatur und ihre Zerstörung durch den Nationalsozialismus* (Munich, 1991), especially ch. 2, part 3; Georg Simmel, "The Metropolis and Mental Life," in *On Individuality and Social Forms: Selected Writings*, ed. Donald N. Levine (Chicago, 1971), 336.
56. *NAZ*, 2 October 1891; *Vorwärts*, 2 October 1891; *BT*, 2 October 1891 M; Theodor Fontane, Brief von 4 Okt. 1891, in Fontane, *Briefe an Georg Friedlaender* (Frankfurt/Main, 1994) 218; *JW*, 22 February 1892, 116.
57. *JW*, 29 January 1892, 54–55; *Rondel v. Worsley*, [1969] 1 A.C. 191 (H.L.); Bramwell, B., in *Johnson v. Emerson and Sparrow*, [1871] L.R. 6 Ex. 329 at 367; Adolf Weissler, *Die Geschichte der Rechtsanwaltschaft* (Leipzig, 1905), 612; Julian Witting, "Kriminal-Verteidiger," *Die Zukunft*, 22 Dezember 1900, 498.
58. Fritz Friedmann, *Die wahren Lehren des Heinze'schen Prozesses für Sitten- und Rechtspflege* (Berlin, 1891), 29; *BT*, 5 November, 1891, GStA Rep. 84a/30075, *Die Bestellung von Offizial-Verteidiger bei den Berliner Gerichten 1891–1906*, 3–4.
59. Michael John, "Between Estate and Profession: Lawyers and the Development of the Legal Profession in 19th Century Germany," in David Blackbourn and Richard J. Evans, eds., *The German Bourgeoisie: Essays on the Social History of the German Middle Class from the Late 18th to the Early 20th Centuries* (London, 1993), 179; GStA Rep. 84a/20152, 20153 and 20154, *Anwaltskammer in Berlin 1879–1899, 1900–1911* and *1912–1928*; Friedmann, *Was ich erlebte!* vol. 1, 107.
60. Dirk Blasius, *Geschichte der politischen Kriminalität in Deutschland 1800–1900* (Frankfurt/Main, 1983), 60; W. L. Guttsman, *The German Social Democratic Party, 1875–1933* (London, 1981), 61; J. C. G. Röhl, *Germany without Bismarck: The Crisis of Government in the Second Reich, 1890–1900* (Berkeley, CA, 1967), 43, 72, 281.
61. *Kölnische Zeitung*, 28 October 1891 1. M.

62. *Kölnische Zeitung*, 4 November 1891 A; *NAZ*, 29 September 1891 M.
63. JM to IM, 6 October 1891, GStA Rep. 77/423/83, *Die Bekämpfung des Zuhältertums*, Bd.1 1891–1897, 2–4.
64. §181a StGB, Olshausen, *Kommentar*, vol. 1, 718; Otto Müller, *Die Lex Heinze* (Freiburg, 1900), 6, 63–67, 120; R. J. V. Lenman, "Art, Society and the Law in Wilhelmine Germany: The Lex Heinze," *Oxford German Studies Review* 8 (1972).
65. Lenman, "Lex Heinze", 87–88; Franz von Liszt, *Lehrbuch des Deutschen Strafrechts*, 21/22 ed. (Berlin, 1919), 350; Olshausen, *Kommentar*, 718, 738–739; *Mordprozess Heinze (Verhandelt vor dem Schwurgericht zu Berlin in den Jahren 1891 und 1892). Der Ursprung der "Lex Heinze." Der unfreiwillige Taufpate der "Lex Heinze"* (Berlin, 1900) (anonymous).
66. *BT*, 5 November 1891, GStA 84a/30075, *Offizial-Verteidiger*, 3–4. The clipping has a covering note: "To his Excellency Mr. State- and Justice Minister Dr. von Schelling."
67. JM to KGP, 12 November 1891, JM to KGP, 9 April 1892, LGP to KGP, 20 January 1894, KGP to JM, 9 February 1894, GStA 84a/30075, *Offizial-Verteidiger*, 6, 33–34, 39–40, 45–47; Hermann Isay, "Die Anwaltschaft in Berlin," in *Aus dem Berliner Rechtsleben*, 111.
68. KGP to JM, 9 February 1894, LGP to KGP, 16 January 1892, GStA 84a/30075, *Offizial-Verteidiger*, 39, 41, 15.
69. Friedmann, *Die wahren Lehren*; Friedmann, *Was ich erlebte!* vol. 1, 119, 129–131; Erich Sello, "Strafprozessreform," *Die Zukunft*, 17 December 1904, 43.
70. Adolf and Max Friedländer, *Kommentar zur Rechtsanwaltsordnung vom 1 Juli, 1878* (Munich, 1920), 97; Fritz Ostler, *Die deutschen Rechtsanwälte 1871–1971*, 2nd ed. (Essen, 1982), 23.
71. Löwe, *Strafprozessordnung, 1907*, 420, 590; *JW*, 22 February 1892, 115–117.
72. *JW*, 22 February 1892, 118.
73. Friedmann, *Was ich erlebte!* vol. 1, 127; *VZ*, 16 March 1892 M; JM and IM to Prussian Ministry of State, 29 October 1891, BA-BL R. 3001/5780, *Sittlichkeitsvergehen*, 53.
74. *JW*, 22 February 1892, 118.
75. Ibid., 115, 118.
76. Ibid., 118–119.
77. Ibid.
78. Ibid.
79. *BT*, 5 November 1891 GStA 84a/30075, *Offizial-Verteidiger*, 3–4; JM and IM to Prussian Ministry of State, 29 October 1891, BA-BL R. 3001/5780, *Sittlichkeitsvergehen*, 52; OSTA KG to ORA, 28 November 1891, BA-BL R. 3005/286, *Ehrengerichtlichen Verfahren*, 2–3.
80. *JW*, 22 February 1892, 121–122, 124.

81. *VZ*, 27 June 1892 A.
82. JM and IM to Prussian Ministry of State, 29 October 1891, BA-BL R.3001/ 5780, *Abänderung von Vorschriften des Strafgesetzbuchs gegen Sittlichkeitsvergehen*, Bd. 2 1890–1892, 52; *VZ*, 27 June 1892 A.
83. *VZ*, 27 June 1892 A, 29 June 1892 M; *Mordprozess Heinze*, 71.
84. *Mordprozess Heinze*, 68.
85. *VZ*, 3 July 1892 S; *Mordprozess Heinze*, 75.
86. "Der Fall Prager und der Fall Brausewetter," *BLA*, 24 January 1892.
87. *BLA*, 9 April 1899 S; *BLA*, 13 April 1899 A; *BLA*, 16 April 1899 S; Maximilian Harden, "Guthmann," *Die Zukunft*, 29 April 1899, 185–190.
88. *DT*, 22 December 1904 A.
89. Maximilian Harden, "Prozess Berger," *Die Zukunft*, 24 December 1904, 413.
90. *BT*, 24 December 1904 A.
91. "Berlin Zweimillionenstadt," *DT*, 31 December 1904 A.

3. Honorable Men

1. David Blackbourn, *The Long Nineteenth Century: Germany 1780–1918* (London, 1997), 411.
2. David Blackbourn, "The German Bourgeoisie: An Introduction," in David Blackbourn and Richard J. Evans eds., *The German Bourgeoisie: Essays on the Social History of the German Middle Class from the Late 18th to the Early 20th Centuries* (London, 1993), 3 and related footnotes; Theodor Fontane, *Die Poggenpuhls* (Stuttgart, 1969), 61; Alfred Kerr, Berliner Brief of 30 September 1900, in *Wo liegt Berlin? Briefe aus der Reichshauptstadt, 1895–1900* (Berlin, 1999), 615–20; Ernst Ottwalt, *Denn sie wissen, was sie tun. Ein deutscher Justiz-Roman* (Berlin, 1931), 92; on officers and civil servants as equivalents to lawyers see *Geheimer Justizrat* Dr. von Wilmowski, "Die Thätigkeit des Ehrengerichtshofes für die Rechtsanwälte," *JW*, 14 June 1892, 289 ff; Ute Frevert, "Bourgeois Honor: Middle-Class Duelists in Germany from the Late Eighteenth to the Early Twentieth Century," in Blackbourn and Evans, *Bourgeoisie*, 256.
3. Hermann Müller, *Die Preussische Justizverwaltung: Eine systematische Darstellung der die administrativen Geschäfte der Justiz betreffenden Vorschriften*, 6th ed., vol. 1, 461, 464–465, 447, 463, 549; LGP I to KGP, 20 September 1888, KGP to JM, 4 October 1888, GStA Rep. 84a/40297, *Acta Personalia des Justiz-Ministeriums betreffend den Landgerichtsdirektor Lüty*, 7–8, 12–13.
4. *Berliner Börsen Zeitung*, 30 October 1907 M, GStA Rep. 84a/49839, *Die Strafsache gegen den Schriftsteller Harden wegen Beleidigung des Grafen Moltke*, 41; *DT*, quoted in *Die Post*, 25 April 1908 M, GStA Rep. 84a/49832, *Die Strafsache gegen den Fürsten Eulenburg*, 49; on honor as a public quality see definitions quoted by Ute Frevert in "Bourgeois Honor," 255.

5. Ralph Angermund, *Deutsche Richterschaft 1919–1945: Krisenerfahrung, Illusion, politische Rechtsprechung* (Frankfurt/Main, 1990), 23; Tilmann Krach, *Jüdische Rechtsanwälte in Pressen: Über die Bedeutung der freien Advokatur und ihre Zerstörung durch den Nationalsozialismus* (Munich, 1991), 36–37, 415; Simone Ladwig-Winters, *Anwalt ohne Recht: Das Schicksal jüdischer Rechtsanwälte in Berlin nach 1933* (Berlin, 1998), 11; Deutscher Juristinnenbund e.V., *Juristinnen in Deutschland. Die Zeit von 1900 bis 1998*, (Baden-Baden, 1998).
6. Franz Hoeniger, *Berliner Gerichte*, Grossstadt Dokumente, vol. 24 (Berlin, 1905), 62–63; Fritz Friedmann, *Was ich erlebte! Memoiren* (Berlin, 1911), vol. 1, 103, 117.
7. Hoeniger, *Berliner Gerichte*, 41, 64–65; Friedmann, *Was ich erlebte!* vol. 1, 117, 119–120; Angermund, *Richterschaft*, 23; Julian Witting, "Kriminal-Verteidiger," *Die Zukunft*, 22 December 1900, 505–506; Thomas Ormond, *Richterwürde und Regierungstreue. Dientsrecht, politische Betätigung und Disziplinierung der Richter in Preussen, Baden und Hessen 1866–1918* (Frankfurt/Main, 1994), 169, 341; Fritz Ostler, *Die deutschen Rechtsanwälte 1871–1971*, 2nd ed. (Essen, 1982), 129–132.
8. Hoeniger, *Berliner Gerichte*, 59.
9. Hoeniger, *Berliner Gerichte*, 60; Friedmann, *Was ich erlebte!* vol. 2, 4; Maximilian Harden, "Landgerichtsdirektor Schmidt," *Die Zukunft*, 16 June 1894, 490.
10. Drescher to JM, 1 January 1893, GStA Rep. 84a/49803, *Strafsache gegen den Schriftsteller Maximilian Harden in Berlin wegen Majestätsbeleidigung, 1893*, 3–8; Friedmann, *Was ich erlebte!* vol. 2, 8–9; Harden, "Landgerichtsdirektor Schmidt," 486.
11. Schelling to Drescher, 11 April 1893, Drescher to Schelling 9 May 1893, GStA Rep. 84a/49803, *Majestätsbeleidigung, 1893*, 28–29, 42–44. On the Schmidt case see also "Merkblatt: Ausführungen des Reichstagsabg. über Eingriffe der Preussischen Justizverwaltung in die Unabhängigkeit der Richter," GStA Rep. 84a/2944, *Richter und Staatsanwälte: Allgemeine Bestimmungen über die Anstellung im höhern Justizdienst, 1927–1930*, 3ff.
12. *VZ*, 5 June 1894 A; 6 June 1894 A.
13. Harden, "Landgerichtsdirektor Schmidt," 488. On Harden generally see Harry F. Young, *Maximilian Harden, Censor Germaniae: The Critic in Opposition from Bismarck to the Rise of Nazism* (The Hague, 1959); B. Uwe Weller, *Maximilian Harden und die "Zukunft"* (Bremen, 1970).
14. 1st STA LG I to JM, 2 May 1892, "Auszug aus den Akten in der Strafsache," GStA Rep. 84a/16772, *Versuchter Mord and Anstiftung zum Mord an Dr. Georg Prager durch den Handlungsgehilfen Max Schweitzer und Eugenie Prager aus Berlin 1892–1896*, 8–11, 45–51.
15. *BLA*, 20 January 1892 M.
16. "Der Fall Prager und der Fall Brausewetter," *BLA*, 24 January 1892; *BLA*, 22

January 1892 A; E. Löwe, *Die Strafprozessordnung für das Deutsche Reich*, 12th ed. (Berlin, 1907), 706–707, (emphasis added); *BLA*, 29 January 1892 A; *Vorwärts*, 30 January 1892; *VZ*, 24 May 1892 M; *VZ*, 22 April 1892.

17. *Berliner Volksblatt*, 4 December 1886, 5 December 1886; *TR*, 5 December 1886.
18. Report, Opinion, and Judgment of the *Ehrengerichtshof*, 27 April, 1888, BA-BL R. 3005/169, *Ehrengerichtliches Verfahren gegen den Rechtsanwalt Artur Stadthagen zu Berlin, 1888*, 30–33, 58–59; Stadthagen's written defense, 19 October 1892, Report, Stadthagen's written defense, 31 October 1892, BA-BL R. 3005/304, *Ehrengerichtliches Verfahren gegen den Rechtsanwalt Arthur Stadthagen in Berlin, 1892*, 45–46, 49–50, 54, 107.
19. Report, BA-BL R. 3005/304, *Ehrengerichtliches Verfahren*, 107–108.
20. Stadthagen's written defense, 31 October, 1892, Stadthagen's written defense, 19 October, 1892, Report, in Ibid., 46–47, 107; *VZ*, 29 April 1892 M, 30 April 1892 A; *Vorwärts*, 29 April 1892.
21. Stadthagen's written defense, 31 October 1892, BA-BL R. 3005/304, *Ehrengerichtliches Verfahren*, 52.
22. Ibid., 54–55.
23. Judgment of the Supreme Honor Court, 17 November 1892, BA-BL R. 3005/304, *Ehrengerichtliches Verfahren gegen den Rechtsanwalt Arthur Stadthagen in Berlin, 1892*, 133–134; *Entscheidungen des Ehrengerichtshofes für die deutsche Rechtsanwälte*, vol. 6, 1892–1893 (Berlin, 1894), 227–228.
24. *Das Kleine Journal*, 14 June 1894, GStA Rep. 84a/49620, *Die Untersuchung wider den früheren Rechtsanwalt Arthur Stadthagen zu Berlin*, 11–12 (see also the second volume of this file: GStA Rep. 84a/49621, *Die Untersuchung wider den früheren Rechtsanwalt Arthur Stadthagen zu Berlin*); Walther Killy and Rudolf Vierhaus, eds., *Deutsche Biographische Enzyklopädie*, vol. 9 (Munich, 1998), 431.
25. Hermann Ahlwardt, *Neue Enthüllungen: Judenflinten* (Dresden, 1892), and *Judenflinten: II. Theil* (Dresden, 1892); accounts of the trial in *BT*, 29 November to 10 December, 1892; Hugo Friedlaender, "Der Judenflinten-Prozess," in *Interessante Kriminal-Prozesse von kulturhistorischer Bedeutung*, vol. 1 (Berlin, 1910), 143–156; O. Bähr, "Der Prozess gegen Ahlwardt," *Grenzboten* IV 1892, GStA Rep. 84a/15114, *Prozess gegen Ahlwardt wegen der antisemitischen Druckschrift "Judenflinten," 1892–1894*, 165; Justus Olshausen, *Kommentar zum Strafgesetzbuch für das Deutsche Reich*, 9th ed. (Berlin, 1912), 743, 752, 759, 772.
26. *BT*, 10 December 1892 A; "Die innere Politik der Woche," *KZ*, 11 December 1892 S; *SZ*, "Rechtspflege. Der Prozess Gegen Ahlwardt," 4 January 1893; O. Bähr, "Der Prozess gegen Ahlwardt," *Grenzboten* IV 1892, GStA Rep. 84a/15114, *Prozess gegen Ahlwardt*, 165; "Pressstimmen über den Prozess Ahlwardt," *BT*, 12 December 1892 A.

27. This is a paraphrase from *VZ*, 10 May 1894 A.
28. *BT*, 8–9 May 1894; Bernt Engelmann, *Die Unsichtbare Tradition, vol. 1, Richter zwischen Recht und Macht. Ein Beitrag zur Geschichte der deutschen Strafjustiz von 1779 bis 1918* (Cologne, 1988), 254 ff.
29. Reports from *BT* and *VZ*, 9–10 May 1894; *BT*, 8 May 1894 A.
30. 1st STA LG I to JM, 10 May 1894, GStA Rep. 84a/49684, *Strafverfahren gegen Sozialdemokratische und bürgerliche Zeitungsredakteure*, 11–12; *BT*, 9 May 1894 A, 10 May 1894 M.
31. "Die innere Politik der Woche," *KZ*, 13 May 1894 S; *BT*, 11 May 1894 M, 11 May 1894 A; *VZ*, 10 May 1894 A.
32. Deputy Singer in the Reichstag, *Reichstag, 29. Sitzung*, 1 February 1896, 689; "Die innere Politik der Woche," *KZ*, 13 May 1894 S; LGP I to KGP and OSA KG, 16 May 1894, KGP and OSA to JM 18 May 1894, GStA Rep. 84a/49684, *Strafverfahren gegen Sozialdemokratische und bürgerliche Zeitungsredakteure*, 15, 18.
33. *BT*, 22 December, 1895, 11, 12, 16, and 20 January 1896.
34. Alfred Kerr, Berliner Brief of 25 December 1895, in *Wo liegt Berlin?* 110; *BT*, 2 February 1896.
35. *Reichstag, 29. Sitzung*, 1 February 1896, 701; Engelmann, *Unsichtbare Tradition*, 256; *BT*, 2 February 1896; Maximilian Harden, "Brausewetter", *Die Zukunft*, 25 January 1896, 192; Fritz Friedmann, *Was ich erlebte!* vol. 1, 128; Reichsgerichtsrat O. Bähr, "Der Prozess gegen Ahlwardt," *Grenzboten* IV 1892, GStA Rep. 84a/15114, *Prozess gegen Ahlwardt*, 165; Richard Grelling, "Epilog zum Fall Brausewetter," *BT*, 2 March 1896.
36. Julian Witting, "Kriminal-Vertheidiger," *Die Zukunft*, 22 December 1900, 495. Witting was Maximilian Harden's brother; like Harden, he had opted for a more Germanized name than their original Witkowski. Young, *Harden*, 5–6.
37. Adolf Weissler, *Die Geschichte der Rechtsanwaltschaft* (Leipzig, 1905), 536–537; Erich Sello, "Munckel," *VZ*, 15 April 1903 M; Friedmann, *Was ich erlebte!* vol. 1, 104–106.
38. Sello, "Munckel"; Hoeniger, *Berliner Gerichte*, 53.
39. See Werner Sarstedt, "Max Alsberg, ein deutscher Strafverteidiger. Festvortrag vor der Deutschen Strafverteidiger-Tagung am 13.10.1977 in Bonn," in Jürgen Taschke, ed., *Max Alsberg—Ausgewählte Schriften* (Baden-Baden, 1992), 28; Hoeniger, *Berliner Gerichte*, 55; Richard Finger, *Die Kunst des Rechtsanwalts: Eine systematische Darstellung ihrer Grundfragen unter besonderer Berücksichtigung der ehrengerichtlichen Rechtsprechung*, 2nd ed. (Berlin, 1912), 245.
40. Konrad H. Jarausch, *The Unfree Professions: German Lawyers, Teachers and Engineers, 1900–1950* (New York, 1990). Kenneth Ledford's argument is a variant: "German lawyers did not abandon liberalism so much as they ran out of solutions when their liberal practices failed at every turn to protect their profes-

sional interests." Kenneth F. Ledford, *From General Estate to Special Interest: German Lawyers 1878–1933* (Cambridge, UK, 1996), 295.

41. BM, 10 December 1912; Curt Riess, *Der Mann in der schwarzen Robe: Das Leben des Strafverteidigers Max Alsberg* (Hamburg, 1965), 35.
42. Weissler, *Rechtsanwaltschaft*, 616, and generally 608–616.
43. Annual Reports of the Berlin Lawyers' Chamber, GStA Rep. 84a/20152, *Anwaltskammer in Berlin 1879–1899;* and GStA Rep. 84a 20153, *Anwaltskammer in Berlin 1900–1911*.
44. Gordon to the EGH, 13 April 1897, BA-BL R. 3005/436, *Ehrengerichtliches Verfahren gegen die Rechtsanwälte Edmund und Alfred Ballien in Berlin, 1897,* 14–15, 20–21.
45. Report, 27 May 1897, Judgment of the Supreme Honor Court, 30 June 1897, in Ibid., 67, 77, 79.
46. Report, BA-BL R. 3005/616, *Akten in dem ehrengerichtlichen Verfahren gegen den Rechtsanwalt Dr. Alfred Ballien in Berlin, 1903,* 19; Lawyers' Chamber in Berlin, Annual Report for 1902, GStA Rep. 84a/20153, *Anwaltskammer in Berlin 1900–1911,* 113.
47. Judgment of the Supreme Honor Court, 11 June 1903, BA-BL R. 3005/616, *Ehrengerichtliches Verfahren,* 30.
48. Lawyers' Chamber in Berlin, Annual Report for 1903; Lawyers' Chamber in Berlin, Annual Report for 1904; Lawyers' Chamber in Berlin, Annual Report for 1906; GStA Rep. 84a/20153, *Anwaltskammer in Berlin, 1900–1911,* 120–121, 154, 183; Ballien's written defense, 29 June 1908, BA-BL R. 3005/855, *Akten in dem ehrengerichtlichen Verfahren wider den Rechtsanwalt Dr. Alfred Ballien in Berlin, 1908,* 11–12; *Handbuch über den königlich preussischen Hof und Staat für das Jahr 1918* (Berlin, 1918), 851.
49. Fritz Friedmann, *Was ich erlebte!* vol. 1, 111; Hoeniger, *Berliner Gerichte,* 53. The story of Friedmann's expulsion from the bar can be found in his memoirs, *Was ich erlebte!* (Berlin, 1911), vol. 2, chapters 3–5; and in the files of the *Ehrengerichtshof:* BA-BL R. 3005/107, *Akten in dem ehrengerichtlichen Verfahren wider die Rechtsanwälte Bruno Saul und Dr. Fritz Friedmann in Berlin, 1885;* BA-BL R. 3005/380, *Ehrengerichtliches Verfahren gegen den Rechtsanwalt Dr. Fritz Friedmann in Berlin, 1896.*
50. Ladwig-Winters, *Anwalt,* 223. For the Eulenburg case see *inter alia* Hans von Tresckow, *Von Fürsten und anderen Sterblichen: Erinnerungen eines Kriminalkommissars* (Berlin, 1922), 133–210; Maximilian Harden, *Prozesse: Köpfe III. Teil* (Berlin, 1913), 169–286, 409–508; Karsten Hecht, *Die Harden Prozesse: Strafverfahren, Öffentlichkeit und Politik im Kaiserreich* (Ph.D. diss., Ludwig-Maximilian-University, Munich, 1997), ch. 11; Isabel V. Hull, *The Entourage of Kaiser Wilhelm II 1888–1918* (Cambridge, UK, 1982), ch. 5.
51. Friedmann, *Was ich erlebte!* vol. 1, 117; Friedmann, "Juristische Glossen zum Ahlwardt Prozess," *Die Zukunft,* 17 December 1892, 554–555.

52. *BT,* 1 November 1900 A; *BT,* 2 June 1901 S.
53. *BT,* 7 December 1900 A.
54. *BM,* 10 December 1912; Alfred Kerr, Berliner Brief of 30 May 1897, in *Warum Fliesst der Rhein nicht durch Berlin? Briefe eines europäischen Flaneurs* (Berlin, 1999), 111; *BT,* 1 June 1901 A; *BT,* 2 June 1901 S.
55. Ute Frevert, *Ehrenmänner. Das Duell in der bürgerlichen Gesellschaft* (Munich, 1991), 11, 16–17; for Sello's literary activity see Chapter 4.
56. GStA Rep. 84a/17202, *Beleidigung durch Harriet Platho aus Charlottenburg und durch den Kaufmann Hugo Arndt aus Berlin in Zusammenhang mit dem Prozess gegen den Bankier August Sternberg wegen Sittlichkeitsverbrechen, 1900;* Judgment of the Ninth Criminal Chamber, 21 December 1900, GStA Rep 84a/17192, *Strafsache gegen den Bankier August Sternberg wegen Sittlichkeitsverbrechen,* 74–75; *BT,* 13 November 1900 A, 14 December 1900 A, 20–22 December 1900; Maximilian Harden, "Prozess Sternberg," *Die Zukunft,* 29 December 1900, 525–534.
57. *BT,* 20 December 1900 A, 21 December 1900 A.
58. *BT,* 22 December 1900, 2 June 1901 S.
59. *BT,* 1 June 1901, 2 June 1901 S.
60. Judgment of the EGH, 13 October 1902, BA-BL R. 3005/596, *Ehrengerichtliches Verfahren gegen den Rechtsanwalt Justizrat Dr. Erich Sello in Berlin,* 24.
61. Report, BA-BL R. 3005/1037, *Akten in dem ehrengerichtlichen Verfahren wider den Rechtsanwalt Dr. Karl Liebknecht in Berlin, 1912, 1914,* 56. Today, the visitor to the law library of Humboldt University in former East Berlin may surf the Web under a stained glass window depicting Liebknecht, Lenin, and Luxemburg frowning seriously at their law books; in other panels they seem to be dispensing legal advice to suitably grateful peasants.
62. Helmut Trotnow, *Karl Liebknecht (1871–1919): A Political Biography* (Hamden, CT, 1984), 65. The Judicial Code specified high treason as the one criminal offense in which the Imperial Supreme Court had original jurisdiction.
63. Annual Report, 1908, GStA Rep. 84a/20153, *Anwaltskammer in Berlin 1900–1911,* 223; *BT,* 30 April 1908 A.
64. Judgment of the EG, 29 April 1908, BA-BL R. 3005/869, *Akten in dem ehrengerichtlichen Verfahren wider Rechtsanwalt Dr. Karl Liebknecht aus Berlin, 1908,* 3–7; *BT,* 30 April 1908 A; *Die Entscheidungen des Ehrengerichtshofes für deutsche Rechtsanwälte,* vol. 14, 1908–1909 (Berlin, 1910), 83; Annual Report, 1908, GStA Rep. 84a/20153, *Anwaltskammer in Berlin 1900–1911,* 223.
65. Annual Report, 1911, GStA Rep. 84a/20154, *Anwaltskammer in Berlin 1912–38,* 11; Judgment of the EG, 11 October 1911, BA-BL R. 3001/4420, *Eingaben in ehrengerichtlichen Angelegenheiten,* unpaginated.
66. ORA to EGH, 22 May 1914, Beschluss of the EGH, 29 May 1914, Liebknecht to ORA, 24 September, 1914, BA-BL R. 3005/1037, *Akten in dem ehrengerichtlichen Verfahren wider den Rechtsanwalt Dr. Karl Liebknecht in Berlin, 1912,*

1914, 43; GSA KG to the EG in Berlin, 21 October 1911, ORA to Staatssekretär des Reichsjustizamts, 2 October 1914, JM to Staatssekretär des Reichsjustizamts, 27 October 1914, BA-BL R. 3001/4420, *Eingaben,* unpaginated.

67. Riess, *Alsberg,* 21–22.
68. *BM,* 24 December 1912, GStA Rep. 84a/20446, *Landgericht I Allgemeines,* 1911–1914, 123; Judgment of the EG, 27 November 1912, BA-BL R. 3005/1142, *Ehrengerichtliches Verfahren gegen die Rechtsanwälte Dr. Walther Jaffé und Dr. Max Alsberg zu Berlin,* 2–4.
69. Judgment of the EG, 27 November 1912, BA-BL R. 3005/1142, *Ehrengerichtliches Verfahren,* 6–7, 9, 16, 19–20, 27.
70. Ibid., 16–18.
71. *BZ am Mittag,* 23 October 1911, BA-BL R. 3001/4404, *Rechtsanwälte Angelegenheiten,* unpaginated; Judgment of the Honor Court, 27 November 1912, BA-BL R. 3005/1142, *Ehrengerichtliches Verfahren,* 21.
72. Judgment of the EG, 27 November 1912, BA-BL R. 3005/1142, *Ehrengerichtliches Verfahren,* 28–30, 40.
73. Judgment of the EGH, 11 October 1913; in Ibid., 79–80, 83–84.
74. Jürgen Taschke, "Einleitung," in Taschke, ed., *Ausgewählte Schriften,* 9.
75. The quote actually describes what Harden felt could be expected of a Berlin lawyer arguing a case in Frankfurt-on-Oder on behalf of the notorious killer August Sternickel. Harden, "Sternickel," in *Prozesse,* 522–523.
76. As for instance in the cases of Wilhelm Bruno Gehrt and Paul Krantz; see Erich Frey, *Ich beantrage Freispruch: Aus den Erinnerungen des Strafverteidigers Prof. Dr. Dr. Erich Frey* (Hamburg, 1959), 269–404.
77. Quoted in Jarausch, *Unfree Professions,* 13.
78. Finger, *Kunst,* 94–95, 26–27.
79. Peltasohn in the *Abgeordnetenhaus,* 5 February 1910, GStA Rep. 84a/2941, *Richter und Staatsanwälte,* 120; Ostler, *Rechtsanwälte,* 130–131.
80. *VZ,* 14 April 1903 A; JM to OLG presidents, 21 February 1914, GStA 84a/2942, *Richter und Staatsanwälte,* 24.

4. Justice Is Blind

1. Ludwig Flatau, *Mehr Schutz für die Rechtspflege! Legislative Betrachtungen über einige Prozesse aus der letzten Zeit* (Berlin, 1901), 17, 63, 69, 82.
2. Ibid., 11, 21, 39.
3. Ibid., 47–48, 49–53; *BT,* 14 February 1901.
4. Geoff Eley, *Reshaping the German Right: Radical Nationalism and Political Change after Bismarck* (New Haven, CT, 1980), 194. Generally: David Blackbourn, "The Politics of Demagogy in Imperial Germany," in *Populists and Patricians: Essays in Modern German History* (London, 1987), 217–245; David

Blackbourn, *The Long Nineteenth Century: Germany 1780–1918* (London, 1997), 411–16; Margaret Lavinia Anderson, *Practicing Democracy: Elections and Political Culture in Imperial Germany* (Princeton, NJ, 2000); Jonathan Sperber, *The Kaiser's Voters: Electors and Elections in Imperial Germany* (Cambridge, UK, 1997).

5. Steven E. Aschheim, *The Nietzsche Legacy in Germany, 1890–1990* (Berkeley, CA, 1992); Blackbourn, *Long Nineteenth Century*, 351–399; Flatau, *Mehr Schutz*, 74.

6. The classic texts of the so-called "Free Law Movement" are Oskar Bülow, *Gesetz und Richteramt* (Leipzig, 1885); Eugen Ehrlich, *Freie Rechtsfindung und Freie Rechtswissenschaft* (Leipzig, 1903); Hermann Kantorowicz, *Der Kampf um die Rechtswissenschaft* (Heidelberg, 1906). See also Karl Larenz, *Methodenlehre der Rechtswissenschaft*, 6th ed. (Berlin, 1991); Franz Wieacker, *Privatrechtsgeschichte der Neuzeit. Unter besonderer Berücksichtigung der deutschen Entwicklung*, 2nd ed. (Göttingen, 1996).

7. Georg R. Schroubek, "Zur Tradierung und Diffusion einer europäischen Aberglaubensvorstellung"; Albert Lichtblau, "Die Debatten über die Ritualmordbeschuldigungen im österreichischen Abgeordnetenhaus am Ende des 19. Jahrhunderts," in Rainer Erb, ed., *Die Legende von Ritualmord. Zur Geschichte der Blutbeschuldigung gegen Juden* (Berlin, 1993), 21, 267–292; Christoph Nonn, "Zwischenfall in Konitz. Anti-Semitismus und Nationalismus im preussischen Osten um 1900," *Historische Zeitschrift* 266 (1998): 387–418; Julius H. Schoeps, "Ritualmordbeschuldigung und Blutaberglaube. Die Affäre Buschoff im niederrheinischen Xanten," in Jutta Bohnke-Kollwitz et al., eds., *Köln und das rheinische Judentum* (Cologne, 1984), 286–299; Arthur Nussbaum, *Der Polnaer Ritualmordprozess. Eine kriminalpsychologische Untersuchung aus aktenmässiger Grundlage* (Berlin, 1906).

8. See Schoeps, "Ritualmordbeschuldigung," 286–290; GStA Rep. 84a/16771, *Strafsache gegen Heinrich Oberwinder wegen Beleidigung*; Hugo Friedlaender, "Der Xantener Knabenmord," in Friedlaender, *Interessante Kriminalprozesse von kulturhistorischer Bedeutung*, vol. 1 (Berlin, 1910), 69–70. The murder in Konitz has recently become the subject of a very fine social-historical study: Helmut Walser Smith, *The Butcher's Tale: Murder and Anti-Semitism in a German Town* (New York, 2002).

9. *BT*, 1 October 1902 A; Paul Block, "Das Räthsel von Konitz III," *BT*, 10 November 1900 A; Nonn, "Zwischenfall," 391; *BT*, 30 September 1902 M; Hugo Friedlaender, "Die Ermordung des Gymnasiasten Ernst Winter in Konitz," in *Interessante Kriminalprozesse von kulturhistorischer Bedeutung*, vol. 3 (Berlin, 1911), 76, 78.

10. Friedlaender, "Die Ermordung des Gymnasiasten Ernst Winter in Konitz," 105; OSA Marienwerder to JM, 24 April 1900, OSA Marienwerder to JM, 2 May

1900, GStA Rep. 84a/57471, *Ermordung des Gymnasiasten Ernst Winter*, vol. 1, 29, 30, 51.
11. OSA Marienwerder to JM, 2 May 1900, GStA Rep. 84a/57471, *Ermordung des Gymnasiasten Ernst Winter*, 52.
12. Paul Block, "Konitzer Auslese," *BT*, 12 November 1900 A; Friedlaender, "Die Ermordung des Gymnasiasten Ernst Winter in Konitz," 118–136; Isenbiel to JM, 28 July 1900, GStA Rep. 84a/16784, *Strafsache contra Boetticher und Genossen*, 1–2; Isenbiel to JM, 22 June 1900, GStA Rep. 84a/57471, *Ermordung des Gymnasiasten Ernst Winter*, 273–274.
13. Isenbiel to JM, 2 November 1900, GStA Rep. 84a/16784, *Strafsache contra Boetticher und Genossen*, 7–11.
14. *BT*, 2 October 1902 A, 3 October 1902 M, 6 October 1902 A.
15. *BT*, 10 October 1902 M, 12 October 1902 S; Isenbiel to JM, 6 July 1903, *Staatsbürger Zeitung*, 14 October 1903, 15 November 1903, GStA Rep. 84a/16784, *Strafsache contra Boetticher und Genossen*, 77–78, 90, 92.
16. *BT*, 21 March 1903 M; Hugo Friedlaender, "Das spiritistische Medium Anna Rothe," in Friedlaender, *Kriminalprozesse*, vol. 1, 242–243.
17. Friedlaender, "Das spiritistische Medium," 208; Maximilian Harden, "Anna Rothe & Co.," *Die Zukunft*, 4 April 1903, 43; Erich Sello, "Der Prozess Rothe," *Die Zukunft*, 18 April 1903, 93–94.
18. Sello, "Der Prozess Rothe," 95–96, 98.
19. Judgment of the 9th *Strafkammer, Landgericht* I, 21 December 1900, GStA Rep. 84a/17192, *Strafsache gegen den Bankier August Sternberg*, 10–11.
20. LGP II to KGP, 17 March 1896, GStA Rep. 84a/20442, *Landgericht Berlin I Allgemeines, 1896–1901*, 44; *BT*, 30 October 1900 A; Maximilian Harden, "Moabiter Dramaturgie," *Die Zukunft*, 17 November 1900, 264, 267.
21. Maximilian Harden, "Prozess Sternberg," *Die Zukunft*, 29 December 1900, 531, 533; Julian Witting, "Justizchronik," *Die Zukunft*, 12 January 1901, 85.
22. Hans von Kahlenberg (Helene von Monbart), *Nixchen: Ein Beitrag zur Psychologie der höheren Tochter* (Vienna, 1904).
23. It is Herbert's account of being with "Isolde": "She is very close to me, naked, soft, fragrant . . . I kiss her. I hold her tender, smooth body. I press her to me." Kahlenberg, *Nixchen*, 69.
24. Isenbiel to OSA KG, 30 April 1902, OSA KG to JM, 11 May 1902, GStA Rep. 84a/17332, *Strafsache gegen die Schriftsteller Helene von Monbart in Berlin-Steglitz und den Verlagsbuchhändler Karl Reissner wegen des unsittlichen Inhalts der Novelle "Nixchen," 1902–1904*, unpaginated.
25. OSA KG to JM, 6 May 1902, OSA KG to JM, 11 May 1902, OSA KG to JM, 12 December 1902, GStA Rep. 84a/17332, *Nixchen*, unpaginated; Harden, "Nixchen," 427–428.
26. OSA KG to JM, 8 June 1903, Isenbiel to JM, 24 September 1903, Isenbiel to JM,

25 October 1903, 1st STA LG II to JM, 18 March 1904, GStA Rep. 84a/17332, *Nixchen*, unpaginated; Harden, "Nixchen," 428–429.
27. 1st STA Neu-Ruppin to JM, 19 July 1904, KGP and OSA KG to JM, 4 September 1904, OSA KG to JM, 15 January 1906, GStA Rep. 84a/17332, *Nixchen*, unpaginated; Harden, "Nixchen," 429–430.
28. See discussion of the Plötzensee case in Chapters 1 and 5; Maximilian Harden, "Sextuor," *Die Zukunft*, 26 November 1910, 279; A. O. Weber, *Lieber ins Zuchthaus als entmündigt! Nachklange zum Schoenebeck-Prozess* (Berlin, 1912), 9; OSA KG to JM, 2 November 1912, GStA Rep. 84a/20891, *Staatsanwaltschaft beim Landgericht Berlin I Allgemeines, 1905–1913*, 190.
29. Franz von Liszt, *Die Reform des Strafverfahrens* (Berlin, 1906), 14; Richard Finger, *Die Kunst des Rechtsanwalts: Eine systematische Darstellung ihrer Grundfragen unter besonderer Berücksichtigung der ehrengerichtlichen Rechtsprechung*, 2nd ed. (Berlin, 1912), 10, 96.
30. See *inter alia* George L. Mosse's introduction to Max Nordau, *Degeneration* (Lincoln, NE, 1993); Susanna Barrows, *Distorting Mirrors: Visions of the Crowd in Late Nineteenth Century France* (New Haven, CT, 1981); Daniel Pick, *Faces of Degeneration: A European Disorder, c. 1848–c. 1918* (Cambridge, UK, 1989). Richard Wetzell has recently demonstrated the role of this discourse in the shaping of German criminology: Richard Wetzell, *Inventing the Criminal: A History of German Criminology 1880–1945* (Chapel Hill, NC, 2000), chs. 1 and 2.
31. Erich Sello, *Zur Psychologie der cause célèbre. Ein Vortrag* (Berlin, 1910), 19–21, 30–31, 43. On the Polna case see Arthur Nussbaum, *Der Polnauer Ritualmordprozesss. Eine kriminalpsychologische Untersuchung auf aktenmässiger Grundlage* (Berlin, 1906).
32. Julian Witting, "Justizchronik," *Die Zukunft*, 12 January 1901, 83–86.
33. O. G. Schwartz, *Strafrecht, Strafprozess: Ein Hilfsbuch für junge Juristen* (Berlin, 1907), 249; Hans von Tresckow, *Von Fürsten und anderen Sterblichen: Erinnerungen eines Kriminalkommissars* (Berlin, 1922), 201; Erich Sello, "Strafprozessreform," *Die Zukunft*, 17 December 1904, 380–381; Sello, *Psychologie*, 40; Fritz Friedmann, *Hau ist kein verstockter Mörder! Kritische Studie* (Berlin, 1907), 27–28; Max Alsberg, *Der Fall des Marquis de Bayros and Dr. Senerau. Ein Beitrag zur Lehre der unzüchtigen Schrift und unzüchtigen Darstellung* (Berlin, 1911), 8, 36, 39–40.
34. Johannes Werthauer, *Strafunrecht. Beitrag aus der Praxis zur Ermittlung und Beseitigung der strafrechtlichen Uebelstände, insbesondere zur Ersetzung des Strafgedankens durch den Erziehungsgedanken* (Berlin, 1919), 4; Johannes Werthauer, *Moabitrium. Szenen aus der Grossstadt-Strafrechtspflege*, Grossstadt-Dokumente, vol. 31 (Berlin, 1908), 9–24.
35. Werthauer, *Moabitrium*, 25–29.
36. Ibid., 6–7.

37. Johannes Werthauer, *Wie leicht man sich strafbar machen kann* (Berlin, 1912); Werthauer, *Strafunrecht*.
38. Erich Sello, *Die Irrtümer der Strafjustiz und ihre Ursachen. Erster Band: Todesstrafe und lebenslänglicher Zuchthaus in richterlichen Fehlspruchen neuerer Zeit* (Berlin, 1911), 1, 2, 466–468; Sello, *Die Hau-Prozesse und ihre Lehren. Auch ein Beitrag zur Strafprozessreform* (Berlin, 1908), 130–134.
39. Max Alsberg, *Justizirrtum und Wiederaufnahme* (Berlin, 1913), iii, xiii–xv; Oliver Wendell Holmes, Jr., *The Common Law* (New York, 1991), 1.
40. Alsberg, *Justizirrtum*, 3–4, 7–11, 26–29, 30.
41. Michael John, *Politics and the Law in Late Nineteenth-Century Germany: The Origins of the Civil Code* (Oxford, 1989); Wieacker, *Privatrechtsgeschichte*; Uwe Wesel, *Geschichte des Rechts: Von den Frühformen bis zum Vertrag von Maastricht* (Munich, 1997); Eberhard Schmidt, *Einführung in die Geschichte der deutschen Strafrechtspflege*, 3rd ed. (Göttingen, 1995); Larenz, *Methodenlehre*; Karlheinz Muscheler, *Relativismus und Freirecht. Ein Versuch über Hermann Kantorowicz* (Heidelberg, 1984); Gnaeus Falvius (Hermann Kantorowicz), *Der Kampf um die Rechtswissenschaft* (Baden-Baden, 2002), 5; Bülow, *Gesetz und Richteramt*, 30–31; Max Weber, "The Formal Qualities of Modern Law," in *Max Weber on Law in Economy and Society*, trans. Edward Shils and Max Rheinstein (Cambridge, MA, 1954), 309.
42. Karlheinz Muscheler, *Hermann Ulrich Kantorowicz. Eine Biographie* (Berlin, 1984), 32; Kantorowicz, *Kampf*, 23–24, 45; Weber, "The Rational and Irrational Administration of Justice," in Weber, *Law*, 355–356; Weber, "The Formal Qualities of Modern Law," 321, 306–307.
43. Sello, *Psychologie*, 41–42.
44. Siegfried Kracauer, *The Mass Ornament: Weimar Essays* (Cambridge, MA, 1995); Max Horkheimer and Theodor W. Adorno, *Dialectic of Enlightenment* (New York, 2002).
45. Andreas Roth, *Kriminalitätsbekämpfung in deutschen Grossstädten 1850–1914: Ein Beitrag zur Geschichte des strafrechtlichen Ermittlungsverfahren* (Berlin, 1997), 52–53; *BLA*, 14 April 1899 M.
46. *BLA*, 21 April 1899 M; Langenbruch, "Guthmann-Graphologen," *Die Zukunft*, 6 May 1899, 280.
47. Meerscheidt-Hüllessem, "Vorbereitung und Bearbeitung von Kapitalsachen," 15 May 1899, "Vorbereitung und Bearbeitung von Kapitalsachen," 7 August 1899, BLHA Rep. 30 Berlin C, Tit. 198B/1932, *Vorbereitung*, 3–4, 13.
48. Meerscheidt-Hüllessem, "Vorbereitung und Bearbeitung von Kapitalsachen," 7 August 1899, in Ibid., 14–18.
49. *BT*, 2 February 1901, *BM*, 2 February 1901, Provisional Agreement of 26 July 1900, BLHA Rep. 30 Berlin C, Tit. 198B/1932, *Vorbereitung*, 73, 92.
50. Paul Lindenberg, *Berliner Polizei und Verbrechertum* (Leipzig, 1892), 36–37;

Tresckow, *Fürsten,* 115; Simon A. Cole, *Suspect Identities: A History of Fingerprinting and Criminal Identification* (Cambridge, MA, 2001), 34–49; Roth, *Kriminaliätsbekämpfung,* 101–103; Special Report of Criminal Inspector Meerscheidt-Hüllessem, 5 December 1895, Conference on the evaluation of the Bertillon system in the federal states of the German Reich, *Freisinnige Zeitung,* 22 January 1902, BA-BL R. 3001/5446, *Das Bertillon'sche System 1895– 1930,* 46ff, 89ff, 106.

51. On the Kwilecki case see: Hugo Friedlaender, "Prozess wider das Grafen-Ehepaar Kwilecki wegen Kindesunterschiebung," in *Interessante Kriminal-Prozesse von kulturhistorischer Bedeutung,* vol. 1 (Berlin, 1910), 13–45; *BT,* 26 October–26 November 1903; BA-BL R. 3001/5314, *Äusserungen der Presse über den Fall Kwilecki;* Friedrich Karl Kaul, "Graf oder Weichenstellersohn? Der Fall Kwilecki," in *Von der Stadtvogtei bis Moabit. Ein Berliner Pitaval* (East Berlin, 1965), 277–310. A discussion of the case has also recently formed part of a dissertation: Gerd Linnemann, *Klassenjustiz und Weltfremdheit. Deutsche Justizkritik 1890–1914* (Ph.D. diss., University of Kiel, 1989).
52. Friedlaender, "Prozess wider das Grafen-Ehepaar," 26–30.
53. Wetzell, *Inventing,* especially 28–31; Peter Gay, *The Cultivation of Hatred* (New York, 1993), 155–157; Carlo Ginzburg, "Clues: Roots of an Evidential Paradigm," in *Clues, Myths, and the Historical Method,* trans. John and Anne Tedeschi (Baltimore, 1992), 123; Cole, *Suspect Identities,* 94–95, 97–118; Richard J. Evans, *Rituals of Retribution: Capital Punishment in Germany, 1600–1987* (London, 1997), 437.
54. Tresckow, *Fürsten,* 55, 115; David Blackbourn, *Marpingen: Apparitions of the Virgin Mary in a Nineteenth Century German Village* (New York, 1995), 209–214.
55. Jens Dobler, "Leopold von Meerscheidt-Hüllessem (1849–1900)," *Archiv für Polizeigeschichte,* vol. 9, part 3, 1998: 73–79, 77–78.

5. "Were People More Pitiless Fifteen Years Ago?"

1. *BM,* 1 January 1910; Joachim Radkau, *Das Zeitalter der Nervosität. Deutschland zwischen Bismarck und Hitler* (Munich, 2000), 204, 207.
2. Alfred Kerr, Berliner Brief of 30 September 1900, in *Wo liegt Berlin? Briefe aus der Reichshauptstadt, 1895–1900* (Berlin, 1999), 616; "Shopping. Eine neue Sitte in Berlin," *BT,* 16 August 1908 S; *BM,* 10 January 1910, 11 January 1910.
3. Horst Bosetzky, *Berliner Bahnen* (Munich, 2000); *BM,* 1, 6, and 7 January 1910.
4. Hermann Sudermann, *Stein unter Steinen. Schauspiel in vier Akten* (Stuttgart, 1905). On Sudermann: Alfred Kerr, Berliner Brief of 12 April 1896, in *Wo liegt Berlin?* 144. *Stein unter Steinen* was filmed several times, including in 1916 with Emil Jannings.

5. Carl Zuckmayer, *Der Hauptmann von Köpenick. Theaterstücke* (Frankfurt/Main, 1995). The play has been filmed several times, most famously in 1956, directed by Helmut Käutner and starring Heinz Rühmann.
6. *BT*, 1 December 1906 A, 2 December 1906 S; Walter Bahn, *Meine Klienten: Beiträge zur modernen Inquisition*, Grossstadt-Dokumente, vol. 42 (Berlin 1908), 80–81, 83–84. Rixdorf Police President to Berlin Police President, 14 August 1906, LB Pr. Br. Rep. 30/99, *Personal-Akten des königlichen Polizei-Präsidiums zu Berlin betreffend Wilhelm Voigt*, 24.
7. *BT*, 1 December 1906 A, 2 December 1906 S; Judgment of the Third Strafkammer LG II, 1 December 1906, GStA Rep. 84a/15388, *Strafsache gegen Wilhelm Voigt*, 70–71; *Retentum*, 27 October 1906, LB Pr. Br. Rep. 30/99, *Personal-Akten des königlichen Polizei-Präsidiums zu Berlin betreffend Wilhelm Voigt*, 36.
8. Bahn, *Meine Klienten*, 70; *Der Tag*, 4 December 1906, GStA Rep. 84a/15388, *Strafsache wider Wilhelm Voigt*, unpaginated.
9. *BT*, 1 December 1906 A; *KZ*, 2 December 1906 S; Winfried Löschburg, *Ohne Glanz und Gloria. Die Geschichte des Hauptmanns von Köpenick* (Berlin, 1996), 175; Wilhelm Voigt, *Wie ich Hauptmann von Köpenick wurde* (East Berlin, 1986), 125.
10. *BT*, 1 December 1906 A.
11. *BT*, 1 December 1906 A; Judgment of the 3rd Strafkammer LG II, 1 December 1906, GStA Rep. 84a/15388, *Strafsache wider Wilhelm Voigt*, 61–62.
12. *BT*, 1 December 1906 A; Robert von Hippel, "Der 'Hauptmann von Köpenick' und die Aufenthaltsbeschränkung bestrafter Personen," *Deutsche Juristen-Zeitung* 11, no. 23 (1906); *BT*, 2 December 1906 S.
13. Judgment of the 3rd Strafkammer LG II, 1 December 1906, GStA Rep. 84a/15388, *Strafsache wider Wilhelm Voigt*, 71; *BT*, 1 December 1906 A.
14. *BT*, 2 December 1906 S; Judgment of the Third Strafkammer LG II, 1 December 1906, GStA Rep. 84a/15388, *Strafsache wider Wilhelm Voigt*, 76–78; Voigt, *Hauptmann von Köpenick*, 130–131. Where a person commits several different offenses through one and the same action, German law calls this *Idealkonkurrenz*; the Reich Criminal Code stipulation that the highest punishment should be determinative is known as the *Absorbtionsprinzip*. O. G. Schwarz, *Strafrecht, Strafprozess: Ein Hilfsbuch für junge Juristen* (Berlin, 1907), 78.
15. *BT*, 2 December 1906 S; Voigt, *Hauptmann von Köpenick*, 132. Since prison (*Gefängnis*) was considered to be two-thirds as serious as hard labor (*Zuchthaus*), Voigt's sentence amounted to 8/15 of the maximum.
16. Bahn, *Meine Klienten*, 71, 76; Paul Lindau, *Ausflüge ins Kriminalistische* (Munich, 1909), 265; "Die Polizeiaufsicht," *VZ*, 3 December 1906 A, "Barbarisches in unserer Rechtspflege," *National Zeitung*, 3 December 1906 A, *BM*, 2 December 1906, *BT*, 3 December 1906, *Das kleine Journal*, 3 December 1906, GStA Rep. 84a/15388, *Strafsache wider Wilhelm Voigt*, unpaginated. No one else

seems to have reported Dietz's remark as Bahn did, and it stands somewhat in opposition to other comments Dietz is reported to have made at the trial. He suggested that Voigt could not have expected exculpatory evidence to make a great difference in the sentencing outcome, and in the oral reasons for judgment the court said it could not assess the hardness of the sentence after so many years: *BT,* 1 December 1906 A, 2 December 1906 S.

17. *KZ,* 21 August 1908 M; Lindau, *Ausflüge,* 268; *BM,* 2 December 1906, *Berliner Börsen Zeitung,* 2 December 1906 M, GStA Rep. 84a/15388, *Strafsache wider Wilhelm Voigt,* unpaginated.

18. Judgment of the Third Strafkammer LG II, 1 December 1906, GStA Rep. 84a/15388, *Strafsache wider Wilhelm Voigt,* 79; Karl Binding, "Das Problem der Strafe in der heutigen Wissenschaft," in Thomas Vormbaum, ed., *Strafrechtsdenker der Neuzeit* (Baden-Baden, 1998), 438.

19. Nieberding to Beseler, 8 December 1906, Beseler to Nieberding, 21 December 1906, GStA Rep. 84a/15388, *Strafsache wider Wilhelm Voigt,* 16.

20. JM to 1st STA LG II, 10 July 1908, 1st STA LG II to JM, 22 July 1908, JM to IM, 27 July 1908, JM to Kaiser, 8 August 1908, Kaiser to JM, 15 August 1908, JM to 1st STA LG II, 17 August 1908, in ibid., 55, 58–59, 81, 91, 92, 94; Regierungspräsident Breslau to police President Berlin, 7 October 1908, LB Pr. Br. Rep. 30/99, *Personal-Akten des königlichen Polizei-Präsidiums zu Berlin betreffend Wilhelm Voigt,* 88.

21. See Gary D. Stark, "Pornography, Society and the Law in Imperial Germany," *Central European History* 14, no. 3 (September 1981): 200–229; Stark, "Cinema, Society, and the State: Policing the Film Industry in Imperial Germany," in Gary D. Stark and Bede Karl Lackner, eds., *Essays on Culture and Society in Modern Germany* (College Station, TX, 1982), 130; R. J. V. Lenman, "Art, Society and the Law in Wilhelmine Germany: The Lex Heinze," *Oxford German Studies Review* 8 (1972): 86–113; Magnus Hirschfeld, *Von einst bis jetzt* (Berlin, 1986).

22. On this theme see Richard J. Evans, *Rituals of Retribution: Capital Punishment in Germany, 1600–1987* (London, 1997), especially 402–20; Peter Fritzsche, *Reading Berlin 1900* (Cambridge, MA, 1996), especially 158–161; and Peter Fritzsche, *A Nation of Fliers: German Aviation and the Popular Imagination* (Cambridge, MA, 1992), 9–58.

23. Fritzsche, *A Nation of Fliers,* 9–17.

24. *Die Zeit am Montag,* 3 and 10 December 1906, *BM,* 4 and 6 December 1906, *Reichsbote,* 5 December 1906, *BT,* 17 and 18 August, 1908, *Reichsbote,* 19 August 1908, GStA Rep. 84a/15388, *Strafsache wider Wilhelm Voigt,* unpaginated; Voigt, *Hauptmann von Köpenick,* 144–148; Löschburg, *Ohne Glanz,* especially chs. 14 and 15.

25. *Leipziger Neueste Nachrichten,* 20 August 1908, GStA Rep. 84a/15388, *Straf-*

sache wider Wilhelm Voigt, unpaginated; "Zeppelin oder Voigt?" *DT,* 23 August 1908, Sontags-Beilage.

26. "Verirrungen und Verzerrungen," *DT,* 8 August 1908 A; "Grete Beier und Hau," *DT,* 18 August 1908 M; "Schwächen und Schäden im Rechtsleben. Von einem Richter," *DT,* 19 August 1908 M; "Zeppelin oder Voigt?" *DT,* 23 August 1908, Sontags-Beilage. On the Hau and Beier cases: Erich Sello, *Die Hau Prozesse und ihre Lehren* (Berlin, 1908); Fritz Friedmann, *Hau ist kein verstockter Mörder! Kritische Studie* (Berlin, 1907); Jakob Wassermann, *Der Fall Maurizius* (Munich, 1997); Hugo Friedlaender, "Grete Beier, Tochter des Bürgermeisters Beier zu Brand," in *Interessante Criminal-Prozesse,* vol. 6, 278–322; Evans, *Rituals,* 401–403.

27. *Reichsbote,* 19 August 1908, *Leipziger Neueste Nachrichten,* 20 August 1908, GStA Rep. 84a/15388, *Strafsache wider Wilhelm Voigt,* unpaginated.

28. Paragraph 40 Prussian Criminal Code, Paragraph 51 Reich Criminal Code, in Justus Olshausen, *Kommentar zum Strafgesetzbuch für das Deutsche Reich,* 9th ed. (Berlin, 1912), 220–221.

29. Radkau, *Zeitalter,* 234, 236; Dirk Blasius, *Einfache Seelenstörung. Geschichte der deutschen Psychiatrie 1800–1945* (Frankfurt, 1994), 61–62.

30. Richard Wetzell, *Inventing the Criminal: A History of German Criminology 1880–1945* (Chapel Hill, 2000), especially 73–106.

31. Wetzell, *Inventing,* 79; Blasius, *Seelenstörung,* 75; Gabriel Finder, "The Medicalization of Wilhelmine and Weimar Juvenile Justice," paper presented at the Workshop on Crime and Criminal Justice in Modern Germany, 1870–1960, German Historical Institute, Washington, DC, May 10–11, 2001, 10.

32. Hugo Friedlaender, "Die Ermordung des Justizrats Levy," *Interessante Kriminalprozesse von kulturhistorischer Bedeutung,* vol. 9 (Berlin, 1913), 231–234; *BT,* 21 October 1896 M, 1 December 1896 A.

33. Friedlaender, "Die Ermordung des Justizrats Levy," 227–229; *BT,* 1 December 1896 A; *Die Zukunft,* 31 October 1896, 198. The *Tageblatt's* examples of Werner's diction were "eventuell" and "dass lasse ich dahingestellt."

34. *Die Zeit am Montag,* 22 February 1904, March 1904 (illegible date), BA-BL R.3001/5655, *Äusserrungen der Presse über die Strafvollstreckung und das Gefängniswesen,* unpaginated; *BT,* 15 May 1905 A, 17 May 1905 A, 18 May 1905 M.

35. *BT,* 6 June 1905 M. Compare the speech which Leppmann gave at the 27th Deutscher Juristentag, as reported in Wetzell, *Inventing,* 91–92.

36. *BT,* 18 May 1905 M, 9 June 1905 A, 15 June 1905 A.

37. *BT,* 22 September 1913 A, *BZ am Mittag,* 22 September 1913, BLHA Rep. 30 Berlin C, Tit. 198 B/1384, *Knabenmord in Berlin,* unpaginated.

38. *BT,* 22 September 1913 A, 23 September 1913 A; Regina Stürickow, *Der Kommissar vom Alexanderplatz* (Berlin, 1998), 22–28.

39. Gennat has recently been the subject of a popular biography: Regina Stürickow, *Der Kommissar vom Alexanderplatz* (Berlin, 1998); more scholarly treatments of his work appear in Evans, *Rituals*, 577–582, and Hsi-Huey Liang, *Die Berliner Polizei in der Weimarer Republik* (Berlin, 1977). There is an affectionate portrayal of him in Erich Frey, *Ich beantrage Freispruch: Aus den Erinnerungen des Strafverteidigers Prof. Dr. Dr. Erich Frey* (Hamburg, 1959), especially 169–195, and he figures as Commissar Lohmann in the classic Fritz Lang film *M*.
40. Stürickow, *Kommissar*, 31; *BZ am Mittag*, 22 September 1913, BLHA Rep. 30 Berlin C, Tit. 198 B/1384, *Knabenmord in Berlin*, unpaginated.
41. *BZ am Mittag*, 22 September 1913, BLHA Rep. 30 Berlin C, Tit. 198 B/1384, *Knabenmord in Berlin*, unpaginated.
42. *BZ am Mittag*, 22 September 1913, BLHA Rep. 30 Berlin C, Tit. 198 B/1384, *Knabenmord in Berlin*, unpaginated; *BT*, 23 September 1913 A; *KZ*, 23 September 1913 A.
43. See Wetzell, *Inventing*, chs. 2 and 3.
44. Paragraph 175 of the Reich Criminal Code, Olshausen, *Kommentar*, 693; *BT*, 23 September 1913 A; *KZ*, 23 September 1913 A. On Hirschfeld: GStA Rep. 84a/17333, *Verbreitung unsittlicher Schriften und Beleidigung durch den Praktischen Arzt Dr. Magnus Hirschfeld aus Berlin Charlottenburg, 1903–1905*; Jens Dobler, "Leopold von Meerscheidt-Hüllessem (1849–1900)," *Archiv für Polizeigeschichte*, vol. 9, part 3 (1998): 73–79; Dobler, "Hans von Tresckow (1866–1934)," *Archiv für Polizeigeschichte*, vol. 10, part 2 (1999): 47–52; Magnus Hirschfeld, *Von einst bis jetzt* (Berlin, 1986).
45. *BLA*, 24 September 1913 M, BLHA Rep. 30 Berlin C, Tit. 198 B/1384, *Knabenmord in Berlin*, unpaginated; *BT*, 23 September 1913 A, 24 September 1913 M; *KZ*, 24 September 1913 M.
46. *BLA*, 24 September 1913 M, BLHA Rep. 30 Berlin C, Tit. 198 B/1384, *Knabenmord in Berlin*, unpaginated; *KZ*, 24 September 1913 A.
47. *KZ*, 1 October 1913 M, 20 October 1913 M; *TR*, 30 September 1913 A.
48. Hugo Friedlaender, "Ein Liebesdrama im Berliner Tiergarten: Die 20 jährige Kontoristin Hedwig Müller wegen Ermordung ihres Geliebten Reimann vor den Geschworenen," in *Interessante Kriminalprozesse von kulturhistorischer Bedeutung*, vol. 10 (Berlin, 1913), 201; *BM*, 4 October 1913.
49. Friedlaender, "Liebesdrama," 208–211.
50. Ibid., 218.
51. Ibid., 219–220.
52. Ibid., 233.
53. Ibid., 239.
54. *BM*, 4 October 1913; Friedlaender, "Liebesdrama," 225.
55. *BM*, 7 October 1913; Friedlaender, "Liebesdrama," 249–250.

56. *BM*, 7 October 1913; Friedlaender, "Liebesdrama," 250.
57. *BM*, 7 October 1913; Friedlaender, "Liebesdrama," 251.
58. *BM*, 4 and 5 October 1913.
59. *BM*, 8 October 1913; Friedlaender, "Liebesdrama," 255–256, 260.
60. *BM*, 8 October 1913.
61. *BM*, 8 October 1913; Friedlaender, "Liebesdrama," 263–265; E. Löwe, *Die Strafprozessordnung für das Deutsche Reich*, 12th ed. (Berlin, 1907), 724–725.
62. *Die Post*, 8 October 1913 M; *KZ*, "Aus anderen Blättern," 9 October 1913; "Lehren aus drei Schwurgerichtsverhandlungen", *KZ*, 20 October 1913 M; "Zeitungsschau," *TR*, 9 October 1913 M.
63. Quoted in *KZ*, "Aus anderen Blättern," 9 October 1913.
64. "Zeitungsschau," *TR*, 8 October 1913 M, 11 October 1913 M; "Innere Politik der Woche," *KZ*, 12 October 1913 S.
65. *KZ*, 15 October 1913 A; *KZ*, "Aus anderen Blättern," 9 October 1913.
66. *Die Post*, 2 October 1913 A; "Innere Politik der Woche," *KZ*, 12 October 1913 S.
67. Abgeordnetenhaus, 5 February 1914, Abgeordnetenhaus, 6 February 1914, GStA Rep. 84a/2942, *Richter und Staatsanwälte: Allgemeine Bestimmungen über die Anstellung im höhern Justizdienst, 1913–1922*, 14–15, 21.
68. *BM*, 9 and 14 January 1910, 5 March 1910; *BT*, 1 May 1910 S, 2 May 1910 A; Paragraph 216 Reich Criminal Code, Olshausen, *Kommentar*, 11th ed., (1927), 961–965.
69. Hugo Friedlaender, "Der Raubmörder Hennig," *Interessante Kriminal-Prozesse von kulturhistorischer Bedeutung*, vol. 1 (Berlin, 1910), 60–65; Fritzsche, *Reading Berlin*, 159–160; Police President to IM, 27 January, 1907, IM to Police President, 8 February, 1907, BLHA Rep. 30 Berlin C, Tit. 198 B/1693, *Raudmörder Hennig*, 85–88; *BT*, 5 December 1906 A.
70. Judgment of the Jury Court, Landgericht III, 7 July 1911, BLHA Rep. 30 Berlin C. Tit. 198B/1018, *Schwurgerichtssache gegen Hartmann 1911*, 52–53.
71. *BLA*, 19 October 1907, BLHA Rep. 30 Berlin C. Tit. 198 B/47, *Fall Waldeck*, unpaginated; *BLA*, 19 December 1909 M, BLHA Rep. 30 Berlin C. Tit. 198 B44, *Grabowski Gattenmord*, unpaginated; Evans, *Rituals*, 467–468 and Statistical Appendix, 913 ff.
72. Evans, *Rituals*, 437, 470–477; Blasius, *Seelenstörung*, 61–116; Dieter Langewiesche, *Liberalism in Germany*, trans. Christiane Banerji (London, 2000), 126–127; Thomas Kühne, *Handbuch der Wahlen zum Preussischen Abgeordnetenhaus 1867–1918. Wahlergebnisse, Wahlbündnisse und Wahlkandidaten* (Düsseldorf, 1994), 54–61.
73. *BM*, 24 January 1910.
74. Hans Land, *Staatsanwalt Jordan. Ein Berliner Roman* (Hamburg, 1922), 9, 33.
75. *Die Zeit am Montag*, 6 January 1908, GStA Rep. 84a/49840, *Die Strafsache gegen den Schriftsteller Harden wegen Beleidigung des Grafen Moltke. Beiakten*

enthaltend Zeitungsberichte, vol. 2, 64; "Eulenburg Schauspiele. Umriss und Stimmungen," *Volks-Zeitung,* 1 July 1908, GStA Rep. 84a/49833, *Die Strafsache gegen den Fürsten Eulenburg,* 11; *KZ,* 7 October 1913 M; *BM,* 25 April, 1908, GStA Rep. 84a/49832, *Strafsache gegen den Fürsten Eulenburg,* 48; *Hamburger Nachrichten,* 24 October 1907 A, GStA Rep. 84a/49839, *Strafsache gegen den Schriftsteller Harden wegen Beleidigung des Grafen Moltke. Beiakten enthaltend Zeitungsberichte,* vol. 1, 4e.
76. Evans, *Rituals,* 479–480.

Epilogue

1. Erich Frey, *Ich beantrage Freispruch: Aus den Erinnerungen des Strafverteidigers Prof. Dr. Dr. Erich Frey* (Hamburg, 1959), 488.
2. On this legislation see David Blackbourn, *The Long Nineteenth Century: Germany 1780–1918* (London, 1997), 408.
3. Hans von Tresckow, *Von Fürsten und anderen Sterblichen: Erinnerungen eines Kriminalkommissars* (Berlin, 1922), 239–240; Frey, *Freispruch,* 12; KGP to JM, 17 October 1914, GStA Rep. 84a/20447, *Landgericht I Allgemeines, 1914–1915,* 122; GStA Rep. 84a/20259, *Im Kriege gefallene Justizbeamte und Rechtsanwälte 1914–1918,* 18, 30, 40, 51; GStA Rep. 84a/2942, *Richter und Staatsanwälte,* 21, 120, 121.
4. KGP to Berlin LGPs and AGPs, 27 August 1915, GSA KG to JM, 29 July 1917, 1st STA LG I 25 June 1917, GStA Rep. 84a/20253, *Misc. inkl. Ansteigen der Geschäfte bei den Staatsanwaltschaften, 1915–1918,* 26, 154–156.
5. Leo Haber, "Richterstellung und Richteraufgaben im deutschen Prozesse," *Deutsche Richterzeitung,* 1 February 1917, GStA 84a/2942, *Richter und Staatsanwälte,* 39; *BT,* 21 November 1916, GStA Rep. 84a/20154, *Anwaltskammer in Berlin 1912–1928,* 167.
6. Bendix to Ministry of State, 14 November 1918, GStA 84a/2942, *Richter und Staatsanwälte,* 79; Kurt Tucholsky, "Deutsche Richter," in *Politische Justiz* (Reinbek bei Hamburg, 1990), 27; OSA Mehliss, "Strafjustizreform," *Deutsche Allgemeine Zeitung,* 28 March 1922, GStA Rep. 84a/2942, *Richter und Staatsanwälte,* 263; Emil Julius Gumbel, *Vier Jahre politischer Mord* (Berlin, 1922).
7. Frey, *Freispruch,* 204; *Montag Morgen,* 24 October 1927, GStA Rep. 84a/20304, *Vorwürfe gegen die Justizverwaltung,* 205; "Erziehung zum Verbrechen. Missbrauch der Bewährungsfrist. Einige Proben aus Moabit," *Deutsche Zeitung,* 24 April 1930, GStA Rep. 84a/20309, *Vorwürfe gegen die Justizverwaltung 1929–1931,* 13. Examples of traditional procedural thinking after the advent of the Third Reich are, among others, the manner in which the *Reichsgericht* handled the notorious Reichstag fire trial in 1933 and the bizarre internal debate between 1938 and 1941 regarding whether or not it was proper for a "German"

defense counsel to act for a "Jewish" defendant. On the former see, *inter alia,* Ingo Müller, *Hitler's Justice: The Courts of the Third Reich,* trans. Deborah Lucas Schneider with an introduction by Detlev Vagts (Cambridge, MA, 1991), 27–35; on the latter, BA-BL R. 3001/Alt R.22/1079, *Generalakten des RJM betrff. Verteidigung in Strafsachen 1934–1943,* 205–278.

8. For Liszt's very liberal views on the rights of the defense, see the summary of his lecture on the subject in the *Berliner Tageblatt,* 9 January 1901 M; for his position on the jury court see his pamphlet, *Die Reform des Strafverfahrens* (Berlin, 1906).

9. Richard J. Evans, *Rituals of Retribution: Capital Punishment in Germany, 1600–1987* (London, 1997), 469; Richard Finger, *Die Kunst des Rechtsanwalts: Eine systematische Darstellung ihrer Grundfragen unter besonderer Berücksichtigung der ehrengerichtlichen Rechtsprechung,* 2nd ed. (Berlin, 1912), 19–20; David Halpert, *Die Harmlosen und ihre Verhaftung. Eine kritische Studie* (Berlin, 1899), 17–18.

10. Hugo Friedlaender, *Kulturhistorische Kriminal-Prozesse der letzten vierzig Jahre* (Berlin, 1908), 77.

11. "Eine Erinnerung an den Heinze-Prozess," *TR,* 5 October 1913 S.

12. Cossmann's story, like Alfred Ballien's, can be found in many *Ehrengericht* files at the Bundesarchiv Berlin-Lichterfelde: R.3005/491/1a *Ehrengerichtliches Verfahren gegen den Rechtsanwalt Dr. Richard Cossmann in Berlin* (1898); R.3005/491/1b, *Cossmann* (1930); R.3005/491/5, *Dr. Cossmann Wiederaufnahmeanträge* 1930—; R.3001/4428, *Eingaben in ehrengerichtlichen Angelegenheiten.* A few basic biographical facts about Cossmann appear in Simone Ladwig-Winters, *Anwalt ohne Recht: Das Schicksal jüdischer Rechtsanwälte in Berlin nach 1933* (Berlin, 1998), 115.

13. BLHA Rep. 30 Berlin C, Tit. 198 B/1555, *Verstorbene Mörder und hingerichtete Verbrecher.* The *Berliner Tageblatt* report on the first day of Berger's trial notes that he was born 26 May 1869 in Quedlinburg. *Berliner Tageblatt,* 12 December 1904 A.

14. *Berliner Allgemeine Zeitung,* 19 June 1909, "Handstreich des 'Hauptmanns von Köpenick,'" Death Certificate, LB Pr. Br. Rep. 30/99, *Personal-Akten des königlichen Polizei-Präsidiums zu Berlin betreffend Wilhelm Voigt,* 117, 135–136; vol. 2, unpaginated.

15. LB Rep. 358/899, *Strafsache contra Knopf.*

16. Harry F. Young, *Maximilian Harden, Censor Germaniae: The Critic in Opposition from Bismarck to the Rise of Nazism* (The Hague, 1959), 246–248.

17. *Handbuch über den königlich preussischen Hof und Staat, 1908–1910* (Berlin, 1908–1910).

18. Curt Riess, *Der Mann in der schwarzen Robe: Das Leben des Strafverteidigers Max Alsberg* (Hamburg, 1965), 329, 331–332. On Alsberg see also Jürgen

Taschke, ed., *Max Alsberg—Ausgewählte Schriften* (Baden-Baden, 1992), especially introductory material by Taschke, Sarstedt, Jungfer, and Krach. On Werthauer, see Ladwig-Winters, *Anwalt,* 219, where the information on the date of death is curiously vague—1936/37.

19. Chodziesner to President of the Rechtsanwaltskammer, 24 June 1936, BLHA Rep. 4a/7326, *Kammergericht Berlin Personalakten, Ludwig Chodziesner,* 37; Ladwig-Winters, *Anwalt,* 111.
20. GSA KG to JM, 16 December 1944; BA-BL Rep. R. 3001/Alt R. 22/050682, *Reichsjustizministerium Personalakten: Walter Bahn,* 14–18.
21. "Nach der Zerstörung der Elisabeth-Kirche. Seit mehr als 50 Jahren leistet es sich Berlin, den Schinkel-Bau immer noch zu vernachlässigen," *Berliner Zeitung,* 27 December 1999, 13; Helmet Engel et al., eds., *Geschichtslandschaft Berlin: Ort und Ereignisse,* vol. 2: *Tiergarten* (Berlin, 1987), 217, 232; "Justitia lebt im Armenhaus," *Tagesspiegel,* 5 February 2001.
22. Frey, *Freispruch,* 488.

Archival and Primary Sources

Archival Sources

Geheimes Staatsarchiv Preussisicher Kulturbesitz (GStA)

I Hauptabteilung, Repositur 77. *Innenministerium*

114/222. *Die Jahresberichte des Justizministers über die Justizverwaltung in der Preussischen Monarchie sowie die Jahrbücher der Preuss. Gerichtsverfassung*, vol. 1 1837–1899.

423/83. *Die Bekämpfung des Zuhältertums*, vol.1 1891–1897.

I Hauptabteilung, Repositur 84a. *Justizministerium*

2941-5. *Richter und Staatsanwälte: Allgemeine Bestimmungen über die Anstellung im höhern Justizdienst, 1867–1935.*

8255. *Meineid 1872–1930.*

9786. *Zeitungsartikel des Kriegsgerichtsrats Elsner v. Gronow zum Metternich-Prozess im "Tag" mit der Forderung nach Schutz des Gerichts vor Beleidigungen und dem Vorschlag zu Verfahrensänderungen 1911.*

15114. *Prozess gegen Ahlwardt wegen der antisemitischen Druckschrift "Judenflinten," 1892–1894.*

15388. *Strafsache wider Wilhelm Voigt.*

16413. *Betrug, Beleidigung und Erpressung durch den Zeitungsverleger und Redakteur Wilhelm Friedenstein aus Berlin 1889–1892.*

16422. *Betrug durch die Witwe Anna Rothe geborene Zahl aus Schöneberg, 1903.*

16771. *Strafsache gegen Heinrich Oberwinder wegen Beleidigung.*

16772. *Versuchter Mord und Anstiftung zum Mord an Dr. Georg Prager durch den Handlungsgehilfen Max Schweitzer und Eugenie Prager aus Berlin, 1892–1896.*

16781-2. *Konizter Mord Presse-Ausschnitte.*

16784. *Strafsache contra Boetticher und Genossen.*

16819. *Doppelmörder Gerth.*

17192-3. Strafsache gegen den Bankier August Sternberg wegen Sittlichkeitsverbrechen.
17195. Äusserungen der Presse betreffend Verbrechen und Vergehen wider die Sittlichkeit.
17202. Beleidigung durch Harriet Platho aus Charlottenburg und durch den Kaufmann Hugo Arndt aus Berlin in Zusammenhang mit dem Prozess gegen den Bankier August Sternberg wegen Sittlichkeitsverbrechen, 1900.
17332. Strafsache gegen die Schriftsteller Helene von Monbart in Berlin-Steglitz und den Verlagsbuchhändler Karl Reissner wegen des unsittlichen Inhalts der Novelle "Nixchen," 1902–04.
17333. Verbreitung unsittlicher Schriften und Beleidigung durch den praktischen Arzt Dr. Magnus Hirschfeld aus Berlin Charlottenburg, 1903–1905.
20152-4. Anwaltskammer in Berlin, 1879–1928.
20201. Die zur Beförderung in höhen Stellen geeigneten richterlichen Beamten und Staatsanwälte, 1900–1920.
20250-1. Zeitungs-Auschnitte über wirkliche oder vermeintliche Missstände bei Gerichten des Kammergerichtsbezirks.
20253. Misc. inkl. Ansteigen der Geschäfte bei den Staatsanwaltschaften, 1915–18.
20254-5. Akten betr. Miscellanea Berlin Bezirks-Akten, 1919–22.
20256. Misc. betr. Rechtsanwälte, 1923–1926.
20259. Im Kriege gefallene Justizbeamte und Rechtsanwälte, 1914–1918.
20361. Gesetz zur Wiederherstellung des Berufsbeamtentums betr. Staatsanwälte.
20363. Durchführung des Berufsbeamtengesetzes bezgl. Rechtsanwälte und Notare, 1933.
20423-7. Landgericht Berlin III Allgemeines, 1906–33.
20442-51. Landgericht Berlin I Allgemeines, 1896-1931.
20475. Rechtsanwälte bei dem Landgericht I Berlin, 1892–3.
20507-8, Landgericht Berlin II Allgemeines, 1895–1906.
20890. Staatsanwaltschaft bei dem Landgericht I Allgemeines, 1893–1905.
20891-3. Staatsanwaltschaft beim Landgericht I, 1905–1929.
20959. Neu-Organisation der Gerichte für Berlin und Umgebung. Aufsicht im Kriminalgerichtsgebäude.
30075. Die Bestellung von Offizial-Verteidiger bei den Berliner Gerichten, 1891–1906.
30295. Charakterverleihung als Justizrat oder Geheimer Justizrat an Rechtsanwälte und Notare, 1907–17.
40297. Acta Personalia des Justiz-Ministeriums betreffend den Landgerichtsdirektor Lüty.
49620-1. Die Untersuchung wider den früheren Rechtsanwalt Arthur Stadthagen zu Berlin.
49684. Strafverfahren gegen sozialdemokratische und bürgerliche Zeitungsredakteure wegen Beleidigung der Berliner Polizei, 1894–1895.

49721. *Strafsache gegen Kaliski und Genossen.*
49803. *Strafsache gegen den Schriftsteller Maximilian Harden in Berlin wegen Majestätsbeleidigung, 1893.*
49804. *Strafsache contra den Schriftsteller Maximilian Harden in Berlin No. 41 u. 45 der "Zukunft" von 1893.*
49818. *Strafsache contra den Schriftsteller Maximilian Harden in Berlin wegen Majestätsbeleidigung, 1898.*
49831-2. *Strafsache gegen den Fürsten Eulenburg.*
49838. *Acta des Justizministeriums betreffend: Die Strafsache gegen den Schriftsteller Harden wegen Beleidigung des Grafen Moltke.*
49839-40. *Strafsache gegen den Schriftsteller Harden wegen Beleidigung des Grafen Moltke: Beiakten enthaltend Zeitungsberichte.*
57471. *Ermordung des Gymnasiasten Ernst Winter in Konitz,* Bd. I.

Brandenburgisches Landeshauptarchiv

Pr. Br. Repositur 4a. *Kammergericht Berlin Personalakten*

7326. *Justizrat Ludwig Chodziesner.*
7763. *Rechtsanwalt Dr. David Halpert.*

Repositur 30 Berlin C. Tit. 198 B. *Berlin Mordkommission*

18. *Anna und Hermann Heinze.*
25. *Fall Ernestine Machus.*
44. *Grabowski. Gattenmord.*
47. *Fall Waldeck.*
56. *Fall Josefa Arend.*
1018. *Schwurgerichtsache gegen Hartmann 1911.*
1384. *Knabenmord in Berlin.*
1555. *Verstorbene Mörder und hingerichtete Verbrecher.*
1690-3. *Raubmörder Hennig.*
1932. *Vorbereitung der Polizei auf die Bearbeitung von Kapitalverbrechen.*
1936. *Organisation der Berliner Kriminal Polizei um die Jahrhundertwende.*

Bundesarchiv Berlin-Lichterfelde

NY 4011. *Nachlass Hans Litten.*

R. 3001/Alt R. 22. *Reichsjustizministerium 1933–1945*

4202.
1079. *Generalakten des RJM betrff. Verteidigung in Strafsachen 1934–43.*
50682. *Reichsjustizministerium Personalakten: Walter Bahn.*

50682. *Reichsjustizministerium Personalakten: Hans-Joachim Litten.*

R. 3001. *Reichsjustizamt/Reichsjustizministerium, 1871–1933*

4404. *Rechtsanwälte Angelegenheiten.*
4420. *Eingaben in ehrengerichtlichen Angelegenheiten.*
4429. *Entscheidungen des EGH 1917–1924.*
5314. *äusserungen der Presse über den Fall Kwilecki.*
5446. *Das Bertillon'sche System 1895–1930.*
5653-5. *Äusserrungen der Presse über die Strafvollstreckung und das Gefängniswesen, 1877–1934.*
5780-2. *Abänderung von Vorschriften des Strafgesetzbuchs gegen Sittlichkeitsvergehen, 1890–98.*
5993. *Zeitungsausschnitte über Strafrecht Bd. XI 1915–1924.*
6157. *Majestätsbeleidigung.*

R. 3005. *Ehrengerichtshof für die deutschen Rechtsanwälte*

107. *Akten in dem ehrengerichtlichen Verfahren wider die Rechtsanwälte Bruno Saul und Dr. Fritz Friedmann in Berlin, 1885.*
169. *Ehrengerichtliches Verfahren gegen den Rechtsanwalt Artur Stadthagen zu Berlin, 1888.*
216. *Ehrengerichtliches Verfahren gegen den Rechtsanwalt Artur Stadthagen zu Berlin, 1889.*
286. *Ehrengerichtliches Verfahren gegen die Rechtsanwälte Dr. David Richard Cossmann und Dr. Karl Emanuel Arthur Theodor Alfred Ballien in Berlin.*
304. *Ehrengerichtliches Verfahren gegen den Rechtsanwalt Arthur Stadthagen in Berlin, 1892.*
380. *Ehrengerichtliches Verfahren gegen den Rechtsanwalt Dr. Fritz Friedmann in Berlin, 1896.*
436. *Ehrengerichtliches Verfahren gegen die Rechtsanwälte Edmund und Alfred Ballien in Berlin, 1897.*
489. *Akten in dem ehrengerichtlichen Verfahren gegen den Rechtsanwalt Dr. Alfred Ballien in Berlin, 1898.*
491/1a. *Ehrengerichtliches Verfahren gegen den Rechtsanwalt Dr. Richard Cossmann in Berlin, 1898.*
491/1b. *Cossmann 1930.*
491/5. *Dr. Cossmann. Wiederaufnahmeanträge 1930 –*
596. *Ehrengerichtliches Verfahren gegen den Rechtsanwalt Justizrat Dr. Erich Sello in Berlin.*
616. *Akten in dem ehrengerichtlichen Verfahren gegen den Rechtsanwalt Dr. Alfred Ballien in Berlin, 1903.*
678. *Akten in dem ehrengerichtlichen Verfahren gegen den Rechtsanwalt Dr. Alfred Ballien in Berlin, 1904.*

671. *Ehrengerichtliches Verfahren gegen den Rechtsanwalt Dr. Karl Schwindt in Berlin, 1904.*

777. *Akten in dem ehrengerichtlichen Verfahren wider den Rechtsanwalt Dr. Alfred Ballien in Berlin, 1906.*

855. *Akten in dem ehrengerichtlichen Verfahren wider den Rechtsanwalt Dr. Alfred Ballien in Berlin, 1908.*

869. *Akten in dem ehrengerichtlichen Verfahren wider Rechtsanwalt Dr. Karl Liebknecht aus Berlin, 1908.*

1037. *Akten in dem ehrengerichtlichen Verfahren wider den Rechtsanwalt Dr. Karl Liebknecht in Berlin, 1912, 1914.*

1142. *Ehrengerichtliches Verfahren gegen die Rechtsanwälte Dr. Walther Jaffé und Dr. Max Alsberg zu Berlin.*

Landesarchiv Berlin (LB)

Pr. Br. Rep. 30. *Königliches Polizei-Präsidium zu Berlin*

99. *Personal-Akten des königlichen Polizei-Präsidiums zu Berlin betreffend Wilhelm Voigt.*

Rep. 358. *Generalstaatsanwaltschaft beim Landgericht Berlin*

899. *Strafsache contra Knopf.*
243. *Strafsache gegen Gerth*

Printed Primary Sources

Newspapers and Periodicals

Berliner Lokal-Anzeiger
Berliner Morgenpost
Berliner Tageblatt
Berliner Volksblatt
Deutsche Tageszeitung (Berlin)
Die Neue Zeit (Berlin)
Entscheidungen des Ehrengerichtshofes für die deutsche Rechtsanwälte (Berlin)
Juristische Wochenschrift (Berlin)
Kölnische Zeitung
Kreuzzeitung (Berlin)
Preussische Jahrbücher (Berlin)
Reichsgesetzblatt (Berlin)
Staatsbürger Zeitung (Berlin)
Statistisches Jahrbuch der Stadt Berlin (Berlin)

Tägliche Rundschau (Berlin)
Tagebuch (Berlin)
Vorwärts (Berlin)
Die Zukunft (Berlin)

Books and Pamphlets

Ahlwardt, Hermann. *Neue Enthüllungen: Judenflinten*. Dresden: Verlag der Drückerei Glöss, 1892.
———. *Judenflinten: II. Theil*, Dresden: Verlag der Drückerei Glöss, 1892.
Alsberg, Max. *Der Fall des Marquis de Bayros und Dr. Semerau: Ein Beitrag zur Lehre von der unzüchtigen Schrift und unzüchtigen Darstellung*. Berlin: Alfred Pulvermacher & Co., 1911.
———. *Justizirrtum und Wiederaufnahme*. Berlin: Langenscheidt, 1913.
Apfel, Alfred. *Behind the Scenes of German Justice: Reminiscences of a German Barrister, 1882–1933*. London: John Lane, 1935.
Architekten Verein zu Berlin. *Berlin und seine Bauten*. Berlin: W. Ernst & Son, 1896.
Aus dem Berliner Rechtsleben: Festgabe zum XXVI. Deutschen Juristentage. Berlin: Verlag von Franz Vahlen, 1902.
Bahn, Walter. *Meine Klienten: Beiträge zur modernen Inquisition*. Grossstadt-Dokumente vol. 42. Berlin: H. Seemann Nachf., 1908.
———. *Der Prozess der Frau Schoenebeck-Weber*. Berlin: Steinitz, 1910.
Berliner Humor vor Gericht: Heitere Scenen aus den Berliner Gerichtssälen. Berlin: Hugo Steinitz Verlag, 1905.
Der Konitzer Blutmord vor dem Berliner Gericht: Die Verhandlungen des Presseprozesses gegen die "Staatsbürger-Zeitung" vor der II. Strafkammer des Königl. Landgerichts I, 30. September bis 11. Oktober 1902. Berlin: Verlag der Staatsbürger-Zeitung, 1902.
Der Mordprozess Heinze: (Verhandelt vor dem Schwurgericht zu Berlin in den Jahren 1891 und 1892). Der Ursprung der "Lex Heinze." Der unfreiwillige Taufpate der "Lex Heinze." Berlin: Gnadenfeld, 1900.
Ensor, R. C. K. *Courts and Judges in France, Germany and England*. Oxford: Oxford University Press, 1933.
Exner, Franz. *Studien über die Strafzumessungspraxis der deutschen Gerichte*. Leipzig: Wiegandt, 1931.
Finger, Richard. *Die Kunst des Rechtsanwalts: Eine systematische Darstellung ihrer Grundfragen unter besonderer Berücksichtigung der ehrengerichtlichen Rechtsprechung*, 2nd ed. Berlin: Struppe & Winckler, 1912.
Flatau, Ludwig. *Mehr Schutz für die Rechtspflege! Legislative Betrachtungen über einige Prozesse aus der letzten Zeit*. Berlin: J. Edelheim, 1901.
Fontane, Theodor. *Die Poggenpuhls*. Stuttgart: Reclam, 1969; East Berlin: Verlag der Nation, 1980.

———. *Romane*. Düsseldorf: Artemis & Winckler, 1998.

Frey, Erich. *Ich beantrage Freispruch: Aus den Erinnerungen des Strafverteidigers Prof. Dr. Dr. Erich Frey.* Hamburg: Bluchert, 1959.

Friedenstein, Wilhelm. *Ein Justizmord und der Herr Landgerichtsdirektor Brausewetter in Berlin: Ein Beitrag zur Frage der Wiedereinführung der Berufungsinstanz in Deutschland.* Leipzig: A. Schulz, 1892.

Friedlaender, Hugo. *Kulturhistorische Kriminal-Prozesse der letzten vierzig Jahre.* Berlin: Continent, 1908.

———. *Interessante Kriminalprozesse von kulturhistorischer Bedeutung.* 10 vols. Berlin: Hermann Barsdorf Verlag, 1910–1913.

Friedländer, Adolf, and Max Friedländer. *Kommentar zur Rechtsanwaltsordnung vom 1 Juli, 1878.* Munich: J. Schweitzer Verlag, 1920.

Friedmann, Fritz. *Die wahren Lehren des Heinze'schen Prozesses für Sitten- und Rechtspflege.* Berlin: Hermann Lazarus, 1891.

———. *Hau ist kein verstockter Mörder! Kritische Studie.* Berlin: Alfred Pulvermacher and Co., 1907.

———. *Was ich erlebte! Memoiren.* 2 vols. Berlin: Alfred Pulvermacher and Co., 1911.

Frohme, Karl. *Politische Polizei und Justiz im monarchistischen Deutschland.* Hamburg: Auer, 1926.

Gumbel, Emil Julius. *Vier Jahre politischer Mord.* Berlin: Verlag der neuen Gesellschaft, 1922.

———. *Vom Fememord zur Reichskanzlei.* Heidelberg: L. Schneider, 1962.

Güstrow, Dietrich. *Tödlicher Alltag: Strafverteidiger im Dritten Reich.* Berlin: Severin & Siedler, 1981.

Halpert, David. *Die Harmlosen und ihre Verhaftung: Eine kritische Studie.* Berlin: Stankiewicz, 1899.

———. *Der Prozess Sternberg: Kriminalistische Randglossen.* Berlin: Martin Hildebrandts Verlag, 1900.

Handbuch über den königlich preussischen Hof und Staat für das Jahr 1918. Berlin, 1918.

Harden, Maximilian. *Prozesse: Köpfe III. Teil.* Berlin: Verlag Erich Reiss, 1913.

Hirschfeld, Magnus. *Von einst bis jetzt.* Berlin: Verlag Rosa Winkel, 1986.

Hoeniger, Franz. *Berliner Gerichte.* Grossstadt Dokumente vol. 24. Berlin: H. Seemann Nachf., 1906.

Hohenlohe-Schillingsfürst, Chlodwig Fürst zu. *Denkwürdigkeiten der Reichskanzlerzeit,* Osnabrück Federal Republic of Germany: Biblio Verlag, 1967.

Kahlenberg, Hans von (Helene von Monbart). *Nixchen: Ein Beitrag zur Psychologie der höheren Tochter.* Vienna: Wiener Verlag, 1904.

Kempner, Robert M. W. *Ankläger einer Epoche: Lebenserinnerungen.* Frankfurt: Ullstein, 1983.

Kerr, Alfred. *Wo liegt Berlin? Briefe aus der Reichshauptstadt, 1895–1900*. Berlin: Siedler Verlag, 1999.

———. *Warum Fliesst der Rhein nicht durch Berlin? Briefe eines europäischen Flaneurs*. Berlin: Aufbau Verlag, 1999.

Land, Hans. *Staatsanwalt Jordan: Ein Berliner Roman*. Hamburg: Gebrüder Enoch, 1922.

Landsberger, Artur. *Die Unterwelt von Berlin: Nach den Aufzeichnungen eines ehemaligen Zuchthäuslers, mit einer Schlussbetrachtung von Dr. Max Alsberg*. Berlin: Paul Stegemann Verlag, 1929.

Lindau, Paul. *Ausflüge ins Kriminalistische*. Münich: Albert Langen, 1909.

———. *Der Prozess Graef*. East Berlin: Verlag Das Neue Berlin, 1985.

Lindenberg, Paul. *Berliner Polizei und Verbrechertum*. Leipzig: Philipp Reclam, 1892.

Liszt, Franz von. *Die Reform des Strafverfahrens*. Berlin: J. Guttentag, 1906.

———. *Lehrbuch des deutschen Strafrechts*. 21st and 22nd ed. Berlin: de Gruyter, 1919.

Lorenz, Karl et al., eds. *Justus von Olshausen's Kommentar zum Strafgesetzbuch für das Deutsche Reich*. 11th ed., 2 vols. Berlin: Verlag von Franz Vahlen, 1927.

Löwe, E. *Die Strafprozessordnung für das Deutsche Reich*. 12th ed. Berlin: J. Guttentag, 1907.

Müller, Hermann. *Die preussische Justizverwaltung: Eine systematische Darstellung der die administrativen Geschäfte der Justiz betreffenden Vorschriften*. 2nd ed. Berlin: Reinhold Kühn, 1883.

———. *Die Preussische Justizverwaltung: Eine systematische Darstellung der die administrativen Geschäfte der Justiz betreffenden Vorschriften*. 6th ed., 2 vols. Berlin: Reinhold Kühn, 1909.

Müller, Otto. *Die Lex Heinze*. Freiburg: C. Lehmann's Nachf., 1900.

Nordau, Max. *Degeneration*. Introduction by George L. Mosse. Lincoln: University of Nebraska Press, 1993.

Nussbaum, Arthur. *Der Polnaer Ritualmordprozess: Eine kriminalpsychologische Untersuchung aus aktenmässiger Grundlage*. Berlin: A. W. Hayns Erben, 1906.

Olshausen, Justus. *Kommentar zum Strafgesetzbuch für das Deutsche Reich*. 9th ed. Berlin: Verlag von Franz Vahlen, 1912.

Ostwald, Hans. *Das Berliner Dirnentum*. Leipzig: Verlag von Walther Fiedler, 1905.

Ottwalt, Ernst. *Denn sie wissen, was sie tun: Ein deutscher Justiz-Roman*. Berlin: Malik-Verlag, 1931.

Reidnitz, Georg. *Juristenbildung, insbesondere die Vorbildung der Rechtsanwälte in ihrer Entwicklung bis heute*. Mainz: Verlag der Zentralbuchhandlung Deutscher Rechtsanwälte, 1911.

Ring-Zborow, Joé von. *Enthüllungen zum Sternberg Prozess und der Oberstaatsanwalt: Die Staatsbürger Zeitung bei der Arbeit*. Berlin: H. Shildberger, 1900.

Rosenfeld, Ernst Heinrich. *Der Reichs-Strafprozess: Ein Lehrbuch*. 4th and 5th eds. Berlin: J. Guttentag, 1912.

Scheffler, Karl. *Berlin: Ein Stadtschicksal*. Berlin: Verlag Erich Reiss, 1910.

Schneidt, Karl. *Der Plötzensee-Prozess und seine Bedeutung*. Berlin: Neue Verleger-Gesellschaft, 1906.

Schwarz, O. G. *Strafrecht, Strafprozess: Ein Hilfsbuch für junge Juristen*. Berlin: Carl Heymans Verlag, 1907.

Sello, Erich. *Die Hau-Prozesse und ihre Lehren: Auch ein Beitrag zur Strafprozessreform*. Berlin: Marquardt & Co., 1908.

———. *Zur Psychologie der cause célèbre: Ein Vortrag*. Berlin: Verlag von Franz Vahlen, 1910.

———. *Die Irrtümer der Strafjustiz und ihre Ursachen: Erster Band: Todesstrafe und lebenslängliches Zuchthaus in richterlichen Fehlsprüchen neuerer Zeit*. Berlin: R. von Decker's Verlag, 1911.

Sling (Paul Schlesinger). *Richter und Gerichtete*. Munich: Rogner & Bernhard, 1969.

———. *Der Fassadenkletterer vom 'Kaiserhof.'* East Berlin: Verlag Das Neue Berlin, 1989.

Sudermann, Hermann. *Stein unter Steinen: Schauspiel in vier Akten*. Stuttgart: J. G. Cotta'sche Buchhandlung Nachf., 1905.

Tergit, Gabriele (Elise Hirschmann). *Blüten der zwanziger Jahre: Gerichtsreportagen und Feuilletons, 1923–1933*. Berlin: Rotation Verlag, 1984.

Tovote, Heinz. *Heimliche Liebe: Novellen*. Berlin: F. Fontane & Co., 1893.

Tresckow, Hans von. *Von Fürsten und anderen Sterblichen: Erinnerungen eines Kriminalkommissars*. Berlin: F. Fontane & Co., 1922.

Voigt, Wilhelm. *Wie ich Hauptmann von Köpenick wurde: Mein Lebensbild*. East Berlin: Eulenspiegel Verlag, 1986.

Wassermann, Jakob. *Der Fall Maurizius*. Munich: DTV, 1997.

Weber, A. O. *Lieber ins Zuchthaus als entmündigt! Nachklange zum Schoenebeck-Prozess*. Berlin: Kleines Journal, 1912.

Weissler, Adolf. *Die Geschichte der Rechtsanwaltschaft*. Leipzig: C. E. M. Pfeffer, 1905.

Werthauer, Johannes. *Moabitrium: Szenen aus der Grossstadt-Strafrechtspflege*. Grossstadt-Dokumente vol. 31. Berlin: H. Seemann Nachf., 1908.

———. *Wie leicht man sich strafbar machen kann*. Berlin: Langenscheidt, 1912.

———. *Strafunrecht: Beitrag aus der Praxis zur Ermittlung und Beseitigung der strafrechtlichen Uebelstände, insbesondere zur Ersetzung des Strafgedankens durch den Erziehungsgedanken*. Berlin: Alfred Pulvermacher and Co., 1919.

Wertheim, Gertrud. *Meine Glaubwürdigkeit im Metternich-Prozess.* Berlin: Kleines Journal, 1911.

Zarnow, Gottfried. *Gefesselte Justiz: Politische Bilder aus deutscher Gegenwart.* Vol. 1. Munich: Lehmann, 1931.

———. *Gefesselte Justiz: Politische Bilder aus deutscher Gegenwart.* 2nd ed., vol. 2. Munich: Lehmann, 1932.

Zuckmayer, Carl. *Der Hauptmann von Köpenick: Theaterstücke.* Frankfurt/Main: Fischer, 1995.

Index

Adversarial procedure, 22–23, 32
Ahlwardt, Hermann, 117–118
Alberti, Conrad, 172
Alexanderplatz, 12–13
Alsberg, Max, 14, 29, 53, 125, 134, 137–143, 164, 165, 168–169, 213–214, 230
Anti-Semites, 88, 117–118, 120, 122, 130–131, 148–153, 211–212, 224–225
Anti-Socialist Law *(Sozialistengesetz)*, 85
Arson, 27
Assessoren, 107, 223–224
Association for the Protection of the Interests of Women Workers, 114
"Aulus Agerius," 31, 32–33

Bahn, Walter, 51, 184, 185, 187, 231–232
Ballien, Alfred, 46, 68–69, 70, 71, 72, 75, 76, 77, 78, 82, 83–85, 90, 91, 92–97, 97–99, 126–128
Beate, Ferdinand, 52
Beier, Grete, 193–194
Bendix, Ludwig, 225
Berger, Theodor, 51–52, 58, 101–102, 229
Berger trial (1904), 51–52, 101–102
Berlin, 6, 11–18, 41, 47, 55–60, 81–82, 103, 179–180
Berlin, Lucie, 101–102
Berlin Lawyers' Association *(Berliner Anwaltsverein),* 113, 140
Berliner Börsen-Zeitung, 106, 188
Berliner Lokal-Anzeiger, 49, 93, 99, 101, 112–113, 172, 202
Berliner Morgenpost, 49, 125, 179, 188, 203, 207, 209, 216

Berliner Tageblatt, 48, 49, 51–2, 65, 84, 88–89, 96, 102–103, 118–119, 120, 121, 122, 132, 135, 180, 196–197, 198, 214, 224–225
Berliner Zeitung, 118
Bertillon system, 174–176
Beseler, Justice Minister Max von, 139, 144, 184, 189–190
Bierwagen, Bruno, 202, 210
Binding, Karl, 20, 189
Bismarck, Chancellor Otto von, 13, 19, 85, 111, 181
Bötticher, Paul, 151–153
Braun, Commissar Alexander, 61, 64–65, 101, 149–150
Braun, Nightwatchman Friedrich, 55, 57, 60–61, 63, 76–77
Brausewetter, Superior Court Director Georg Robert, 51, 112–123
Braut, State Advocate, 129–130, 132, 133
Bruhn, Wilhelm, 151–153
Bülow, Oskar, 170
Buschoff, Adolf, 148
Buschoff trial (1892), 148–149
BZ am Mittag, 18, 49, 200

Caprivi, Chancellor Leopold von, 111
Center Party, 88
Chodziesner, Ludwig, 14, 128, 230–231
Cities, culture of, 11–12, 78–80, 179–180, 210
Civil Code *(Bürgerliches Gesetzbuch),* 170
Code of Civil Procedure *(Zivilprozessordnung),* 169

Code of Criminal Procedure *(Straf-prozessordnung),* 17, 19, 23–26, 28–29, 92, 113, 115, 141, 169
Cohn, Dr. Toby, 206–207, 208, 209, 210
Conservatives, attitudes to criminal law of, 3, 189–194, 202, 210–212
Contempt of court *(Ungebühr),* 94, 138
Cossmann, Richard, 46, 68–69, 70, 71, 72, 76, 77, 82, 83–85, 90, 91, 92–96, 97–99, 229
Courthouses, 15–18, 31, 47, 65–66, 184, 232–233
Courts of Appeal *(Oberlandesgerichte),* 26, 29, 33
Criminal chambers *(Strafkammern),* 17, 28–29, 34–37, 38, 43–44, 47, 124
Criminology, 79, 100, 168, 181, 195
"Crisis of confidence in justice," 226

Death penalty, 19, 20, 181, 194, 212, 214–215
Defense lawyers, 39, 41–42, 44–46, 66, 71, 83–85, 88–91, 92–97, 113–114, 116–117, 123–144
Dettmann, Constable Albert, 64
Deutsche Juristen-Zeitung, 189
Deutsche Richterverein, 109
Deutsche Richterzeitung, 109, 144, 224
Deutsche Tageszeitung, 102, 103, 106, 192–194, 212
Deutsche Zeitung, 226
Deycks, Vincenz, 53, 66, 123–124
Dietz, Superior Court Director, 185, 186, 187, 188, 218
Drescher, First Prosecutor, 110–111, 118
Dueling, 62, 130, 133–134

Ehrlich, Eugen, 7, 170
Eulenburg, Prince Phillipp zu, 52, 128, 218
Exner, Franz, 7, 22

Festungshaft. See Prisons
Finger, Richard, 7, 125, 143, 161, 162, 227
Fingerprints, 172, 176–177
First World War, impact on Berlin courts of, 223–225
Flatau, Ludwig, 38–39, 145–146
Fontane, Theodor, 49, 68, 82, 83, 105
Forensic science, 62, 63, 171–172, 173–177

Frankfurt School, 172
Fraud *(Betrug),* 154, 155
Frederick II, 1
Free law movement, 7, 19–20, 147, 170–171, 189
freie Advokatur, 84–85, 108, 126
Frey, Erich, 11, 14, 37, 52, 64, 142, 220, 223, 225, 232, 234
Friedenstein, Wilhelm, 51
Friedlaender, Hugo, 57, 154, 203, 228
Friedmann, Fritz, 39, 42–43, 44–46, 53, 84, 90, 91, 108, 110, 121, 122, 123, 124, 128, 164
Friedmann, Leonhard, 140, 206, 209
Fuchs, Ernst, 7, 170
Fuld, Ludwig, 83

Galton, Francis, 176–177
Gefängnis. See Prisons
Gennat, Commissar Ernst, 37, 199
Germania, 151, 211
Gordon, Adolf von, 126
Gross, Hans, 172, 177, 215
Grosse, Willy, 196–198
Grossmann, Carl, 37
Grosz, Georg, 225
Gumbel, Emil Julius, 1, 225
Guthmann, Hugo, 25, 100–101
Guthmann trial (1899), 25, 100–101, 102, 172–173
Gysae, State Advocate, 207, 208–209

Halpert, David, 51, 227–228
Hamburger Nachrichten, 218
Harden, Maximilian, 18, 39, 46, 47, 51, 58, 101, 102, 106, 110–112, 122, 142, 154, 156, 157, 160, 161, 184, 197, 218, 230
Hart, H. L. A., 4
Hartmann, Albert, 215
Hau, Carl, 193–194
"Hauptmann von Köpenick." *See* Voigt, Wilhelm
Heinze, Anna, 64, 69, 70, 72–73, 74, 75, 76, 77, 87, 97–99, 228–229
Heinze, Hermann, 25, 64, 69, 70, 73, 74, 75, 76, 77, 78, 87, 97–99, 228–229
Heinze trial (1891–1892), 25, 46, 65–99, 100, 102
Hennig, Rudolf, 188, 214

Herrfurth, Interior Minister Ernst Ludwig, 86–87, 93
Hippel, Robert von, 185, 189
Hirschfeld, Magnus, 178, 200, 201
Hoeniger, Franz, 44, 48, 49, 53–54, 108, 109, 124, 128
Hoffmann, *Medizinalrat* Dr., 199, 206, 208
Holmes, Oliver Wendell Jr., 168
Holthoff, Aurel, 123–124
Homicide, 27, 61, 62; unpremeditated murder, 98, 201–202, 208, 214; grievous bodily harm causing death, 99, 202; "killing on the express and serious demand of the victim," 214, 216
Honor Court (Berlin), 92–96, 114, 115–116, 126, 127, 133, 135, 136, 140
Honor Courts *(Ehrengerichte)*, 91, 126
Hyan, Hans, 48, 216
Hysteria, 195, 206–210

Imperial Supreme Court *(Reichsgericht)*, 26, 29, 114, 135, 156, 159, 208
Inquisitorial procedure, 22, 23, 32
Insanity defense, 194–213, 216
Isenbiel, First Prosecutor Hugo, 38, 39–42, 106, 131, 132, 151–152, 158, 159, 160, 217–218, 227–228, 230

Jaffé, Walther, 138, 139–141
Jeserich, Court Chemist Dr., 172
Jews: persecuted by the Nazis, 3–4, 52, 230–231; in the legal professions, 107, 108–109, 224–225; accused of "ritual murder," 148–150, 153
Judges, 2, 4, 24, 27, 33, 34, 37, 38, 41, 43–44, 46, 53, 90, 105–111, 115, 121–123, 142–143, 213, 223–224, 228
Judicial Code *(Gerichtsverfassungsgesetz)*, 19, 25, 30, 33, 111
Jünnemann, Hans, 213–214
Jünemann trial (1910), 213–214
Juristische Wochenschrift, 83, 144
Jurors, 26, 68, 83, 146, 163–165, 198–199
Jury courts *(Schwurgerichte)*, 16–17, 34, 146, 164

Kaliski, Julius, 38, 197
Kaliski trial, 38, 160, 197–198
Kammergericht, 1, 29, 33, 90

Kantorowicz, Hermann, 7, 170–171
Kerr, Alfred, 12, 13, 18, 48, 105, 121, 130
Kiaulehn, Walther, 12, 18, 53
Klähn, Otto, 199
Kleines Journal, 188
Kölnische Zeitung, 87, 120, 211
Konitz, 149–150
Kortum, *Geheimer Rat* Dr., 207–208
Kreuzzeitung, 49, 81, 118, 119–120, 188, 202, 210, 211, 212, 218
Kwilecka, Countess, 128
Kwilecki trial (1903), 128, 175–176

Land, Hans, 217
Langbehn, Julius, 79
Lassalle, Ferdinand, 123
Law of Association (Prussian), 114
Lawyers' Chamber (Berlin), 85, 92, 107, 113–114, 116, 127–128, 136
Lawyers' Chambers *(Anwaltskammern)*, 91
Lawyers' Code *(Rechtsanwaltsordnung)*, 91–92, 115, 116
Lay-judge courts *(Schöffengerichte)*, 17, 26–27
Legal positivism, 2, 4, 9, 19–20, 147, 170
Legal profession, 83–85, 88–97, 105–110, 113–114, 116, 123, 126, 127–128, 140, 142–143
Legal realism, 6–7
Leipziger Neuste Nachrichten, 192, 194
Leppmann, *Medizinalrat* Dr., 197–198, 199–200
lèse majesté *(Majestätsbeleidigung)*, 36
Levy, Meyer, 196
lex Hagemann, 35
lex Heinze, 87–88
Libel *(Beleidigung)*, 117–118, 152–153
Liberals, 3, 17, 145–147, 154, 161, 181, 216
Liebknecht, Karl, 38, 90, 134–137, 168, 200, 213
Liebknecht, Wilhelm, 134
Lindau, Paul, 184, 187, 188, 218
Liszt, Franz von, 20, 143, 155, 161, 181, 189, 195, 227
Llewellyn, Karl, 6
Local Courts *(Amtsgerichte)*, 17, 26
Lombroso, Cesare, 79, 176
Löwenstein, Siegfried, 168

Meerscheidt-Hüllessem, Inspector Leopold von, 62, 75, 82, 173–174, 177–178
Micro-history, 7–8
Miquel, Finance Minister Johannes von, 47
Moabit, 15–18, 47–54, 104, 232–233
Moltke, Count Kuno von, 46, 218
Monbart, Helene von, 157–160
Mosse, Rudolf, 14, 49
Müller, Hedwig, 203–212
Müller trial (1913), 203–212, 213, 218
Munckel, August, 90, 123–124, 144

Naatz, Willy, 52
National Zeitung, 18, 187
Neue Zeit, 81
Nieberding, Secretary of State for Justice Rudolf, 184, 189
Nightwatchmen, 55, 103
Nordau, Max, 79
Norddeutsche Allgemeine Zeitung, 81, 82–83
"Numerius Negidius," 33–34

Oberwinder, Heinrich, 120, 148
Obscenity, 158–160
Ostwald, Hans, 51, 59

Passing off a child *(Kindesunterschiebung)*, 175
Peltasohn, Martin, 143
Perjury, 27, 34
Plötzensee (prison), 15, 160, 197–198
Police (Berlin), 61–63, 82, 173–175, 188
Post, 210, 211, 212
Pound, Roscoe, 6–7
Prager-Schweitzer trial (1892), 99–100, 112–114
Press (Berlin), 5, 41, 42–43, 48–49, 78, 106, 118–120, 181, 191–192
Preussischer Richterverein, 109
Prisons, 15, 19–20
Procuring *(Kuppelei)*, 35–36, 37, 86–88
Prosecutors, *(Staatsanwälte)*, 17, 24–25, 31–34, 37–43, 47, 105–110, 216–217
Prostitution, 58–60, 81, 86–88, 102
Prussian Criminal Code (1851), 19, 194–195
Public opinion, influence on the justice system of, 25, 35, 42–44, 47, 61, 69, 70–71, 78, 84–86, 89, 94–95, 97–98, 104, 106, 120, 121, 141, 146–155, 162–165, 171, 172, 188–190, 212–213, 216, 218

Radbruch, Gustav, 2
Referendare, 107, 223–224
Reich Criminal Code *(Reichstrafgesetzbuch)*, 19–22, 58–59, 88, 117–118, 152–153, 188, 195, 200–201
Reichsbote, 194
Reimann, Georg, 203, 204, 205, 208, 210
"Rental Barracks," 55–56, 101–103
Rieck, Superior Court Director Otto, 46, 68, 69, 70, 71, 72, 73, 74, 76, 77, 78, 93–94, 97–99
Ritter, Josef, 199–202
Ritter trial (1913), 199–202, 210, 212, 213
"Ritual murder," 148, 153
Rosenfeld, Ernst, 32
Rothe, Anna, 153–155
"Rubber Hose Trial" (1894), 118–120
Rule of law, 227–228

Saint Elizabeth's Church, 14–15, 60–61, 232
Saul, Bruno, 85
Savigny, Karl Friedrich von, 30, 32
Scheffler, Karl, 11, 56
Schelling, Justice Minister Ludwig von, 47, 86–87, 89–90, 92, 93, 96, 97, 110–111, 113, 148
Scherl, August, 14, 49
Schlichting, Superior Court Counselor, 198–199, 202, 203, 207, 212, 223
Schmidt, Superior Court Director Alexander, 110–112
Schneidt, Karl, 38, 197–198
Schoenebeck-Weber, Frau von, 51
Schönstedt, Justice Minister Karl von, 150
Schwarz, Otto, 23, 32, 164
Schwindt, Karl, 14, 46, 184
Sello, Erich, 14, 29–30, 51, 91, 123, 124, 125, 128–134, 154–155, 162–163, 164, 165, 167–168
Sentences, 20–22, 86–88, 118, 119, 133, 135, 139, 188, 190, 201–202, 209–210, 214–216, 225
Simmel, Georg, 82
Singer, Bertha, 62, 101
Social Democrats, 3, 80–81, 82, 85, 114, 115, 117, 134, 136, 181, 193, 216

Sociological school (of criminal law), 20, 189
Staatsbürger Zeitung, 5, 130–131, 151–153, 157
Stadthagen, Artur, 90, 114–117, 121, 129
Sternberg, August, 25, 129, 132, 156, 229–230
Sternberg, Dr. Leo, 204, 205, 206, 210, 211–212
Sternberg trial (1900), 25, 40, 42, 129–132, 146, 156–157
Stierstädter, Constable, 129, 131
Störmer, *Medizinalrat* Dr., 176, 199
Strassmann, Professor Dr., 176
Sudermann, Hermann, 182, 187
Superior Courts *(Landgerichte),* 17, 26, 27, 33
Supreme Honor Court *(Ehrengerichtshof),* 92, 96–97, 105, 114, 117, 125, 126–127, 128, 133–134, 135–136, 141

Tagesspiegel, 232
Tägliche Rundschau, 81, 210, 229
Tegal (prison), 15, 191
Theft, 27, 36–37, 41, 58–60, 61–62
Thiel, Commissar, 129, 132
Thiele, Oskar, 43
Third Reich, 2, 3–4, 230–232
Tiergarten, 203, 205
Tietz, Hermann, 179–180
Tönnies, Ferdinand, 78–79
Tresckow, Commissar Hans von, 47, 53, 164, 174, 177, 223
Tucholsky, Kurt, 225

Ullstein, Leopold, 14, 49
Underworld (of Berlin), 57–60, 63, 101

Unger, State Advocate Wilhelm, 68, 71, 72, 97–99

Voigt, Wilhelm, 51, 182–191, 192–194, 229
Voigt trial (1906), 184–189, 218
Vorwärts, 80, 81, 83, 117, 119, 160, 197
Vossische Zeitung, 49, 78, 79–80, 81, 98, 111, 120, 140, 187

Wachler, General Prosecutor, 135, 184
Weber, Max, 170–171
Wehn, Commissar, 149, 199
Weimar Republic, 1, 2, 225–226
Weissler, Adolf, 84, 123, 126
Werner, Bruno, 196
Werthauer, Johannes, 14, 42, 131, 132, 134, 165–167, 168, 230
Wertheim, Alexander, 180
Wertheim, Gertrud, 51, 139
Wertheim, Wolf, 139, 180
Wilhelm II, 1, 35–36, 85–87, 110
Winter, Ernst, 149
Witting, Julian, 84, 123, 157
Wolff-Metternich, Count Gisbert von, 138–139
Wolff-Metternich trial (1911), 138–140
Woyda, Frieda, 129, 156–157
Wronker, Max, 14, 124, 128

Young offenders, 21, 27, 196–197

Zeit am Montag, 160, 197, 218
Zeppelin, Count Ferdinand von, 192–194
Zuchthaus. See Prisons
Zuckmayer, Carl, 182
Zukunft, 165, 172–173, 230